THE
SIX SIGMA
WAY

How to Maximize the Impact of
Your Change and Improvement Efforts

SECOND EDITION

Peter S. Pande
Robert P. Neuman
Roland R. Cavanaugh

New York   Chicago   San Francisco   Athens   London
Madrid   Mexico City   Milan   New Delhi
Singapore   Sydney   Toronto

1R 2 3 4 5 6 7 8 9 0 QFR/QFR 1 9 8 7 6 5 4

ISBN   978-0-07-149732-9
MHID   0-07-149732-3

e-ISBN   978-0-07-182301-2
e-MHID   0-07-182301-8

Library of Congress Cataloging-in-Publication Data
Pande, Peter S.
  The Six Sigma way : how to maximize the impact of your change and improvement efforts / by Peter Pande, Robert Neuman, and Roland Cavanagh. — Second edition.
      pages cm
Includes bibliographical references and index.
  ISBN 978-0-07-149732-9 (alk. paper)—ISBN 0-07-149732-3 (alk. paper) 1. Six sigma (Quality control standard) 2. Quality control—Statistical methods. 3. Continuous improvement process. 4. Production management. I. Neuman, Robert P. II. Cavanagh, Roland R. III. Title.
  TS156.17.S59P36 2013
  658.5—dc23   2013037217

McGraw-Hill Education books are available at special quantity discounts to use as premiums and sales promotions or for use in corporate training programs. To contact a representative, please visit the Contact Us pages at www.mhprofessional.com.

To Anne and Al Pande,
"Six Sigma" parents and my best friends.
—P.S.P.

To my dear wife, Mabel.
—R.P.N.

To my dad, Hale Cavanagh,
who would have been pleased and proud
to see the results of this undertaking.
—R.R.C.

CONTENTS

PART THREE: IMPLEMENTING SIX SIGMA: THE ROADMAP AND TOOLS

INTRODUCTION TO
THE SECOND EDITION

When the first edition of this book was published back in 1999, it was one of only a couple of books on the subject of Six Sigma. Now, hundreds of books, websites, and blogs on Six Sigma (and *Lean* Six Sigma) are sliced into many different specialties and perspectives. It is rewarding to note, though, that our work has stood the test of time: *The Six Sigma Way* has sold more than 200,000 copies and has been translated into more than 20 languages, and *Forbes* magazine called it "one of the most important business books of the past 20 years."

When we wrote the first edition, Six Sigma was still not well understood in business circles: although Motorola had championed Six Sigma in the late 1980s, it was not really well-known until General Electric popularized it in the mid-1990s with the aggressive backing of then-CEO Jack Welch. Hearing GE and others touting its benefits prompted a lot of people to wonder "What is this Six Sigma thing all about?" Many organizations began trying to apply it themselves, which was one of the reasons we wrote the book. We felt then that a lot of misconceptions, misunderstandings, and narrow definitions surrounded Six Sigma and hampered its potential. And while a lot has been learned, good and bad, we feel that is *still* true today: Six Sigma has been packaged and repackaged and sold and resold under many different guises, so a lot of confusion remains about what it really is and how it can really help an organization.

One of the most pervasive problems with and misconceptions about Six Sigma is its name, which draws on statistics even though using statistics is only one (optional) element of the Six Sigma approach! The name *Six Sigma* was almost accidental, but the label has stuck, so we need to simply clarify what the approach really is and how it can help. We continue to use it in the book (not only because it's in the title!) but also because it is still used in many organizations. And even though other terms have become nearly interchangeable with it, including *Lean Six Sigma, process excellence, performance excellence, business process improvement,* and others, all are greatly influenced by Six Sigma principles and practices. In fact, many organizations have chosen their own terminology or brand for the work that comes from Six Sigma to avoid that phrase altogether because it can sound intimidating or strange to a lot of people.

Regardless of what Six Sigma is called, it is still a powerful approach to driving organizational change and improvement, and we—along with our colleagues at McGraw-Hill—felt it was time for a new edition to this book. The fundamental descriptions of what Six Sigma is, how it works, and how *you* can use it and adapt it to the specific needs of *your* organization are still true, accurate, and valid. But we wanted to update and build on the experience of many organizations that have applied Six Sigma over more than a decade, some with great success, some not. With plenty to update, the good news is that most of the core principles and tools still apply and much of the advice we offered in the first edition has proven accurate (even though we wish more had taken it to heart).

Six Sigma's Hidden Truths, Lessons Learned, and Potential Payoffs

To help you get the greatest possible benefit from Six Sigma, it is important to recognize some of the misunderstood truths about what it offers, how it works, and where its real value lies. The truths for the most part are constant; still, we include some "Lessons Learned" based on the much deeper experience of Six Sigma since 1999.

Hidden Truth #1

Six Sigma encompasses a broad array of business concepts, best practices, and skills (some advanced, but a lot common sense) that are essential ingredients for making improvement and change work well. Where it has shown the most impressive and lasting results, Six Sigma *thinking* is really more important than the tools. When it is narrowly defined as "a quality program" or "a statistical approach," the impact is sure to be limited.

Lessons Learned: Far too many organizations and training programs have continued to emphasize tools and projects and overlooked the fundamental Six Sigma dimension of *asking the right questions.* Learning tools and working on projects can only go so far, whereas asking questions and responding effectively can be applied every day.

The Payoff: By balancing the tools and projects with the proactive, creative thought processes that are core to Six Sigma, you will be able to apply it much more broadly and see the impact on not just formal problem solving, but also how people, from leaders to front-line, act and respond every day.

Hidden Truth #2

Look around and you will find many "Six Sigma Ways." Following a fixed prescription, hiring a consultant to tell you what to do, or mimicking another organization is guaranteed to fall short or fail. You need to be guided by your own vision, goals, capabilities, and culture (or "cultures," since most organizations are really a mix) and be prepared to learn and adapt. In addition, the Six Sigma Way is not (or should not be) about solving only certain types of problems. Because it is about thinking as much as tools, it can impact how you address many kinds of challenges.

Lessons Learned: Here, the story is much more positive than under Hidden Truth #1. Most organizations soon recognize that following a standard implementation model for Six Sigma does not work. Only those that have continued to adapt their approach over time have achieved the kinds of results they had hoped for. Persistence, it seems clear, has its rewards.

The Payoff: Building your own Six Sigma way can be a great learning experience, yielding insights into how your business works, what good and bad habits govern your actions, where the biggest opportunities for improvement lie, and how best to capitalize on those opportunities. If you are willing to continue on that Way, it is likely that the biggest benefits lie ahead of you.

Hidden Truth #3

The potential gains from Six Sigma are equally or more significant in services and nonmanufacturing activities as they are in production environments, and even greater when working *across* functions and processes.

As you will see, you cannot apply Six Sigma quite the same way in sales as in manufacturing, but the fundamentals are the same, whether it is measuring performance, finding waste, or implementing a solution.

Lessons Learned: When leaders invest time, working as a team to identify and address key cross-functional opportunities, the outcomes are nearly always positive. By contrast, when Six Sigma is run by department-focused groups that are left to generate their own projects, the outcomes are usually disappointing. One of the biggest remaining upsides of Six Sigma still lies in greater leader and organization-wide ownership; it is much more often relegated over time to a department or group that works only on special projects, having to justify its existence every year.

The Payoff: You can get more mileage from your improvement investment if you look at your opportunities broadly and take on both the cross-functional issues and local problems that have the most impact on your profits and customers. Then it can be more easily linked to what is important to everyone and be integrated into common practice.

Hidden Truth #4

Six Sigma is as much about people excellence and mindset as it is about technical capability and quality. Customer focus, creativity, collaboration, communication, commitment, and openness to change form the foundation of effective improvement, and they start with people. Fortunately, the fundamental ideas of big-picture Six Sigma can inspire and motivate better ideas and performance from people and create synergy between individual talents and technical prowess. To bring forth excellence in people, however, you have to put significant effort into engaging and enabling their contributions.

Lessons Learned: It is here that the impact of Six Sigma is difficult to gauge. So many thousands of people have been trained, examined problems and processes, and implemented improvement, but how has that really affected their ability and attitudes toward continuous improvement? Certainly plenty of people view the whole endeavor as a waste of time, but many others feel it has given them valuable skills, insights, and abilities. In some cases, it has been a life-changing experience.

The best we can conclude after talking to many of these people is that when their Six Sigma story emphasizes people and robust business excellence, the net impression is often very positive. When the

training and themes are technical and narrow, the lasting benefit is
not nearly as strong.

In addition, it is clear that inherent ability in communication, connecting ideas, openness, and flexibility can have a big impact on how
quickly an individual will take to Six Sigma and apply it well. Bringing
these people into the effort early on can make a big difference in the
success of an organizational initiative.

The Payoff: Done right, Six Sigma can help you bring out the best
in people: yourself, your team, your organization. Collectively, it can
and should help your culture evolve to be more responsive, less complacent, and more focused, not to mention more efficient and effective.

Hidden Truth #5

Successful improvement, which is the essence of Six Sigma, can be
thrilling and rewarding, if you can unlock the talent that exists in your
organization. We have seen people rave about the positive changes
that have come to their organization, thanks to the new, smarter way
they are running their business. We have watched executive teams
abandon their decorum, as they race around trying to speed up and
perfect a "broken" process in a Six Sigma workshop. In this book,
we try to share some of the fun and enthusiasm we have seen and
felt about Six Sigma as we describe how to make your efforts successful. (If at times our attempts at sparkling wit fall flat, we apologize in
advance.)

It is a lot of work, too. Any type of Six Sigma effort takes an investment in time and money, effort and energy. Finding the right way to
motivate yourself and others, whether your organization is at the top
of its game or in dire straits, is one of those elusive essentials.

Lessons Learned: Rewards and recognition are valuable in getting
people's attention and promoting involvement, but they have their
limits and potential unintended consequences (as in one client where
first-generation Six Sigma trainees received stock options, prompting a
lot of others to expect the same up-front payoff). Better, we have seen,
to set a vision for change that links the practical/tangible (reducing
costs, growing revenue) and the inspiring (building a great company).
Then connect these goals to people's performance expectations and
measures. Improvement success becomes both a fundamental requirement *and* a cause for celebration.

The Payoff: Done right, the financial gains from Six Sigma may
be exceeded in value by the intangible benefits. In fact, the changes

in attitude and enthusiasm that come from improved processes and better-informed people can be more fulfilling, emotionally, than the financial gains, though of course those are quite important, too! Strive for both, and you are much more likely to achieve your vision and goals.

Key Features of *The Six Sigma Way*

This book is designed with maximum customer satisfaction in mind. We hope that by reading it you gain a complete picture of what is behind the Six Sigma movement, how it has paid off for many organizations, and how you can implement the system so as to best fit your circumstances. Our goal is to provide a flexible resource and reference, whether you have been engaged in Six Sigma for several years or are just starting to learn and apply it.

Here are some of the features that will help you get the most out of the book:

1. **A guide to finding just what you need.** Following this introduction, you will find an overview of each section and chapter, with tips on which pieces to use (or skip over) depending on your objectives and circumstances.
2. **Practical implementation guidelines.** Whether it is fixing a process problem or implementing Six Sigma companywide, we review important information to help you get started and keep moving.
3. **Insights, comments, and examples from real people.** Business leaders, experts, and managers who are using Six Sigma in their organizations share thoughts that have helped reinforce and refine our ideas; we are confident you will learn a lot from them, too.
4. **Case studies based on real companies.** These real examples, with fictional names and details, help you see how Six Sigma can work (and has worked) in many organizations in many different industries. These case studies are set off in tinted boxes, so you can easily discern the examples from the main text.
5. **Real-world stories of Six Sigma success and insights from companies.** These companies are as diverse as Adobe, Macy's, Starwood, and others.
6. **Checklists for many of the essential steps in Six Sigma improvement.** We hope to prepare you to go out and do Six Sigma activities, so we map out key steps to help you make the right choices.

7. **Lists of questions to ask yourself.** Such a list can be essential when preparing for or embarking on a Six Sigma project.

8. **An introduction to advanced techniques.** This book is not meant to be a technical manual; plenty of other texts cover the nuances of process statistics and advanced experimental design. We will, however, help anyone understand what the analytical tools of Six Sigma are, why and how they are used, and when they should be applied. (But remember they are only a small part of what makes Six Sigma pay off.)

9. **Our own perspectives and advice.** In giving you a guide to Six Sigma best practices, we synthesized different viewpoints, guided by our experience and understanding of what works best, when, and how. Some of our thoughts challenge the views of Six Sigma experts; where they do, we give evidence for our perspective. Because we have worked with some of the most visible Six Sigma companies and have applied these concepts in many types of businesses, we believe our views can make Six Sigma even more powerful than it might otherwise be.

A Final Philosophical Word

Lastly, we would like to offer you a theme that we think represents one of the most important aspects of Six Sigma and hence will be key to your success in applying it to your business.

In their book *Built to Last*, James Collins and Jerry Porras provide insights into many of the most successful and admired companies of the twentieth century. The dimension that they found most remarkable among these firms is their ability and their willingness to simultaneously adopt two seemingly contrary objectives *at the same time*. Stability and renewal, big-picture and minute detail, creativity and rational analysis, these forces working together make organizations great. This we-can-do-it-all approach they call the "Genius of the And."

You can see this genius in action in everyday business if you look closely. For example, the best managers are usually those who set broad goals and direction (big picture), yet who can still offer effective input and ask tough questions (the details). In a larger business context, an example of the "Genius of the And" would be a company's constant attention to *both* long-term growth and quarterly results.

The opposite effect, to which lesser organizations fall victim, Collins and Porras dub the "Tyranny of the Or."[1] It is the paralyzing view that we can have it one way or the other, but not *both*.

Six Sigma, we believe, depends on your business learning to exhibit the Genius of the And, and it offers a way to unlock this genius in your own people and processes. Table I.1 provides some examples of those seemingly opposing ideas we encounter in this book that *in fact* are key to success.[2]

As you learn about the what, why, and how of Six Sigma in this book, try to remember that the success you are seeking will be based on your ability to focus on the "And" and not the "Or." The key to unlocking the Genius of the And in you and your organization can be found in these pages. The goal of *The Six Sigma Way* is to enable you to understand *what* Six Sigma is (both a simple and a complex question), *why* it is probably the best answer to improved business performance of the past 20 to 30 years, and *how* to put it to work in the unique environment of your organization. In our mission to demystify Six Sigma for the executive and professional, we hope to show you that it is just as much about a passion for serving customers and a drive for great new ideas as it is about statistics and number-crunching; the value of Six Sigma applies just as much to marketing, service, human resources, finance, and sales as it does to manufacturing and engineering. In the end we hope to give you a clearer picture of how Six Sigma—the *system*—can dramatically raise your odds for staying successful, even as you watch other companies ride one wave of good times only to wipe out on the next. (Our first and last surfing analogy!) Let's get started.

TABLE I.1 "GENIUS OF THE AND" EXAMPLES

Reduce errors to almost none	Get things done faster
Engage people in understanding and improving their processes and procedures	Maintain control of how work gets done
Measure and analyze what we do	Apply creative solutions to "push the envelope"
Make customers extremely happy	Make a lot of money

A GUIDE TO *THE SIX SIGMA WAY*

This book is organized for use by a variety of readers, from Six Sigma novices to people right in the thick of improvement efforts. Although you may prefer to read it from cover to cover, the content is organized in three parts to help you learn about Six Sigma now at just the level of depth you need. You can read the rest of the book later when you need it.

Here is a guide to the content, first by part, then by chapter.

The Major Sections

Part One: An Executive Overview of Six Sigma

For the executive or the newcomer to Six Sigma, Part One provides a thorough overview of key concepts and background including success stories, themes, measurement, improvement strategies, and the Six Sigma roadmap—a five-phase model for building the Six Sigma organization. We also look at how Six Sigma efforts can avoid some of the mistakes that hurt total quality efforts and how to apply Six Sigma in service as well as manufacturing processes or businesses.

Part Two: Gearing Up and Adapting
Six Sigma to Your Organization

This section looks at the organizational challenges of launching, leading, and preparing people for the Six Sigma effort. We examine the key question of whether to start a Six Sigma effort and where to begin your effort. Here is also where you can find out about responsibilities of business leaders, Black Belts, and other roles. Finally, we explore how to choose the right improvement projects.

Part Three: Implementing Six Sigma: The Roadmap and Tools

This section focuses on the how-to of the major components and tools in the Six Sigma system. For those who want to begin doing the work of making Six Sigma gains, or just want to know more about what is really involved in the effort, this section should answer many of your questions. For example, if your concern is about measurement, you can concentrate on Chapter 14; if you are looking at redesigning a process, Chapter 16 will be your focus. We cover some of the more important advanced tools of Six Sigma in this section as well. As a conclusion, we offer a list of Twelve Keys to Success for your Six Sigma journey.

The Chapters

The following quick summary of each chapter focuses on the questions addressed in each.

Chapter 1: A Powerful Strategy for Sustained Success

How does Six Sigma apply to the business challenges of the new century? What are some of the results and successes that have brought Six Sigma to the forefront of business leadership today, including at GE, Motorola, and AlliedSignal? What are some of the key organizational benefits it offers and the themes that drive Six Sigma improvement?

Chapter 2: Key Concepts of the Six Sigma System

What kind of organizational "system" can Six Sigma create and how does in apply to short- and long-term success? What does the *measure* "Six Sigma" mean? What role do customers and defects play in measuring Six Sigma performance? What are the core improvement and management methodologies of Six Sigma? What is the DMAIC model? What really is, or should be, a Six Sigma organization?

Chapter 3: Applying Six Sigma to Service and Manufacturing

Why does Six Sigma hold as much, if not more, promise in service processes and organizations as in manufacturing? What are the keys to making Six Sigma work well and provide results in a service environment? What are the unique challenges that can arise in applying Six Sigma in manufacturing functions, and how do you address them?

Chapter 4: The Six Sigma Roadmap

What is the best sequence for implementing the core competencies of Six Sigma? What are the advantages of the ideal Six Sigma roadmap? What is the value provided by each component to a responsive, competitive organization?

Chapter 5: Is Six Sigma Right for Us Now?

What key questions should we ask to determine whether our organization is ready for and can benefit from Six Sigma? When would Six Sigma *not* be a good idea for a business? What are the cost/benefit considerations when deciding whether to embark on a Six Sigma initiative?

Chapter 6: How and Where Should We Start Our Efforts?

What options can we consider in planning our Six Sigma launch? What are the on-ramps to the Six Sigma roadmap? How do we scale our effort to meet our needs? How can we use an assessment of our strengths and weaknesses to focus our resources? Why is a piloting strategy essential, and how should it work?

Chapter 7: Leadership Actions to Launch and Guide the Effort

What are the key responsibilities for organizational leaders in guiding the effort? How do communication, demand for results, and "change marketing" impact our potential for success?

Chapter 8: Preparing Black Belts and Other Key Roles

What roles are typically needed in a Six Sigma implementation? What is a Black Belt, and what are the options for defining his/her function? How can the various roles be structured and conflicts be avoided? What are the key considerations when choosing members for team projects?

Chapter 9: Training Your Organization for Six Sigma

Does Six Sigma necessarily demand weeks and weeks of training to start? What are the keys to effective Six Sigma training? What are the common elements in a Six Sigma curriculum?

Chapter 10: The Key to Successful Improvement: Selecting the Right Six Sigma Projects

What are the key steps in choosing and setting up Six Sigma improvement projects? How do we decide which improvement model—DMAIC or some other approach—is best for our business?

Chapter 11: Identifying Core Processes and Key Customers (Roadmap Step 1)

What are core processes, and how have they become a key to understanding businesses? What are some common types of core processes, and how do you identify those in your organization? How do you identify the key customers and outputs of your core processes? What is a SIPOC model and diagram, and how can they be applied to a better understanding of our business?

Chapter 12: Defining Customer Requirements (Roadmap Step 2)

Why is having a voice of the customer (VOC) system so critical in business today? What are the key actions and challenges in strengthening your VOC system? How do we identify and specify output and service requirements of our customers? How does better understanding of customer needs link up to our strategy and priorities?

Chapter 13: Measuring Current Performance (Roadmap Step 3)

What are the basic concepts in business process measurement? What are the basic steps in implementing customer- and process-focused measures? How do you effectively carry out data collection and sampling? What types of defect and performance measures are fundamental to the Six Sigma system? How do you calculate "Sigma" for your processes?

Chapter 14: Six Sigma Process Improvement (Roadmap Step 4A)

How do you define, measure, analyze, and improve a key business process, while focusing on identifying and eliminating root causes? What are the basic tools of process improvement, and when can each be used effectively? What are some of the key obstacles to executing a Six Sigma improvement project?

Chapter 15: Six Sigma Process Design/ Redesign (Roadmap Step 4B)

How is Six Sigma process design/redesign different, and why is it a critical element in maximizing business performance? What conditions are essential to take on a process design or redesign project? How does redesign differ in execution from improvement? What special tools and challenges come into play when you are designing/redesigning a business process? How do you test and overcome assumptions that limit the value of redesigned processes?

Chapter 16: Expanding and Integrating the Six Sigma System (Roadmap Step 5)

How do you measure and solidify the gains made through Six Sigma improvement projects? What are the methods and tools of process control? What are the specific responsibilities of and considerations for a process owner? How does the evolutionary discipline of process management support the Six Sigma system and long-term improvement?

Chapter 17: Advanced Six Sigma Tools: An Overview

What are some of the most prevalent power tools of Six Sigma improvement? What role does each play in helping you to understand and improve processes and products/services? What are the basic steps to these sophisticated techniques?

Conclusion: Twelve Keys to Success

What are some of the key actions and considerations any company or leader should keep in mind to make Six Sigma pay off?

AN EXECUTIVE OVERVIEW OF SIX SIGMA

CHAPTER 1

A Powerful Strategy for Sustained Success

The most challenging question confronting business leaders and managers in the new millennium is not "How do we succeed?" It's: "How do we stay successful?"

Business today puts forward a succession of companies, leaders, products, and even industries getting their "15 minutes of fame" and then fading away. Even corporate powerhouses—the IBMs, Fords, Apples, and many others—go through dramatic cycles of near-death and rebirth. It's like riding the wheel of fortune as consumer tastes, technologies, financial conditions, economic crises, and competitive playing fields change ever more quickly. In this high-risk environment, the clamor for ideas on how to get the edge, stop the wheel (while on top, of course), or anticipate the next change gets louder and louder. Hot new answers are almost as common as hot new companies.

Six Sigma can seem like another "hot new answer"—and certainly quite a few organizations have tried to apply it that way. But looking closer, you'll find a significant difference: Six Sigma is not tied to a single method or strategy, but rather a *flexible system* for improved business leadership and performance. It builds on many of the most important management ideas and best practices of the past century, creating a new formula for twenty-first-century business success. It's not about theory, it's about action. Evidence of the power and value of the Six Sigma Way is visible in the significant gains tallied by some high-profile companies and some not-so-high-profile ones, which we will examine in a moment.

In almost an antifad mentality, companies in sectors as diverse as financial services, transportation, health care, government, high-tech, and traditional manufacturing are *quietly* applying Six Sigma and Lean—often disguised under other titles—as the foundation for their improvement efforts. They've joined others who have been more vocal about their initiatives, including 3M, Alstom, BofA, Bombardier, DuPont, FedEx, Intuit, Johnson & Johnson, Pfizer, Tesco, Telefonica, Vanguard Group, Virginia Mason Medical Center, and many others around the world.

Its value and "shelf-life" can be seen just as well in the willingness of companies to reenergize their Six Sigma efforts, building on learnings and even setbacks from their initial endeavors. In its most valuable applications, Six Sigma goes beyond projects and process improvement to help leaders build new structures and practices that strengthen organizational culture and drive sustained higher levels of performance.

To get a broader sense of the popular impact of Six Sigma, consider the volume of these web search results as of August 2013: A query for "Six Sigma" on Google yielded more than 12 million results; on Bing, more than 27 million! Looking for "Six Sigma" in the books category of Amazon reveals more than 5,000 offerings. Certainly, high-volume results are part of the search-engine process: the TV show *Desperate Housewives* garnered 47 million results on Google, but only 2,500 on Amazon. "Theory of relativity" brought up fewer than 6 million Google results and just over 3,700 on Amazon.

Ignoring the question of why we chose those two comparisons, we can see that Six Sigma has gone far beyond being a pet project of a few CEOs to having far-reaching, and perhaps underestimated, impact on global management thinking and improvement efforts. Helping it deliver even *greater* impact is a big reason why we've written this book: because in many cases, the full potential of Six Sigma is still not being realized.

Some Six Sigma Success Stories

Focusing on Six Sigma successes may seem a bit disingenuous: certainly it isn't hard to find plenty of Six Sigma failures and disappointments. Indeed, the disappointing cases offer a lot of lessons, which we will draw on throughout this book. But the successes are important, too, because they provide a hint to the potential of putting smarter improvement practices to work. And because improvement really starts with facing up to the deficiencies and flaws in your business, these successes can suggest areas of opportunity for your organization to apply Six Sigma.

We start with some historical cases: the two companies that together probably had the most influence in making Six Sigma a global improvement. Then we highlight some more focused examples of where Six Sigma has been applied in other organizations and the results achieved. (Others will be profiled elsewhere in the book as well.)

Six Sigma at General Electric

> *Six Sigma has forever changed GE. Everyone—*
> *from the Six Sigma zealots emerging from*
> *their Black Belt tours, to the engineers, the auditors,*
> *and the scientists, to the senior leadership*
> *that will take this Company into the new*
> *millennium—is a true believer in Six Sigma,*
> *the way this Company now works."*
>
> **—GE CHAIRMAN JOHN F. WELCH**[1]

GE is often the first company that comes to mind when people hear the words *Six Sigma* because of the passion and commitment of legendary former chairman and CEO Jack Welch—and the positive results the company achieved:

► GE saved $750 million by the end of Year 3 after implementing Six Sigma and has saved billions of dollars since.

▶ GE's operating margins—which had been in the 10 percent range for decades—hit new records quarter after quarter. When the first edition of this book was published, the numbers were consistently above 15 percent. GE leaders cited this margin expansion as the most visible evidence of the financial contribution made by Six Sigma.

▶ GE's Lighting unit cut invoice defects and disputes with one of its top customers by 98 percent, which speeded payment and improved productivity for both companies.

▶ One of GE Capital's service businesses streamlined its contract review process, leading to faster completion of deals—in other words, more responsive service to customers—and annual savings of $1 million.

▶ GE's Power Systems group addressed a major irritant with its utility company customers, simply by improving the *documentation* provided along with new power equipment. The result: both the utilities and GE saved hundreds of thousands of dollars a year.

▶ The Medical Systems business—GEMS—used Six Sigma design techniques to create a breakthrough in medical scanning technology, reducing the time for full-body scans from 3 minutes to 30 seconds, which also enabled the hospitals to increase their use of the equipment and reduce the cost per scan.

Some might cynically suggest that the only reason people got on board the Six Sigma bandwagon at GE was because Welch insisted on it, which at first was likely the case for a lot of GEers. Over time, though, the number of converts grew—and they played a big role in expanding Six Sigma practices. Dozens of former GE executives who have gone on to other leadership roles—including James McNerney at 3M and now Boeing to Robert Nardelli at Home Depot and Chrysler—have implemented adaptations of Six Sigma as key parts of their strategy.

The impact of Six Sigma at GE can be seen in more subtle ways as well: It became a recurring target of parody for the hit TV comedy *30 Rock* on NBC (longtime unit of GE, now part of Comcast).

Six Sigma at AlliedSignal/Honeywell

AlliedSignal/Honeywell is another Six Sigma prime mover and success story. It was Larry Bossidy—a longtime GE executive who took the helm at Allied in 1991—who convinced Jack Welch that Six Sigma was an approach worth considering. Allied began its own quality improvement activities in the early 1990s and was soon saving more than $600 million a year, thanks to the widespread employee training in and application of Six Sigma principles.[2] Not only were Allied's Six Sigma teams reducing the costs of reworking defects, they were applying the same principles to the design of new products such as aircraft engines, reducing the time from design to certification from 42 to 33 months. The company also credits Six Sigma with increases in both productivity and profit margins.

Allied's leaders view Six Sigma as "more than just numbers—it's a statement of our determination to pursue a standard of excellence using every tool at our disposal and never hesitating to reinvent the way we do things."[3]

As one of Allied's Six Sigma directors put it: "It's changed the way we think and the way we communicate. We never used to talk about the process or the customer; now they're part of our everyday conversation."

AlliedSignal's Six Sigma leadership helped it earn recognition as the world's best-diversified company (from *Forbes* global edition) and the most admired global aerospace company (from *Fortune*).

Six Sigma Around the World

With GE and Allied Signal/Honeywell and others setting an example—and, for some, reenergizing the interest in *quality* that had waned somewhat after disappointment with total quality management (TQM) efforts—literally thousands of organizations and millions of projects have followed in applying Six Sigma. Any listing of results would be a mere drop in the bucket, but here are a few, just to give you a flavor:

Redesigning Production: High-Tech Manufacturing. A telecommunication products company used Six Sigma design techniques to enable greater flexibility and faster turnaround at a key manufacturing facility. At the plant, several specialized products are built on a single production line. Because each customer's order may require different circuit boards, the need to avoid retooling was critical.

Working through alignment of customer needs, product design, and process specifications, retooling was dramatically reduced. The plant was also able to institute parallel processing so that if one area of the line wasn't functioning, work-in-process could be easily rerouted without adding to cycle time. Also, under the new plant design, customer orders are transmitted electronically, where virtual design is applied to speed response.

The Result: Altogether, these innovative changes improved overall cycle time from days to hours, as well as improving productivity and resource management.

Speeding Call Center Performance: Credit Financing. A credit financing center used a Six Sigma team approach to analyze and improve call center operations. The focus was on two objectives: (1) reducing average call answer time, and (2) increasing the percentage of customer issues and questions resolved in the initial call.

The Result: The team "centralized and simplified" the call answering system, cutting average times from 54 seconds to 14 seconds. "First call resolution" jumped from 63 percent to 83 percent.

Seeing Patients on Time: Medical Clinic. The Internal Medicine department of a major health care provider noted high levels of patient dissatisfaction with long waits far beyond their appointment times. A team discovered that patients had a 99 percent likelihood of long waits at some point between check-in and seeing a doctor. By breaking down the process and exploring several hypotheses for delays, the team was able to implement several changes in handling initial patient appointments at the start of the morning and afternoon treatment periods (by getting the *first* appointment started on time, all the subsequent visits could be on time as well).

Results: Late check-ins were reduced from 58 percent to 3 percent and the chance of a patient experiencing a wait-time problem was cut to 23 percent from the original 99 percent. In addition, the improved handling of patients freed up capacity for an additional 70+ appointments per year. These lessons were shared and replicated by other clinics in the system as well.

Thinking Outside the Box: Aerospace Manufacturing. The spare parts marketing and logistics group for an aerospace manufacturing company was looking for ways to take costs and time out of their service to customers. One major cost element was parts packaging: bulk parts shipments from manufacturing plants were unpacked, placed on warehouse shelves, and then picked and repackaged for shipment to customers. By focusing the process design on customer needs and value-adding activities, the spare parts packaging operation was moved from the warehouse to the plants.

The Result: Packaging material cost savings alone were cut by $500,000 per year. The change also contributed to major improvements in on-time delivery, which jumped from less than 80 percent to over 95 percent in about three years.

Settling in the Sailors: U.S. Military. Temporary living allowance costs for sailors and families relocating to an overseas U.S. Navy installation had grown and were having a significant budget impact—not to mention creating dissatisfaction among the ranks and affecting new arrivals' morale and productivity. A Six Sigma team looked at the types of housing and length of delays and found that off-base housing was a major challenge, and that communication between groups responsible for coordinating and approving service member housing was ineffective. Improvements focused on better coordination and establishing stronger ties with off-base housing providers. A significant element of the improvement involved getting buy-in for the changes and adapting behaviors of the staff.

The Result: Average time to place families in housing was reduced from 15.8 to 5.3 days, with savings of more than $700,000 in temporary housing costs (exceeding initial forecasts).

Bringing in the Pounds: Financial Services. The credit card division of a major UK retailer recognized that its effectiveness in collecting overdue payments from cardholders was significantly below where it should be and was impacting overall business results. A first step was to refocus collection agents' time by eliminating administrative tasks—giving them significantly more capacity to contact customers. A variety of new approaches were put in place, with an emphasis on *helping* rather than *pressuring* holders of overdue accounts so they could find a reasonable way to pay their bills. In addition, the company reduced the number of accounts referred to an external debt collection firm, and found its internal efforts were both more successful and cost effective.

The Result: An initial goal of 50 percent collections improvement was actually exceeded, delivering an increase of 65 percent in funds collected per hour of collection agents' time. Overall costs were reduced and customer satisfaction increased.

Improving Complex New Product Development: High-Tech. With a goal of providing more complete and effective solutions for its customers, a major high-tech firm was frustrated to find that new product development efforts involving multiple business units (BUs) were much more prone to delays and excess costs. A Six Sigma team found that 50 percent of the more complex projects were behind schedule, versus 13 percent of single-BU efforts, with significant impact on cost and customer satisfaction. As the group anticipated, the causes of delays were not simple and involved a combination of adjusting attitudes and accountabilities as well as process changes. A key element of the solution was to clarify the interdependencies between elements of the cross-BU projects, which had been misunderstood and a key cause of past delays.

The Result: The changes, implemented for new development efforts, led to a significant improvement in coordination and on-time performance of cross-BU new product introductions. The project helped break down traditional barriers between different business units, which had had separate performance goals and profit measures, so they could work more effectively for the benefit of the *entire* company and its customers.

When reading a summary of these successes, don't be tempted to think they were easy or obvious. Each addressed important, often chronic issues that had either been previously ignored (because no one had looked at them with Six Sigma mindset) or had defied resolution in the past. Throughout this book and in your own efforts, remember that Six Sigma is not *magic*, it's not *easy*, but it can be *powerful*.

The Benefits of Six Sigma

The growth and impact of Six Sigma may be appealing, but with the struggles that so many organizations have gone through over the past several years, it's easy to wonder whether you can afford to apply these methods. If your company is doing well—as GE was in 1995, when Jack Welch launched its effort—why should you consider energizing your organization with Six Sigma practices? What has prompted so many businesses, prominent and modest, to invest in this funny-sounding business approach? While certainly some did so more to copy the big companies—and did not get what they had hoped for—many others have found great impact from it. Drawing from the many success stories and sifting out the challenges that any change effort involves, we can define several benefits that continue to attract companies to the Six Sigma Way:

1. **Six Sigma strengthens your chances for survival and sustained success.** The only way to overcome challenging economic conditions, position your organization for growth, and retain a hold on shifting markets is to constantly innovate and remake the organization. Six Sigma has key ingredients to create the skills and culture for constant revival—what we describe in Chapter 2 as a *closed-loop system.*

2. **Six Sigma sets a performance goal for everyone.** In a company of any size, getting everyone working in the same direction and focusing on a common goal is pretty tough. Each function, business unit, and individual has different objectives and targets. What everyone has in common, though, is the delivery of products, services, or information to customers (inside or outside the company). Six Sigma uses that common business framework—the process and the customer—to create a consistent goal: Six Sigma performance, or a level of performance that's about as close to perfect as most people can imagine. Companies that understand their customers' requirements (and who shouldn't?) can assess their performance against the Six Sigma goal of 99.9997 percent "perfect"—a standard so high that it makes most businesses' previous views of "excellent" performance look pretty weak. Figure 1.1 contrasts the number of problems that would be found with a goal of *99 percent quality* versus a goal of Six Sigma performance (99.9997 percent). The difference is pretty startling.

3. **Six Sigma enhances value to customers.** When GE began its Six Sigma effort, executives admitted that the quality of the company's products was not what it should be. Although its quality was perhaps better than that of its competitors, Jack Welch stated, "We want to make our quality so special, so valuable to our customers, so important to their success that our products become their only real value choice."[4] This same discovery has been made by many organizations who have since embarked on Six Sigma efforts: what was thought to be "pretty good" performance has turned out to be much farther from customers' expectations than had been assumed. Moreover, with tighter competition in every industry and huge

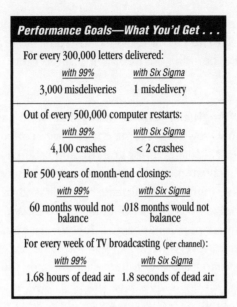

FIGURE 1.1   99% QUALITY VERSUS SIX SIGMA PERFORMANCE

challenges for government agencies, schools, and others, delivering just good or defect-free services and products is not enough. The focus on customers at the heart of Six Sigma means learning *what* value means to customers (and prospective customers) and planning *how* to deliver it to them profitably.

4. **Six Sigma boosts the return and accelerates the rate of improvement.** This benefit may be the most critical contribution Six Sigma can offer. Most organizations, likely including yours, are seeking to get better, somehow, every day. Few businesses or agencies begin Six Sigma from a standing start. But existing efforts far too often fail to deliver the level of change you need or that your competition and markets demand. The competitor who can convert its "improvement investment" into real results is much more likely to win the race. By borrowing tools and ideas from many disciplines, Six Sigma provides a foundation and flexible way to accelerate and have an impact on your improvement work: boosting performance while also "improving *improvement*."

5. **Six Sigma promotes learning and cross-pollination.** The 1990s saw the birth of the "learning organization," a concept that appeals to

many but seems hard to put into action. AlliedSignal leaders have commented that "everyone talks about learning, but few succeed in weaving it into the fabric of everyday life for so many employees."[5] Six Sigma is an approach that can increase and accelerate the development and sharing of new ideas throughout an organization. Even in a company as diverse as GE, the value of Six Sigma as a learning tool is seen as critical. Skilled people with expertise in *processes* and how to manage and improve them can be shifted from, say, GE Plastics to GE Capital, not only with a shorter learning curve but actually bringing with them *better* ideas and the ability to apply them more quickly. Ideas can be shared and performance compared more readily. Piet van Abeelen, who was GE's chief Six Sigma quality officer (and who reported directly to then-CEO Jack Welch and subsequent CEO Jeffrey Immelt) has noted that in the past, a manager in one part of the organization could discount input from a counterpart in another area: "Your ideas won't work, because I'm different." Van Abeelen says Six Sigma eliminates those defenses: "Well, cry me a river. The commonalities are what matter. If you make the metrics the same, we can talk."[6]

6. **Six Sigma executes strategic change.** Introducing new products, launching new ventures, entering new markets, acquiring new organizations—what were once occasional business activities are now daily events in many companies. Better understanding of your company's processes and procedures will give you a greater ability to carry out *both* the minor adjustments and the major shifts that twenty-first-century business success will demand.

The Tools and Themes of Six Sigma

Like most great inventions, Six Sigma is not "all new." While some themes of Six Sigma arise out of more recent breakthroughs in management thinking, many have their foundation in common sense. Before you dismiss that origin as no big deal, we'd remind you of a saying we picked up once while working in Europe: "Common sense is the least common of the senses." From a "tools" perspective, Six Sigma is a pretty vast universe. The following list summarizes many— but by no means all—of the most important Six Sigma methods:

- ▶ Continuous improvement
- ▶ Lean thinking
- ▶ Root cause analysis
- ▶ Change management
- ▶ Process design/redesign
- ▶ Business process management
- ▶ Analysis of variance
- ▶ Balanced scorecards
- ▶ Voice of the customer
- ▶ Theory of constraints
- ▶ Creative thinking
- ▶ Design of experiments
- ▶ Process management
- ▶ Statistical process control

The more we have learned over the years about the Six Sigma system, the more we have come to see it as a way to link together—and even to implement—many otherwise disconnected ideas, trends, and tools in business today. Some of the "hot topics" that have direct application or can complement a Six Sigma initiative include:

- ▶ E-commerce and services
- ▶ Enterprise resource planning
- ▶ Lean manufacturing
- ▶ Customer relationship management systems
- ▶ Strategic business partnerships
- ▶ Knowledge management
- ▶ Activity-based management
- ▶ The process-centered organization
- ▶ Globalization
- ▶ Just-in-time inventory/production

Six Themes of Six Sigma

We close out this introductory look at Six Sigma by distilling the critical elements of this leadership system into six themes. These principles—supported by the many Six Sigma tools and methods we present throughout this book—will give you a preview of *how* you can make Six Sigma work for your business.

Theme One: Genuine Focus on the Customer

During the big total quality push of the 1980s and 1990s, dozens of companies wrote policies and mission statements vowing to "meet or exceed customer expectations and requirements." Unfortunately, however, few businesses tried hard to improve their *understanding* of customers' requirements or expectations. Even when they did, customer data-gathering typically was a one-time or short-lived initiative that ignored the dynamic nature of customer needs. (How many of your customers want the same stuff today as five years ago? Two years ago? Last month?)

In Six Sigma, customer focus becomes the top priority. For example, the measures of Six Sigma performance begin with the customer. Six Sigma improvements are defined by their impact on customer satisfaction and value. We will look at why and how your business can define customer requirements, measure performance against them, and stay on top of new developments and unmet needs.

Theme Two: Data- and Fact-Driven Management

Six Sigma takes the concept of *management by fact* to a new, more powerful level. Despite the attention paid in recent years to measures, improved information systems, knowledge management, and so on, it should come as no shock to you to hear that many business decisions are still being based on opinions and assumptions. Six Sigma discipline begins by clarifying *what* measures are key to gauging business performance; then it applies data and analysis so as to build an understanding of key variables and optimize results.

At a more down-to-earth level, Six Sigma helps managers answer two essential questions to support fact-driven decisions and solutions:

1. What data/information do I *really* need?
2. How do we *use* that data/information to maximum benefit?

(A warning, however: One of the missteps that has hampered the value of Six Sigma in quite a few cases has been taking this "data-driven" theme too far. The goal should be *smarter* and more effective use of facts in setting priorities, defining needs, and developing solutions. But it does *not* mean banning intuition or good judgment from the management toolkit, and it does not mean that every conclusion needs statistics to back it up.)

Theme Three: Process Focus, Management, and Improvement

In driving improvement, processes are where the action is. Whether designing products and services, measuring performance, improving efficiency and customer satisfaction, or even running the business, Six Sigma positions the *process* as an essential vehicle of success.

Of course, pointing out that processes are key to improvement is not brand new to Six Sigma. The difference is an emphasis on the linkages *between* processes—from macro to micro, departmental to cross-functional, current state to future state. In fact, processes become the context for understanding what those all-important facts and data really mean. If we see a change in "the numbers," the only way to explain it is by looking at the process, or how the work is done. This "boundaryless" view of the process and business system also drives the teamwork needed to effect sustainable change.

Bottom line: Every dollar of efficiency gains or new revenue contribution that Six Sigma has helped deliver has come from some enhancement of the business system: that is, a process.

Theme Four: Proactive Management

Most simply, being *proactive* signifies acting in advance of events—the opposite of being *reactive*. In the real world, though, proactive management means making *habits* out of what are, too often, neglected business practices: defining ambitious goals and reviewing them frequently; setting clear priorities; focusing on problem prevention versus firefighting; questioning *why* we do things instead of blindly defending them as "how we do things here."

Being truly proactive, far from being boring or overly analytical, is actually a starting point for creativity and effective change. Reactively bouncing from crisis to crisis makes you busy or gives you a false impression that you're on top of things. In reality, it's a sign of a manager or an organization that's lost control.

Six Sigma, as we will see, encompasses tools and practices that replace reactive habits with a dynamic, responsive, proactive style of management. Considering today's slim-margin-for-error competitive environment, being proactive is the only way to be.

Theme Five: Change Management

Amidst the emphasis on tools and methods to drive improvement, probably the most overlooked theme of Six Sigma is *people*.

Any organizational change demands new practices, behaviors, attitudes, and often skills. No degree of *technical* Six Sigma mastery will yield any benefit unless you can engage the people who lead, manage, and—most important—do the work. The good news is that some of the fundamental practices of Six Sigma contribute to clarifying the need for change and why a particular solution is the right choice (e.g., a good "problem statement" should describe the issues that demand improvement). But tools alone are often not enough. Change agents under Six Sigma learn (or *should* learn) to assess the "people landscape" and build messages and plans to help each key group or individual through a change process (there's that word again).

All of the most effective, sustained examples of Six Sigma success have *change management* as a key ingredient and priority.

Theme Six: Drive for Perfection;
Tolerance for Failure

This last theme may seem contradictory. How can you be driven to achieve perfection and yet also tolerate failure? In essence, though, the two ideas are complementary. No company will get anywhere close to Six Sigma without launching new ideas and approaches, which always involves some risk. If people who see a possible path to better service, lower costs, and new capabilities (i.e., ways to be closer to perfect) are too afraid of the consequences of mistakes, they'll never try. The result: stagnation, putrefaction, death. (Pretty grim, eh?)

Fortunately, the techniques we will review for improving performance include a significant dose of risk management (if you're going to fail, make it a safe failure). The bottom line, though, is that any company that makes Six Sigma its goal will have to constantly push to be ever more perfect (because the customer's definition of "perfect" will always be changing) while being willing to accept—and manage—occasional setbacks.

Conclusion: Where You Stand

We would be surprised if you weren't saying to yourself right about now: "We're already *doing* some of those things." But remember, we've already noted that much of Six Sigma is not new. What *is* new is its ability to bring together all these themes into a coherent management process.

As you review this introduction and guide to the Six Sigma Way, we encourage you to take stock of what you are already doing that supports the themes or tools of Six Sigma and keep doing them. Meanwhile, be honest about your business's strengths and weaknesses. By contrast, businesses or managers who puff out their chests and claim to have all the answers are invariably the ones in greatest danger; they stop learning, fall behind, and end up having to scramble to catch up—if it isn't too late. (We see this scenario in some high-flying companies, including Six Sigma practitioners, even in the face of clear signals of trouble in their market or industry.)

So perhaps the final theme of Six Sigma is *avoid complacency*. Clearly, the greatest successes—including ones we will discuss throughout this book—involve organizations where people at all levels are willing to face up to challenges and shortcomings, learn from them, and start setting priorities to correct them.

So we urge you to keep an open mind and look for ways—big or small—to improve your improvement effort. In the remaining sections of the book, we will show you, first in an overview, and then in greater depth, how to find your own route on the Six Sigma Way.

With that in mind, let's take a closer look at how Six Sigma works.

CHAPTER 2

Key Concepts
of the
Six Sigma System

Like all systems, Six Sigma is made up of essential *components* that combine to drive improved business performance. After looking in Chapter 1 at some of the results and key themes of Six Sigma, we will now dig deeper into the questions "What is Six Sigma?" and "Why Six Sigma?" by describing in greater detail some of the key elements of the system.

A Six Sigma Vision of Business Leadership

Creating a Closed-Loop System[1]

Imagine a young child is learning how to ride a bike, and that you as parent, relative, or neighbor, are there to help and offer encouragement. You want to see the kid succeed—much as an investor wants to see its business offspring thrive. You give the kid a push, and for a while you watch him or her ride beautifully: balanced, head erect, proud. "Look, I'm doing it!" you hear, just before the kid runs off the path and into a bush. Of course, you're well aware that kids learning to ride bicycles fall off and run into the bushes pretty often at first, so you just pick up and put that child right back onto the bike (with tear drying as needed).

Businesses, too, get off course, fall down, run into the bushes. And if they are lucky—or if they catch themselves fast enough—companies too can just brush themselves off and get back on the path. If the mistake is too serious, however, its bike-riding days are over; the company is out of business for good.

Both successful bike riding and successful business management (over the long term) rely on the same thing: a *closed-loop system* in which both the internal and external sorts of information (i.e., feedback or stimuli) tell the rider/manager how to correct course, stay upright, and steer successfully. A good closed-loop system should work even on a winding path or in a treacherous business environment. But as we can see around any schoolyard, bike riding comes a lot more naturally than managing a business. Long after most kids are riding with no hands—or even getting into "extreme" bike stunts—businesses are still wobbling uncertainly down the path, hoping no one has decided to put in a curve lately.[2]

Six Sigma is based in large measure on creating a closed-loop business system that is sensitive enough to reduce the company's "wobbling" and keep it safely on the often-twisted path to performance and success (see Figure 2.1). In this case, though, instead of a bike the vehicle is the *process* (or actually, many processes). The internal "stimuli" (like the inner ear) are the measures of activity inside the process. As for the external feedback elements, the ones that tell the company

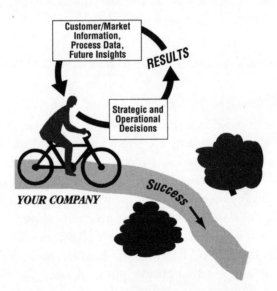

FIGURE 2.1   A CLOSED-LOOP SYSTEM:
STAYING ON THE PATH TO SUCCESS

if it has met its goals and is still on the right path, they include profits, customer satisfaction, and a variety of other data sources.

In the vocabulary of Six Sigma, the wobbling or inconsistency of a business system is *variation*. The types of bad variation that have a negative impact on customers we call *defects*. And the approaches used to create, monitor, and improve that closed-loop business system we'll call *process management*, *process improvement*, and *process design/redesign*.

System Alignment: Tracking the Xs and Ys

Some concepts from algebra are commonly used to describe this closed-loop concept in Six Sigma companies. (It isn't too technical, so hang in there.) In Figure 2.2, you see a model of a company as seen from a process-flow perspective:

▶ On the far left are the inputs to the process (or system).
▶ In the middle is the organization or process itself (depicted as a process map or flowchart).
▶ Finally, on the far right are the all-important customer, end products, and (let's hope) profits.

In Figure 2.3, we add some letters that represent measures or "variables" at different points in the system. The "Xs" that show up in the input and process flow would be indicators of change or performance in the upstream portions of the system. The "Ys" on the right represent measures of the business's performance—like the final score in a game. The formula $Y = f(X)$ ("Y is a function of X") is just a mathematical way of saying that changes or variables in the inputs and process of the system will largely determine how the final score—or Ys—turn out.

The trick of the closed-loop business system is twofold:

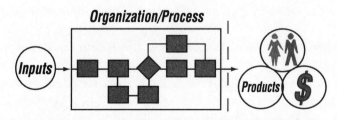

FIGURE 2.2   THE BUSINESS PROCESS MODEL

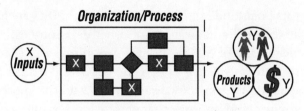

X - Input or Process Variable;   Y - Output Variable

$$Y = f(X)$$

FIGURE 2.3   UPSTREAM (X) AND DOWNSTREAM (Y) VARIABLES

1. To figure out *which* of the Xs, or variables, in the business process and inputs have the biggest influence on the Ys, or results.
2. To use the changes in the overall performance of the process (the Ys, as well as other external factors) to adjust the business and keep it moving on a profitable path.

At Six Sigma companies, this language of Xs and Ys becomes routine. Still, these variables tend to take on a variety of meanings; for example, Y can mean:

▶ Strategic goal
▶ Customer requirement
▶ Profits
▶ Customer satisfaction
▶ Overall business efficiency

and X can mean:

▶ Essential actions to achieve strategic goals
▶ Quality of the work done by the business
▶ Key influences on customer satisfaction
▶ Process variables such as staffing, cycle time, amount of technology, etc.
▶ Quality of the inputs to the process (from customers or suppliers)

Most companies and managers have a weak understanding of the relationship between their own Xs and Ys. They keep their corporate bikes on the path just through luck or by making a lot of *major* corrections as they go. By using Six Sigma methods to understand the system and the variables, a company can learn to monitor and respond to the feedback so that its path forward feels smoother and faster. Like a skilled bicycle rider, it can "automatically" respond to signals from its processes, suppliers, employees, and especially customers and competitors, thereby achieving new levels of strength and performance.

An Introduction to Sigma Measurement (aka "the Big Y")

It's time to explain in more detail both the original meaning of the term *Six Sigma* and the measure it describes. At this point we will look only at some of the concepts behind Six Sigma measures and what those measures *are*. For more on how to calculate it, you can take a look at Chapter 13.

Sigma, Standard Deviation, and Eliminating Variation

The lower-case letter *sigma* (σ in the Greek alphabet) is a symbol used in statistical notation to represent the standard deviation of a population. Standard deviation (as you may recall from statistics courses) is an indicator of the amount of variation or inconsistency in any group of items or process. For example, when you buy fast food that is nice and hot one day and lukewarm the next—that's variation. Or if you buy three shirts of the same size and one is too small, that's also variation. In fact the possible variations are infinite because *everything* varies to some degree or another; variation is a part of life.[3]

The Evils of Variation. In discussing variation, Six Sigma people tend to use words like *evil* and phrases like "the enemy"—almost as if the diabolical Professor Variation (Dr. Evil's cousin?) were plotting to take over the world. In fact, however, variation is no joke when it affects customers. For example, if I am asking for a home loan and the lending company says it will take "about two or three weeks" to get an answer (indicating a lot of variation in their process), that may have a big impact on whether I decide to do business with that lender. For if I do, who knows whether I will get the money on time?

Here's another example: When arriving at your destination on a plane trip, you never know whether it will be 5 minutes or 20 minutes before your luggage gets to baggage claim, so you may wait around for

15 minutes when you could have been making phone calls, reading, buying frozen yogurt, or engaging in some other useful activity.

Variation in products is a critical concern, too. Here are just a few examples:

▶ With complex electronics or mechanical parts, variations in current or width or weight from item to item can add up (sometimes called "tolerance stacking") until the whole thing falls apart.

▶ If your company makes a part that another company puts into its product, your inconsistency/variation may require extra effort for them to get your part to work—not a good value proposition for your customer.

▶ Finally, if a consumer buys a toaster that browns one piece of toast but burns the next—and you never touched the settings—that can waste a lot of bread.

The Advantages of Taking a Variation Perspective. Looking at variation helps management to much more fully understand the *real* performance of a business and its processes. In the past—and still often today—organizations measure and describe their efforts in terms of averages: average cost, average cycle time, average shipment size, and so on. But averages can actually *hide* problems by disguising variation.

For example, if you promised customers that orders for custom parts would be filled within six working days of the date they were ordered, you might find it good news to learn that your *average* order-to-delivery performance is at 4.2 days. Unfortunately, that average number could miss the fact that—due to wide variation in your process—more than 15 percent of orders are arriving in *more* than six days (i.e., *late!*). Without reducing the overall variation, you would have to reach an average delivery time of *two* days just to get all orders to meet your six-day commitment. By significantly reducing the variation, however, you can achieve an average delivery time of five days while having *no* late deliveries. Thus, understanding and addressing variation can benefit both you and your customers, because you no longer have to compensate for unpredictable efforts just to meet customers' requirements (e.g., in most cases, a five-day average delivery time is less expensive to achieve than a two-day).

The objective in driving for Six Sigma performance is to reduce or narrow variation to such a degree that six sigmas—or standard deviations of variation—can be squeezed within the limits defined by the customer's specifications. For many products, services, and processes, that goal means a huge, and tremendously valuable, degree of improvement.

Macy's achieved exactly that level of extreme improvement in its furniture delivery business. Peter Longo, president of Logistics & Operations for Macy's Inc., describes how the company, which is one of the top three furniture retailers in the country (in terms of size), wanted to improve its profitability and improve its growth, especially after the company's leadership recognized that its delivery service was "hated" by its customers. At the time, delivery was viewed as a purely operational, functional activity. Because Six Sigma teaches that an organization should always start with the customer and work backwards, Macy's began a structured process of data gathering. One of the first things it learned from these data was that one of the company's key assumptions about delivery was flat-out wrong. The delivery operations managers believed (without data or statistics to back up that belief) that the single most important aspect of home delivery for customers was the excellent, perfect condition of the merchandise when it was delivered. The managers felt, *"Who would argue with that?"*

Although the condition of the merchandise upon delivery is an important factor, once managers started gathering customer information, they learned that the single most important attribute that customers are looking for is to be on time. So they worked on improving what they call the "delivery window," which at first asked customers to stay home all day, then narrowed that delivery window to four hours. As they reduced the variation in performance for the four-hour time window and moved toward achieving Six Sigma performance, they were able to offer the customer a two-hour time window and consistently achieve performance levels that exceeded expectations. And that's really hard to do! Macy's recognized that timely delivery was the factor the customer wanted and expected.

While Macy's and its customers enjoy good/outstanding performance within the two-hour time window, they continue to apply Six Sigma methodology to reduce defects and increase the percentage of the time the company delivers within the promised delivery window.

Reaching this goal will in turn enable more opportunities to WOW the customer.

How did Macy's do it? They threw out all of their legacy "tribal knowledge" and kept building the model around fixing what the customer said was either a frustration or implementing what represented the customer ideal. In the process, Macy's built what is now called "5-star delivery," which ranks as the preeminent home-delivery service in the country. In fact, among all the indices that Macy's as a corporation measures, the 5-star delivery system is ranked #1 in service attributes over everything else they do, including its best stores.

Customers, Defects, and Sigma Levels

Former Motorola quality manager Alan Larson, who worked closely with the late Bill Smith—the man credited with developing the Six Sigma measurement system—says the simplicity of the approach we are about to explore is one of its big advantages. Larson explains, "It's really a *math* system, not a statistical system. The beauty is, all you need to know is how to count, how to add, and how to divide—you don't have to be a statistician."

The first step, fundamental to Six Sigma, is to clearly define what the customer wants as an explicit requirement. In Six Sigma language these requirements are often called critical-to-quality (CTQ) characteristics. (We could also call them *key results*, or *Ys* of the process, or *specification limits*.) The next step is to count the number of *defects* that occur. We've used that term a lot already, but we need to give it a clear definition now:

> A defect is any instance or event in which the product or process fails to meet a customer requirement.

Once we've counted defects, we can calculate the yield of the process (percentage of items *without* defects) and use a handy table to determine the Sigma level.

Sigma levels of performance are also often expressed in defects per million opportunities (DPMO), also shown in Figure 2.4. DPMO simply indicates how many errors would show up if an activity were to be repeated a million times. By factoring in opportunities for defects in the calculation, Motorola made it more realistic to equate

Simplified Sigma Conversion Table:		
If your Yield is ...	Your DPMO is ...	Your Sigma is ...
30.9 %	690,000	1.0
69.2	308,000	2.0
93.3	66,800	3.0
99.4	6,210	4.0
99.98	320	5.0
99.9997	3.4	6.0

FIGURE 2.4   SIMPLIFIED SIGMA CONVERSION TABLE

performance across different processes. We cover DPMO calculation in Chapter 13, but for now you can think of it simply as another way to describe the quality or capability of a process.

Summary of Sigma Measure Benefits

Companies adopting the Six Sigma system have found that the Sigma scale approach to evaluating process performance offers them some significant advantages. Here's a quick recap:

1. **Sigma measures start with the customer.** Sigma measures demand a clear definition of what the customer's requirements are. That clarity can benefit both you *and* the customer, in terms of thinking through what's really important.
2. **Sigma measures provide a consistent metric.** With their focus on defects and defect opportunities, Six Sigma measures can be used to measure and compare different processes throughout an organization or between organizations. Once you've defined the requirement clearly, you can define a defect and measure almost any type of business activity or process. Here's just a tiny sample:

   ► Typos in a document
   ► Long hold times in a call center
   ► Late deliveries
   ► Incomplete shipments
   ► Medication errors
   ► Power outages

- ► Systems crashes
- ► Parts shortages
- ► Postsale repairs
- ► Expense check discrepancies

3. **Sigma measures link to an ambitious goal.** Having an entire organization focused on a performance objective of 99.9997 percent perfect can create significant momentum for improvement. The Six Sigma measurement approach—provided you invest some thought and effort in setting it up properly—can create a common "measurement language" for all parts of a business.

Sigma Measures: Considering Your Options

It's important to note that there's nothing mandatory about using the Sigma scale. It is possible, first of all, to achieve Six Sigma performance and never look at a Sigma conversion table. Also, various other valid ways can be used to measure and express the performance of a process or product/service—often labeled *key process or performance indicators* (KPIs).

In fact, since Six Sigma was first introduced, many companies have found that the use of the sigma measure is not as critical as simply *finding the right way to measure what they do.* So overall, while the concept of sigma measures is useful, you should view the adoption of Sigma scale measures as an optional element of the Six Sigma system. More important is to ensure effective measures that are meaningful to your organization, customers, and staff.

A final point: None of these measures of results (or Ys, as shown in Figure 2.3) will improve your performance by themselves. Without methods for analysis and improvement—and data to determine what makes the organization work more effectively—KPIs, DPMO, or Sigma represent just a final report card. Let's look next at the methods that drive Six Sigma improvement.

Six Sigma Improvement and Management Strategies

Customer knowledge and effective measures are the fuel of the Six Sigma system. The engine they propel is made up of three basic elements (see Figure 2.5), all of them focused on the *processes* of your

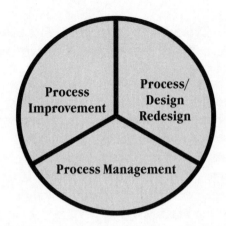

FIGURE 2.5   THREE SIX SIGMA STRATEGIES

organization. Linking these approaches is one of the most important (and least recognized) innovations that Six Sigma brings. Let's take a closer look at each one.

Strategy #1: Process Improvement— Finding Targeted Solutions

The term *process improvement* refers to a strategy of developing focused solutions so as to eliminate the root causes of business performance problems. Other terms that have been used synonymously include *continuous improvement*, *incremental improvement*, or *kaizen*, which is Japanese for "continuous improvement." In essence, a process improvement effort seeks to *fix* a problem while leaving the basic structure of the work process intact. In Six Sigma terms, the emphasis is on finding and targeting solutions to address the "vital few" factors (the Xs) that cause the problem or pain (the Y). Thus, the vast majority of Six Sigma projects are process improvement efforts.

To illustrate the our point, we describe a fictitious company throughout the rest of this chapter. We prefer using a fictitious example to citing a real example because we have seen how difficult it often is for companies in one industry—say, pharmaceuticals—to apply something to their own business if the example is from a different industry—for example, automobile manufacturing. We realize that the following example is a bit fanciful, but it does get our point across!

Case Study #1: Applying Six Sigma to a Transportation Company

Imagine that you're in the water transportation business, and your market niche is to row people in a small boat across a quarter-mile-wide channel. Your typical customer is on a weekday picnic or a weekend outing, so the leisurely row across the channel meets their requirements perfectly.

On some weekdays, though, more and more of your customers are commuters trying to avoid traffic to and from the bridge over the channel. Their speed requirements are a little more stringent; these folks want to get to the other side as quickly as possible. In addition, you can only take three people at a time, which means a line is starting to form on the landings on either side of the channel.

As you gather data, you find it is taking you an average of 7.5 minutes in each direction to cross the channel—and that your slow cycle time is creating the backups at the dock. Your problem is obvious: The boat (your process) is currently too slow.

In a brainstorming meeting with your management team (your spouse, kids, and some neighbors, actually), you develop a list of ways to improve the boat/process so that it will go faster and increase your capacity. Some of the ideas include:

- ▶ Row harder! (You wonder: "Are they calling me lazy?")
- ▶ Have one person on each oar.
- ▶ Get bigger oars.
- ▶ Give the passengers paddles.
- ▶ Put up a sail.
- ▶ Scrape the barnacles off the boat.
- ▶ Toss out extra weight. (You think: "But I like to bring a beer when I'm rowing!")
- ▶ Add an outboard motor.
- ▶ Add a big, huge outboard motor!

At first, you're not sure which idea is best. So you gather some more data and find that two solutions are most cost-effective and address the real root causes of your slow trips. You decide to scrape the boat and to increase your stroke rate by 10 per minute; and sure enough, you cut your round-trip time by three minutes.

In a few months, though, you've attracted more business and the "problem" is back: lines at the dock. Your next solution is to buy a moderate-sized outboard motor, which you can afford now, thanks to your increased revenues. The motor works great, and the boat/process is really humming along. You've managed to take a 15-minute round-trip and cut it to 5 minutes. The Sigma Shores Transportation Company (your new company name) is thriving. Customers are thrilled! And you've just successfully implemented two rounds of process improvement.

Strategy #2: Process Design/Redesign— Building a Better Business

One of the reasons business leaders lost patience with quality initiatives back in the 1980s was the slow pace of improvement they seemed to generate. That frustration opened the door to the reengineering boom of the early to mid-1990s. Even though reengineering ended up producing its own disappointments, it did offer an important perspective on driving better business performance: *Incremental improvements alone don't allow you to keep up with the rapid pace of change in the areas of technology, customer demands, and competition.*

That's why Six Sigma brings together *both* process improvement and design/redesign, incorporating them as essential, complementary strategies for sustained success. In the design/redesign mode, the objective is not to *fix* but rather to *replace* a process (or a piece of a process) with a new one. It also ties into product and service design— often called *Six Sigma design*—in which Six Sigma principles are used to create new goods and services tightly linked to customer needs and validated by data and testing.

In today's business world, no company is likely to stay on top for long if it does not rethink at least some key processes on a regular basis. Chuck Cox, a speaker, consultant, and coauthor of a book on process and product design, says a good rule of thumb probably is to "redesign major processes every five years. Things change that fast."

Let's see how that works at our transportation company.

Case Study #1 Continued: Major Redesign at Sigma Shores Transportation

The success of process improvement at your water transportation business is exceeding your wildest dreams. Lines at the landings are even longer than before. Also, you're getting requests from customers to transport them down the channel and out into the bay—not only a long trip, but dangerous for your little boat. It's becoming clear that your boat/process isn't up to the job anymore. It has reached what process design experts would call its *entitlement*—the limit of its capability as currently designed. When a work process hits that barrier (i.e., when the structure or basic premises of a process aren't keeping up with changing needs or opportunities), the only real recourse is to design a new process. In other words: Time to get a new boat!

Just making that fairly simple decision can open up a whole new panorama of innovations that weren't there for you when you were limited to "fixes." The implications of process design or redesign—as here, in getting a new boat—can be enormous. First of all, a new boat or a new process can be a big investment. But plenty of other factors must be considered as well:

▶ **Skills.** Do you know how to operate a bigger boat? You, or anybody who's working with you, will need to be trained and perhaps even certified to handle the new equipment and procedures. People may find themselves in completely new jobs they hadn't expected to be filling—or may not even want.

▶ **Customers.** How will they respond to a new boat? Will the intimate service and easy access of the rowboat be missed too much? Can you continue to attract enough customers to your crossing? Why do your customers really come to you—for the transportation or for the "rowboat experience"?

▶ **Competitors.** Will major ferry companies or other boating entrepreneurs invade your market? Will you sustain enough business to fully engage the new, bigger boat?

▶ **Other processes and facilities.** You and a few helpers have been able to handle ticket-taking, reservations, embarkation and debarkation, and the maintenance of your outboard-powered rowboat.

With a big new boat, however, processes on either side of the channel will need to be improved or redesigned, too.

Still, despite all of these worries and considerations, you realize you have no choice. Without the significant (exponential) leap in performance that your new boat surely will bring, your business will stagnate and likely lose its edge in the local transportation market. So you go ahead and make the major investment in time, money, and creativity to upgrade your processes, and you buy a shiny new, 30-passenger mini-ferry. Through careful design, planning, and testing, the new Sigma Shores Ferry is successfully launched—and you've reached a whole new level of performance.

Strategy #3: Process Management— The Infrastructure for Six Sigma Leadership

The third key strategy of Six Sigma is the most evolutionary. It involves a change in focus from oversight and direction of *functions* to the understanding and facilitation of *processes*, the flow of work that provides value to customers and shareholders. In a mature process management approach, the themes and methods of Six Sigma become an integral part of running the business:

- ► Processes are documented and managed end-to-end, and responsibility has been assigned in such a way as to ensure cross-functional management of critical processes.
- ► Customer requirements are clearly defined and regularly updated.
- ► Measures of outputs, process activities, and inputs are thorough and meaningful.
- ► Managers and associates (including "process owners") use the measures and process knowledge to assess performance in real time and take action to address problems and opportunities.
- ► Process improvement and process design/redesign—built around the improvement tools of Six Sigma—are used to constantly raise the company's levels of performance, competitiveness, and profitability.

We've described process management as *evolutionary*, because it is an approach that organizations tend to learn and develop slowly. The growth of process management as a practice actually parallels the expansion of Six Sigma into a complete management system. Let's see how process management works at our transportation company.

Case Study #1 Continued: Sigma Shores Institutes Process Management

Having totally revamped your business and processes in upgrading to a new ferry, you now make a vow: "Never again will I let an opportunity as big as this one sneak up on me." So you take steps to establish a more proactive, customer- and process-focused approach to managing the business. You assign your top staff members to take charge of key activities: promotions and sales, customer reservations and embarkation, onboard operations, landing and debarkation. Rather than "departments" you describe these as "processes," each defined by a process map and tracked by key measures.

At Sigma Shores Ferry, each manager keeps track of his or her critical process, communicating with counterparts so as to ensure smooth handoffs (of customers, in particular) and to share useful data. Your customer acquisition (i.e., sales) process owner expands your customer and competitive research efforts, thereby giving you better, more up-to-date information on how your service is performing and on any opportunities or threats. Having key measures on arrival times, service factors, customer boarding, and boat efficiency (e.g., fuel usage) helps you make a healthy profit while maximizing customer satisfaction. Your organization is no longer lurching from crisis to crisis; it's a finely tuned machine.

As you begin to solidify your Six Sigma–based management system, new employees are trained in a common model that guides any process improvement or design/redesign project. This model, which you call define, measure, analyze, improve, and control (DMAIC), gives your people a consistent way to manage change and improvement in your growing organization.

The DMAIC Six Sigma Improvement Model: Define-Measure-Analyze-Improve-Control

Many improvement models have been applied to processes over the years since the quality movement began. Most of them are based on the steps introduced by W. Edwards Deming—Plan-Do-Check-Act (PDCA)—which describes the basic logic of data-based process improvement:[4]

- ▶ **Plan.** Review current performance for issues and gaps. Gather data on key problems. Identify and target root causes of problems. Devise possible solutions, and plan a test implementation of the highest potential solution.
- ▶ **Do.** Pilot the planned solution.
- ▶ **Check (*or* study).** Measure the results of the test to see whether the intended results are being achieved. If problems arise, look into the barriers that are obstructing your improvement efforts.
- ▶ **Act.** Based on the test solution and evaluation, refine and expand the solution to make it permanent, and incorporate the new approach wherever applicable. *Then, start over. . . .*

In *The Six Sigma Way*, we will use and refer to a five-phase improvement cycle that has become increasingly common in Six Sigma organizations: define, measure, analyze, improve, and control—or DMAIC (pronounced "deh-MAY-ihk") (see Figure 2.6).[5] Like other improvement models, DMAIC is grounded in the original PDCA cycle; however, we will be using DMAIC to apply to *both* process improvement and process design/redesign efforts. Therefore, whenever we refer to "DMAIC projects" throughout the remainder of this book, we are talking about efforts using either Six Sigma improvement strategy. Figure 2.7 provides a diagram of the major DMAIC activities, comparing the *process improvement* to the *process design/redesign* paths.

Conclusion: Defining the "Six Sigma Organization"

To close out this discussion of the key concepts of Six Sigma, let's take a brief look at the notion of a Six Sigma organization. Our proposed

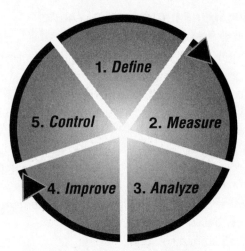

FIGURE 2.6   THE DMAIC SIX SIGMA IMPROVEMENT MODEL

definition of a *Six Sigma organization*—and the one we will be using in this book—is this:

> An organization that is actively working to build the robust themes and practices of Lean Six Sigma (regardless of whether it is *called* Six Sigma) into its daily activities and is showing significant improvements in process performance and customer satisfaction.

Now for a few notes to accompany that definition.

1. To qualify, you do not need to have achieved actual Six Sigma levels of performance (99.9997 percent perfect) on any process. Most people realize now that a so-called Six Sigma organization such as GE has never actually reached this quality nirvana all across the board. But don't get discouraged: Just taking all your processes to *Four* Sigma (99.37 percent yield) would be an enormous achievement for any company we can think of.

2. Simply using sigma measures or a few tools does not qualify a company to be a Six Sigma organization either. Our definition makes the criteria tougher by demanding a *broad scope* of activity and commitment. A real Six Sigma organization should be one that has taken up the challenge of measuring, prioritizing, and continuously improving in critical areas. The objective then is to build a capability

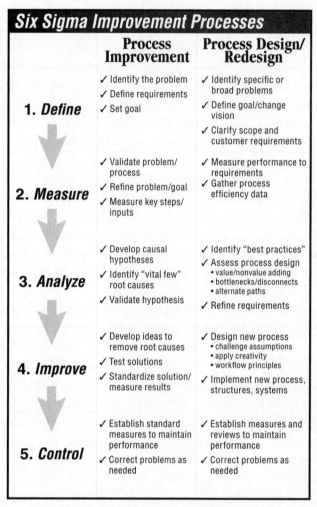

Six Sigma Improvement Processes		
	Process Improvement	**Process Design/ Redesign**
1. Define	✓ Identify the problem ✓ Define requirements ✓ Set goal	✓ Identify specific or broad problems ✓ Define goal/change vision ✓ Clarify scope and customer requirements
2. Measure	✓ Validate problem/ process ✓ Refine problem/goal ✓ Measure key steps/ inputs	✓ Measure performance to requirements ✓ Gather process efficiency data
3. Analyze	✓ Develop causal hypotheses ✓ Identify "vital few" root causes ✓ Validate hypothesis	✓ Identify "best practices" ✓ Assess process design • value/nonvalue adding • bottlenecks/disconnects • alternate paths ✓ Refine requirements
4. Improve	✓ Develop ideas to remove root causes ✓ Test solutions ✓ Standardize solution/ measure results	✓ Design new process • challenge assumptions • apply creativity • workflow principles ✓ Implement new process, structures, systems
5. Control	✓ Establish standard measures to maintain performance ✓ Correct problems as needed	✓ Establish measures and reviews to maintain performance ✓ Correct problems as needed

FIGURE 2.7   OVERVIEW OF PROCESS IMPROVEMENT AND PROCESS DESIGN/REDESIGN PATHS IN DMAIC MODEL

for improvement that enables sustained performance and the ability to adapt to new challenges or—to borrow a theme from AlliedSignal—to "create a culture of continuous renewal."

3. You don't have to call it Six Sigma to be a Six Sigma organization. The system, the methods, and the commitment are much more important than the name you give to your effort. In fact, we often advise clients to find a "brand" for continuous improvement efforts that fits their organization and is more appealing than "Six Sigma" or

"Lean." Although these terms are still popular, they can sound a bit strange to people in the organization. And, unfortunately, enough cases of what you might call "Six Sigma malpractice" have occurred that some people associate the concepts and tools themselves with their ineffective application. Although it is a bit like watching three-year-olds play tennis and concluding that tennis is a terrible game, it's also understandable. So be smart about what you call *your* Six Sigma efforts, and don't take the name as mandatory.

For example, at leading communication and graphics software company Adobe Systems, their adaptation of Six Sigma is called Business Process Improvement (BPI), because "people are less spooked by that term," says Devin Rickard, senior manager of Business and Process Improvement. In fact, the company is moving to make even that term more user-friendly. As Rickard explains, "We're in the process right now of further defining the brand within the company: we found there tends to be a preconceived understanding—or lack of understanding—and a negative reaction to the term 'BPI,' so we've been rebranding around the term 'Simplify.' Our goal is to simplify how our employees get their jobs done on a day-to-day basis and to simplify the lives of our customers and the interactions that they have with our company. It's not that we don't utilize or are not proponents of Six Sigma, but quite often, in the language that we use in trying to drive that cultural change, we will not necessarily refer to Six Sigma and BPI, but we're focusing on communicating to our people that 'we're trying to simplify our jobs and how we get things done at Adobe.'"[6]

In fact, one of Rickard's colleagues who came from another large technology company told Rickard that the term *BPI* was "the very first thing we need to change." Rickard understood, because technology companies often operate under the preconceived notion of what business process improvement is, and it's not necessarily positive. Rickard believes it's important to find a way to be able to communicate in the language of the business without intimidating people or driving them off because they're thinking "this is another one of those quality improvement efforts that we're going to hear a lot about for six months, and then it's going to just blend into the woodwork and eventually go away."

That's why Adobe decided to brand everything around *simplicity*, because they want to help people—both the company's customers and its employees—to simplify. As Rickard explained, "People don't need to be concerned about *how* we go about doing that and what tools we're using. The important thing for them to realize is we're here to partner with them to make it easier for them to do their jobs and to deliver quality to our customers. As long as we stay focused on that, then the results are what become important. In order to get those results, we are applying Six Sigma, but we don't necessarily market Six Sigma as 'Six Sigma' internally, because we don't want to cloud the message, which is simply that we're here to drive improvement for the company, to make it easier for our employees to get their jobs done and for our customers to do business with us. So we just use the tagline 'simplify.'"

At Starwood Hotels and Resorts, some divisions use the name Six Sigma, while other divisions have moved to calling their improvement efforts "Operations Excellence" or "Operational Innovation." Starwood operates a wide array of well-known hospitality brands including Westin, Sheraton, W, St. Regis, Le Meridien, and others, and it has divisions all over the world. The North America team decided to stick with the Six Sigma name. Brian McGuire explains why: "We just knew that SS already had such a strong brand name that we'd been working so hard to develop, so we decided not to change the name. Starwood's Six Sigma team made some subtle tweaks about not holding onto projects, and we didn't beat our chests, saying 'here's another Six Sigma project'; instead, we did the work for whatever discipline needed to roll it out, and then we let them be the face of it and take all the credit and get the buy-in from their constituents in the field. We held onto the Six Sigma name, and it's still strong today at Starwood." Adobe Systems' Rickard emphasizes that the selection of the language you use always depends on your audience. You have to understand your customer, understand your audience, and understand what their tolerance is. As he says, "There are a whole host of 'organ-rejection' words, and if you use those terms in the wrong context, your audience will immediately reject whatever it is you're trying to focus the conversation on at the time. . . . For some people, it's 'Six Sigma'; for other people, it's 'process'; for still others, it's 'business process improvement.'"

He goes on to say, "Tech companies tend to be more sensitive to terminology than other companies, and depending on who you're talking to in a tech company, they're going to be more sensitive to or tolerant of those terms. If I'm talking to people in order management, or simulation operations, you can use the term 'process' and they completely get it, and they understand the importance of process to how well they deliver. On the other hand, if you start talking about 'process' in the sales organization, they're going to see process as more of a necessary evil: they may not like the process, but they understand that they need to follow a process. Finally, if you use the word 'process' to people in engineering, that's a word they believe should be banned from the lexicon entirely. So what term you use really just depends on your audience."

As more and more organizations have adopted Six Sigma—in earnest or just for show—the term *Six Sigma organization* in many ways has fallen by the wayside. But that should not diminish the impact that using the practices of Six Sigma can have for an organization. Despite its detractors and misapplications, Six Sigma is still the "best seller" in improvement approaches worldwide today.

CHAPTER 3

Applying Six Sigma to Service and Manufacturing

A common concern of managers and business leaders is: "How can Six Sigma apply to *my* organization?" We have heard this question hundreds of times, and it seems to come most often from people in service- or transaction-based areas, who wonder how this supposedly manufacturing-oriented discipline will help them. Manufacturing managers have their doubts as well, especially because many manufacturing processes have already been through intense *quality* scrutiny. Thus in this chapter we will look at some compelling reasons why *both* service and manufacturing operations can benefit from a Six Sigma discipline, and show you how to adapt your approach to meet unique challenges in either arena.

First let's clarify the terms we'll be using:

▶ **Service processes and businesses.** When throughout this chapter we talk about *services* or *service and support* processes, what we mean is any part of a company not directly involved in designing or producing tangible products. It can mean sales, finance, marketing, procurement, customer support, logistics, or human resources and more in *any* organization, from a steel company to a bank to a retail store. A few of the other words used to describe these activities include *transactional, commercial, nontechnical, support,* and *administrative.*

▶ **Manufacturing processes.** By *manufacturing* we mean only those activities relating to the development and production of tangible products. Other terms used to describe these are *plant floor, production, a fab,* and sometimes *engineering* and *product development.* These categories are quite broad, of course. For instance, we find a large variation among service processes, as between a call center and a consulting firm. Likewise many differences exist between a company that manufactures coffee cups and another that makes semiconductors. Nevertheless, the issues involved in making Six Sigma effective tend to be most similar *within* these two categories of service and manufacturing. Although as we will see, it's likely that your service activities will benefit most from the Six Sigma approach.

The Changing Role of Manufacturing

These days, purely "manufacturing" companies do not exist.

Designing, producing, and/or selling manufactured products is still, of course, the core business of many companies. The need to provide defect-free products (those that work as expected and meet customer requirements) is more important than ever. Nevertheless, the success of a manufacturing firm is hardly guaranteed solely by producing defect-free goods. A successful manufacturing business needs to master many competencies, including the following:

▶ Keeping track of new technologies and being able to develop them rapidly into viable products.
▶ Understanding existing and emerging customer needs that can be met by improved processes and/or new/improved products.
▶ Establishing and managing supplier networks so as to ensure a timely supply of parts and raw materials.
▶ Taking, processing, and filling customer orders accurately—including building to unique specifications as needed—and profitably.
▶ Adapting to shifting market conditions.
▶ Determining the best "sourcing" strategy to provide optimal value and retain competitive advantage.

On this last point, the once-simple answer for many companies has been to move production to China or another developing manufacturing location to achieve lower costs. This option has proven to be more dynamic over time as costs in one area increase and the added complexities and costs of global logistics are included in the equation. Some hints today indicate that U.S. and European firms may be looking to "redomesticate" key portions of their production to get closer to some markets.

Although determining the right approach to sourcing any firm's manufacturing efforts is a complex challenge, what's certain is that using the best facts, customer knowledge, and processes to execute the best mix requires capabilities pretty close to those of Six Sigma.

Service Process Opportunities—and Realities

As the role played by services in boosting business competitiveness grows, so too does the evidence of plenty of untapped potential in these activities. Consider the following factors:

- ▶ Research has shown that the costs of poor quality (rework, mistakes, abandoned projects, etc.) in service-based businesses and processes typically run as high as 50 percent of total budget. (In manufacturing operations, it is estimated at about 10–20 percent.)
- ▶ These cost data match with our experience and that of many others who find that administrative and service processes, prior to improvement, perform in a range of 1.5 to 3 sigma (yields of 50–90 percent).
- ▶ Analyses of service processes often reveal that less than 10 percent of total process cycle time is devoted to real work on tasks that are important to paying customers. The remainder of the effort and time is used up in waiting, rework, moving things around, inspecting to catch defects, and nonessential activities.

What Makes Six Sigma in Services More Challenging?

Some important, understandable reasons help to explain why service-based activities often have more pent-up opportunities for improvement than manufacturing operations, including:

Service Work Processes Are Often Invisible. In most fabs and factories, you can see, touch, and even follow work product through a process. Take a simple production process such as making a hamburger. When you order a meal at a fast-food place, you expect to receive it in just a little more time than it takes to cook and assemble the burger—and usually that's what happens. Buns, patties, and ingredients, once they are picked up to make your burger, are cooking or moving most every second on the way to your tray or paper bag. It is not easy to hide a patty and a bun in your "out basket" or e-mail folder on the burger production line.

Likewise on a typical plant floor, bottlenecks, slowdowns, scrap, and rework show up quickly to the trained eye. Here's a vivid example. We worked at a bottling plant that would divert any unfilled bottles into a large glass recycling bin: Every defective bottle would loudly *crash* and shatter as it fell into the scrap pile! So too, if you ever see a flame (or "flare") burning over an oil refinery; it is not there as a decoration: it is a sign something is not working right in the plant.

By contrast, the *work product* of most service processes is much harder to spot by simple observation: information, requests, orders, proposals, presentations, meetings, signatures, invoices, designs, and ideas. As more and more service processes revolve around information handled in computers and networks, the work product becomes virtual, flowing from screen to screen or server to server as mere electrons. In fact, with e-mail and the Internet, a service-based process can jump from location to location all around the world instantly. That capability can be a big advantage, of course, in the globalized economy, but it sure does make an understanding of how the work gets done even harder to come by.

Brian McGuire, vice president of operations at Starwood Hotels confirms this difficulty: His company started using Six Sigma in 2001, but "it took us five to six years to see what a good DMAIC project looks like at a hospitality company, since we were the first ones to use Six Sigma in a hospitality setting. There wasn't a roadmap, and we were figuring it out as we went along, and through some missteps and mistakes, we figured out what it looked like. Then we had a template to go forward with, and then we really started seeing some of the meatier SS projects kicking off around 2008 through today, and we became a little bit pickier about the scope of projects that we went after, because we had better experience in knowing what a good project looked like."

Just as big a challenge can be servicepeople's beliefs about their work. Because their processes are often not tangible and can be driven by personal style and circumstance, people working at key functions such as sales, marketing, and even software development are notorious for commenting: "We don't have a process." Actually, they do—usually several of them. But these people are so close to the processes that it can be a challenge to get them to recognize them.

As an example, in health care organizations, a common phenomenon is for each nurse, at the start of his or her shift, to rearrange the work area or patient room to fit personal preference—a sign that the process that *does* exist is not standard, but rather based on who's doing the work. That may not seem like a big deal, until you think about the time spent by all the nurses in all the clinics and hospitals that might be better used caring for the patients.

Service Workflows and Procedures Are Often Continuously Evolving. When you make a change in a production process, it usually takes some work: things get moved, raw materials are sent to different locations, and tooling and procedures are changed. For that reason, changes to manufacturing processes usually are given a high level of deliberation. In fact, making *planned* change more rapid and efficient is a key to success in today's manufacturing environment.

Outside of manufacturing, though, a formal process can be changed quickly, especially if it's a simple change and hasn't gotten itself too ingrained in people's habits. Responsibilities can be shifted, forms revised, new steps added, guidelines altered, and so on, without any capital investment or serious deliberation. Many changes arise out of individual, even spur-of-the-moment decisions, with ramifications that may be small. Add up all the individual choices and changes though, and the overall impact can be huge. As a result, service processes in many businesses evolve, adapt, and *grow* almost continuously (not exactly like viruses—but it's a tempting analogy). If this evolution were purposeful and well-thought-through, it would be fine, but more often it is much closer to random and reactive.

Lack of Facts and Data Make It Difficult to Measure Service Performance. In light of the previous point, it isn't astonishing that the hard facts on the performance of service processes often are pretty skimpy-looking. The data that do exist are narrowly focused, anecdotal, and/or subjective. Even though the nature of these processes makes them inherently more difficult to measure, it can be done, and done well, once the process itself begins to be better understood.

For example, noting and tracing problems in a service process is usually more challenging than in a plant or production facility. Backlogs, rework, delays, and the costs of working on them are hard to spot. It is possible to track the expenses of a department or work group, but tying those costs to specific process activities is still tricky.[1]

Pick up almost any manufacturing or quality engineering trade publication and you will see a slew of ads for production-monitoring and -testing equipment. Measurement for manufacturing is a multibillion-dollar industry. In action, manufacturing measurement can be impressive. For example, a medical products plant in Texas has a display showing various aspects of its production line including a continuous readout on cost-per-unit, in fractions of a cent, updated every few seconds.

Except for volume measurement in computer networks and customer call centers, though, service process managers can't just plug in a machine to do their measurements for them. For instance, one company has been working on streamlining its loan document closure process. They learned—surprise!—that dozens of people independently have been checking up on and trying to solve problems with loan packets, resulting in a significant amount of redundant time and effort. However, accurately *measuring* the time and cost of the rework and redundancy is difficult, because those tasks make up a relatively small slice of many different peoples' workdays.

Service Processes Lack the "Head Start" That Manufacturing Has. Inspectors, quality-control staff, quality engineers, and process improvement gurus have been prowling manufacturing floors for decades. After all, the discipline of maximizing efficiency helped to make the United States the productivity leader of the world in the two decades after World War II. It was as other economies caught up with and passed key industries in the effectiveness or quality of their products that American corporate leadership received a startling wake-up call.

Fortunately, however, service process improvement has caught up to manufacturing on many levels. In fact, as much—if not more—impact in organizational benefit comes from nonproduction-type processes as from manufacturing. Six Sigma is no longer thought of as just for manufacturing.

Patricia Small, vice president of Global Learning and Development at Cartus, a leading corporate relocation and business services firm, has firsthand experience in handling this issue. Cartus helped companies relocate and transfer more than 160,000 people to 165 countries around the world in 2012, using Six Sigma to ensure results-driven performance for its clients. Because Cartus is a service organization, Small recognizes that one of the challenging aspects of her job of training people in how to apply Six Sigma is how it applies to service: "It's much easier for people to understand some of the concepts if I use a manufacturing example and then translate it over to a service example, rather than trying to start with a service example, because that seems rather abstract to them. In contrast, manufacturing examples are very concrete."

Making Six Sigma Work in Services

The following tips for making Six Sigma more effective in services are really just broad suggestions. It is up to you to make them fit your specific organization, products, customers, and so on. Overall, however, these ideas should help you to get results in a service arena faster, with greater positive impact, and with better buy-in from the "this doesn't apply to us" skeptics you're likely to run into.

Services Tip #1: Start with the Process. Ever go to a dance or a party where at the end, someone turns up the lights? It's usually a bit of a shock, maybe a little sad, but also gives you a chance to see things more clearly. Some of the discoveries might include:

- What the people at the party (including you) really look like.
- Who's there whom you may not have seen before.
- How the room has been arranged.
- Where the games or activities were held that you missed.
- What a mess the place is!

In most service organizations, starting to investigate processes is like turning up the lights. Though often something of a rude awakening, it also can be an enlightening event that gets the Six Sigma effort off to a fast start. As people discover what's really going on, they can recognize that one party seems to be over but that another one—cleaning the place up—is just getting under way.

Incidentally, starting with the process is not a bad idea in manufacturing environments either; it just tends to be more critical for services.

Services Tip #2: Fine-Tune the Problem. When the bright lights come on, it takes a few seconds for your eyes to adjust. So too, when you shine a light on service processes, it takes a while for a group to see and understand the issues around them as clearly as they should, which is to be expected. The only way to get a really clear perspective is to get to work detailing your processes and customer requirements, and the issues affecting them.

In the meantime, though, fuzzy vision and an overeagerness to "straighten this place up" can lead to projects or improvement initiatives that are not well defined. The temptation may be to tackle large, unwieldy issues or to launch dozens of minor projects simultaneously, which can raise frustration levels and thereby damage your credibility.

The discipline of effective project selection and problem definition is essential in manufacturing, too. It just tends to be more difficult to choose and scale projects in service environments at the outset of the Six Sigma effort. (For more on the "how-to" of project selection, see Chapter 10.)

Services Tip #3: Make Good Use of Facts and Data to Reduce Ambiguity. One of the biggest obstacles to generating measurable improvement in the service arena is the fact that things often are not well described or defined. For example, product specifications in manufacturing often are noted precisely—literally in milliseconds and microns—while in services they are usually sketchy if they exist at all. That means that as you start to shed light on processes and customers in a service environment, a high priority should be to translate ambiguity into clear performance factors and measures throughout your operations. The ability to define and measure intangibles, the more subjective factors, is one of those unique skills that is a must in service processes but often is a nonissue in manufacturing. In fact, we've worked with quite a few Six Sigma and quality experts with terrific skill and experience in manufacturing, who have trouble adjusting to the greater ambiguity of services. One of the concepts covered in Chapter 13—operational definitions—becomes critically important to create meaningful service process requirements and measures.

Patricia Small of Cartus confirms how the process works in her company's service business: Cartus sends business to certain vendors—especially in the moving services functions—based on metrics Cartus has of those vendors' past performance. That process now is more data driven, which it wasn't before. She explains: "We had data, of course, but since we started using Six Sigma, our people *really* speak in terms of data now: you don't even come to the table without data now. And that's one of the lessons we learned: we had to change our mentality from people just saying, 'This is a really big problem,' to a point where people wouldn't come to a meeting without having done their homework about how big the problem is and what might be causing it."

Small also notes that in a service business, it's easy for every complaint to turn into a gigantic crisis: "Service people are accustomed to thinking in terms of reaction and emotion and experience, so they really needed to change their mindset to 'How can I measure progress?' Measurement is a key point: rather than hitting the panic button, we needed to step back from the problem and look at it logically. We firmly believe the principle of 'If you can't measure a problem, you can't fix it.' Yet that's something our people needed to get creative about: 'How do I measure a customer's experience?' Yet there are ways you can."

Lower volumes in some service processes pose an extra challenge, as they can in manufacturing, too. (See the Applied Materials example later in this chapter, on page 54.) If you're completing only a few dozen "deals" in a month, or you have a tightly focused, intimate customer base, getting large amounts of hard data will be difficult if not impossible. But that shouldn't excuse you from managing your business on a basis of facts and data—you will just need to gather and analyze the data differently. You will still be able to *improve* your processes, too. (For more on that, see "Measuring Rare or Low-Volume Activities" in Chapter 13 on page 203.)

Services Tip #4: Don't Overemphasize Statistics. This notion has been a source of controversy over the history of Six Sigma. For quite a while, our suggestion to avoid getting too enamored of applying statistics was drowned by the clamor for ever-more-sophisticated analytical methods—a kind of improvement tools arms race. But over the years, as individuals have been trained in a vast number of statistical methods, many of which are rarely if ever *used*, the arms race has thankfully subsided in most quarters. The greater emphasis on and impact of Lean methods, which use process and data but usually eschew statistically derived proof, has also helped restore balance to the debate.

The experience of one of our service clients helps illustrate why we urge you to avoid feeling like you are only "doing Six Sigma" if everything is quantified and statistically verified: This firm—an innovator in financial services—was enjoying tremendous growth. When we began working with them, they were turning *away* business and hiring more than 200 new people per month. It was, however, a good news/bad news scenario. Senior management of the company recognized that too many of the new people were being put to work just to deal with the problems created by a chaotic environment.

Less than a year after launching several high-priority improvement projects and introducing Six Sigma and teamwork skills, this company was able to significantly shift its management approach, making it more proactive, fact-based, and cooperative. They achieved major savings and streamlining of inefficient processes, enabling them to handle the company's aggressive growth targets. They retained their fast-paced, entrepreneurial spirit, but channeled those energies more effectively into what their customers and market needed. We heard many of their people comment on how much the Six Sigma skills improved their approach to problems and processes, and the whole atmosphere of the company.

As we talked over their keys to success with the company's Six Sigma vice president, he quickly noted, "I'd say one of the best choices we made was not to push people into heavy statistics right away." His reason was simple, if twofold: that the people who aren't used to technical processes and measurement aren't ready for more sophisticated tools, and that the data they have available isn't ready for advanced analysis.

Adobe is another company that believes in not overemphasizing statistics: in fact, one of their critical success factors was their pragmatic approach to applying Six Sigma. Devin Rickard says, "We jokingly refer to it as 'Stealth Sigma.' We make sure that how we apply the different tools of Six Sigma doesn't take precedence over the business problems we're trying to solve. We're very sensitive to the culture of the company, so we make sure the Black Belts who are working on the projects really understand and speak the language of the business, and we make sure our business partners aren't overwhelmed with having to learn a lot of new terminology or new concepts related to Six Sigma. Ultimately, that's really the responsibility of our Black Belts, to know what those concepts are and how to apply the right tools at the right time. We want to give our business partners confidence that we understand the problems they're faced with, that we have a very effective set of Six Sigma tools that we can apply, that we can identify the changes that are necessary, and that we can successfully implement those changes."

This is not to say using statistics to better understand data, find causes, and validate outcomes is not, at times, essential. But from the outset, it's most important to Six Sigma improvement that people in services *or* manufacturing learn to ask critical questions about their processes and customers:

- ▶ "How do we really know that?"
- ▶ "Is there some way we can test our assumptions?"
- ▶ "What are the data telling us?"
- ▶ "Is there a *better* way to do this?"

Manufacturing Challenges

Your attempt to apply Six Sigma to manufacturing will bring with it some unique challenges, too. The following are some of the most prevalent difficulties you should be mindful of, along with some suggestions to help you overcome them.

Manufacturing Challenge #1: Adopting a Broader Perspective

People on the plant or shop floor have always tended to be somewhat isolated from the rest of the business. And as manufacturing activity becomes an ever-smaller proportion of the overall activity of a business, the risks of isolation from other groups in the company and from external customers increase. The Six Sigma system, though, demands communication and coordination all along your company's critical processes, as well as the demolition of the barriers between manufacturing and the rest of the world. Two key messages arise when manufacturing groups can begin to see their role as integrated into the entire business:

1. **Most problems are not manufacturing problems.** Folks in production will benefit when they and others in the business begin to see data proving what they already had suspected: that unclear orders, last-minute changes, parts and staffing shortages, engineering/ design errors, and so on have a greater impact on delivering the right stuff to the customer on time than do defects on the plant floor. For example, see the GE Power Systems story in Chapter 1 on page 5.

   Givaudan is another company that proves this point. This Switzerland-based company is the global leader in the fragrance and flavors industry: it makes products that are used by other companies that make foods, beverages, consumer goods, and fragrances. Givaudan uses automated equipment that assembles or pours anywhere from 10 to 40 different fragrance ingredients to make a particular product, for such client companies as Unilever and Lancôme. It's a highly customized process, because every product has its own distinct formula, whether shampoo, soap, laundry detergent, or fine perfume.

   In one of Givaudan's plants, the time gap between the first ingredient and the last ingredient was as much as 12 hours, which meant that for much of that time, they were just waiting for the next ingredient. So Givaudan's operations people looked at how they were managing the equipment and how people were communicating, and within a couple of weeks, they were able to reduce that 12-hour time to about 2 hours. That reduction enabled them to streamline the entire process and potentially deliver orders to customers quite a bit sooner.

2. **Manufacturing needs to become an active participant in the entire process.** Just because barriers to Six Sigma often are not the production group's "fault" doesn't mean that improvement isn't their responsibility. The manufacturing folks in many organizations need to be educated on their role in helping to solve "upstream" issues as well as dealing with challenges faced by such "downstream" activities as warehouses and customer service.

One way to change the internal focus of manufacturing is to target Six Sigma improvement projects that demand cross-functional cooperation, including manufacturing. For example, involving people from the plant floor to improve order fill rates will help change the view that *making* the product is a distinct and unrelated activity from selling or delivering it.

The other terrific opportunity for a broader perspective comes through using Six Sigma methods to better integrate product design/development (aka new product introduction) and manufacturing. Some of the most impressive success stories in Six Sigma annals involve using key customer feedback to create refined or totally new products, and then using advanced Six Sigma methods to ensure that the new products can be produced at a Six Sigma level of quality.

Manufacturing Challenge #2: Moving Past Certification to Improvement

A few years back we heard a manager at a computer systems manufacturer complain about his problem in getting new production and testing equipment properly calibrated. As we probed into the problem, he described the company's equipment acquisition process, which surprisingly involved receiving new equipment *twice:* once when it was delivered by the manufacturer, and the second time from a vendor who had calibrated the equipment.

We were asking some obvious questions, such as "Why don't you have the equipment vendor send the items *directly* to the calibrator?" Or better yet, "Why not make the *vendor* responsible for calibrating it?" Then a manager from the company's quality group spoke up: "ISO-9000 requires us to do it this way," he explained.[2]

The emphasis on various manufacturing certifications and audits—ISO-9000 being the most prevalent—can, in our experience, hamper a company's *improvement* efforts. And clearly, in this example, the excuse that certification *requires* a circuitous (and problem-filled) process is just not true. It is true, however, that once a process has been "certified," it tends to be perceived as "law." The too-common case in a certified environment is that once a process has been documented and approved, it is hell-on-earth to improve it.

Of course, more enlightened companies do use their certification efforts to examine and improve their processes. Using certification efforts and the information they provide about process performance can be a valuable complement to Six Sigma, but it usually takes some effort to create a common language between the keepers of the quality management system (such as ISO) and the improvement needs of the business.

Manufacturing Challenge #3: Adapting Tools to Your Manufacturing Environment

So far we have talked about manufacturing as if every production operation were the same, which of course is not at all the case. Making auto engine parts is a distinctly different process from refining chemicals; bottling bleach is different from building computer monitors. We cannot of course even begin to tell you just how you will need to adapt Six Sigma methods so as to optimally fit every type of manufacturing environment. It is important to recognize, though, that you *will* need to flex Six Sigma techniques to make them do their best for you.

We can use one company's experience as a great example here. Applied Materials, the world's leading manufacturer of equipment for semiconductor plants (or "fabs" as they're usually called), first got involved in Six Sigma way back in the late 1980s.

The challenge for Applied Materials Manufacturing in adopting Six Sigma, however, was in using concepts like defects per million opportunities. "We manufacture pieces of equipment that are room-sized," explains Dave Boenitz, then-head of the Applied Materials Quality Institute. "We deal in hundreds of units, not millions. Each unit is comprised of eight, ten, twelve, fifteen *thousand* parts. So if you were to look at a sigma level per unit, it would be very difficult comparing apples to apples. You could definitely look at a million opportunities in one of our systems, but it's a matter of finding out *which* million opportunities you're going to measure."

The approach Applied has concentrated on to reduce defects has been "mistake proofing"—a diligent effort to find and prevent all kinds of mistakes and errors in a process (described in more detail in Chapter 17). "We just have not put energy into the Sigma or DPMO measures, because we don't see what the value-add is going to be." But the improvements Applied makes are just as valid.

Conclusion: Making Six Sigma Work Best for You

If there's one theme we're likely to overstate in this book, it's the need to select, apply, and adapt Six Sigma methods and ideas to fit your organization's needs and readiness. As soon as any consultant, guru, or author tells you "Here's how you have to do it," we recommend that you politely excuse yourself and leave the room. The *real* answer to how you can best implement Six Sigma in your business is, as we've noted, "It depends."

Fortunately, Six Sigma is a robust system; even with the challenges likely to arise in your organization. Whether in service or manufacturing, you can be successful if you remember, and remind others, that Six Sigma is not really a program or a technique. It's a flexible but essential way to make your business more responsive, efficient, competitive, and profitable.

With that in mind, let's turn to Chapter 4, for an overview of the five steps on the Six Sigma roadmap.

CHAPTER 4

The Six Sigma Roadmap

In this chapter we conclude our executive overview with a look at the ideal roadmap for establishing the Six Sigma system and launching improvements. These five steps, depicted in Figure 4.1, feature what we would suggest are core competencies for a successful twenty-first-century organization:

1. Identify core processes and key customers.
2. Define customer requirements.
3. Measure current performance.
4. Prioritize, analyze, and implement improvements.
5. Expand and integrate the Six Sigma system.

Advantages of the Six Sigma Roadmap

The roadmap is not the only path to Six Sigma improvement; you will likely need to adjust the order of these steps, or even start more than one of them simultaneously. In Part Two we will look at ways to adapt the roadmap, based on your organization's specific needs and goals. What makes this path "ideal," however, is that, taken in this order, these activities build up the essential foundation that will then support and sustain Six Sigma *improvement*. Specifically, the roadmap's advantages include:

▶ A clearer understanding of the business as an interconnected system of processes and customers.

FIGURE 4.1   THE SIX SIGMA ROADMAP

- ► Better decisions and uses of resources to get the greatest possible amount of benefit out of your Six Sigma improvements.
- ► Shorter improvement cycle times, thanks to better up-front data and selection of projects.

▶ More accurate validation of Six Sigma gains, whether in dollars, defects, customer satisfaction, or other measures.

▶ A stronger infrastructure, to support change and sustain results.

This roadmap is guaranteed to win a poll as the ideal implementation approach among Six Sigma veterans, as well. Everyone we have worked or spoken with who has been involved in a Six Sigma launch—executives, implementers, and team members—agrees that this is the path they *should* have followed in the past and *would* follow if given the chance to in the future.

As an example here, one of our clients (a unit of GE) spent nearly two years launching dozens of Six Sigma improvement projects—in essence, starting at the roadmap's Step 4. Despite their best intentions and efforts to make those projects pay off, the rate of success did not meet expectations. Projects took longer than expected, and results tended to dissipate after the teams had disbanded. Over time, the firm's top leaders began to realize that one source of their trouble was that, in the words of their number-two executive, "We didn't really know what we should be working on. Like other companies, most of our projects were *internally* focused."

Having gained that insight the hard way, this company had to backtrack in order to fulfill some of the earlier tasks on the roadmap. For example, they have now installed systems and processes to gather real-time "voice of the customer" data (Step 2), as well as measures to evaluate performance against customer "critical to quality" (CTQ) criteria (Step 3). Their improvements now are focused on real customer needs, firmly backed up by data.

Step 1: Identify Core Processes and Key Customers

As businesses become more dispersed and global, customer segments more narrow, and products and services more diverse, it gets tougher and tougher to see the "big picture" of how the work actually gets done. By taking Step 1, you begin to bring that big picture into clearer focus by defining your critical activities and getting a grasp of the broad structure of your business system.

The objective of Step 1 is to create a clear, big-picture understanding of the most critical cross-functional activities in your organization and how they interface with external customers. This objective is applicable to an entire organization or any segment of it. Even a department or function that serves internal customers (e.g., human resources, information technology, or facilities) has its own core processes that deliver products, services, and value to customers.

The deliverable of Step 1 is a "map" or inventory of value-delivering activities in your organization, driven by three questions:

1. What are our core or value-adding processes?
2. What products and/or services do we provide to our customers?
3. How do processes flow across the organization?

The knowledge to be gained from Step 1 is important as a prerequisite for the customer knowledge-building activities of Step 2. A more significant benefit of this high-level inventory, however, is the new, clearer understanding gained about the organization as a whole. If it is already clear to you how and why it is such a great idea, you can jump down to Step 2.

If you're still not sure why the big picture of your customers and core processes is needed, come with us on a trip to Company Island.

Case Study #2: Company Island Lacks a Bird's-Eye View

Company Island is a land much like many corporations or even departments. On the island are several rivers (processes) that flow to the sea and deliver nutrients (products and services) to various and sundry fish (customers). Life is pleasant, though busy, on Company Island. Most of the time, people spend their days tending to their small stretch of a river, or helping make sure the fish come get their nutrients. (Other nearby islands—Competitor Island, Upstart Island, Cash Cow Island, etc.—also are trying to lure the fish.)

The trouble is, life on Company Island is a lot more complicated than even the island's leaders are aware of. For example, along the shore, it turns out that the rivers don't come to the sea in a single broad channel. Instead it's more like a delta, with lots of small rivulets. Some of these may deliver lots of good food to the fish, others may be dumping toxic waste. Big fish get a lot of attention, while the smaller ones are ignored (or sometimes vice versa).

On shore, it's equally complicated. Some streams end nowhere; others meander so much that they take forever to get to the sea. Some tributaries are uncharted and untended by the professional managers (Company Island has a great business school), so they get overgrown and silted up. In fact, in some places well-intentioned islanders have actually built dams that block a river's flow, leaving downstream islanders mighty thirsty and unhappy with their upstream colleagues.

Sometimes, a few folks on Company Island see the problems that need attending to and fix them; unfortunately, a good proportion of those fixes actually hurt things going on downstream or in other rivers. (Islanders who work the shore and tend the fish tend to yell loudest when that happens.)

If those folks could just get more people together to talk about what's happening in the various regions of Company Island, they could piece together a true, complete map of the place. With that bird's-eye view, it would be much easier to identify where the fish are well fed and where they're "fed up" and ready to head for another island. Also, Company Islanders could then figure out which rivers are the most treacherous or slow-moving, and shift their attention to those major trouble spots.

"Mere myth!" you may shout. "Our 'island' is a paradise by comparison!" another may claim. Cold reality would indicate, however, that few organizations really have a true understanding of the lay of the land. The existing maps often are woefully inaccurate, particularly when organizational islands, unlike physical ones, can and do change quickly.

Anyway, we hope you get the point of Company Island: It's difficult to manage, let alone improve, an organization when working with only a ground-level, incomplete picture of how it works and what it does. Step 1 of the ideal Six Sigma roadmap is the place where you begin to chart your island.

Step 2: Define Customer Requirements

One of the discoveries often admitted to by business leaders and managers after embarking on Six Sigma is that, to quote one executive, "We really didn't understand our customers very well." We also saw how this problem happened at Macy's in our earlier example about furniture delivery: the company *believed* its customers were most concerned about having their furniture arrive in perfect condition, when the data revealed that customers took that factor as a given but were even *more* interested in having it delivered within a specific delivery window so they wouldn't have to wait around all day. Clearly, getting good customer input on your company's needs and requirements may be the most challenging aspect of the Six Sigma approach. As we see in Chapter 12, it takes much more than the occasional survey to figure out what your customers really want at a given moment.

Step 2 has two objectives:

1. To establish standards for performance that are based on actual customer input, so that process effectiveness/capability can be accurately measured and customer satisfaction predicted.
2. To develop or enhance systems and strategies devoted to ongoing "voice of the customer" data gathering.

The deliverable sought in Step 2 is a clear, complete description of the factors that drive customer satisfaction for each output and process (aka requirements or specifications) in two key categories:

1. Output requirements that are tied to the end product or service that make it work for the customer (what quality gurus have called "fitness for use")
2. Service requirements that describe how the organization should interact with the customer.

The rationale behind Step 2 is that if you don't know what customers want, it is quite difficult to give it to them. Moreover, in the context of achieving Six Sigma performance, you cannot develop meaningful measures until you have clear, specific requirements. You may gather data while turning up relatively few defects, but entirely ignore other areas where you are falling short.

The further rationale for Step 2 is one of attitude. What's gotten many companies—even entire industries—into serious trouble in the past is a "we know what's best for the customer" mentality.[1] Almost as bad is the misguided belief that "we're really tuned in to the needs of our market," when in fact the company is out of touch with changing demands. Arrogance or ignorance may have been tolerable 20 years ago, but in today's competitive environment either one is a sure predictor of trouble.

In the twenty-first century, it will be the companies that really listen to their customers that are most likely to see long-term survival and success.

Step 3: Measure Current Performance

While Step 2 defines what customers want, Step 3 looks into how well you are delivering on those requirements today, and how likely you are to do so in the future. On a broader level, performance measures focused on the customer serve as the starting point for establishing a more effective measurement system.

The objectives of Step 3 are to accurately evaluate each process's performance against definable customer requirements and to establish a system for measuring key outputs and service features.

The desired deliverables are as follows:

- ▶ **Baseline measures:** Quantified evaluations of current/recent process performance
- ▶ **Capability measures:** Assessment of the ability of the current process/output to deliver on requirements through Sigma scores for each process, which allow comparison of distinctly different processes
- ▶ **Measurement systems:** New or enhanced methods and resources for ongoing measurement against customer-focused performance standards.

Note that measurement systems should also capture data on the efficiency of your processes: costs per output, energy or material consumption, rework, and so on. You can have happy customers and highly inefficient operations, which makes for an unprofitable formula.

The need for an accurate grade of performance against customer requirements should be obvious. Several other benefits of Step 3, however, make it much more valuable than a report card:

- ▶ **Creating a measurement infrastructure.** This foundation gives you the power to follow changes in performance—good or bad—and to respond promptly to warning signs and opportunities. Over time, these data become key inputs to the responsive, always-improving Six Sigma organization.
- ▶ **Setting priorities and focusing resources.** Even in the short term, knowledge derived from these measures drives decisions as to where to make the most urgent and/or high-potential improvements. The impact is a higher return on investment for process design, redesign, or improvement projects (Step 4).
- ▶ **Selecting the best improvement strategies.** Having accurate process capability measures allows you to gauge the real nature of performance issues: Are they occasional problems or minor issues, or situations implicitly demanding that an entire product line or process be revamped?
- ▶ **Matching commitments and capabilities.** Ever hear salespeople wonder in frustration, "How come we can't do this for the customer?" Or people in operations complaining about "impossible commitments" made by the sales force? Better communication alone won't resolve these disconnects, which in many businesses are some of the most challenging and costly. You need to have the added advantage of the knowledge gained through Six Sigma methods—both about what customers really want and what the organization can actually *deliver*.

Step 4: Prioritize, Analyze, and Implement Improvements

Now that you are equipped with facts and measures, not just anecdotes and opinions, you are ready at Step 4 to start cashing in on the real payoff of Six Sigma.

One objective of Step 4 is to identify high-potential improvement opportunities and develop process-oriented solutions supported by factual analysis and creative thinking. Another objective is to effectively implement new solutions and processes and provide measurable, sustainable gains.

The deliverables of Step 4 are as follows:

▶ **Improvement priorities:** Potential Six Sigma projects assessed based on their impact and feasibility
▶ **Process improvements:** Solutions targeted to specific root causes (aka continuous or incremental improvements)
▶ **New or redesigned processes:** New activities or workflows created to meet new demands, incorporate new technologies, or achieve dramatic increases in speed, accuracy, cost performance, and so on (aka Six Sigma design or business process redesign

The rationale for improving business processes probably needs no explanation. A key to success in the Six Sigma system is to choose your improvement priorities carefully and not to "overload" the organization with more activities than it can handle. The value of the improvement methods applied in Step 4 is that they encompass the best techniques for driving out defects and improving process efficiency and capacity. Six Sigma techniques and tools can be applied to large, complex business problems or to fairly simple process improvement opportunities.

Step 5: Expand and Integrate the Six Sigma System

Real Six Sigma performance will not come to you through a wave of improvement projects. It can be achieved only through a long-term commitment to the core themes and methods of Six Sigma.

One objective of Step 5 is to initiate ongoing business practices that drive improved performance; another objective is to ensure constant measurement, reexamination, and renewal of products, services, processes, and procedures. Step 5 is the place where your organization works hard to achieve the vision of a Six Sigma organization.

The deliverables of Step 5 are:

▶ **Process controls:** Measures and monitoring to sustain performance improvement
▶ **Process ownership and management:** Cross-functional oversight of support processes, with input from voice of customer, voice of market, voice of employee, and process measurement systems

▶ **Response plans:** Mechanisms to act based on key information so as to adapt strategies, products/services, and processes
▶ **Six Sigma culture:** An organization positioned for continuous renewal, with Six Sigma themes and tools an essential part of the everyday business environment

Perhaps the strongest rationale for Step 5—the place where you take on the chore of building a long-term vision of a Six Sigma organization—is to consider the possibility of *not* doing it.

It is a few years from now. You have been watching more than a few customers defecting to an upstart competitor, a company that claims to have put a Six Sigma system in place. As you investigate, you learn that this growing business does in fact have some advantages over your older, less-responsive company, such as:

▶ An accurate, well-channeled customer feedback system
▶ Well-integrated, "seamless" processes, with smooth handoffs and cooperation up and down the line
▶ Timely measurement systems that track not just dollars but also defects, changes in key activities, variations in key inputs like raw materials, etc.
▶ Expertise in correcting problems and making improvements, either by fine-tuning processes or by creating entirely new processes, products, or services to meet changing customer needs

How comfortable would you be with that type of competition? Can you be confident that tomorrow a similar firm won't start making inroads into your profits or market share? How would you defend yourself against that type of competitor? If such questions make you squirm even a bit, it is an indication that Step 5 should be made a key element in your Six Sigma efforts.

Recapping the Executive Summary

As we close out Part One of *The Six Sigma Way*, we offer you five summarizing subsections just as a reminder of *what* Six Sigma is and *why* it offers so many potential benefits to any organization.

Definition of Six Sigma

Six Sigma can be defined in several ways:

▶ It's a way of measuring processes.
▶ It's a goal of near-perfection, represented by 3.4 defects per million opportunities (DPMO).
▶ It's an approach to changing the culture of an organization.

Most accurately, though, Six Sigma is a broad and comprehensive *system* for building and sustaining business performance, success, and leadership.

In other words, Six Sigma is a context within which you will be able to integrate many valuable but often disconnected management "best practices" and concepts, including systems thinking, continuous improvement, knowledge management, mass customization, and activity-based management.

Six Essential Themes

The vision of a Six Sigma organization embraces all of these six themes:

1. **A genuine focus on the customer,** backed by an attitude that puts the customers' needs first, as well as by systems and strategies that serve to tie in the business to the voice of the customer.
2. **Data- and fact-driven management,** with effective measurement systems that track both results and outcomes (Ys) and process, input, and other predictive factors (Xs).
3. **Process focus, management, and improvement,** as an engine for growth and success. Processes in Six Sigma are documented, communicated, measured, and refined on an ongoing basis. They are also *designed* or *redesigned* at intervals to stay current with customer and business needs.
4. **Proactive management,** involving habits and practices that anticipate problems and changes, apply facts and data, and question assumptions about goals and "how we do things."
5. **Change management,** engaging the people of your organization to unlock their ideas and energies, while helping them adapt to new practices and improve performance.

6. **A drive for perfection, and yet a tolerance for failure,** that gives people in a Six Sigma organization the freedom to test new approaches even while managing risks and learning from mistakes, thereby raising the bar of performance and customer satisfaction.

History and Evolution

Six Sigma was developed at Motorola in the late 1980s as an adaptation of total quality management, providing a clear focus on improvement and helping to accelerate the *rate* of change in a competitive environment. The concept, tools, and system of Six Sigma—many of which have been around for decades—have evolved and expanded through the years, which has helped to continually rekindle interest and redouble efforts at process and quality improvement. Because Six Sigma and its cousins like Lean, Theory of Constraints, and so on are fairly easy to *try* but hard to *sustain*, many organizations have experienced several iterations of continuous improvement, but all are based on a common set of principles that are integrated into Six Sigma.

Results and Opportunities

At early adopters such as GE and Honeywell, Six Sigma yielded billions in gains in a few years and has taken root—with modifications—as a part of the business culture. Of the many organizations worldwide that have taken up the Six Sigma (or Lean Six Sigma) banner over the past decade and more, many have achieved significant results and have developed thousands of improvement-trained "experts" who continue to lead improvement efforts. Still, creating a sustainable *culture* of continuous improvement has been an elusive goal for many organizations.

The opportunities open to your business will depend on your current performance and defect levels, your competitive position, and so on. If yours is a *service*-based process or organization, you may actually have a much greater potential for improvement than does a product or manufacturing organization.

Implementation

It is essential that your organization develop its own strategy and plan for launching and integrating Six Sigma. Many experienced users would endorse some version of these five basic steps:

1. Identify core processes and key customers.
2. Define customer requirements.
3. Measure current performance.
4. Prioritize, analyze, and implement improvements.
5. Manage processes for Six Sigma performance.

Still, as we will see in the chapters of Part Two, many options are open to you as you seek to define goals and to execute Six Sigma.

PART TWO

GEARING UP AND ADAPTING SIX SIGMA TO YOUR ORGANIZATION

CHAPTER 5

Is Six Sigma Right for Us Now?

Embarking on a Six Sigma initiative begins with a decision to *change*—specifically, to learn and adopt methods that can boost the performance of your organization. In its most ambitious applications, Six Sigma can be a more fundamental change than, say, a major acquisition or a new systems implementation, because Six Sigma affects *how* you run the business. The depth of impact on your management processes and skills will vary, of course, with how extensively you want to apply Six Sigma tools and the results you are seeking.

The starting point in gearing up for Six Sigma is to verify that you're ready to—or need to—embrace a change that says "There's a better way to run our organization." This decision shouldn't be a rote, number-crunching-based decision; you will need to consider a number of essential questions and facts in making your readiness assessment, which are covered in this chapter.

Six Sigma Readiness

1. Assess the Outlook and Future Path of the Business

A first step is a general review of the condition of your organization today and its outlook for the future, both in the short and the long term. Key questions are listed in Exhibit 5.1.

Exhibit 5.1

KEY QUESTIONS TO ASSESS THE FUTURE PATH OF YOUR BUSINESS

■ *Is the strategic course clear for the company?*
  • Do we have a strong sense of what value we offer to the market and to our customers?
  • Is there a plan to adapt the strategy to potential or pending changes in our markets, technologies, and so on?
■ *Are our chances good for meeting our financial and growth goals?*
  • Is the business in a healthy enough state that it has the needed cash and capital to provide customer and shareholder value?
  • Can we meet the expectations of analysts and investors?
  • Do we have a strong theme or vision for the future of the organization that is well understood and consistently communicated?
■ *Is the organization good at responding effectively and efficiently to new circumstances?*
  • Will we be able to plan and manage change (new products, acquisitions, growth, etc.), or are we more likely to be reacting to internal and external events?
  • Are we creating truly innovative new products and services that will keep us in the lead?
  • How stable are our customers' needs? Our technologies?
  • How able are we to maintain and improve our intellectual capital?

Generally good prospects make it less likely that you need Six Sigma to sustain your success, as long as you're being realistic about your future. Complacency and/or overconfidence, however, always are dangerous in the twenty-first-century business environment. Thus it's a good idea to discount any rosy predictions as a hedge against unforeseen events.

In fact, a positive outlook can also be seen as a compelling reason in *favor* of Six Sigma. Along with those companies that have embarked on Six Sigma to stave off future disaster, plenty have taken on Six Sigma in the midst of strong growth and positive projections. For example, one of our clients—an integrated logistics company—has grown tenfold over the past decade and has good reason to project similar gains as large firms continue to outsource their logistics and warehousing efforts. Nonetheless, they are taking on Six Sigma to help leverage and guarantee their growth and competitive position.

2. Evaluate Your Current Performance

Even if your organization's situation appears very positive, continued scrutiny and recognition of issues or weakness is essential. Six Sigma makes it easier to be more honest and accurate in assessing where you are today; the more you can use hard data to answer the questions listed in Exhibit 5.2, the better.

Exhibit 5.2

QUESTIONS TO ASK WHEN EVALUATING YOUR COMPANY'S CURRENT PERFORMANCE

- *What are our current overall business results?*
  - Are we meeting sales and profit goals?
  - Are any areas (products, business units) underperforming?
  - How well are we performing against key indicators—and are those measures truly meaningful (for example, based on real data)?
  - Is our output performance subject to a lot of variation?
- *How effectively do we focus on and meet customer requirements?*
  - Do we even understand what our customers need?
  - How would we describe our relationships with key customers/ segments? What would *they* say?
  - Do we compete mainly on price—and might we find better ways to convey value to our customers?
  - Does our service match the quality of our products, and vice versa?
  - How successful are our new products or services when released to the market?
  - Are we able to satisfy one player in our supply chain but not others?

■ *How efficiently are we operating?*
  • What level of rework and waste exists in our processes?
  • Are we so "busy" solving problems and fighting fires that we never take time to improve things?
  • What's our cost per unit—is the trend improving or getting worse?
  • Are our support processes—finance, human resources, facilities, and information technology—enhancing our ability to deliver value to customers, or simply enforcing rules and policies?
  • How smoothly do our new products or services reach the market?

While this assessment can yield a variety of insight and/or additional questions, from a "Should we take up Six Sigma?" perspective, you need to look at these basic issues:

▶ **Is there enough room for improvement to make Six Sigma worthwhile?** If everything is humming along just fine and the money is rolling in, you may decide the potential payoff from Six Sigma isn't worth the effort. On the other hand if you see some major improvement opportunities—financial and/or competitive—that's a sign that Six Sigma may be a worthwhile option. For some organizations, too, the potential value of Six Sigma lies in improving the culture or habits of the business (e.g., converting from a reactive, "seat-of-the-pants" style to a more responsive or proactive management approach). However, because the negative impact of a reactive culture will show up in increased costs, you should be able to back up the need to "improve our culture" by pointing to concrete financial benefits to be gained.

▶ **Where are the best opportunities for improvement?** This part of the assessment can give you initial insights into those high-priority needs on which your first Six Sigma projects may focus.

▶ **How effective are our customer knowledge and measurement systems?**

The harder you found it to answer these three questions, the more seriously you should consider adopting Six Sigma methods to help you strengthen your "voice of the customer" and measurement capabilities.

3. Review Systems and Capacity for Change and Improvement

A third major factor in deciding whether to launch Six Sigma is the organization's existing improvement processes and its ability to undertake a new initiative. Exhibit 5.3 lists some of the questions you should consider here.

Exhibit 5.3

QUESTIONS TO ASK ABOUT YOUR CAPACITY FOR CHANGE AND IMPROVEMENT

- *How effective are our current improvement and change management systems?*
  - Do we already have efforts under way to improve our performance, measures, systems, and so on?
  - Are the improvement efforts well-coordinated, or are they disconnected (aka "shotgun") solutions?
  - Do data sufficiently support the choice of improvement priorities and result measurements?
  - How well do we implement solutions and changes—both from a technical and a people perspective?
  - Have we integrated continuous improvement into our business culture?
  - Are we good at making changes and flexing to meet new business challenges?
  - Is our quality effort/group focused on improvement, or just on control?
- *How well are our cross-functional processes managed?*
  - Do our people understand the entire process or just their own narrow slice?
  - Do we provide enough opportunities for our people to learn more about the business as well as about the key skills that drive people's performance?
  - Would we be able to adapt quickly to new customer demands or tighter requirements?
  - Do functional groups interact well, or do barriers exist between departments?

- • Are decisions subject to a lot of reviews or checks, or do we
  trust our people to make the call?
- ■ *What other change efforts or activities might conflict with or
  support a Six Sigma initiative?*
  - • Are recent acquisitions, new product introductions, strategy
    changes, systems implementations, or other "big" initiatives
    likely to consume people's attention and resources?
  - • Would other changes make potential Six Sigma solutions
    obsolete?
  - • Can Six Sigma be used to help leverage a new initiative (e.g., to
    help integrate processes in a merger or redesign activities for a
    new information system)?

The purpose of this third assessment element is to test the timing
and readiness of the business for a possible Six Sigma effort. Even if
assessment factors 1 (future prognosis) and 2 (current performance)
make a strong case to initiate Six Sigma, your business may already be
capable of dealing with the challenges. Or your people, systems, and
resources may already be all wrapped up in making other efforts or
changes, in which case you'd have trouble making the commitment of
leadership, time, and energy, not to mention money, that a Six Sigma
effort demands.

For example, when Givaudan implemented SAP, that technology
provided a new way to dig into data and get more detailed information
on a global level about how the company was doing and what factors
were driving sales. Once Givaudan started digging into its data,
managers became even more interested in finding methodologies
for how to improve. Willem Mutsaerts, Global Head Operations
Fragrances at Givaudan, describes what happened when the company
discovered Six Sigma:

> We started projects left and right, and even though we were
> informed that Six Sigma is a high-impact initiative, we were laugh-
> ing because we thought we could do things in six months and then
> go back to doing what we were always doing. But now it's three
> years later, and we're still at the beginning stages of this journey,
> because it's a complete change.

Initially, we focused on specific opportunities and projects where we felt we could improve. Then, based on our success stories, we decided to roll out Six Sigma globally and to engrain Black Belt education into our DNA. Change management takes more time than simply having consultants come in, do a Six Sigma project, and then leave after six months. Our positive experience with our Six Sigma projects made us realize that we should acquire this knowledge inside, so our journey will be much more intensive and longer. We're training people now in Six Sigma, and we have between 10 and 20 people trained as Black Belts.

When Six Sigma Is *Not* Right for an Organization

First, let's remind ourselves that Six Sigma can be applied as a *targeted* approach, so a limited implementation may always be feasible. Nevertheless, we can look at the flipside of the preceding assessment to identify conditions in which it probably would be best to say "No thanks" (for now) to Six Sigma efforts. Conditions that might indicate a "no-go" decision on Six Sigma include the following:

▶ **You already have in place a strong, effective performance and process improvement effort.** If systems and tools are in place to support ongoing problem solving and process design/redesign, Six Sigma may not add much value—and might even confuse people.

▶ **Current changes already are overwhelming your people and/ or resources.** An organization can handle only so much turmoil at once. Lumping Six Sigma on top of one or more other major business upheavals could prove to be the proverbial straw on the camel's (your company's) back. However, beware of making the "we're too busy" argument, which often ends up as a weak excuse for never doing the tough work it takes to become a truly outstanding organization. Just as with getting married or having children, you cannot pinpoint a "perfect" time. Your success will have a lot more to do with how well you integrate and use Six Sigma to support other, existing changes.

▶ **The potential gains are not there.** Six Sigma demands an investment. If you cannot make a solid case for future or current return, it may be best to stay away—at least until you have figured out exactly how and when it might pay off.

Summarizing the Assessment: Three Key Questions

At the end of a review of your business, including its future and current states, and its organizational factors, the objective is to decide whether take on, or at least seriously consider, a Six Sigma initiative for the organization. The specifics boil down to three key questions:

1. Is change (whether broad or targeted) a critical business need now, based on bottom-line, cultural, or competitive needs?
2. Can we come up with a strong strategic rationale for applying Six Sigma to our business? (Which is another way of saying, "Will it get and hold the commitment of business leadership?")
3. Will our existing improvement systems and methods be capable of achieving the degree of change needed to keep us a successful, competitive organization?

If your answers are *Yes, Yes,* and *No,* you may well be ready to explore further how to adopt Six Sigma in your organization. By the way, these three questions also may be found in the Six Sigma Start-Up Worksheet in Exhibit 6.2. (The lower half of the worksheet focuses on finding the type of effort that makes the best sense for you, based on the discussions in the following chapter.)

Six Sigma from a Cost/Benefit Perspective

Though we touched on several factors relating to the potential value and feasibility of Six Sigma, the blunt question we often hear posed by executives and managers is this: "Exactly what is Six Sigma going to cost, and what kind of return can we expect it to bring us?" Unfortunately, that question cannot be answered without examining the improvement opportunities present in your business, and then planning your implementation to see what the relative payoff will be. We can, however, offer you a bit of guidance on how to estimate—and manage—your likely return.

Estimating Potential Benefits

You can most accurately define possible financial gains from Six Sigma by evaluating the costs of rework, inefficiency, unhappy or lost customers, and so on, and then estimating the amount by which you think you can *reduce* them. For example, if you've developed measures of defects per million opportunities (DPMO), you would determine the average cost of each defect (taking into consideration people, material, and other factors) and total savings for an *x* percent defect reduction. The more specifically you can define these numbers, called *costs of poor quality* (COPQ), the more accurate your estimates will be.

The type of assessment will never be perfect, however, for the following reasons among others:

1. Because it would be a huge amount of work to quantify costs for *all* the problems in any organization, you will likely have to rely instead on guesstimates, or the broader overview assessment described earlier.
2. Knowing what extent of savings is possible (what "x percent" really means) will really be just a guess until someone actually starts analyzing the problem and the possible solutions to it—in other words, only *after* you've started doing the real work of Six Sigma improvement.
3. External impacts are hard to quantify. For example, it is challenging to project just how many new customers you will gain, or existing ones you will prevent from defecting, simply by improving a key process. A certain level of Six Sigma effort is based on *faith* that better management and data will translate into better market image and customer loyalty.
4. You won't be able to work on everything, and the choice of improvement projects will significantly impact the early success and financial benefit of the Six Sigma initiative. We cover improvement project selection in detail in Chapter 10, where we seek to ensure that you will target the optimal opportunities.

Probably the best way to get good estimates of potential Six Sigma financial benefits is to take a combined approach. First, conduct a detailed financial benefit assessment of several representative improvement opportunities. Then, project how many similar opportunities exist across the organization to give you a more solid answer to the "How much can we gain?" question, but remember that it will still be an estimate.

Determining Lead Time for Results

We once had a colleague who displayed the following saying on her desk: "Everything takes longer than you expect, even when you expect it to take longer than you expect." That wonderful truism could be applied to many things, but it sure can hold true for Six Sigma results. Improvement projects can exceed their predicted completion times by months, especially when those projects haven't been well defined to begin with. Predicting when you will see real dollars or major customer impact will depend a lot on *what* you choose to work on.

Still, it is relevant and important to wonder what the lead time for a payoff will be. Generally you should figure *six to nine months* for the first wave of DMAIC projects to be completed and results to be concrete. Of course, you *can* push for faster results and look for "quick win" opportunities. Giving people coaching from an experienced person as they work through their "learning curve" can be a good way to accelerate efforts although it also may boost your costs. Based on our experience and the many companies we have observed, it would be a mistake to forecast big tangible gains much sooner than that for a couple of reasons:

1. **It takes time to sift through and target the right or best opportunities for projects.** This lesson is a difficult one to learn: you probably know *lots* of things that need improvement, but often those are just initial ideas that require time and even some up-front work to validate.

2. **Confirming results does not happen immediately.** Green Belts and Black Belts or improvement project leaders often focus their attention on a deadline to implement their solution, which becomes the date everyone has in mind. In reality, it may take days, weeks, or even months to gather data and verify the impact of the improvement. In the meantime, people get frustrated and unnecessary doubts arise.

Timing of when you begin can affect how results are calculated as well. We know of several organizations that have set goals for improvement impact during a fiscal year period, but then delayed launching projects until midyear, making it quite a scramble to "cash in" under the deadline. Thus, if a pay-as-you-go implementation is critical, you may want to consider how to schedule your Six Sigma launch so as to achieve your results time frame. You can also consider how to manage your *costs* so that the urgency of a payoff won't be as great.

The Costs of Six Sigma Implementation

Back in the 1970s, total quality guru Philip Crosby wrote a successful book entitled *Quality Is Free*, suggesting that eliminating waste and poor quality would drive a handsome payoff far exceeding the investment. For many organizations, Crosby's hypothesis is certainly true, but it doesn't mean you can unlock those benefits without some seed money. So if you can't find *any* budget to support a new or rejuvenated Six Sigma effort, you may just have to wait.

Some of the most important Six Sigma implementation costs—or investments—will include:

► **Direct payroll.** Individuals dedicated to the effort full time. (See Chapter 8, Preparing Black Belts and Other Key Roles.)
► **Indirect payroll.** The time devoted by executives, team members, process owners, and others to such activities as measurement, voice of the customer data gathering, and improvement projects.
► **Training and consulting.** Teaching people Six Sigma skills and getting advice (from folks like us) on how to make the effort successful can be a significant investment, too.
► **Improvement implementation costs.** Expenses to install new solutions or process designs can range from a few thousand dollars to millions—especially for IT-driven solutions. (But keep in mind that you're likely *already* making these investments, and their payoff may not be very positive.)

Other expenses to keep in mind include travel and lodging, facilities for training, and office and meeting space for teams.

Estimating and Managing Your Costs and Returns

Estimates of *your* Six Sigma costs will depend on your implementation speed, the scale of your effort, and your general risk profile when it comes to investing in the potential gains of the initiative. Many of the factors impacting your investment decisions, including your overall objective, staffing, training, and project selection, are covered in the subsequent chapters of Part Two.

The example of our client, GE Capital Services (GECS), may be encouraging. GECS launched Six Sigma in 1996 and spent about $53 million the first year—a number driven more by speed and scale than by a concern for controlling costs. (It was not Six Sigma on a shoestring!) However, the initiative reportedly paid for itself that same year, with $53 million in gains and savings. In year 2, 1997, Six Sigma expenditures at GECS rose to $88 million, but gains were pegged at $261 million—a $173 million *profit*. In year 3, the profit reported was $310 million over expenses of $98 million.[1] The scale is usually different for organizations that have followed GE, but we have seen only a few instances where the investment was not at least a break even.

How can you optimize *your* Six Sigma return on investment (ROI)? Primarily by making careful, smart decisions as to where the investment is most likely to pay off. We have observed and worked with companies that probably spent more than was necessary to get results from their Six Sigma efforts. On the other hand, trying to do Six Sigma "on the cheap" can be a bad move. It can adversely affect the quality of the training and advice you receive; but more importantly it sends the wrong message to the organization about the seriousness of your commitment. When you ask people to invest their energy and enthusiasm in improving the business—which often involves sacrifices to their personal time, potentially risky career decisions, and stepping outside their comfort zone to try new skills and tools—the company has to show its willingness to sacrifice, too.

Cost/Benefit and Your Six Sigma Launch

The question raised at the start of this section was "Exactly what is Six Sigma going to cost, and what kind of return can we expect it to bring us?" By now we hope you understand why we believe that a strictly cost/benefit–based decision on a Six Sigma start-up is usually not the best approach. (The exception would be for a limited, one- or two-project effort.) For most companies, the issues that affect potential return are much too broad and the cost/benefit estimates too sketchy to base your decision on that ratio alone. We suggest that the culture and climate factors cited earlier in this chapter (i.e., the organization's readiness for change, the ability to track and understand customer needs, the tendency to go with "firefighting" versus fire *prevention*, etc.) should have as much influence on your Go/No-go decision as any hard dollar estimates.

If Six Sigma continues to look attractive to your organization at this point, the next meaningful question you should be asking is "How do we ensure that our Six Sigma effort works well and yields a significant return in both the short term and long term?" Answering that question will be our focus through the remainder of Part Two.

CHAPTER 6

How and Where Should We Start Our Efforts?

The first important choice you have to make in your Six Sigma launch, and one that affects your costs and the potential size and speed of your return on investment, boils down to asking "Where do we begin?" You can use the Six Sigma roadmap that was introduced in Chapter 4 to frame and guide these start-up decisions. In this chapter, we actually look at two ways to approach your initial implementation decisions. The first is based on criteria that affect the scale and urgency of your effort; the second is an assessment of your strengths and weaknesses in what we call the *core competencies* of the Six Sigma system.

Where to Start: Objective, Scope, and Time Frame

"How *should* your organization begin its push toward Six Sigma performance?" When tough questions about Six Sigma are posed, we tend to fall back on one of these two answers: "It depends" and "God only knows."

Because the second answer leaves us unable to consult further, we try to narrow down "It depends." Fortunately for us, decisions on how to tailor your approach clearly rest on three primary factors: your objective, your scope, and your time frame. These elements are interrelated, but looking at them one at a time provides some guidelines on how to make your start-up decisions. As we review these criteria, you should recognize that information drawn from the Six Sigma readiness assessment, covered in Chapter 5, can be a big help in your implementation choices.

Clarifying Your Objective

What do you want your Six Sigma efforts to accomplish?

Every business wants results from Six Sigma, but the type of result or change that is needed (or feasible) can vary significantly. For example, Six Sigma may be attractive as a way to address nagging problems in terms of product failures or gaps in customer service. Then again, you may be part of a profitable, growing business, but recognize that your success is creating a reactive management culture that threatens future growth. Each of these scenarios leads to a different type of Six Sigma effort.

We previously defined three broad levels of objective—business transformation, strategic improvement, and problem solving (see Figure 6.1)—based on the scale of impact you want to make on the

Objective	Description
Business Transformation	A major shift in how the organization works; aka "culture change." Examples: • creating a customer-focused attitude • building greater flexibility • abandoning old structures or ways of doing business
Strategic Improvement	Targets key strategic or operational weaknesses or opportunities. Examples: • speeding up product development • enhancing supply chain efficiencies • building e-commerce capabilities
Problem Solving	Fixes specific areas of high cost, rework, or delays. Examples: • shortening application processing time • reducing parts shortages in West • decreasing volume of past-due receivables

FIGURE 6.1   THREE LEVELS OF SIX SIGMA OBJECTIVE

organization. It is tempting, of course, to say "I want it *all*!" But identifying which is your primary driver for Six Sigma (for now, at least) will help you to arrive at the best start-up strategy.

Assessing Your Scope

What segments of the organization can or should be involved in your initial Six Sigma efforts?

Scope can be influenced by your position in the organization. If, for example, you head an information technology group, you may have the authority and resources to launch a Six Sigma change effort in IT, but certainly not across the entire corporation. Even so, it is possible you will want to try to influence your organization's leaders to begin a companywide effort. In fact, one of our clients did begin to implement its Six Sigma effort based just on some early suggestions coming from the vice president of IT.

Another element of scope revolves around the basic question, "What's feasible?" It may not be realistic to take on every business activity simultaneously. Even at GE, some businesses and processes were not included in the initial Six Sigma wave. Sales processes, for instance, didn't receive any focused attention until more than a year into the effort. Businesses such as NBC (now part of Comcast) started a little later, too. Scrutiny of your core processes or business operations can provide valuable input as you seek to focus your initial scope.

Determining feasibility always involves trade-offs (as we said, "It depends"). The three main factors that come into play in most cases are the following:

1. **Resources.** Who are the best candidates to participate in the effort? How much time can people spend on Six Sigma efforts? What budget can be devoted to the start-up? What other activities will compete for resources?
2. **Attention.** Can the business focus on many start-up efforts at the same time? Will you or other leaders be overwhelmed as you try to guide too many activities simultaneously?
3. **Acceptance.** If people in a certain area (function, business unit, department, etc.) are likely to resist, for whatever reason, it may be best to involve them later. It is the organizational change version of the adage "Choose your battles."

Defining Your Time Frame

How long are you—or the powers-that-be—able/willing to wait to get results?

In other words, "urgency" or "patience" or "degree of panic" might be more accurate here than "time frame." A long lead time for a payoff can be frustrating; companies can be like kids on a car trip ("Are we there yet?"). The time factor, in fact, has the strongest influence on most Six Sigma start-up efforts, and for good reason.

Chuck Cox, one-time head of quality efforts for the server division of computer firm Groupe Bull and longtime Six Sigma consultant, noted: "You can't persuade the senior guys to break loose the resources and lead the charge unless they see a pretty immediate return on the investment." To Cox, getting gains in a quick-start mode is the best way to prove both the concept and value of Six Sigma.

Cox also agreed, however, that short-term gains are not the main point. The real goal is to create an organization that can effectively hang on to "a loyal customer base," something that can happen only with a long-term, integrated effort. The danger of a purely project-based, problem-solving approach is that you never raise the scope of your work so as to really capitalize on the Six Sigma system.

On-Ramps to the Six Sigma Roadmap

Possible starting points—corresponding to the objective for your Six Sigma effort—are presented in Figure 6.2 as on-ramps to the road-map. It's even possible to take more than one on-ramp at a time—a neat trick, as long as you are careful not to spread your resources and energies too thinly. After we explain the on-ramps, we will present a start-up scenario to illustrate each category.

Business Transformation On-Ramp

The top on-ramp in Figure 6.2 is for those who have the need, vision, and patience to launch Six Sigma as a full-scale change initiative. At the outset it may be more feasible—and a worthwhile learning exercise—to concentrate on developing a map of a few core processes, rather than trying to identify and define all processes at once. In addition, taking the business transformation on-ramp does not close down the other ones for you. In fact, usually it is smart to approach any organizational change as a multifaceted effort.

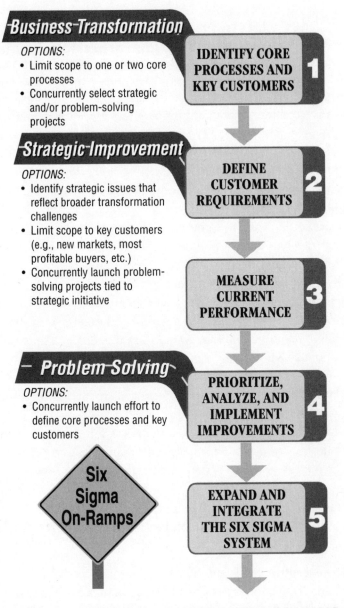

FIGURE 6.2 ON-RAMPS TO THE SIX SIGMA ROADMAP

Case Study #3: Using Six Sigma for Business Transformation at Miracle Semiconductor

The leaders of Miracle Semiconductor have agreed that their organization needs to be rejuvenated if it is going to survive for more than a few years. Miracle makes specialty digital components for small appliances and for increasingly high-tech durable goods such as cars and dishwashers. Though profitable, Miracle's growth has been slowing over the past two years. As demands from customers become increasingly challenging, Miracle's strength—engineering and technical sophistication—is being spread thin. At the same time, the company is weak in creating those partnerships with customers that create the kind of give-and-take needed to develop truly excellent custom products.

The idea of Six Sigma as a focal point for change actually began with the vice president of engineering, who heard about the concept in an executive MBA seminar. He first shared his thoughts with the head of marketing. Then together, they brought up the idea in a senior management meeting, where they were able to get agreement from the other top executives that the company's engineering-based culture needed to be replaced with one that balances technical creativity with a customer-responsive attitude.

"A New Miracle" was chosen as the theme for the effort. The executive group began to talk informally with managers and team members about their ideas, and then announced the initiative at a web-based videoconference linking the company's locations in Asia, Europe, and the Americas.

Two major efforts were established as the first priorities in A New Miracle:

- ▶ The executive group and two levels of management began to hold a series of meetings designed to create a high-level map of the businesses, showing links between departments and critical interfaces with customers and prospective customers.
- ▶ A cross-functional team was formed to assess issues relating to development of proposals for prospective customers, with the goal of identifying three to four specific improvement projects by the end of the quarter.

"I know we need to beef up our technical resources," said Miracle's president, "but we'll just be wasting our time if we don't get these things done first."

The Strategic Improvement On-Ramp

The middle on-ramp in Figure 6.2 is the one that offers the most options. A strategic improvement effort can be limited to one or two key pilot improvement projects, or it can engage a whole wave of teams and training aimed at addressing a strategic weakness. It can set the stage for a more ambitious business transformation initiative, or simply involve a focused improvement campaign that exists in a longer-term context.

Strategic improvement also can be aimed at building one of the key infrastructure elements or core competencies of the Six Sigma system (e.g., measurement or voice of the customer systems).

Case Study #4: Using Six Sigma for Strategic Improvement at Safety Zone Insurance

Safety Zone Insurance is a life and casualty insurer that sells policies through independent agents in the upper Midwest. Despite several waves of belt-tightening, Safety Zone has one of the highest cost profiles in its market. Its claims service is considered to be outstanding—insured customers actually are quite happy—but it takes Safety Zone a lot of time, with high labor costs, to perform underwriting activities and to issue policies. The delays are an aggravation for agents, who complain about them regularly.

The company's chief operating officer, Eleanor Zone, concluded that just telling people to "cut costs" again won't cut it. "We've got to get smarter about how we handle applications," she exclaimed in frustration, while preparing for the company's shareholder meeting. (Safety Zone stock had just dropped 10 percent over the prior month.)

After the meeting, Zone met with the director of underwriting and suggested that they try a Six Sigma approach to cut costs and application processing time.

"Isn't that a whole 'culture change' thing?" the director asked.

"From what I'm hearing," Zone responded, "we can use Six Sigma methods just to help with critical issues—like fixing our costs. If that works, we can look for other ways to expand it."

Because several agents in Michigan had recently written a letter threatening to stop representing Safety Zone, a team was formed right away to address the problem. Meanwhile, a review committee was formed to gather data about the high costs and the slow processing, with a deadline for a report in two weeks. . . .

The Problem Solving On-Ramp

With an urgency of results driving nearly every Six Sigma start-up, most organizations choose to jump on the problem solving on-ramp first (the third ramp shown in Figure 6.2). And yet, although it is usually the quickest way to a payoff, doing *only* problem solving can also be the riskiest shortcut on the Six Sigma Way. The dangers come in two categories:

1. **Poor project selection.** Without process or customer data, business leaders choose their projects based on mere guesses and assumptions. In this way, you may well end up targeting issues that are annoying, but not really critical to the business or its customers. Another common temptation is to launch too many projects simultaneously.

2. **Limited gains.** The problem-solving methods of Step 4 (process improvement and process design/redesign) are most powerful when driven by a wider focus and a long-term perspective. A real vision of broader change often was missing from TQM problem-solving efforts, which is a big reason why so many companies lost momentum.

If you are among the majority of organizations who want to start Six Sigma improvement projects (Step 4) right away, your best bet is to try to balance the push for immediate results with attention to longer-term goals (Steps 1, 2, 3, and 5). But if *all* you want to do is solve some critical problems, that is okay, too.

Case Study #5: Using Six Sigma for Problem Solving at Acme Products Company

The chief financial officer (CFO) for Acme Products Company was surprised to see Joe Check, eager head of Acme's accounts receivable group, hovering outside her office door. "Come in, Check," she called. "What's up?"

"I've got some interesting stuff I wanted to show you," Joe said. "I've had a couple of people on my staff working on trying to cut the number of accounts sent to collections. We all figured the problems would be with the shakier customers, but we found it's really the top accounts that have outstanding invoices most often."

"You mean we're sending collection agents after our better customers?"

"Almost twice as often as the ones we call the 'deadbeats,'" Joe confirmed.

"Oops," said the CFO. "But hey, if they aren't paying on time, we have to go after them anyway."

"Well, if the invoices had been correct, I'd agree with you. We also found some discrepancies between the sales reps' pricing formulas and the invoicing system. Almost 80 percent of the delayed payments included items that had mismatched pricing."

"How did you figure all this out?"

"Well," Joe explained, "I'd been reading about this Six Sigma improvement stuff, and it seemed interesting. I mean, we spend a lot of time just fixing problems around here that I suppose we shouldn't have at all. So I decided to try it out. We didn't do anything really sophisticated—it was really all about looking at the problem more carefully instead of assuming we knew what was going on. But the guys in the department were pretty impressed."

"I'm pretty impressed, too," the CFO admitted. "I can think of quite a few other areas we could work on."

By the end of the following month, the CFO had announced a pilot Six Sigma effort in finance, involving accounts receivable and investor relations.

The Roadmap and Your Strengths and Weaknesses

An alternative way of defining your Six Sigma priorities based on the Six Sigma roadmap (shown in Figure 4.1) is to assess your capabilities at each step, which represent the core competencies for a successful organization in the twenty-first century. As you ponder your responses to the questions listed in Exhibit 6.1, you will begin to see where your greatest weaknesses lie and where your initial activities might be concentrated.

Exhibit 6.1

QUESTIONS TO HELP IDENTIFY YOUR ORGANIZATION'S STRENGTHS AND WEAKNESSES

- *Step One: The Organization as a Whole*
  - Do we have a clear understanding of how our organization "fits together"?
  - What are the core processes?
  - Which key customers do they serve?
  - Are the interfaces or handoffs between groups clear and well managed?
- *Step Two: Our Customers*
  - How well do we *really* understand our customers?
  - How well do we understand our competitors' customers?
  - Do we have an effective, broad-based voice of the customer strategy?
  - Are mechanisms in place to capture customer and market input so that we can review and analyze it?
  - Is our focus on *both* service and output requirements, or are we ignoring one or the other?
  - Have we translated customer feedback into clear requirements or specifications?
- *Step Three: Our Performance*
  - Are we accurately *measuring* our performance against customer requirements? (Do we really know how well we are doing?)
  - Do measures encompass both service and output specifications?

- Do we have too few measures, or too many?
- Are the data accessible?
- How well do we use measurement data to evaluate and fine-tune our processes/performance?
- Do the people working in the process understand the measures and what to do with the information?
- Are input or process measures in place, to help us see potential problems or opportunities *before* they happen?

■ *Step Four: Problems and Opportunities*
- Do we have any critical problems or opportunities that are calling out for attention?
- Conversely, is every problem urgent, or are we setting effective improvement priorities?
- What's the likely payoff from these problems?
- Are necessary resources being deployed to tackle the problems, or are we solving them with Band-Aids?
- Is a clear, proactive process in place to develop root-cause-focused solutions?
- Are we able and willing to design or redesign processes when their current design is no longer viable?
- Are key leaders engaged in and supporting the improvement efforts?
- Are we measuring results and ensuring that solutions pay off?

■ *Step Five: Ongoing Assessment and Management*
- Have we established responsibility for ongoing assessment and management of our key processes?
- Have we taken steps to ensure that improvements are maintained and that results are being met?
- Are measures captured and reported so we can tell at a glance how the business is performing?
- Are we prepared to manage the business as a closed-loop system?

In some ways, the questions in Exhibit 6.1 offer a more reasoned way of identifying your Six Sigma priorities. Rather than being driven by current issues or concerns, which is the emphasis in the choice of on-ramps, this assessment focuses on the *systemic* strengths and weaknesses of your organization. For example, by improving your knowledge of customer needs, or by strengthening your measurement systems, you create a stronger business while giving Six Sigma teams a better environment, not to mention better data for improvement.

Realistically, though, current issues usually take precedence over systemic challenges. The trick is to focus on the immediate needs of your business even while ensuring that your initial projects lay the groundwork upon which you can build your Six Sigma core competencies.

Piloting Your Six Sigma Effort (aka "Start Smaller and Grow")

Although not every Six Sigma adopter has taken a gradual approach, having supported as well as witnessed many initiatives, we strongly urge you to consider a "piloting strategy" for your effort. For one, the all-in approach is expensive, riskier, and less forgiving of mistakes. A phased launch allows you to assess various elements of your effort— from project selection and measurement to training and engaging people. And it helps you manage your investment so you can gauge the real return sooner and often more accurately.

The common arguments *against* piloting include a need to move fast, lack of resources, and/or a loss of momentum and enthusiasm around the Six Sigma effort. A well-thought-out ramp-up plan shouldn't delay your progress much, however; and by working out the "bugs" in your training, projects, teamwork, and so on, you pave the way for greater results faster.

Patricia Small of Cartus confirms this point: "The whole concept of piloting has made an enormous difference here. When we first started doing Six Sigma, people thought, 'Why waste our time? This is just an added step that you're making us do.' But once we had some early experiences with averting some pretty major mistakes by using a pilot, now no one would implement anything without a pilot. It's just second nature. And that's true even for our people who haven't been through Six Sigma training."

What Should You Pilot?

Piloting can be applied to any aspect of Six Sigma implementation, including:

▶ Orientation of business leaders
▶ Project selection
▶ Project team makeup
▶ Team leader selection
▶ Measurement methods
▶ Training design and content (for audiences including executives, team leaders, team members, etc.)
▶ Training logistics and scheduling

Clearly, the most important pilot subject will be the *results* achieved from the Six Sigma effort. Those results may take a while to measure, however. So by keeping an eye on some of the factors noted here, you can boost the probability of a strong final payoff.

Key Questions for a Piloting Strategy

A piloting strategy starts with the *attitude* that you will manage problems and adopt a continuous improvement approach to your Six Sigma effort. Specifics of a piloting strategy depend on your objective, but asking some basic questions can help to drive any pilot planning:

▶ **How can we test our plan or approach to ensure that it will work?** Look for opportunities for a limited, lower-risk trial of key aspects of the Six Sigma effort. Make sure, though, that any test replicates normal conditions as much as possible, otherwise your pilot data may not represent what will happen later.
▶ **What will we need to measure/observe to see how well our effort is working?** The more specific you can be, the better. Piloting needs to be accompanied by a careful, focused review of what worked and what didn't. Without it, your improvements will be based as much on guesses as on real learning from the pilot.
▶ **How much time will be needed to respond to what we learn from the pilot?** This piece is always a challenge. Most companies, once they decide to launch Six Sigma, want to get it done *yesterday*. But some time for review and refinement is key, if a pilot strategy is to pay off. Therefore we strongly recommend that a period be set aside in your rollout to assess, identify, and implement improvements. Usually, depending on what you are piloting, the review/refinement time can be a couple of weeks or less, after which you can move

forward aggressively and with much more confidence that your efforts will pay off.

It does not mean you cannot succeed with a full-scale, organization-wide rollout. Our client Starwood Hotels and Resorts has been successfully applying and integrating Six Sigma (in hotels!) for more than a decade. Starwood applied what was internally called a Big Bang approach, rolling out training and projects to management teams and staff at most of its international regions in a six-month blitz. At the same time, Starwood also invested significant funds and effort in a six-month "business case" validation and planning phase *before* the Big Bang exploded, and went through several Go/No-go decision points with its executive team during that initial preparation period.

Still, despite the overall success of their initiative, which included a commitment to sustain Six Sigma even after the 9/11 attacks brought Starwood's business to a near standstill, the executive who led the effort and his team felt, in retrospect, that a phased approach would have been better.

(We've also witnessed several cases of the Big Fizzle, most memorably at a South African bank where the CEO led a company meeting where the organization voted overwhelmingly by electronic ballot to embark on a Six Sigma initiative—and then did nothing.)

Six Sigma Start-Up Summary

Let us begin here by reminding you that some of the basic questions related to preparing your effort are found on the Six Sigma Start-Up worksheet shown in Exhibit 6.2.

Now let's summarize some of the most important things you should remember:

▶ **Plan your own route.** Of the many paths to Six Sigma, the best is the one that works for your organization. Steer clear of those who say they have *the* way to implement Six Sigma.
▶ **Define your objective.** Priorities are important. It is okay to apply Six Sigma to solve key problems; it also can be a driver of culture change. Start at the level (or levels) that make the sense given your needs and readiness.

Six Sigma Start-Up Checklist

Part One: Is Six Sigma Right for Us Now? . . .

Assess the current strategic and performance status of your organization (company, business unit, department) and answer the following:

1. Is change a critical business need or opportunity now, based on financial, competitive, or cultural needs?   YES   NO
2. Can we make a strong strategic rationale for applying Six Sigma (in some form) to our business?   YES   NO
3. Will our existing management systems and improvement processes be capable of achieving the degree of involvement essential to our continued success?   YES   NO

If your answers are Yes, Yes, and No, you appear ready to explore further how to adopt Six Sigma in your organization.

Part Two: How and Where Should We Start Our Efforts? . . .

Consider the current mix of activities and priorities in the organization and check *one* of the following statements that best describes your situation:

1. The company is ready for and able to focus on an all-out push to create a "Six Sigma organization."   ☐
2. There are major, high-priority strategic issues or processes in the business that demand focused improvement resources.   ☐
3. Our sense of urgency is such that we need to tackle short-term problems and projects before expanding the Six Sigma process.   ☐

If you chose:
1 – You may be ready for a full Business Transformation. 2 – Your best focus will be on some form of Strategic Improvement. 3 – Immediate process improvement projects are probably your best starting point.

Exhibit 6.2 SIX SIGMA START-UP CHECKLIST

▶ **Stick to what is feasible.** Set up your plans so that they match your influence, resources, and scope. If that means trying Six Sigma methods on a small scale in an area you can manage—hey, that's often a great way to start.

▶ **Use a piloting or phased launch strategy.** You will save time and effort in the long run if you test and improve key aspects of your effort before you roll them out full-scale.

▶ **Balance short- and long-term considerations.** The big drawback of aiming for quick results is the risk of getting stuck working only on short-term projects. Building the core competencies of Six Sigma into your organization (customer knowledge, measurement, proactive improvement, etc.) needs to be a focus as well.

CHAPTER 7

Leadership Actions to Launch and Guide the Effort

It is often noted that success in Six Sigma, whether it is initiating a few projects or changing the organizational culture, requires *leadership support*. In fact, leadership support is critical for many things. The problem with that advice, however, is that *support*, no matter how you define it, is not enough.

For one, a leader or manager can easily say "I support this" and not really mean it. Even when the statement of support is sincere, it may be sitting on thin ice: "I'm in favor of this . . . but will abandon it if other things come up." A third situation—more promising but still challenging—is strong support with no real understanding of what leaders need to do to make Six Sigma successful.

To help overcome this "support fallacy," we prefer terms such as *ownership*, *engagement*, and (perhaps best) *accountability* to describe what effective leadership of Six Sigma requires. The good news is that the effort of leading Six Sigma can be a great opportunity to learn how to be a better leader overall, including the following ways.

1. Leading change—helping an organization adapt and improve—is perhaps the most essential role and skill of leadership today.
2. Guiding Six Sigma efforts can and should prompt leadership teams at all levels to examine, assess, and improve their own management

processes, which have a huge impact on the organization's efficiency, flexibility, strategic focus, and teamwork.

Because these topics are big ones, we will limit our focus in this chapter to describing eight actions that are critical for leaders as you initiate and build a Six Sigma or continuous improvement initiative in your organization. As a warning: avoid the temptation to look at what other companies or leaders have done and just copy them. You can certainly learn from others, but the specifics need to fit *your* circumstances, culture, and goals.

Develop a Strong Vision and Rationale

Leaders should be able to describe—first for themselves, then for others—*why* the Six Sigma system is needed by the organization. "It's the latest big thing," or "Wall Street is really hot on Six Sigma companies" won't cut it. The rationale has to be specific to *your* organization and tie in directly to benefits almost anyone in the company can understand. The most effective or compelling vision is usually one that connects to the core mission of your organization and one that describes how the ability to drive change is integral to achieving that mission.

A good example is how the U.S. Centers for Medicare and Medicaid Services (CMS) described the rationale for its CMS Improvement Initiative. It began with what CMS called the "Three-Part Aim: Better Care for Individuals; Better Health for the Population; Lower Cost Through Improvement." Driving improvement and achieving operational excellence were essential dimensions of this vision: If we expect to influence change in the health care system across America, we have to be constantly enhancing how we do our work."

In addition to linking to your organizational mission or purpose, the rationale for applying Six Sigma should have some urgency tied to it. Even if your organization is in a good position (financially and competitively; or for government or nonprofits, in terms of fulfilling your mission), you can realistically explain that the organization's future success is not guaranteed and requires aggressive action to maintain its edge.

A strong vision should usually include some details of what your desired future state will be. For example, one of our financial service clients tied improvement to having the highest "net prompter score" in its market segment, which means it has the greatest percentage of clients who are willing to *recommend* the firm's services.

A good tagline or slogan can be helpful as well, as long as it is not just used in place of real improvement work. Some good ones include:

▶ "Building an Enduring Great Company"—this is one of our favorites, from a high-tech client
▶ "Creating a Culture of Continuous Renewal"—AlliedSignal/ Honeywell
▶ "Completely Satisfying Customer Needs Profitably"—GE's quality definition

Your vision and rationale can evolve over time as business conditions change. Remember that the *ability to change, adapt, and improve* (in our opinion, at least) is always worth cultivating in any organization.

Actively Participate in Planning and Implementation

As soon as top leaders hand over responsibility to a Six Sigma manager or a consultant, the likelihood of sustained success plummets. Getting expert advice and setting up a core team to drive the initiative are valuable to be sure, but the executive group needs to be involved in and actively endorse all key decisions, for three critical reasons:

1. Each decision and action will involve time and resources (aka money); leaders need to be directly involved to ensure that the focus is truly aligned with organizational needs and that they can explain and guide the efforts.
2. Every step of improvement is a learning opportunity, and many will require adaptation over time. Leaders who don't benefit from those lessons are likely to second guess, make mistakes, and then repeat those mistakes.

3. Leaders' actions will signal their true level of commitment. If people hear talk about improvement needs and goals, but don't see leaders taking true responsibility (investing time, explaining successes and failures, examining and improving their *own* behaviors), they will view it as an optional or short-term distraction (i.e., the "flavor of the month").

These guidelines don't apply simply to the "launch" phase. One of the top reasons why an ambitious vision of creating a continuous improvement culture so often fails is that leaders lose focus or disengage after a few months or a year. The Six Sigma work may continue, but it is relegated to a select few people and projects. Therefore, your start-up plans should focus not just on projects, training, and selecting Belts, but also on integrating improvement strategy and execution into routine management processes.

Devin Rickard of Adobe believes that the executive commitment to Six Sigma at his company is one of the reasons it is so successful: "We make sure we have the right level of executive commitment: they're there not only at the beginning of the project, but they're active and visible throughout the entire project. We really look to them to build a coalition of sponsors, especially when our initiatives are cross-functional in nature, and we look to them to take an active part in propagating the communication down through the organization about what's being done, why it's a priority to the organization, and the level of support that's needed throughout the organization in order to make sure we're successful."

Create a Marketing Strategy and Plan

This practical side of change management should be tailored to fit your vision and scope. If your focus is on "testing" Six Sigma improvement on a few projects, obviously a big organization-wide splash is not appropriate. Key questions to drive your Six Sigma marketing include the following:

- ▶ Who are our key audiences—internal and external?
- ▶ How do we best introduce our plans to ensure a positive reaction?
- ▶ How does the message need to be tailored to different groups?
- ▶ What media, events, and similar activities are appropriate?
- ▶ How do we deal with negative reactions?

The plan should include key terms and phrases, too: *launch, expansion*, and *ongoing support*, for example. The challenge is to develop a marketing plan for Six Sigma that is appealing and challenging, but realistic. Avoid overly optimistic hype.[1]

Keep in mind that marketing Six Sigma as an initiative does not take the place of change management at a project or tactical level. Every improvement action requires some level of active effort to build support and overcome concerns.

Become Powerful Advocates

One strategy that does need to be borrowed from the likes of "early adopters," such as Larry Bossidy of AlliedSignal and Jack Welch at GE, is their continued emphasis of the message that improvement capability is essential to an organization's success. It was not a "nice to have" or an add-on, but rather a vehicle to meet the challenge of tougher competition, economic ups-and-downs, customer demands, and more.

The most effective advocacy must keep in mind some keys to success:

▶ **Avoid "blind faith" statements.** Adopting Six Sigma is never a magic wand. Tough problems attacked by smart improvement methods are still tough problems.

▶ **Create a team of advocates.** If the CEO or Six Sigma vice president is the only committed messenger, the balloon will deflate as soon as he or she leaves the room, or the organization. At every company where the improvement process has been sustained, it became a part of the leadership culture. As evidence: Six Sigma initiatives have been launched by dozens of former GE execs who have taken leadership roles in new organizations.

▶ **Explain (sincerely) what you are doing to improve.** Too often, leaders limit their engagement to telling *others* to make change happen. This guideline will both boost your credibility and help ensure you pay attention to the leadership/management systems that *also* need to be examined and improved.

Over time, integrating messages about improvement capability and impact should become a natural part of your communications, not a special thing. For example, Patricia Small at Cartus described how senior involvement in her company's Six Sigma program was a key factor in its success: in particular, she notes how president and CEO Kevin Kelleher's support of Six Sigma was the primary reason the program kept moving along. "Kevin was very involved in working with our Six Sigma trainees: every time we led a class of Six Sigma individuals, every person from the class was required to meet with him a couple of months after the class, to give him an update on the project they were working on. That was really something that kept people engaged in the learning, instead of just going to the class and saying 'I took Six Sigma' so they could put it on their resumes. Kevin's involvement really got them using it, which is so important because if they didn't use what they learned in the classes, they would forget it very easily.

"Another way Kevin supported Six Sigma was to talk about it at our all-company town meetings and to mention it in company updates. That had a powerful impact on the number of people who were interested in learning more about Six Sigma. I've worked for Cartus for 13 years, most recently in the learning and development aspect of our business, and whenever Kevin mentioned Six Sigma in a publication or a speech, I always had a lot of people interested in taking a Six Sigma class. His support made a visible, measurable difference in people's interest in knowing what Six Sigma was all about and in using it."

Another CEO who championed Six Sigma at a difficult time for business is Barry Sternlicht, who was CEO of Starwood when the company first implemented Six Sigma in early 2001. After the tragedy of 9/11 occurred that same year, Starwood realized it needed to cut costs, and since Six Sigma had just started, many people suggested cutting that program altogether. Brian McGuire recalls how the senior leadership team at the time decided not to eliminate the Six Sigma program. Starwood's approach was that even though no one was traveling then, and even though Starwood's competitors—Hilton, Marriott, Hyatt—were all cutting costs, the senior leadership team that was headed by Sternlicht committed to doubling down on Six Sigma, to working to become more efficient while still keeping the voice of the customer in mind, and partnering with them.

Finally, although it is critical to have top management's support, it is not always necessary to *start* at the top to get that commitment.

Scott Szczepanek, assessment director for BP, pointed this out: "A lot of people argue that you can't do Six Sigma without a top-down mandate. That can be true for organizations that want to run very large projects with very large stakeholder groups. But I've found, at both Sears (where I worked previously) and BP, that it's sometimes better to take a ground-up approach, almost like guerilla warfare, to build support and localized capability through smaller projects that deliver easier benefits to the business. That builds momentum, and then you can ride that wave to the leaders, to get them to support Six Sigma and make it something they really want to support. Both models work—top-down and bottom-up—which you use just really depends on the operating culture of your organization."

Set Clear Objectives

Your goals can be just as important a feature of the marketing effort as your communication plans or theme. Broad business targets (e.g., 10X improvement, Five Sigma in Five Years) are excellent *if* they can be interpreted meaningfully in the trenches. The specific objectives appropriate for your organization will be tailored to the nature and scope of your effort. In any case, they should be understandable, challenging, meaningful, and *not* impossible.

Hold Yourself and Others Accountable

One of the boldest, most effective, and most remarked-on aspects of GE's Six Sigma effort was the linking of 40 percent of every executive's variable compensation (i.e., bonus money) to successful Six Sigma efforts. That feet-to-the-fire incentive sent a strong message to everyone at GE about the importance of Six Sigma and certainly helped keep Six Sigma projects from getting swamped by other priorities.

In stark contrast, we were called in to meet with the president of a client company who was frustrated with the company's quality effort. "I've been pushing people for two years," he complained, "and we still aren't seeing any results." When we asked him what were the *consequences* of that lack of results, however, the leader had no answer for us. The same people who *weren't* achieving improvement goals were being paid and getting bonuses just like always.

Where accountability starts in driving continuous improvement is, without question, with the *leaders* themselves. For example, if an improvement project fails, questions should focus not just on teams or training, but more importantly on what leaders could have done:

- ▶ Were enough resources provided?
- ▶ Was the project well defined?
- ▶ Did I/we listen when problems were raised?
- ▶ Did we provide the needed sense of urgency?

For instance, if *only* the direct reports of the company president in the preceding story had been held accountable for improvements, a lot more would have been achieved.

Included in executive accountability, and extending throughout the organization, is the whole question of aligning compensation and rewards in a way that will foster Six Sigma results. We see a surprising number of instances, in large organizations, where compensation criteria send mixed if not *contrary* signals about what's important. For example:

- ▶ A consumer products company paid commissions to salespeople based on revenue only. As soon as they added profit margin as an element of the compensation, a whole new attitude and set of behaviors emerged that helped align customer behaviors with the business's capability. The result was a win-win for customers and the company.
- ▶ The information technology group at a unit of a *Fortune* 500 firm is given incentives to cut its budget, but without regard to the potential impact on service levels. By contrast, where IT costs are tied directly to the business units they are supporting, more intelligent decisions about priorities and investment are made, and IT becomes much more of a partner with its internal clients. (*Note:* A prerequisite here is the ability to track technology investments to the business unit versus the common "allocation formula.")
- ▶ A product development/marketing department for a large telecommunications company is evaluated on the speed with which new offerings are introduced—meaning that programs are sometimes launched before sales and service people have any

information about them. Organizations that evaluate new product introduction as an end-to-end process that includes production, commercialization, and profitability have a consistently higher level of success—or at least fewer new product introduction fiascos.

Addressing these types of misalignment may be one of the most unrecognized and valuable benefits of Six Sigma. Even though gaining good alignment of goals throughout a company may take a bit of time to achieve, some short-term improvement project solutions hinge on resolving compensation–goal conflicts.

Demand Meaningful Measures of Results

One of the weaknesses of past improvement waves such as total quality management was overreliance on anecdotal results that never seemed to find their way to the bottom line. With Six Sigma, that gap is addressed, and it is important for leaders to maintain the emphasis on ensuring meaningful, credible progress.

At the same time, the lessons of the past decade of Six Sigma have shown that being *too* concerned with "hard currency" savings can have negative consequences as well. If you expect to quantify every benefit down to the dollar, yuan, or euro, you will force people to look only at cost reduction that can be clearly accounted for. That may *sound* fine, but it means avoiding improvements—with clear *customer* benefits that help boost satisfaction and competitiveness—simply because those gains are impossible to validate with the same level of accuracy.

To ensure the right balance and still drive credible, measurable results, leaders should:

▶ Encourage/demand a good "baseline" for each improvement effort. It is impossible to see progress unless you know where you started.
▶ Allow a mix of hard and soft results. Some of your most meaningful improvement will be hard to quantify in money (e.g., cutting weeks out of your new product introduction lead time). But guesstimates are okay if they are based on facts and reasonable assumptions.
▶ Include some culture or climate indicators (e.g., a regular employee survey) and customer metrics (e.g., satisfaction or "net promoter" assessment) to capture the less directly measurable changes of your effort.

► Pay attention to and celebrate small wins. The journey to improvement is often about what you *learn* as much as what you *do*, especially early on. Even projects that fail provide insights, but you need to encourage people to capture the lessons and build on them.

► Be realistic and expect a mix of large and small successes. Some early consultants marketed Six Sigma with ridiculous claims that "average Black Belt projects yield $250,000 in savings." Some executives surprisingly accepted these numbers, ignoring that (1) the projections were based on zero knowledge of the specific business in questions; and (2) the same consultants making these claims would also call averages a poor type of measure. The only way to know what you can gain is to look at your own operations and processes, which takes time and effort. You will usually experience a lot of small to medium-sized results projects, and some major ones, if you're lucky.

Communicate Constantly

One of the realities leaders need to recognize is that messages that *you* are tired of sending are often only *beginning* to be heard by your people, customers, and stakeholders. Connected to your advocacy role and the marketing strategy for Six Sigma is the need to continue repeating the call for change, smarter improvement practices, greater reliance on facts, willingness to challenge assumptions, and progress toward your vision. Noting mistakes and areas where you and the organization do better is okay—in fact, it is critical to the learning and progress.

Ideally, Six Sigma communication over time will be integrated into "what we do" and not seem like something special. But usually that transition takes a while and requires conscious effort. Meanwhile, you also need to beware of sending messages that are misinterpreted. When the leadership team of one of our clients (a corporate services firm with large business clients) began emphasizing the need for financially smarter decisions, people responded by saying, "Well, I guess the 'customer intimacy' days are over," which was *not* the intent at all.

Finally, remember that the best communication is *two-way*, so your emphasis needs to balance both sending and receiving (i.e., listening to your managers and employees).

Be Persistent

Underlying all the keys to success for leaders embarking on, or inheriting, a Six Sigma effort is the need for what quality guru W. Edwards Deming called "constancy of purpose." Because the basic principles of Six Sigma are really commonsense business ideas, they should not be switched on and off. All the organizations we know and have worked with who show the most meaningful benefit from continuous improvement are the ones who *stick with it*, even when major distractions or challenges arise.

Conclusion

Without a doubt, leaders set the tone and direction for the effort. Their actions have the greatest overall impact on the course of the Six Sigma process. Without the input of other key players, however, no leader can effect change or achieve the results that a well-executed Six Sigma initiative can offer. In the following chapter, we look at such other essential roles in your implementation.

CHAPTER 8

Preparing Black Belts and Other Key Roles

One of the best-publicized aspects of the Six Sigma movement is the creation of a corps of continuous improvement experts known variously as Black Belts, Master Black Belts, Green Belts, and Yellow Belts. Although the "Belts" are important, they alone will not ensure you can achieve the change vision or results you target. Other key roles must be considered, as well as important considerations about how you select and deploy your own Belts.

One of your key tasks, as you start on the Six Sigma Way, will be to define the appropriate roles for your organization and to clarify their responsibilities. Those decisions should be driven by a variety of factors, including your Six Sigma objectives, implementation plan, budget, and existing staff and resources. In this chapter, we'll be probing three key questions:

1. What are the major roles to support a sustained Six Sigma capability and culture?
2. What is a Black Belt, and what are the options to best benefit from the Black Belt, Master Black Belt, Green Belt, and Yellow Belt roles?
3. What level and content of training is needed to get your Six Sigma process off the ground and keep it climbing?

Roles in a Six Sigma Organization

We will set aside terms like *Black Belt* and *Master Black Belt* for a moment, and look first at a variety of important Six Sigma job descriptions.[1] These generic roles are not all mandatory. In fact, we would suggest that these be about the *most* you have, as there can be some overlap among these responsibilities as it is. Table 8.1 gives you some of the variations we've seen, including the increasingly common "Belt" titles. Figure 8.1 shows the two options open to you for deploying these different roles, and how their "reporting structures" might work.

The Leadership Group or Council

If they are to build a truly effective improvement capability and drive meaningful results (as described in Chapter 7), executives must have a forum in which they can discuss, plan, guide, and learn from Six Sigma actions and outcomes. Although back in the TQM days, that role was often was delegated to a special "quality council," most organizations taking up the Six Sigma banner have at least tried to invest ownership in the same people who run the organization. Certainly it is a key early step to sending the right message about the importance of improvement to your long-term success.

In addition to the critical leadership tasks we have defined earlier, specific functions of the top management group are listed in Exhibit 8.1.

TABLE 8.1   EXAMPLES OF VARIATIONS IN GENERIC ROLES AND BELT OR OTHER TITLE

Leadership Council	Quality Council, Six Sigma Steering Committee
Sponsor	Champion, Process Owner
Implementation Leader	Six Sigma Director, Quality Leader, Master Black Belt
Coach	Master Black Belt or Black Belt
Team Leader	Black Belt or Green Belt
Team Member	Team Member or Green Belt
Process Owner	Sponsor or Champion

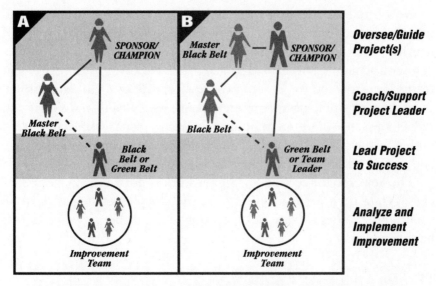

FIGURE 8.1   OPTIONAL SIX SIGMA ROLES AND STRUCTURE

Exhibit 8.1

KEY RESPONSIBILITIES OF THE LEADERSHIP GROUP

- *Establishing the roles and infrastructure of the Six Sigma initiative*
- *Selecting specific projects and allocating resources*
- *Periodically reviewing the progress of various projects and offering ideas and help (e.g., avoiding project overlap)*
- *Serving (individually) as sponsors of Six Sigma projects*
- *Helping to quantify the impact of Six Sigma efforts on the company bottom line*
- *Assessing progress and identifying strengths and weaknesses in the effort (i.e., avoiding complacency)*
- *Sharing best practices throughout the organization and with key suppliers and customers, where appropriate*
- *Acting as roadblock removers when teams identify barriers*
- *Applying the lessons learned to their own individual management styles*

How often a leadership team includes improvement priorities and performance on its agenda can have a big influence on the pace and depth of the overall initiative. For example, convening monthly is a common schedule and is usually adequate. However, if improvement teams are expected to present progress reports to a full committee, several months may pass between updates, which can slow efforts and reduce the sense of urgency. Shorter, more frequent sessions may work better, especially early in the launch phase, in maintaining the pace and energy behind the improvements.

The key is to make sure Six Sigma work is not an optional or special agenda item for leaders. If it is, the chances of success will be small and the organizational learning that can be so valuable will be squandered.

The Sponsor or Champion

A sponsor—a role mentioned in several of our earlier Six Sigma stories—is the manager who oversees an improvement project. This critical responsibility can require a delicate balance. Teams need the freedom to make their own decisions, but they also need guidance from business leaders on the direction of their efforts. Sponsor responsibilities are listed in Exhibit 8.2.

Exhibit 8.2

KEY RESPONSIBILITIES OF THE IMPROVEMENT SPONSOR OR CHAMPION

- Setting and maintaining broad goals for improvement projects under his or her charge—including creating the project rationale—and ensuring that they are aligned with business priorities
- Coaching and approving changes in direction or scope of a project, if needed
- Finding (and negotiating) resources for projects
- Representing the team to the leadership group and serving as its advocate
- Helping to smooth out issues and overlaps that arise between teams or with people outside the team

- *Working with process owners to ensure a smooth handoff at the conclusion of an improvement project*
- *Applying gained knowledge of process improvement to management tasks*

Of all the responsibilities listed in Exhibit 8.2, perhaps the most important to the success of a project and the overall improvement effort lies in helping to clarify and refine the scope of change initiatives. In our experience, many projects slow down or stall simply because the people working on the issue are hesitant to narrow or shift their focus, for fear of disappointing leaders. So they persist in trying to take on *too* much, but end up going nowhere. Few priority issues can be resolved in one step, and the sponsor's help in adjusting the size and direction is critical.

The Implementation Leader

On one hand, the overall ownership of Six Sigma will ideally be in the hands of organizational leaders and managers. On the other hand is still a need for responsibility and resources to guide the execution, resources, and alignment of continuous improvement efforts. Depending on the scale of your efforts, one implementation leader or Six Sigma director may be enough, or you may need a staff to handle this broad set of tasks, listed in Exhibit 8.3.

Exhibit 8.3

KEY RESPONSIBILITIES OF THE SIX SIGMA/CONTINUOUS IMPROVEMENT LEADER

- *Supporting leaders in their activities, including communication, project selection, and project reviews*
- *Identifying and/or recommending individuals/groups to fulfill key roles, including external consulting and training support*
- *Preparing and executing training plans, including curriculum selection and scheduling and logistics*
- *Helping sponsors fulfill their role as supports, advocates, and cheerleaders of the teams*

- *Documenting overall progress and surfacing issues that need attention*
- *Executing the internal marketing plan for the initiative*
- *Ensuring consistency of approach across the organization, while helping each group adapt training, structures, and processes to its own needs*
- *Assessing overall impact, both of projects (return on improvement investment) and culture (how well Six Sigma practices are being integrated into daily practice)*

The talent and energies required for this central guidance role can be enormous. Usually, this person will be more a strategic change agent than a Six Sigma technical expert. He or she really serves as the conscience of effective improvement principles: simultaneously managing politics, logistics, and cultural evolution. So the Six Sigma/continuous improvement leader can have a bigger impact on overall success than any other individual—and should have close links to the executive team.

The Improvement Coach

The coach provides expert advice and assistance to process owners and Six Sigma improvement teams, in areas that may range from project selection to statistics to change management. The coach is the expert in defining and resolving issues successfully, with a level of technical expertise that will vary from business to business based on how the roles are structured and the level of complexity of the problems.

Because the coach is really a *consultant*, one of the keys to his or her success is to define clear agreements on people's roles and the extent of their direct involvement with the projects and processes. The fine line between "helping" and "meddling" often can only be determined according to the needs of the client, so flexibility is important. In addition to technical help, a coach may provide guidance on the responsibilities listed in Exhibit 8.4.

Exhibit 8.4

KEY RESPONSIBILITIES OF AN IMPROVEMENT COACH

- *Helping ensure an improvement opportunity is well defined and scoped*

- *Communicating with and providing feedback to the project sponsor and leadership group*
- *Establishing a firm schedule for the project and adapting when needed, while driving to timely results*
- *Supporting change management and teamwork and dealing with resistance or lack of cooperation from people in the organization*
- *Estimating potential and validating actual results (defects eliminated, dollars saved, etc.)*
- *Guiding a project leader and team on what tools to use, when, and how*
- *Resolving team member disagreements, conflicts, and other issues*
- *Gathering and analyzing data about team activities*
- *Helping teams promote and celebrate their successes*

The Team Leader or Project Leader

The team leader is the individual who takes primary responsibility for the work and the results of a Six Sigma project. Although many assume the project leader is always a Belt, in plenty of cases it is more useful to have a businessperson (not an improvement expert) lead the team, while the Belt (whatever color) serves as a coach. Team leaders' focus may be on core business process improvement or design/redesign, but they also can take on efforts tied to "support systems" such as voice of the customer strategies, measurement and performance indicator reporting, or process alignment and management. As we will see in some of our Six Sigma stories in Part Three, the team leader is critical to keeping a project on track and ensuring that progress continues. Some of his or her specific responsibilities, particularly in an improvement project, are listed in Exhibit 8.5.

Exhibit 8.5

KEY RESPONSIBILITIES OF A SIX SIGMA TEAM OR PROJECT LEADER

- *Reviewing/clarifying the project rationale with the sponsor*
- *Developing and updating the project charter and implementation plan*
- *Selecting or helping to select the project team members*
- *Identifying and seeking resources and information*

- *Defining and helping others in the use of appropriate Six Sigma tools as well as team and meeting management techniques*
- *Maintaining the project schedule and keeping progress moving toward final solutions and results*
- *Supporting the transfer of new solutions or processes to ongoing operations, while working with functional managers and/or the process owner*
- *Documenting final results and creating a storyboard of the project*

The Team Member

Most organizations use *teams* as the vehicle for the bulk of their improvement efforts. The team members provide the extra brains and muscle behind the measurement, analysis, and improvement of a process. They also help spread the word about Six Sigma tools and processes and become part of the bench strength for future projects.

The Process Owner

This person takes on a new cross-functional responsibility to manage an end-to-end set of steps that provide value to an internal or external customer. He or she receives the handoff from improvement teams or becomes the owner of new and newly designed processes. Note that the sponsor and the process owner may be the same person. (For details, see Chapter 16.)

Belt Types and Role Structures

Following our review of the most common roles in a continuous improvement implementation and some options as to their use, we can give you a better understanding of what Black Belt and Master Black Belt mean while also laying out the choices you have for preparing and deploying these individuals.

The stories vary as to how the term *Black Belt* emerged. Clearly, though, it originated at Motorola in the early 1990s and signified individuals possessing special expertise in statistics and technical product/

process improvement. The Black Belt label, of course drawn from the martial arts, suggests a finely honed skill and discipline; the different levels of Yellow, Green, Black, and Master recognize depth of training and experience. In Six Sigma's early days, certification and training for Six Sigma Black Belts was developed in a joint effort among companies including Motorola, Texas Instruments, IBM, and Kodak. It was almost exclusively a technical role, focused on manufacturing and product-related improvements.

Because no official job description or certification exists for Green and Black Belts (by far the most common), the role and the skills that define them have been and remain fairly diverse. Although some organizations, such as the American Society for Quality (ASQ), have a bit more clout in the certification arena, plenty of organizations have developed their own set of criteria and assessment processes, from corporations to universities to consulting firms. Generally, we can outline the levels of Belt-ness in the following way:

▶ **Yellow Belts.** Have some level of training in improvement methods and tools (beyond "awareness") that can be applied to simpler, smaller-scope efforts. Yellow Belts tend to focus more on Lean-oriented methods than analytical variation-reduction skills. Yellow Belts are usually members of improvement teams, rather than leaders.

▶ **Green Belts.** Have fairly in-depth training in improvement project management and tools, including analytical and process streamlining/Lean techniques. Often does not include more in-depth statistical analysis tools. Green Belts typically serve as improvement team leaders, but Six Sigma is only a part-time role for them.

▶ **Black Belts.** Have in-depth training and practice in a full range of improvement methods, including some level of statistical analysis, change management, process flow analysis, and facilitation. Usually, someone who's labeled a Black Belt is (or has in the past) served as a full-time improvement project leader and internal consultant.

▶ **Master Black Belts.** Although this category probably sees the *most* variation, in nearly every case an MBB is a career improvement leader/coach and has a few years of experience in Six Sigma and/ or Lean. Some organizations emphasize technical/analytical skills; others rely on MBBs to conduct training; and in some cases, MBBs pretty much "own" the Six Sigma process, where it unfortunately has been off-loaded by organization leaders (i.e., not a good thing). The Master Black Belt is always a full-time job.

The differing criteria and skill sets for Belts is partly due to the need/desire of organizations to put their own twist on things. But the variation is also *necessary* because, realistically, the types of skills and capabilities needed to "do improvement" differ quite a bit from one type of organization to another (say, a semiconductor manufacturer versus a hotel). It is not, nor should it be, a one-size-fits-all role.

The good news, as noted, is that you don't need to feel beholden to some strict code of Belt certification in determining what the roles should be in your organization. On the other hand, you do have to give it some thought and maintain some reasonable standards or criteria to ensure that the people you rely on as change drivers can really get the job done.

Considerations in Defining the Green and Black Belt Role

How you go about selecting and deploying Lean Six Sigma Belts will be influenced by some of the issues we've noted.[2] You should also consider how you intend to staff the positions and their longer-term value to the organization. Developing management skills and building technical expertise are two such considerations.

Management Skill Development

In some businesses, one of the purposes of Belt development is to upgrade the skills of current/future managers and leaders. In these cases Belt candidates are drawn mainly from the existing ranks and usually are assigned to lead an improvement project. People placed in full-time Black Belt positions are given opportunities for advancement after they finish their "tour of duty."

> *The pros:*
> ▶ Puts people with direct experience of the organization and its processes to work on improvement opportunities.
> ▶ Engages middle managers directly in the Six Sigma effort by assigning them projects.

- Black Belts drawn from inside the organization usually already are familiar with the politics and people in the organization, which means they can select team members, work with sponsors more effectively, and so on.
- If the Black Belts are well known and respected, they can help convince others in the business of the value of the Six Sigma system.
- Instills in management talent the basic Six Sigma knowledge and skills

The cons:

- May draw existing or promising management talent away from day-to-day operations.
- Can lengthen the ramp-up time it takes for inexperienced Black Belts to be trained and to become familiar with Six Sigma methods.

Building Technical Expertise

Another approach is to establish the Black Belt as a permanent position and career path. Companies with this priority will tend to either hire in or select and train people with Six Sigma–focused skills and aptitudes. Though they may lead a project, the role usually fits better under the heading of coach, and their advancement would be within the ranks of the Six Sigma expert group.

The pros:

- Allows Six Sigma expertise to be applied to projects right away (from people hired in).
- Permits a raising of the level of rigor of the training.
- Keeps trained Six Sigma resources focused on sanctioned projects and initiatives, rather than dispersing them back to the organization.
- May allow more projects, if each Black Belt can take on multiple projects.

The cons:

- Technically oriented Black Belts may have less organizational knowledge or experience.
- Misses out on the opportunity to "seed" management and professional ranks with experienced, trained Six Sigma project leaders.

A Hybrid Approach

A mix of these two approaches can often work best: Having some Black Belts come from existing management and professional groups, and selecting others or bringing them into the organization specifically to be the Six Sigma technical expertise. In the hybrid model you would have a choice of calling the temporary group Green Belts or Black Belts, and the technical experts Black Belts or Master Black Belts.

Of course, it isn't essential that you adopt the Belt naming system at all. You could stick with more common terms like *coach* and *team leader*, or create your own names for the roles.

Role-Clarity Issues

Even within a seemingly clear structure, overlapping responsibilities and role confusion can create significant challenges. Sometimes these challenges are due to personal styles or actions. For example, an eager sponsor might feel that he or she is showing real commitment by attending every team meeting, when in fact that is making the team leader feel uncomfortable and unimportant. Then again, if a coach takes a hands-off, you-do-it approach with a struggling team, the group can get frustrated and disillusioned. Thus it is important both to establish clear guidelines for each role and to encourage communication about how individuals can adapt their roles to their personal styles.

Other role conflicts can arise when existing functions seem to overlap with those in the continuous improvement structure. For example, some companies have used auditors or organization development staff to help business units and departments with their improvement efforts. Factoring these people's current responsibilities into the mix of Six Sigma activities is important; ignoring them will only increase the likelihood of confusion or resentment. How you can best resolve role issues is not based on any one formula; the most important objective is to make sure all potentially *duplicate* roles are eliminated.

Selecting Project Team Members

Because so much of the work in Six Sigma is done by teams, our review of roles would not be complete without some tips on *choosing* people for those teams.

One of the more common mistakes in establishing teams of all types is to overload them with too many members, called *overpacking*. We often see this issue in airports and on rental car shuttles when people are trying to move around several *giant* suitcases—apparently thinking they have to prepare for any possible need that might arise during a trip. (Of course, they may just be inveterate shoppers.)

When it comes to teams, it is smarter to recognize that size does matter. Large teams move more slowly, and their members also tend to be less engaged and enthusiastic. You may hear plenty of different "rules of thumb" on team size, but a good optimum number for almost any project team is between five and eight. Beyond that, communication tends to get overly complicated, decisions harder to make, and cohesiveness weak.

Exhibit 8.6 lists some key questions for you to ponder, as an aid to selecting team members.

Exhibit 8.6

QUESTIONS TO ASK WHEN SELECTING SIX SIGMA TEAM MEMBERS

- *Who has the best knowledge of the process being improved and/ or contact with the customer?*
- *Who has the most knowledge about the problem and/or the best access to data?*
- *What key skills or perspectives will be needed throughout the course of the project?*
- *What groups or functions will be most directly affected by the project?*
- *What degree of management/supervisory/frontline representation is likely to be needed?*
- *What skills, functions, or organizational levels can be obtained as needed during the project?*

It is acceptable to *adjust* the membership of the Six Sigma team over the course of a project, especially in the transition from developing solutions to implementing them. Indeed, different skills and talents often are needed to make process improvements work successfully. Also, having a flexible approach to team makeup—as long as it doesn't disrupt the cohesiveness of the group—will help you avoid the overpacking problem.

Once people are on board the Six Sigma effort, the next challenge is to give them the skills, knowledge, and tools they will require if everyone pulling together is going to achieve meaningful change and improvement.

CHAPTER 9

Training Your Organization for Six Sigma

Mastering continuous improvement requires yours to be a *learning organization*, one that is constantly gaining new information and insights from its customers, external environment, and processes; using that knowledge to respond with new ideas, products, services, and improvements; and then measuring the results and learning still more.

Training—or more broadly, capability building—is a key ingredient to achieving success by following the Six Sigma Way, both at the outset and on a sustained basis. Returning to one of our earliest messages in this book, remember that almost every key management skill plays a role at some point in building continuous improvement results and culture. For example, we have trained Six Sigma Belts in a wide array of topics ranging from project management, change management, and consensus and team building, to the tools and techniques of measurement and process analysis. Leaders need to learn how to collaborate among themselves, how to ask questions versus providing answers, and how to overcome the habits that may have gotten them where they are.

In your company's Six Sigma training, you should emphasize the skills and methods your people most need to fulfill their immediate role(s), and then build a more comprehensive *continuous* learning system—both adding and reinforcing.

The Essentials of Effective Six Sigma Training

The keys to good Six Sigma training are not dramatically different from those for any kind of training. In our view, too much of the training offered on the market over-emphasizes technical and analytical knowledge and misses the *people* side of effective change. Likewise, learning is tied strictly to improvement *projects* and fails to include every day thinking and problem solving processes. But through the following essentials, you can help avoid these pitfalls:

- ▶ **Emphasize hands-on learning.** From leaders to experts to practitioners, people in a business learn best when they can put concepts and skills into immediate practice. Ideally, such hands-on work will include efforts exerted on real processes, projects, and improvement needs. For example, Cartus trains employees via a class that runs for two and a half days, then everyone goes off and does a Six Sigma project. Then they come back three to four weeks later and have another two and a half days in the classroom.

- ▶ **Provide relevant examples and links to the "real world."** If your people are going to internalize how Six Sigma will work in your organization, the examples and exercises you provide will have to reflect your business and its specific challenges. Generally, a service business or process needs to use service-related examples; a manufacturing group learns most from plant floor–related scenarios. Even if you haven't done Six Sigma yet, a good training provider who knows the methodologies should be able to come up with some good examples that will work in your environment.

- ▶ **Build knowledge.** With a lot of material to cover for usual Belt training, it is easy to fall into the trap of data dumping. The concepts of Six Sigma can be interesting and exciting, but starting with advanced ideas and jargon will turn people off, or lead them to overcomplicate the improvement work. Establishing a foundation of commonsense principles and ideas—stated in regular language—helps people apply the methods more quickly and sets the stage for learning more sophisticated skills and methods (if needed). It is also important to put tools into a context (e.g., an improvement model like DMAIC, the Six Sigma roadmap) so that their application and relevance are clear. Cartus does this, too, as Patricia Small explains: "It's really important for service people especially not to go gangbusters with all the statistics right off the bat. So our approach to Six Sigma is not 'immerse yourself in two weeks of training and then go do a project.' Instead, we teach our people the concepts and the tools, we give them time to practice, and then present to people and get feedback on how they used the methodology. So we have adapted the Six Sigma rigor to what our employees can digest."

▶ **Cater to a variety of learning styles.** Visuals, games, exercises, and so on should be varied and, for most audiences, include some *fun*.

▶ **Make training something more than learning.** Training is a key element in your Six Sigma marketing plan. It represents a golden opportunity to convey the change vision, gain buy-in, deputize change agents, and clarify the themes of the effort and its value to the business. Look for ways to reinforce those messages during the training.

▶ **Make training an ongoing effort.** One of the comments we most often hear from participants in Six Sigma training is the suggestion that they get "refreshers" on a regular basis. Businesses, however, tend to offer only hit-and-run training. We give kids (ages 5 through 21) about 16 *years* to absorb an education, but people in the working world are expected to learn and master major new concepts and tools in (if they are lucky) three days! Six Sigma (i.e., learning) organizations will almost certainly have to adopt a practice of continuous education and training, just as their processes themselves are in need of continuous renewal and improvement. Considering the speed of change today, occasional once-off learning or cookie-cutter training won't make it.

Again, Cartus is a good example of a company that learned this lesson, as Patricia Small describes: "It's so important to immerse people in the Six Sigma process once you train them. We learned our lesson by having people go through training who were *considering* using it or who *intended to* use it on small projects, but what really happened was they never used what they learned. So we found that you have to be leading at least one major Six Sigma project that you're going to be accountable for, so you can get practice using the tools. I always hear about how important it is to choose the right projects, but it's just as important to *choose the right people* that you're going to train, and then make sure they apply what they've learned once they're back to work."

Planning a Six Sigma Curriculum

Six Sigma successes in organizations of many types have proven that a lot of talent and opportunity is just waiting to be unleashed on making organizations more responsive and efficient. One of the first concerns that arises, though, is "Will it take many weeks of training for us to tap into that potential?"

Our answer would be: "It doesn't have to." Some of the advanced skills of Six Sigma clearly take time to master, especially for those having no background or experience in, for example, statistics or meeting facilitation. On the other hand, people can be prepared in less than two weeks to begin tackling improvement projects, provided the training is well designed and tailored to the participant's current skills, processes, and so on.

Because of the many approaches to and versions of Lean Six Sigma training, it is impossible to suggest a specific curriculum. (Having *developed* many different versions, we sometimes feel the training part of our business specializes in "wheel reinvention.") But some categories and guidelines can help in assessing and developing or buying your own training. Table 9.1 presents an overview of the generic menu: the ranges of days reflect possible differences in the existing knowledge of participants, the amount of hands-on practice, and the depth of content that may be provided.

Please note that we are *not* suggesting that every group mentioned requires all of the training elements noted. In the early 2000s, the phenomenon of "Six Sigma envy" led to some excessively weighty training, which has subsided a bit. The most effective training helps participants both master the challenges of tackling difficult organizational issues while also getting people to understand that improvement can also be done in a few hours if they have the right information and manage the risks.

TABLE 9.1 A MODEL SIX SIGMA TRAINING CURRICULUM

Orientation to Six Sigma Concepts	Basic continuous improvement principles; review of business need for Lean Six Sigma; brief practice and/or simulation; overview of roles and expectations	All	1–2 days
Leading and Sponsoring Six Sigma Efforts	Role requirements and skills for leadership council and sponsors; project selection and portfolio management; reviewing team projects; change management	Business leaders; Implementation leaders	1–2 days
Six Sigma Processes and Tools for Leaders	Condensed and adapted in-struction in Six Sigma measure-ment and analysis processes/tools	Business leaders; Implementation leaders	3–5 days
Leading Change	Concepts and practices for setting direction, promoting, and guiding sustained organizational change	Business leaders; Implementation leaders; Coach/Black and Green Belts; Team leaders	2–5 days
Six Sigma/Lean Improvement Core Skills Training	Process improvement, design/redesign, and essential measure-ment and improvement tools—plus change management prin-ciples and methods	Team leaders/Black Belts; Managers/Green Belts; Team members; Project sponsors	6–10 days
Collaboration and Team Leadership Skills	Skills and methods for developing consensus, leading discussions, conducting meetings, and managing disagreement	Business leaders; Coaches/Master Black Belts; Team leaders/Black Belts; Managers/Green Belts; Team members	2–5 days
Intermediate Six Sigma Measurement and Analytical Tools	Technical skills for more com-plex project challenges: sam-pling and data collection; statis-tical process control; statistical tests; changeover; correlation and regression; basic design of experiments; etc.	Coaches/Master Black Belts; Team leaders/Black Belts	2–6 days

continued

TABLE 9.1   A MODEL SIX SIGMA TRAINING CURRICULUM (continued)

Advanced Six Sigma Tools	Modules in specialized skills and tools: quality function deployment; advanced statistical analysis; advanced DOE; Taguchi methods; etc.	Coaches/ Master Black Belts; Internal consultants	Varies by topic
Process Management Principles and Skills	Defining a core or support process; identifying critical outputs, requirements, and measures; monitoring and response plans	Process owners; Business leaders; Functional managers	2–5 days

CHAPTER 10

The Key to Successful Improvement: Selecting the Right Six Sigma Projects

We once conducted an informal poll of colleagues who have been involved in Six Sigma and other process improvement initiatives, and found an unanticipated consensus: Each person identified *project selection* as the most critical, and most commonly mishandled, activity in launching Six Sigma. It is a simple equation: well-selected and well-defined improvement projects equal better, faster results. The converse equation is also simple: Poorly selected and defined projects equal delayed results and frustration.

In fact, one of the strongest arguments in favor of following the ideal Six Sigma roadmap (see Figure 4.1) is that doing so allows you to much more effectively select your improvement target areas and build a more effective priority-setting process.

Project Selection and Priority Management Essentials

Let's begin by looking at some of the keys to effective project selection, which will set the stage for us to offer you steps to ensure you do it well. We believe that four steps are essential:

1. Provide guidance to leaders.
2. Launch a reasonable number of projects.
3. Scope projects properly.
4. Focus on *both* efficiency and customer benefits.

Let's take a closer look at each of these essentials in a bit more detail.

Provide Guidance to Leaders

Leaders need to master many skills that are key to guiding a Six Sigma initiative. Of these, project selection and priority setting usually have the most immediate impact, so should be top priority in the learning and support effort. Most effective in our experience is a facilitated meeting or working session where a *team* of leaders can work through possible issues, select a target set of efforts, and develop an initial rationale for improvement priorities and projects. Through this work, leaders discover (or are reminded) that effective improvement efforts should emphasize the following:

- ▶ Problems, not solutions
- ▶ Meaningful opportunities but manageable scope
- ▶ A mix of efforts, like a well-balanced investment portfolio
- ▶ Solid links to business strategy and goals (not just learning projects)
- ▶ Opportunities to expand or leverage success

Launch a Reasonable Number of Projects

"But what's wrong with working on lots of things at once?" you may ask. Well, imagine you are standing in front of a group of 15 people and gently tossing three or four basketballs at them. Chances are, someone will reach out and catch the balls. Now let's say you are throwing out more but smaller balls, say 10 or 15 tennis balls. The chance is greater that one or two will hit the floor, but if you use a gentle toss, most will still be caught.

Instead, what if you were to ever so gently toss a few handfuls of dried beans at the group? No matter what, of course, most of them would land on the ground or a tabletop.[1]

The moral: People and organizations can focus on only so many things at one time.

In the urgency to get results, it is easy to bombard an organization with many basketballs and beans. Too large a wave of projects can drown leaders' ability to track and guide them. Too many projects scatter people's attention and sap their ability to implement them well. For example, GE made the admitted mistake of requiring every manager to complete a personal (or "desktop") Six Sigma project. Many of these individual projects were makeshift, even trivial, which reduced the overall benefit of the effort.

Scope Projects Properly

A persistent challenge is trying to solve world hunger. A Belt or team can spend months trying to make headway on an extremely big, weighty issue, thereby frustrating the team and trying the leaders' patience. The ideal is to strike a balance between two broad criteria. We suggest your mantra for project selection become: *meaningful* and *manageable*. Usually, this means keeping the assignments reasonably small and highly focused.

Organizations continue to struggle with scoping, from our observation, either because they think it means shying away from potential big wins or because they are not prepared to invest the time needed up front to determine the best places to focus. The better choice, however, is to produce results on some narrower efforts—with the learning they offer—and move on to the next issue or segment of the problem.

Focus on *Both* Efficiency and Customer Benefits

Some executive groups, early in a Six Sigma effort, demand to know when and where their efforts would yield home runs, those quick-strike big-dollar gains. For most businesses, however, early-inning home runs occur only through cost cutting and efficiency improvements. This desire for big-dollar savings from Six Sigma can be a good thing as long as it is balanced by an understanding that short-term financial gains are only a part of the potential benefit. More often the greatest upside potential comes through improvements in competitive position and market strength, even though the payoff may take longer.

Let's look now at an example—or dramatization—of how projects tend to be chosen and expectations set.

Case Study #6: Using Six Sigma to Improve Efficiency and Reduce Costs at the Perfecto Pasta Company

Senior managers of the Perfecto Pasta Company were concerned about flat growth in sales and profits. Even though their market, packaged noodles sold in stores, was growing at double-digit-plus rates, Perfecto's numbers had held steady, meaning that their share of the market had declined from 25 percent to just 13 percent. Compared to other packaged-pasta companies, Perfecto's profit margins were low as well.

Perfecto's top management was introduced to Six Sigma concepts by a consultant who promised he could deliver them big bottom-line savings within six months. Excited by the concepts they heard and by the prospect of turning around the business, the group decided to launch these three pilot Six Sigma efficiency-boosting projects:

▶ Reduce waste on the number-three vermicelli production line (estimated saving: $100,000/quarter)
▶ Streamline the order entry and fulfillment process, including implementation of a new, industry-tailored ordering software system, PastaPower™, and the likely layoff of 25 people (estimated saving: $250,000/quarter)
▶ Speed up the invoicing and cash application process to improve cash flow and reduce outstanding receivables (estimated saving: $80,000/quarter)

The announcement of the new initiative was well received by stock analysts, and Perfecto's share price responded with a 15 percent gain in two weeks. "They're going to hit some real home runs with this one," said one of Perfecto's stock watchers as he upgraded the company from "sell" to "maintain."

When the projects paid off, company leaders initially rejoiced. Total savings were projected to be about $2 million a year. The joy was dampened, however, when Perfecto's market share continued to fall, down to below 10 percent.

As it turned out, competitors had gained an edge over Perfecto by tailoring their shipments to retailers so as to fit the noodle preferences of each store's consumers. (In some areas shoppers prefer rigatoni, while in others, manicotti and bow-tie noodles are the leaders.) Perfecto had continued to offer a standard order mix of eight pasta products.

Perfecto finally had to sell out to one of its upstart competitors, the formerly tiny NoodleCorp. Perfecto's president was asked why the Six Sigma effort hadn't addressed the tailored-delivery issue: "Do you know how long it would have taken for us to make any money on that?" he responded angrily.

Now, of course, your company won't necessarily go under, like Perfecto, if early continuous improvement projects focus only on internally driven savings. Certainly, the gains that can be realized through enhanced efficiencies and reduced rework are tremendous in many organizations. The push for quick gains alone, however, means delaying those longer-term benefits of Six Sigma that target *customers*: satisfaction, service, value, and product performance. Such a commitment to making *customers* the sole focus of your project selection is rare, and it requires some real executive discipline. We are aware of only one major industrial company, a more recent Six Sigma adopter, which has explicitly stated that efficiency improvement is *not* a priority of their initiative, whereas customer loyalty is.

Our best advice is to balance projects so that they include *both* externally and internally directed improvement opportunities.

Steps Toward Effective Project Selection

Good project selection is itself a process; if you follow it well, you can improve your "hit rate" substantially. Presented next are some key questions and steps that will help drive the project selection process. Our assumption here is that projects are being chosen by a group, usually of senior managers. If you are choosing projects on your own for your organization, the same considerations apply.

Choosing Sources for Improvement Project Ideas

As is true of any process, inputs are key to an effective result (i.e., "garbage in, garbage out"). If you take into consideration only a few anecdotal pieces of data as you decide where to focus your Six Sigma efforts, you are that much more likely to have irrelevant or unmanageable projects. Steps 1 through 3 in the Six Sigma roadmap are designed not only to provide you with a better understanding of your customers, business, and processes, but also solid information on improvement priorities. Absent those steps, sources of project ideas are described in the following sections.

External Sources of Project Ideas. These ideas from external sources fall into three categories:

1. Voice of the customer
2. Voice of the market
3. Comparison with competitors

In essence, these sources identify opportunities to better meet customer requirements, respond to trends in the market, or counter competitor strategies and capabilities. Sources for this kind of information can vary widely from trade and business articles, to competitor/market research, to feedback from salespeople. Exhibit 10.1 lists some questions you should consider about these sources.

External Sources of Project Ideas. These inputs help you to identify challenges that your business faces in defining and/or achieving its market and customer strategies. Again, Exhibit 10.1 lists some questions they should help you answer. Some of the best improvement opportunities arise from these questions because of their clear value both to the company and to its positioning vis-à-vis the outside world.

Internal Sources of Project Ideas. The frustrations, issues, problems, and opportunities visible inside your operations are the third key source of possible Six Sigma projects. You can label these internal sources "voice of the process" and "voice of the employee." Again, Exhibit 10.1 lists some questions for you to consider in listening to these voices. The goal here is to pay closer attention to various people's perspectives on ways in which processes can be improved to the benefit of the business, customers, shareholders, and employees.

Exhibit 10.1

KEY QUESTIONS TO ASK WHEN IDENTIFYING POSSIBLE SIX SIGMA PROJECTS

- *Where are we falling short in meeting customer needs?*
- *Where are we behind our competitors?*
- *How will the market be evolving? Are we ready to adapt?*
- *What new needs are on the horizon for customers?*
- *What barriers lie between us and our strategic goals?*
- *What new acquisitions need to be integrated so that they are profitable and aligned with our desired market image?*
- *What new products, services, locations, or other capabilities do we hope to launch to better provide value to customers and shareholders?*
- *What major delays slow down our process?*
- *Where does a high volume of defects and/or rework occur?*
- *Where are the costs of poor quality (COPQ) increasing?*
- *What concerns or ideas have employees or managers raised?*

Understanding Types of Improvement Projects

Early applications of Six Sigma focused on a fairly narrow range of problems where the objective was to reduce defects and/or manage variation. As useful as that kind of focus was, it created challenges to organizations that aspired to build a more robust continuous improvement capability and culture. For one, not every critical problem is best addressed as defect reduction; and frankly, as a theme for culture change, it is not the sexiest or most inspiring call to action. In addition, it led to people to ask: "Is this problem a good one for Six Sigma, or not?" which meant these commonsense methods were considered *optional* and therefore not truly common practice.

Many organizations recognize this issue and overcome the limited application of Six Sigma (more explicitly adding Lean concepts and tools helped), but in dozens of other companies, Six Sigma is marginalized and applied to only a small proportion of change efforts—usually those run by the specially trained Belts.

The reality is that Six Sigma principles can be applied to *any* issue, though the "how" needs to be adjusted according to the type of challenge. Here is a brief overview of the most common types, and what differentiates them:

▶ **A Quick Win.** When the problem, solution, and implementation are well understood, and risks of failure low, why not just *do it*? Some might say this philosophy is not really Six Sigma, but it is still useful and appropriate to apply Six Sigma concepts to ensure or enhance quick win results. For example, testing impact on the customer or looking at how to measure the benefits can turn a reactive fix-it action into a much bigger win.

▶ **A Rapid Improvement.** Also known as *kaizen* efforts or "Work Out," rapid improvement is best applied to smaller-scope opportunities where causes are fairly clear and solutions can be developed by a small team. Although many variations on this approach are possible, in every case the improvement discipline of Lean Six Sigma helps ensure the problem is clearly defined, that facts and ideas are kept in balance, and that ideas are converted into improved processes and observable results.

▶ **A Streamlining Effort.** When the objective is to reduce waste, eliminate red tape, and/or speed up a process, a Belt and team will draw more from the Lean toolkit. (These tools in reality *were* included in many original versions of Six Sigma training, and a lot of early successes at places like GE Capital focused on reducing cycle time.) Depending on the scope of the process being improved, streamlining projects may break up into a variety of subprojects and include quick wins, rapid improvements, and so on.

▶ **An Analytical or Root Cause–Focused Project.** These best fit the original textbook Six Sigma project definition, where the goal is to ferret out the causes of errors, variation, defects, or other performance issues. The depth of analysis can vary a lot depending on the type and complexity of the problem and the risks of a mistake. (The false assumption that statistical verification would be essential to every project is one reason why Six Sigma has at times been viewed as "too onerous.")

▶ **A Design or Redesign Initiative.** Covered in some depth in Chapter 15, this approach focuses on situations where simply *fixing* the current process is not enough, either because it is beyond repair or because external conditions (e.g., customer requirements, technology) have made it potentially obsolete.

It is not always easy, or possible, to know what types of projects you have until you dig into them a little further. Most important, if you want your Six Sigma efforts to achieve their potential, is to skip the question "Should this be a Six Sigma improvement or not?" and focus instead on "What are the most important problems or opportunities for us to be working on, based on our needs, goals, and resources?"

Defining Criteria for Project Selection

One of the challenges of managing effective improvement efforts—as in many business decisions—is to agree not just on what to do, but also on what *not* to do. Lots of things are important. The key word is *priority*: Which problems/opportunities will you tackle *first*?

The best project selection is based on identifying the issues/opportunities that best match your current needs, capabilities, and objectives. Exhibit 10.2 is a generic list of possible criteria to include in your project selection process, grouped into three categories: results or business benefits, feasibility, and organizational impact.

Exhibit 10.2

POSSIBLE CRITERIA FOR SELECTING SIX SIGMA PROJECTS

■ *Results or Business Benefits Criteria*
1. **Impact on external customers and requirements.** How beneficial or important is this problem/opportunity to our paying customers or key external audiences (e.g., shareholders, regulators, supply chain partners)?
2. **Impact on business strategy, competitive position.** What value will this potential project have in helping us to realize our business vision, implement our market strategy, or improve our competitive position?

3. **Impact on core competencies.** How will this possible Six Sigma project affect our mix and capabilities in core competencies? (Could involve strengthening a core competency or off-loading an activity no longer deemed a key internal skill?)

4. **Financial impact (e.g., cost reduction, improved efficiency, increased sales, market-share gain).** What is the short-term dollar gain likely to be? Long-term? How accurately can we project these numbers? (Beware of inflating possible gains beyond what's realistic.)

5. **Urgency.** What kind of lead time do we have to address this issue or capitalize on this opportunity? (*Note: Urgency* is distinct from *impact*; a small problem can be urgent, and a huge issue can have a long lead time.)

6. **Trend.** Is the problem, issue, or opportunity getting bigger or smaller over time? What will happen if we do nothing?

7. **Sequence or dependency.** Are other possible projects or opportunities dependent on dealing with this issue first? Does this issue depend on other problems being addressed first?

■ *Feasibility Criteria*

8. **Resources needed.** How many people, how much time, and how much money is this project likely to need?

9. **Expertise available.** What knowledge or technical skills will be needed for this project? Do we have them accessible and available?

10. **Complexity.** How complicated or difficult do we anticipate it will be to develop the improvement solution? To implement it?

11. **Likelihood of success.** Based on what we know, what is the likelihood that this project will be successful (in a reasonable timeframe)?

12. **Support or buy-in.** How much support for this project can we anticipate from key groups within the organization? Will we be able to make a good case for doing this project?

■ *Organizational Impact Criteria*

13. **Learning benefits.** What new knowledge about our business, customers, processes, and/or the Six Sigma system might we gain from this project?

14. **Cross-functional benefits.** To what extent will this project help to break down barriers between groups in the organization and create better whole-process management?

As extensive is this list of criteria in Exhibit 10.2, you may have other criteria that are relevant to your organization. You should *not* use all these factors in your project selection; instead, choose the five to eight that are most relevant criteria today. Where possible, it is smart to stick to the criteria for which you have more factual answers. Remember, the objective is to target the best priorities to fit your specific business and organizational needs and to deliver successful improvement that can build Six Sigma capability.

When you have a long list of potential improvement needs, it may be a good idea first to narrow the list down by using some qualifying criteria (e.g., minimum potential dollar benefits; benefits to external customers) or type of group-voting process. To gain a more careful assessment, note that scoring each possible project on each of your chosen criteria will give you a comparison and show which best supports all the factors for a worthwhile project. A criteria matrix can help structure your comparison of the projects.

However you use or define the criteria for project selection, remember that there are lots of reasons to consider a project to be worthy of the DMAIC process, as well as many things to watch out for before formally launching a project. Fundamentally, these reasons all go back to our two macro criteria: Is the project *Meaningful*, and is it *Manageable*?

Creating the Project Rationale

The end product of the selection effort is a description of the issue, value, and broad goal or expectations of the team assigned to a project. The project rationale establishes direction for an improvement team leader in choosing team members (if it is up to him/her to assemble the team) and in developing an initial plan for execution of the project. Done well, the rationale also becomes a communication tool and even something of an internal marketing document that helps to explain the purpose of the project to others in the organization.

Most importantly, the rationale (sometimes called a "business case," "project mission," or "purpose statement") provides a starting point for an improvement team to create its *charter* or similar overview document. Common elements of a project rationale statement include the following:

- ► **A description of the issue or concern.** It is important not to assign cause or blame for the problem/opportunity.
- ► **The focus of this specific project (optional).** Sometimes more than one project can be launched to work on various aspects of a large (world hunger–like) problem/opportunity.
- ► **A broad goal or type of results to be achieved.** Normally, a rationale should *not* include a target; it is more appropriate for the team to set its own specific goal or target, with the support of the project sponsor or champion.
- ► **An overview of the value of the effort.** What is the financial, customer, strategic, or other benefit of addressing the project, and why is it being done now?
- ► **Project parameters and expectations.** This element can give the team some understanding of the resources they have available to them, what solutions they may *not* consider, and so on.

Your project rationale statements may include other elements or leave some of these out. If you have an existing project definition format or document, it could be used as a rationale statement. In other words, we recommend you use what works in your own business.

Overall, it is important to strike a balance between giving clear guidelines to a team on project direction and expectations, while not overly narrowing options or dictating solutions. As we will see in Chapter 14, one of a Six Sigma improvement team's first tasks will be to interpret and prepare its own starting document based on the project rationale created by business leaders.

Before we wrap up this section and move on to choosing your Six Sigma model, let's take a look at the "dos and don'ts" of selecting projects, listed in Exhibit 10.3.

Exhibit 10.3

"DOS AND DON'TS" FOR SELECTING PROJECTS

- ■ Do—*Base your improvement project selection on solid criteria.*
  - Balance results, feasibility, and organizational impact issues. Good project selection can be a key to early success.
- ■ Do—*Balance efficiency/cost-cutting with externally focused customer-value projects.*
  - The customer-focus theme is a source of Six Sigma's strength. Putting your energies into short-term savings only sends the wrong signal and reduces your chance of boosting customer satisfaction and loyalty.
- ■ Do—*Prepare for an effective handoff to the improvement team.*
  - A technique such as the project rationale can give a good start to a project by defining clear issues and objectives.

- ■ Don't—*Choose too many projects.*
  - Improvement takes care and feeding on the part of leaders and experts, especially at the beginning. Avoid the temptation to overextend your resources and capabilities.
- ■ Don't—*Create world-hunger projects.*
  - Even more common than "too many" is "too big." Better to get a too-small project done more quickly—as long as the results are meaningful—than to have a too-big project drag on for months.
- ■ Don't—*Fail to explain the reasoning for the projects chosen.*
  - Everyone has problems *they* think should get top priority. Ensuring support for the ones you choose means providing a good rationale for your priorities.

Choosing Your Improvement Model

A final consideration in defining your Six Sigma approach is what improvement model to adopt. Although it directly affects primarily Step 4 in the Six Sigma roadmap, the choice of models will also affect how you conduct your training and how you "market" the Six Sigma initiative.

As we explained in Chapter 2, many companies have adopted the DMAIC model—define, measure, analyze, improve, control—or some variation of it for their Six Sigma improvement projects and as an enterprise change framework. We use those five steps as our guiding framework throughout *The Six Sigma Way*. However, if your organization already uses or has taught people a process improvement or redesign method, it is by no means mandatory that you abandon it in favor of DMAIC. And frankly, some people's past experience with overly technical applications of Six Sigma make them wary of DMAIC; they assume it is a complicated or hard-to-use process. If you see this type of resistance in your organization, applying a different model may be smarter.

Whatever improvement or problem-solving model you arrive at, it should not be difficult to adapt the actions covered in Chapters 14 and 15 to your existing improvement process. But do pay attention to some of the benefits DMAIC thinking brings to improvement efforts, so you can emphasize them in the model you do apply.

Features or Advantages of DMAIC

Making a Fresh Start. If your existing continuous improvement model is perceived to be part of a failed or discredited quality initiative or if it is used only rarely, DMAIC (or some other valid model) may help you to position Six Sigma as a truly different, better approach to business improvement. This "clean break" may help you avoid opening old wounds or reviving animosities created in a previous push for improvement. Explained properly, it can signal that the business has learned from its past efforts and is embarking on a new and improved path: Six Sigma.

Giving a New Context to Familiar Tools. Introducing a new (and better) improvement model is a positive rationale for giving people a fresh opportunity to learn and practice familiar tools, as well as to add new ones.

Creating a Consistent Approach. A lasting effect of the waves of quality training that assaulted many companies from the 1970s through the 1990s is the existence of *different* improvement models within the same company. If cross-functional efforts are to work on an end-to-end process, a common method and vocabulary are essential. Thus a decision to pick one model and stick with it may be an important way for your business to tap into the power of Six Sigma.

Putting a Priority on Customers and Measurement. Another potential advantage of the DMAIC model is the emphasis it places on these two critical components of the Six Sigma system. For example, validating customer requirements is a key sub step of the define phase, but was not to be found in most of the older quality models. Measurement is specifically addressed in other improvement roadmaps, but in the DMAIC process, measurement is presented more as a foundational, ongoing effort than as simply a task.

Conclusion

Again, building a continuous improvement culture does not depend on a single essential model. Most important is to provide a clear, shared set of steps that encourage people to review priorities and clarify goals, apply facts and data, challenge assumptions, and base solutions on good reasoning and risk management, and finally to assess outcomes and learn from the effort.

Having laid out many of the key decisions and some of the challenges associated with defining and designing Six Sigma for your organization, we turn next in Part Three to *making it happen*.

PART THREE

IMPLEMENTING SIX SIGMA: THE ROADMAP AND THE TOOLS

CHAPTER 11

Identifying Core Processes and Key Customers
(Roadmap Step 1)

In Chapter 4 we introduced the example of Company Island, a place where a lot of stuff is flowing around, but no one really has a grasp of the big picture. Whether you start your Six Sigma effort with Step 1 or loop back to this effort later, the objective here is to develop the high-level view of the organization—in essence, a map of your island that shows how essential work gets done.

The mapmaking approach described here is somewhat like putting a puzzle together. We begin by forming a basic idea of how the puzzle should look—just as you get from the top of the puzzle box. Then we assemble the edges of the puzzle first or because we are delicately balancing two metaphors, we define the coastline of the island where it links up with its customers. Then, we assemble the internal pieces of the puzzle, adding clarity to the basic image we first described. As with a puzzle this process will involve some trial and error and, like mapmaking, some research, too. Usually, as the picture emerges it looks a little different from what you expected, much as seeing a map of a place you have visited often can reveal facts you never knew.

The following are the three main activities associated with identifying core processes and key customers:

1. Identify the major core processes of your business (covered in Step 1A in this chapter).
2. Define the key outputs of these core processes and the key customers they serve (covered in Step 1B in this chapter).
3. Create a high-level map of your core or strategic processes (covered in Step 1C in this chapter).

As we discuss these steps, we assume for the most part that the organization we are mapping is an entire business or operating unit. It is possible, though, to use the same approach to map a *segment* of the organization including those areas (e.g., finance, human resources, or information technology) that provide services or products primarily to *internal* customers. Even small islands can use the Six Sigma system to improve their performance.

To bring to life many of the key steps, challenges, and tools of the Six Sigma Way, in Part Three we will feature a series of stories or scenarios of real but fictionalized companies that are putting their best effort forward to accomplish the tasks we describe. The first of the organizations we meet is a consumer products company. Others will include a transportation company, an electronics marketer/ manufacturer, and an insurance company. (*Note*: The scenarios we're presenting are based on real events, but the names and organizations have been fictionalized.)

Step 1A: Identify Core Processes

By *core process* we mean a chain of tasks that usually involve various departments or functions and deliver value (products, services, support, information) to external customers. Alongside the core or "value stream" processes, each organization has a number of *support* or *enabling processes* that provide vital resources or inputs to the value-producing activities.

Step 1A begins by describing three important concepts behind the idea of a core process: the concept of work as a process, cross-functional management, and the value chain. Then, we describe generic core processes and support processes. Next, we explain how you can define and tailor your organization's core processes, and we offer a case study to show how one company did exactly that. Then we will move on to Step 1B.

Concept #1: Work as a Process

Starting with Frederick Taylor and proceeding through the quality gurus of the 1980s and 1990s, the *process* has been an important theme for management theorists and practitioners. In the early days of modern manufacturing, the scale of production and degree of specialization were limited, and the processing of goods for customers was still clearly at the core of the business. As industrial organizations and competition grew, however, the work processes were overlaid and sometimes obscured by functional management structures and specialization of skills. The work processes were still going on, but the primary management focus was on "our function" and the individual's attention on "my task."

When the quality movement brought the process back into focus, it was and can still be difficult for people to see their work in this somewhat familiar way. Over the years, however, the idea that business success is driven by understanding and improving work processes has become a basic management principle through the influence of Six Sigma and related methods.

Concept #2: Cross-Functional Management

Frustration with functional and hierarchical business structures is nothing new. Some of the most persistent jokes, satires, and complaints about corporations through the years have been aimed at the empires and bureaucracies that hamper good decision making and responsiveness. As early as the 1920s, organizations such as General Motors were using interdivisional relations committees to deal with the friction generated between line and staff divisions, and between the various functional areas created within GM's decentralized organization.[1]

Efforts to break through the organizational barriers have been made countless times in the history of modern business, through reorganizations, restructurings, management shake-ups, and so on, and they happen often today. Cross-functional project and management teams have been tried as a force to break down the walls between groups. Although teamwork can help, just forming a team does little to remove the attitudes and structures that create the walls.

As businesses have begun to understand the difference between a process and a department and to map processes *across* functional boundaries, the real key to the cross-functional cooperation has appeared.

Concept #3: The Value Chain

Showing how work passes through various departments is terrific; however, a truly powerful model for management must show a clear strategic benefit. Thus, other than eliminating some squabbles and bureaucratic snags, how can cross-functional processes be used to improve business competitiveness and profitability? The third concept, the value chain, provides the answer.

The *value chain*, as defined by Harvard's Michael Porter in his 1985 book *Competitive Advantage*, is a way of representing an organization as "a collection of activities that are performed to design, market, deliver, and support its product."[2] Three dimensions of the value chain (or value stream) concept finally bring the core process idea into focus:

1. **The value chain reinforces the key interconnectedness of business activities and corporate success.** Each function plays a part (or should) in the basic goal of the organization: to provide some unique value to its market and customers. Any break or weak link in the chain (e.g., interfunctional rivalries) diminishes the value provided.
2. **Even though each function contributes to value, some play a primary role, others a secondary one.** Primary functions are "involved in the physical creation of the product [or service] and its sale and transfer to the buyer as well as the after-sale assistance."[3] Functions categorized as support activities by Porter include human resources, finance, procurement and even (gasp!) senior management. (Of course, anyone who has worked around large companies for a while knows that "support" functions often have greater clout or get more attention than do the "primary" ones—a corporate case of the tail wagging the dog.)
3. **Value chains are defined at the operating-unit level of an organization.** A corporate-wide value chain, encompassing various business units, would be meaningless.

In his initial work, Porter was not actually an advocate for a process view of the business. The value chain activities he describes are more akin to departments or functions tied to the traditional organization-chart view of a business. Still, the relevant message for companies trying to define and prioritize their business processes is clear: Those processes that provide products and services to customers are primary and others are secondary.

A Sampling of Core Processes

For any enterprise, certain activities are essential. In your organization they may be called something different or broken into smaller chunks, but the following list is a good starting point to help you ensure you include all the primary processes.

- ▶ **Customer acquisition.** The process of attracting and securing customers for the organization.
- ▶ **Order administration.** Activities meant to interpret and track requests for products or services from customers.
- ▶ **Order fulfillment.** Creation, preparation, and delivery of the order to the customer.
- ▶ **Customer service or support.** Activities designed to sustain customer satisfaction after delivery of an order.
- ▶ **New product/service development.** Conception, design, and launch of new value-adding services to customers.
- ▶ **Invoicing and collections (optional).** Whether "getting paid" is really a core, versus support, process is open to interpretation. Although technically it is not part of value delivery, it is a key part of a win-win relationship with customers, and hence of your financial success. Therefore it certainly is reasonable to consider it a core process.

An Overview of Support Processes

In the support functions of an organization, standard processes provide key resources or capabilities that enable the core processes to perform. These functions are a little more specific. Here we take various *departments* and divide them into their key processes:

- ▶ **Capital acquisition.** Provision of financial resources for the organization to do its work and execute its strategy.
- ▶ **Asset maximization.** Deployment of existing capital (especially money) to create the greatest possible return in alignment with the firm's value strategy.
- ▶ **Budgeting.** The process of deciding how funds will be allocated over a period of time.
- ▶ **Recruitment and hiring.** Acquisition of people to do the work of the organization.
- ▶ **Evaluation and compensation.** Assessment and payment of people for the work/value they provide to the company.
- ▶ **Human resource support and development.** Preparation of people for their current jobs and future skill/knowledge needs.
- ▶ **Regulatory compliance.** Processes ensuring that the company is meeting all laws and legal obligations.
- ▶ **Facilities.** Provision and maintenance of physical plant and equipment so that the business can perform its functions.
- ▶ **Information systems.** Movement and processing of data and information to expedite business operations and decisions.
- ▶ **Functional and/or process management.** Systems and activities to ensure effective execution of the work of the business.

After reading these support process descriptions, you may be thinking, "This is *weird*!" Well, we warned you that the "functional" view of the organization is so deeply ingrained in our minds that, when we change the context to flow of work and value provided, it seems strange and disorienting. But it is also true that the list just presented is only *one* way out of many to define these processes. How *you* do it will almost certainly be different and make more sense for your organization.

Defining and Tailoring Your Core Processes

One of the first things to recognize in trying to list the primary or core processes in your organization is that there is no "right" or "wrong." In some instances how you define core processes may be guided by the need to send a message to the organization. We recently spoke with a senior executive who reorganized his company under what were called four "pillars"—create, deliver, care, and support—encompassing three core and various enabling processes. Each pillar involves a great deal of detail, but as a unifying theme for the company, the pillar concept is effective. As another example, one of our clients developed a fairly simple model of what they call their strategic processes, shown in Figure 11.1. Each person in the organization is able to identify his or her own contribution to one or more of these core processes.

Putting together your model of core processes may take some time and thought. Then too, how many you identify will vary with your business and with factors such as strategy and history. As a rule of thumb, however, most operating units should have between four and eight high-level primary processes. Asking the following questions can help you to determine them.

1. **What are the major activities through which we provide value—products and services—to customers?** This question gives you a starting point to identify your core processes with *value* as the primary definer of a *core* activity. Be careful not to include activities that are very important to you (e.g., legal or regulatory compliance)

Strategic Processes

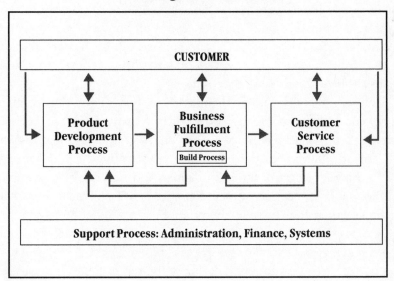

FIGURE 11.1   EXAMPLE: SIMPLIFIED STRATEGIC PROCESSES MODEL

but that do not add value to customers. (We encounter this notion again when we look at value analysis in Chapter 15.)

2. **How could we best describe or name these processes?** You can refine the names later, but give them a label to start with. Try to avoid using a department or function name. No true core process happens within a single department.

3. **What are the primary (one to three) critical outputs of each process that we can use to evaluate its performance/capability?** The quality of the end product delivered to the customer is the most important success criterion for a process. If you identify many outputs from a core process, you may not have defined the process specifically enough or perhaps you lumped together several business units.

Now that you have an overview of how to define core processes, let's see how one company tackled this problem.

Case Study #7: FieldFresh Looks at the Big Picture to Define Its Core Processes

The FieldFresh company has been packing and selling canned and frozen fruits and vegetables through retail stores in the Midwest for more than 60 years. The FieldFresh brand has benefited greatly from its strong reputation for quality and from the loyalty of consumers in its eight-state market area. FieldFresh is still and always has been profitable, but the company is aware that even though times have changed a lot in six decades, things at FieldFresh have not.

FieldFresh today is run by a handful of top managers, all with 20 or more years with the company and most of whom are getting close to retirement. It has always been a close-knit, family-oriented company (it is not uncommon for parents and their offspring to both work at FieldFresh), with a strong sense of tradition and a high level of commitment to employees and customers. The heads of FieldFresh's four main functional groups (advertising and promotion, manufacturing, accounting, and personnel) have done an excellent job running their individual departments. Each has a firm grasp of his or her area, but because they have worked together so long and know the business so well, the four have kept operations among the different functions flowing smoothly and effectively.

The biggest concern for the FieldFresh leaders—prompted by pressure from the company's board of directors—is how the company will weather the changes in its industry as well as the pending turnover in top management. "You've been really lucky," commented FieldFresh board member Marla Jones, president of a local bank. "So many companies like FieldFresh have had the rug pulled out from under them because they failed to adapt and prepare for change. You're still doing fine, but the question is: 'How will FieldFresh make it in the new century?'"

FieldFresh Leaders Consider Their Challenge

At first members of management resisted as "meddling" the challenging comments made by some members of the board of directors. Over time, however, most of the top five executives at FieldFresh—President Elliott Peardale and his four department vice presidents—began to acknowledge the validity of the issue. "We've got some great people here," said Peardale, "but we've not helped them learn the business to the degree we might have. After all, we've handled every top decision pretty much by ourselves."

At the urging of another board member, who happens to be chairman emeritus of the business department at the state's top university, FieldFresh's top leaders attended a one-day seminar on the concepts behind the Six Sigma approach to business management. After the workshop, the group met at their weekly lunch to share their thoughts on the ideas they heard.

"Sounds too much like all that quality b——!" pronounced Jimmy Haricot, manufacturing vice president.

"Don't judge too fast, Jimmy," responded Brenda Lechosa, head of advertising and promotion. "It got me thinking that we've set this company up for trouble. The only people who really understand this entire company are us. We know the customers, we know the departments, we know the background. And even then, I think we're in the dark on more stuff than we'd like to admit."

"Brenda's right, I'd say." That was accounting vice president Hal Krautmeyer. "I can't hand things off to anyone else in the department for more than a couple of weeks. When I come back from vacation I have a stack of backlogged issues to work on. When Millie and I head for Arizona permanently in a couple of years, are you guys going to hang around and pay the bills?"

"We did try some of that TQM stuff, you know, a few years back," commented Peardale, "and it didn't get us much. I can see why Jimmy's skeptical."

"But this seems different to me," persisted Lechosa. "They said Sigma Six, or whatever you call it, is about fixing problems, but I really liked the part about looking at the business in a new way."

"What would be 'new'?" asked Haricot. As the manufacturing head, he typically played the role of nuts-and-bolts skeptic on the FieldFresh team.

Personnel leader Al Funghi finally weighed in: "To me, what's new is a way to show others in the company how we work together. We keep saying we can't hand over responsibility to people, but we haven't really tried. Maybe if we helped them understand the company as well as we do, they could do more."

"I don't need any teams to start fixing a bunch of imaginary problems in the plants!" protested Haricot.

"Jimmy," said Peardale, "I don't think that's the suggestion."

"No way," agreed accounting's Krautmeyer. "I don't think fixing problems is the answer for us—at least not right away. But if we could start showing people how the company works—and maybe see ways for it to work better—we might all be able to retire when we want to, instead of working here till we're all eighty-something."

"That's what I'm saying," agreed Lechosa. "But I'd add one thing: I think there's more at stake than our retirement. I just think we can't expect our brand loyalty and tradition to carry us forever. The way we've run the company probably won't work for the next generation."

"You know," said Peardale, almost interrupting the advertising manager. "I guess that's what has been bothering me for quite a while now, but I hadn't been able to explain it. It's hard to admit, but it's time we updated things at FieldFresh if we're going to leave a good situation behind when we leave." The consensus was strong enough that the managers decided to take a first step on the Six Sigma roadmap and create a process-focused map of the FieldFresh organization.

FieldFresh Gets to the Core of the Matter

A month later, the five top managers at FieldFresh arrived at work for an early 7:00 a.m. meeting. Their agenda was to identify the major or core processes of their business. Jimmy Haricot agreed to give it a try; the other executives were convinced it would be a good idea. They brought in a facilitator to help them, recommended by one of the board members.

Their first list was a mix of lots of activities or groups, including payroll, grower relations, invoicing, media buying, label design, and so on. "This is a mess," complained personnel director Al Funghi. "We're doing something wrong."

"You know," said Jimmy, who was trying to be cooperative, "weren't we supposed to look at the stuff that focuses on the customer *only*?"

Everyone agreed they had gotten off track. With the help of the facilitator, they began to move the noncore activities to a separate list of support functions and processes and to reorganize the core processes by major categories. It was a struggle, and by the end of the session at 10:30 a.m. they were exhausted. "We'd better noodle this over a little," said Peardale.

In between meetings, Brenda Lechosa called the people who had given the initial workshop and got some advice. When they met for another 7:00 a.m. session a week and a half later, she passed along the input: "They suggested we try to avoid naming any process after a department. We have to think cross-functionally and focus on the major value-adding activities."

At the end of another couple of hours work—and a fair amount of verbal arm-wrestling—they had reduced the list to the following four core processes:

- ► Product supply
- ► Product development
- ► Production and distribution
- ► Consumer and retailer marketing

They then created a list of what they decided to call support processes, following a simple naming convention:

- ► People support
- ► Financial support
- ► Infrastructure support
- ► Strategic support

They sketched a diagram of these lists, which the facilitator put into a more presentable graphic (see Figure 11.2).

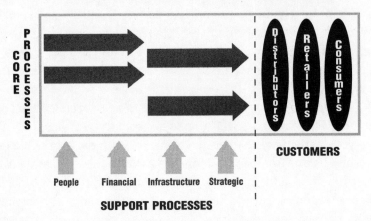

FIGURE 11.2   FIELDFRESH CORE AND SUPPORT PROCESSES

Step 1B: Define Your Key Process Outputs and Key Customers

Although it is the easiest part of Step 1, it has its traps, too. The challenge is to avoid pushing too many items or work products into the category of *outputs*. If yours is like most organizations, a lot of "stuff" is getting produced every day, and some of it may end up in the hands of your customer. From a strategic or core process standpoint, however, only the final product or the primary output is relevant for now.

It is not at all mandatory that core process outputs be delivered to external, paying customers. For example, the output of a customer acquisition process is some type of agreement to do business with a customer (e.g., an order, distribution agreement, contract, statement of work, policy, etc.) The external customer usually receives some verification of the deal, but the primary customer of that core process will be the *next* core process (e.g., order administration or production).

Let's return to our case study and look at the outputs for company processes at FieldFresh.

Case Study #7 Continued: The Outputs of the FieldFresh Processes

Each of the vice presidents at FieldFresh was given an assignment: to draft a definition of the major outputs and customers of the core processes they had identified. Because a customer could be a person or a group of people, they decided it would be okay to name a department as the customer of a core process, even though it might be the first step in another process.

For example, accounting's Hal Krautmeyer took "product development." He listed three outputs, each with different customers:

Output 1: Product formula; *Customers:* Plant Technical Support, Grower Relations

Output 2: Process specifications; *Customer:* Plant Engineering

Output 3: Consumer test data; *Customers:* Promotions Planning, Brokers/Distributors.

Al Funghi of HR was asked to work on "product supply." It had one major output:

Output 1: Produce (raw material); *Customers:* Plant Technical Support (which handles recipe-based products), or Production (which receives any fresh-canned or fresh-frozen items directly).

Step 1C: Create High-Level Core Process Maps

The last step you should take in assembling the process map puzzle is to identify the major activities that make up each core process. (As an option, you can create high-level diagrams of support processes as well.)

A SIPOC diagram is one of the most useful and often-used techniques of process management and improvement. It presents an at-a-glance view of work flows. The name comes from the five elements in the diagram:

▶ Supplier—the person or group providing key information, materials, or other resource to the process
▶ Input—the "thing" provided
▶ Process—the set of steps that transforms and ideally, adds value to the input
▶ Output—the final product of the process
▶ Customer—the person, group, or process that receives the output

Often, key requirements of the input and output are added, making it more like SIRPORC. (No one seems to use that term, though—maybe because it sounds like a royally honored pig.)

SIPOC can be a big help in getting people to see the business from a process perspective. Here are just a few of its advantages:

1. It displays a cross-functional set of activities in a single, simple diagram
2. It uses a framework applicable to processes of all sizes, even an entire organization
3. It helps maintain a big-picture perspective, to which additional detail can be added

By linking SIPOCs end-to-end across an organization (i.e., where the output of one process becomes the input of another), you can develop a high-level process diagram of the entire company.

The first two tasks covered in this chapter have given us a good start on a SIPOC diagram: Identify the process broadly by name and define the output and customer. We are interested in the suppliers and inputs as well as a more detailed description of the process.

Identifying Suppliers and Inputs

To identify the suppliers and inputs to a process, you first need to know at what point—where, when, and with what action—the process *starts*. Detecting this starting point is usually not too difficult when defining the major processes for an organization; you can simply identify at what point the previous (or upstream) process leaves off and what inputs are passed along to the next process.

Generally it is best to limit inputs to items consumed during the process and *not* to include equipment, facilities, or other relatively permanent infrastructure. First of all, it is much simpler: If you included every piece of software, desk, telephone, and machine used in most processes, the list would be *long*. More importantly, an ultimate goal of diagramming the process is to understand the flow and variation in the work over time. Stuff that is more or less permanent actually becomes part of the process, and we can measure its effect on the work there, but not as an input.

The following are some easy questions for you to ask to aid in identifying suppliers and inputs:

▶ **What key materials, information, or products are provided to the process?** The most critical input to any core process is the "thing" being worked on. In an assembly plant, it is parts; in a lending company, it is a loan request; at an airline company, it is a passenger. Other key inputs will be essential to the success of the process also, such as a work order at the assembly plant, customer data at the lending company, and passenger reservations at the airline.

▶ **Which of these inputs are absolutely essential to the process work as being performed?** Focus only on such critical inputs. If the work can get done well without it, it isn't critical.

▶ **Are they consumed or used during the process or passed through to the customer as an output?** If neither is true, it may be a tool, but it probably is not an input.

▶ **Who provides those inputs?** Once you define the input, its usually easier to identify the process suppliers.

Diagramming the Process

The *P* segment of a SIPOC is best done as a block diagram, with each box representing major activities or subprocesses. Unlike a more detailed process map or flowchart, a block diagram usually is a simple, straight-line flow, with no decision points, rework loops, or alternate paths shown. To avoid getting into too much detail, you should limit the process to 4–10 blocks. It can be tricky, though, because the detail tends to come out anyway. For that reason we usually recommend using an *affinity* method to build the high-level block diagram. In the affinity technique, a group lists ideas and then organizes (or, in the ize-ization of our vocabulary, *affinitizes*) them into meaningful categories. What emerge are usually the high-level steps. Once you name the steps or tasks, you can order them into a (roughly) sequential set or activities—the *process*. For the business's high-level processes, even these process blocks will in most cases be broad and cross-functional.

Let's return to our case study and see how FieldFresh identified its suppliers and inputs and created a series of process maps.

Case Study #7 Continued: FieldFresh Identifies Its Suppliers, Inputs, and Processes

The FieldFresh management group was happy with the list of outputs and customers they each had drawn up individually.

Brenda Lechosa of advertising offered an idea: "If our next step is to map out these processes, I think some of the directors and managers would be really helpful. And it would save us some time having to do this all ourselves."

The group was willing to give it a try. So they drew up a roster of four process committees to identify inputs and suppliers and create a series of high-level process maps.

All four committees made presentations of their core process SIPOC maps in an all-managers meeting held at a local conference center. An example, from the product supply process, is shown in Figure 11.3. After the presentation, Peardale announced to the assembled management group that FieldFresh was initiating an effort, which he called "FieldFresh 3000," to position the company for competitiveness and growth "all the way to the next millennium."

The process committees that worked on the core process maps would continue to work on defining and measuring the requirements of each key activity. "We're going to take this a step at a time," he cautioned the group. "We still don't know whether this Six Sigma approach is really right for FieldFresh. But the signs so far look pretty good."

Using the Core Process Maps

The core process definition becomes the starting point for Step 2 in the Six Sigma roadmap, and where we begin to identify requirements for the processes. At the same time, the value of the whole-organization view of the business as a network of key processes can help create a new understanding of the business and its interdependencies.

FieldFresh **Product Supply Core Process**

Inputs	Outputs
Product Formulas	*Produce at Plant*
Sales Forecasts	*Grower Contracts*

FIGURE 11.3   FIELDFRESH PRODUCT SUPPLY CORE PROCESS

Just as at FieldFresh, the act of defining a process model of the organization can be an eye-opener and a way of focusing attention on such questions as "Why do we do it this way?"; "Are these activities really important?"; "How effectively are these two processes connecting?"

These questions arise all the time in a Six Sigma–savvy organization, which is why we suggest defining the core processes as the ideal starting point for the effort. Before moving on to Step 2, let's see how FieldFresh benefitted from its work during this step of Six Sigma. At the end of the chapter, Exhibit 11.1 provides a list of "dos and don'ts" to help *you* identify *your* organization's core processes and key customers.

Case Study #7 Conclusion: The Follow-Through at FieldFresh

In the ensuing months, the FieldFresh management group became a much more open place to work. It turned out that a lot of ideas and information had been bottled up in the director and manager ranks. Those ideas began to come forth as these key people offered ideas on how to measure their performance and how to better communicate with customers.

At the end of the following year, Elliot Peardale announced his retirement as president and handed over the reins of the company to Brenda Lechosa. Two other vice presidents retired, but they were replaced with directors from inside the business who know and understand the FieldFresh culture and tradition.

Lechosa pledged to continue the FieldFresh 3000 effort, but said it would gradually be phased into a new management practice model based on the Six Sigma system.

From a business results perspective, FieldFresh continued to revamp outdated processes and over time established better collaborative relationships with its distributors and with retailers. Publicity gained through stories appearing in several regional newspaper business sections ("FieldFresh Refreshes" and "A New President and New Practices") mirrored a sales rebound, as FieldFresh managed to update its brand identity without losing its strong reputation.

Jimmy Haricot, back for a visit to the office after a month of fishing in Wyoming, told his longtime colleague Lechosa that "The place looks just the same, but I can tell the atmosphere is a lot different. I may just come out of retirement to run the plants for you again."

Lechosa looked at him over her glasses.

"Not!" he added.

The former vice president and the new president both laughed heartily.

Exhibit 11.1

"DOS AND DON'TS" FOR IDENTIFYING CORE PROCESS AND KEY CUSTOMERS

- Do—*Focus on activities that directly add value to customers.*
  - You can include support processes in your work as well, but the priority should be to understand and improve things that drive the business's success.
- Do—*Stay at a high level.*
  - As soon as you get into too much detail, you lose the big-picture perspective that is one of the biggest benefits gained by defining core processes.
- Do—*Involve a mix of people.*
  - It takes cross-functional input to describe cross-functional processes. Use this opportunity to take a new look at how the business unit operates.

■ Don't—*Overload the process with inputs and outputs.*
  • Only rarely do you want more than a few key inputs and one to
    three key outputs.
■ Don't—*Look upon your core processes as unchangeable.*
  • The point of the Six Sigma system is to make your business
    more successful by creating skills and structures that support
    any change needed to meet changing customer and competi-
    tive needs.

$$\boxed{\text{CHAPTER 12}}$$

Defining Customer Requirements
(Roadmap Step 2)

This chapter is all about what may be the most important new core competency your organization will need to develop in the twenty-first century. Understanding what customers really want and how their needs, requirements, and attitudes change over time requires a combination of discipline, persistence, creativity, sensitivity, science, and sometimes luck.

The final products of this Six Sigma activity, in its most comprehensive form, include the following:

- ► A strategy and system for continually tracking and updating customer requirements, competitor activities, market changes, and so on; aka, a "voice of the customer" (VOC)[1] system.
- ► A description of specific, measurable performance standards for each key output, as defined by the customer(s)
- ► Observable and (if possible) measurable service standards for key interfaces with customers
- ► An analysis of performance and service standards based on their relative importance to customers and customer segments and their impact on business strategy.

The tasks you must undertake to develop these deliverables are as follows:

1. Gather customer days and develop your "voice of the customer" strategy (described in Step 2A in this chapter).
2. Develop performance standards and requirements statements (covered in Step 2B in this chapter).
3. Analyze and prioritize these requirements, and evaluate them per your organization's business strategy (covered in Step 2C in this chapter).

Achieving the first task, an ongoing customer feedback system, is really a long-term goal. In the initial stages of a Six Sigma effort you are likely to focus on high-priority input from customers rather than revamp your entire customer-monitoring effort. Because the ability to really listen to the customer is so critical to business success, however, we will begin with that major initiative.

Step 2A: Gather Customer Data, and Develop a "Voice of the Customer" Strategy

It is easy to assume that most companies have a pretty good handle on their customers' needs or have people and mechanisms in place to keep tabs on them. Certainly a lot of money is spent on market research and customer surveys by companies of all types, perhaps including yours. We would suggest, however, that many of the practices in use today, to keep tabs on customers' needs, create a false sense of security. When they are examined more closely, many companies are likely to come to the same conclusion as that reached by an executive at a large insurance company: "We began to realize we didn't understand our customers as well as we thought we did."

Gathering Customer Data

Certainly improved data mining technologies, coupled with the electronic trail many of us leave through web searches, social media, purchase history, and so forth, are providing companies with a growing—and sometimes troubling—access to consumer preferences and needs. But we suggest that taking advantage of what might be viewed as invasive methods is not being customer-focused either if consumers are not happy about it. (We will leave the big ethical questions for another book.)

Even with these technology advances, the vast majority of organizations large and small (businesses, government agencies, health care providers, and more) don't have access to these insights, and often seem to be surprisingly detached from the needs and perspectives of their customers.

As an example, one of our clients, a maker of hip, youth-oriented shoes and apparel, organized its development and product introduction cycle around producing a large, full-color printed product catalog for use by its immediate customers: retail buyers. Noting how much time, cost, and anxiety went into this production, we suggested that maybe it wasn't all that useful to their customers and better ways to share product information might be used. Because it was 2009, the option of moving the whole thing online was not some crazy, new-fangled idea. And as a freewheeling and successful business (the CEO came to work in shorts and flip-flops), you might not expect this company to be married to an old-fashioned catalog. Nevertheless, the idea of eliminating the printed book was unnerving, and it took several months for them to realize their buyer clients would have much preferred information they could search easily, use when needed, and did not weigh several pounds.

To drive really meaningful improvement, a clear understanding of and attention to the needs of customers is mandatory, both to help you deliver more effectively on their core needs, but also to avoid the traps—like our shoe company client—where your *assumptions* about what customers want can leave you in your competitors' dust or have you spending time and money on meeting obsolete needs. Even if you work in an internal support organization such as IT or human resources, your success depends (or should) on how well you help your internal customers reach their key goals.[2]

Voice of the Customer Essentials

Whether you develop this core competency internally or rely on outside resources to serve as your ears to the market, you will need to recognize some of the essentials of an effective voice of the customer system:

- ► Make your VOC system a continuous effort.
- ► Clearly define your customers.

- ▶ Avoid the squeaky wheel syndrome.
- ▶ Use a broad array of methods to find out what your customers want.
- ▶ Seek specific data, and watch for trends.
- ▶ Use the information you obtain.
- ▶ Set realistic goals.
- ▶ Be ready to challenge your own assumptions.

The next sections describe these essentials in greater detail before we move on to Step 2B.

Make Your VOC System a Continuous Effort. The first principle of an effective VOC system is that it must become a constant priority and focus. The now-and-then approach that served in the past is no longer sufficient, in light of today's speed of change. Organizations that fail to keep their eyes and ears open are those most likely to be asking "What the heck happened?" as they watch their fortunes fall.

Clearly Define Your Customers. In Chapter 11, we outlined how to build a more comprehensive view of your core processes and key customers. Looking more carefully at the question "Who are our customers?" can bring a real awakening to a business and its leaders as well.

Quite a few organizations have already been through this awakening. For example, a common discovery is that a small proportion of customers contributes the lion's share of revenues. Often, too, the costs of supporting some customers turn out to make them *unprofitable*. Some intelligent strategic improvements have been made in recent years to better segment customer groups. Companies are getting more adroit at aligning their product offerings, services, and features—as well as their costs—with the profile of each group: a win-win strategy. In other instances, the tough decision is made to abandon a customer segment or to focus efforts on serving those customers whose needs best match the company's strategy.

Our objective in this chapter is to help you design or improve your systems for understanding and defining customer requirements and market trends—not to question your business's strategy. Nevertheless, how you define your strategy and differentiate your customers will have a big impact on the accuracy of your data and the resources needed to establish a voice of the customer system.

Avoid the Squeaky Wheel Syndrome. It is human nature to pay attention to the unusual—or the annoying. It is not necessarily a bad business practice, either. Upset customers, or those with special needs and demands, can test your organization's ability to rise to challenges and develop new capabilities. And you certainly don't want those squeaky, ticked-off clients and customers running around telling their colleagues/ friends about their horrible experience doing business with you.

When the squeaky wheel drowns out everything else, though, it is a serious issue. Your sample of customer data is incomplete and the conclusions you are likely to draw about your market or customers are liable to be wrong. Six Sigma voice of the customer systems will have to be tuned to hear more than just high-pitched whines.

A corollary to the squeaky wheel syndrome is the tendency to interpret the voice of the customer as meaning just your existing customers. An opposite, equally serious mistake is to seek input only from prospective customers while ignoring the people currently helping you to pay the bills (an issue one especially tends to find in sales-driven organizations that are always looking for the "next deal").

Aldie Keene, a partner with the Indianapolis-based Customer Loyalty Research Center, is a veteran of hundreds of customer-focused research projects done for many of the top companies in the United States. Keene says one of the biggest stumbling blocks that organizations trip over is "getting information from the wrong customers." He often sees companies that design products and services to a specific target customer segment. "Then, of course, they sell to anybody that comes in the door." Later, in testing customer satisfaction, "guess who turns out to be the most dissatisfied? A large percentage are ones that weren't targeted by their product/service strategy."

Beyond talking to and listening to the wrong audience, Keene notes, companies then *react* to the negative data: "They say, 'Whoa, we're really doing a bad job.' And they point fingers: 'You, over there—get better!' All without understanding who's really included in the negative responses and why they're unhappy."

The key, not surprisingly, is to balance and diversify your efforts to learn from a variety of groups, including:

► Current, happy customers
► Current, unhappy customers (that includes both those who complain and those who don't)

▶ Lost customers
▶ Competitors' customers
▶ Prospective customers (i.e., those who haven't purchased from you or your competitors, but are potential buyers of your products/ services)

Use a Broad Array of Methods to Find Out What Your Customers Want. Fulfilling the essentials of a twenty-first-century voice of the customer system, as we described it thus far, will demand a wider arsenal of techniques than most organizations employ today. For example, market or customer surveys may be excellent for getting targeted information and preference rankings, but not allow detailed follow-up. Many traditional techniques, including interviews and focus groups, have the disadvantage of being direct observation tools; that is, subjects are aware you are asking them what they think. It no longer comes as a surprise that customers often will say one thing and do another.

Figure 12.1 presents a list of traditional and new-generation voice of the customer data-gathering techniques. The new-generation list, you should note, tends to include more indirect methods of assessing customer needs and preferences by their behavior versus what they say. The best mix of methods will depend a lot on your customers, market, resources, and the type of data you need. It is beyond the scope of this book to cover the how-to of all these methods; most important is that you recognize the need to evaluate, and in many cases strengthen, your existing customer data-gathering approaches.

Voice of the Customer/Market Methods

Traditional . . .	New Generation . . .
• Surveys	• Targeted and multilevel interviews and surveys
• Focus groups	
• Interviews	• Customer scorecards
• Formalized complaint systems	• Data warehousing and data mining
• Market research	• Customer/supplier "audits"
• Shopper programs	• Quality function deployment

FIGURE 12.1   ADVANCES IN VOICE OF THE CUSTOMER METHODS

Seek Specific Data, and Watch for Trends. One of the core requirements of a voice of the customer system will be your ability to identify customer requirements while catching trends, thus helping to keep you ahead of changes in market preferences, aware of new challenges, and so on. Having access to specific data is key to developing objective, accurate standards and measuring performance. However, a big-picture perspective is essential, too, or you may miss new opportunities, or curves in the road, that leave you out of sync with customers and vulnerable to competitors.

Getting specifics from customers is tough. It is not always easy to communicate effectively. Customers have plenty of demands on their time; they also may be unwilling to disclose sensitive information. It takes a lot of time and resources to probe sufficiently and/or analyze data to clearly specify what customers want and need.

Another obstacle: Your customers may be incapable of defining for you any clear requirements. A salesperson in a Six Sigma workshop we once conducted commented: "There are a lot of ignorant customers out there." In the case of many businesses, her comment was absolutely correct: Customers do not understand your product or service as well as you do, which makes it tough for them to give you clear, specific requirements. In the process of gathering the voice of the customer, you may also need to *educate* your customers so that they are better prepared to define their own needs.

Use the Information You Obtain. It has become almost a truism in companies today to say that although all the data you need are available, nobody can tell you where to find it. Or that key information is distributed (posted on the intranet, etc.), but no one uses it. The point is that just gathering customer input does not close the loop; voice of the customer data become valuable only when and if they are analyzed and acted upon. Even organizations that already have sophisticated and effective customer data-gathering systems still encounter the problem of getting executives and managers to *pay attention* to the data.

Aldie Keene notes that many sources of customer input that most companies already have could be consolidated and compared, enabling them to draw a much clearer picture of customer relationships and thereby to make predictions of future behavior. "Very few of our clients make even that most rudimentary connection to try to integrate that information to say 'What does it all mean together?'"

Another key question, then, is "How will your business effectively assimilate and take action on customer and market data?" The broad answer: Develop new processes to handle that information so that it can be applied to improved decisions and more effective responses to changes and opportunities.

The executive team of one of our clients created a process they call "Strategic Find and Solve"—a great example of the kind of loop-closing effort that puts business leaders on the front line in terms of using customer and market data. When they are working on the basis of varied inputs (including one-on-one interviews and targeted market research), a firm's top managers are able to make more informed decisions as they adjust product and service offerings and launch efforts to create or improve processes. Although this process is still being worked out, it is much more than a once-a-year strategic planning session.

Failing to disseminate customer-focused knowledge throughout the organization can also be a serious weakness, notes Aldie Keene. "Where you can effectively get employees to understand customer information, you've laid the groundwork for change to occur. I think most companies would be shocked at how bad their internal communication is with respect to customer information—how few employees really get it."

Finally, because the starting point for information is customers themselves, it is important that your findings—and the responses to them—be conveyed back to those customers. Customer Loyalty Research Center studies show dramatically higher satisfaction scores among customers who receive feedback versus those who hear nothing.

Set Realistic Goals. Creating and maintaining a comprehensive system to gather and use customer input and market data cannot be accomplished overnight. If you are lucky, your organization will have a strong existing foundation to build on, and you can focus on addressing your weaknesses (paying special attention to the essentials just reviewed). If you have no foundation, the challenge is greater, though the discoveries you make may be even more valuable. Either way, targeting new efforts to gather inputs and understand customer requirements is a smart approach. Based on your inventory of core processes and customers, you may select one or a few areas on which to start, and build from there.

Be Ready to Challenge Your Own Assumptions. What you observe and learn from voice of the customer efforts may surprise you. And when those messages contradict what you always *thought* was important to customers, it can be easy to deny or ignore them. Your best response, however, should be the exact opposite: finding the hidden disconnects between what customers would like and what you are doing may be the source of some of the biggest improvements you can make.

Step 2B: Develop Performance Standards and Requirements Statements

Gaining insights into customer needs and behaviors, whether those insights come from existing data or enhanced voice of the customer systems, is the starting point from which you can begin to establish clear guidelines for performance and customer satisfaction. After you complete Step 2A and have your concrete requirements defined, you can measure your actual performance and assess your strategy and market focus against customers' demands and expectations.

Types of Requirements: Output and Service

A first step in defining your customers' specific needs is to understand and differentiate between two critical categories of requirements: output requirements and service requirements. These categories are described in the following paragraphs.

Output Requirements. These features and/or characteristics of the final product or service are delivered to the customer at the *end* of the process. Of the many types of output requirements, they all link to the usability or effectiveness of the final product or service in the eyes of the customer. In many cases output requirements can be defined fairly specifically and objectively, as long as the customer knows what s/he wants. A list of output requirements for a complex product or service can be long.

Service Requirements. These guidelines indicate how the customer should be treated/served during the execution of the process itself. Service requirements tend to be much more subjective and situation-sensitive than output requirements, which means they are usually tougher to define concretely.

Why Distinguish Between Output and Service Requirements?

Comparative examples of service and output requirements are shown in Figure 12.2. How well you rise to the challenge of understanding and differentiating between service and output requirements will depend quite a bit on how well you have clarified your process and its interfaces with the customer. Some factors could be classified as either output or service requirements, depending on how you define the process, so it is not always a black-and-white judgment. In our experience, though, it is "cleanest" to consider as output requirements only those tied to the conclusion of the key transaction or delivery of the final product or service.

A helpful concept for you to employ as you seek to identify service requirements is the "moment of truth"—a term coined by Jan Carlzon, former head of SAS, the Scandinavian airline. It is defined as any instance in which a customer can form an opinion (positive or negative) about your organization.[3] In Figure 12.3 we provide some examples of moments of truth in a retail store process and in a financial service activity.

We have three major reasons for stressing the distinction between output and service requirements and for suggesting that you do the same:

Reason #1. Everyone Has These Requirements. Just because your company manufactures printed circuit boards or soccer balls does not mean your customers don't have service-driven requirements. How

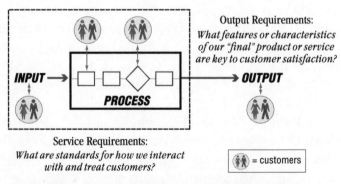

Output Requirements:
What features or characteristics of our "final" product or service are key to customer satisfaction?

INPUT → PROCESS → OUTPUT

Service Requirements:
What are standards for how we interact with and treat customers?

= customers

FIGURE 12.2   CUSTOMERS, PROCESSES, AND SERVICE AND OUTPUT REQUIREMENTS

Service Requirements		Output Requirements	
Process	Typical Req'ts	Output	Typical Req'ts
Auto Sale/ Purchase Process	• Prompt attention (<2 minutes) • Lack of pressure (check with customer every 10 minutes) • Ability to test drive (All cars available to exit lot)	**Automobile**	• Engine starts in .5 seconds • Gas mileage equal to or better than rated • Door locks operate properly
Mortgage Loan Application/ Approval Process	• Complete loan application per customer's schedule • Include checklist of necessary documents with application • Notify applicant of decision within 15 days	**Mortgage Loan**	• Funded upon close of escrow • Accurate data on loan papers • Favorable interest rate
Wholesale Packaged Foods Ordering Process	• Customer-friendly order process (faxable form) • Notify customer when shipment leaves dock (call or fax) • Follow up with customer to ensure satisfaction with order (on-time arrival, product undamaged)	**Shipment of Packaged Foods**	• Delivered by date requested • Full pallet load • Intact (undamaged) product

FIGURE 12.3   EXAMPLES: SERVICE AND OUTPUT REQUIREMENTS

your salespeople treat them, the ease of getting questions answered, and many other factors constitute the service requirements for your business.

Reason #2. Customers Often Pay Equal, If Not Greater, Attention to Service Requirements. Consider a recent flight from New York to Dallas. All the key output requirements were met: the flight was on time, the plane landed at the correct airport, and all passengers' bags arrived safely. But those same passengers griped for days afterward about the 45-minute wait to check in at the gate at JFK. The reverse effect can happen, as well: When our friend Greg picked up his new cell phone, the car power adapter didn't work, but because the customer service person was so good at getting him a replacement, he was quite happy overall.

Reason #3. Building Toward Six Sigma Performance Means Monitoring and Improving Both the Output and Service Dimensions. One unfortunate tendency lately has been to segregate the "product" and "service" components of customer satisfaction. For example, plenty of specialized books and articles describe the managing of quality of service; while many of the most-read quality books are chock-full of product quality–related (i.e., output) examples. This separation makes sense insofar as the two dimensions do pose different challenges and can require different techniques to define and measure. The result in many cases, however, has been an emphasis on one dimension over the other, which means you are really managing only part of the customer relationship.

Organizational "silos" also will tend to aggravate problems by obscuring the view of the tight links between service performance standards and output requirements. Until the two categories are better linked, your business will be particularly vulnerable to suboptimized efforts (i.e., conflicting goals or practices in different departments that reduce the overall effectiveness and/or efficiency of a process).

Eliminating "defects" in service encounters can be just as important to meeting customers' needs as creating defect-free products. We suggest that if you look at both dimensions, output and service, from the beginning, you will develop a better understanding of your customers and be able to focus your efforts most effectively so as to boost satisfaction and competitiveness.

Getting to Specifics: Writing Requirement Statements. A *requirement statement* is a brief but thorough description of the performance standard established for an output or service encounter. Composing statements of requirement is not easy. For example, if you have sketchy or conflicting customer input, it can be a big challenge to succinctly nail down requirements. But even *with* good data it is easy to be vague or to violate some of the guidelines of a well-stated requirement.

First, let's establish some goals for a well-written requirement statement or performance standard. Then we will look at how to actually compose good statements. An effective requirement statement will do the following:

1. **Link to a specific output or "moment of truth."** A requirement cannot be meaningful unless it describes issues relating to a specific

product, service, or event. Figure 12.4 offers some examples of moments of truth.

2. **Describe a single performance criterion or factor.** It should be clear what the customer is looking for or will be evaluating (e.g., speed, cost, weight, taste, etc.). Usually describing the factor is not difficult, but the temptation is to lump factors together.

3. **Be expressed using observable and/or measurable factors.** For a less tangible requirement, some effort may be required to translate it into something observable. If you find it difficult to imagine a way to observe whether a requirement has been met, you know your description is still too vague.

4. **Enable you to establish a level of "acceptable" or "not acceptable" performance.** The requirement should help establish the standard for a defect. Some requirements will be binary, which means they are either met or not. Others will require a clear definition of the customer's specifications (e.g., must weigh more than 2 and less than 3 pounds).

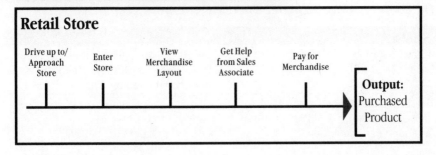

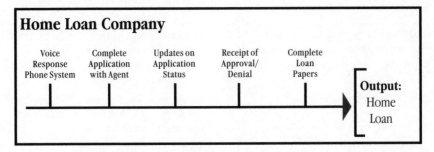

FIGURE 12.4   EXAMPLES: MOMENTS OF TRUTH

5. **Be detailed, but concise.** One of the big shortcomings of requirement statements comes from being too brief. It can be hard to assess
   a process or service based on shorthand requirements. At the same
   time if statements are too wordy, no one reads them. The trick, of
   course, is to strike a balance.
6. **Match or be validated by the voice of the customer.** Most importantly, the requirement or specification needs to fit the need/
   expectation of the customer. Each requirement inside the process
   should likewise be able to be *linked* to an external customer requirement (or why is it a requirement?).

Some Requirement Statement Examples

Table 12.1 provides some contrasting examples of poor and effective
customer performance standards.

Some questions you should ask to test your requirement statements
include the following:

▶ Does this requirement really reflect what's important to our
  customers?

TABLE 12.1   REQUIREMENT STATEMENT EXAMPLES

Rapid delivery	Orders delivered within three working days of purchase order receipt. (POs must be received by 3 p.m.)
Treat all patients like family. (This is fine as a guiding principle, but not as a requirement statement.)	• Greet patients within 20 seconds of entry into waiting area. • Address all patients by "Mr." or "Ms." and last name. • Address patients by first name if permission is given by patient. Etc.
Make products easy to assemble and not requiring too much technical expertise.	All model 1200 bicycles able to be assembled by any adult in 15 minutes or less, using only a wrench and screwdriver.
Liberal returns policy.	Any returned item retailing for less than $200 accepted with no questions and with full cash refund.
Simple application.	Application form length maximum of two pages.

▶ Can we check to see whether and/or how well the requirement has been met?

▶ Has this requirement been stated so that it is easily understood?

Steps Toward Defining Requirements

We can break down the process of clarifying customer requirements into six main steps.

1. **Identify the output or service situation.** This is the key starting point: requirement for *what?*

2. **Identify the customer or customer segment.** Who will receive the product or service? The more narrowly you can focus, the easier it usually will be. When thinking of external customers, be sure to differentiate between distributors or supply chain partners and end users or consumers.

3. **Review available data on customer needs, expectations, comments, complaints, etc.** Use objective, quantified data where possible to define the requirements. Try at all costs not to guess what is important to customers or to base requirements on anecdotal input only.

4. **Draft a requirement statement.** Here you confront the big challenge of translating what customers want into something observable and then defining a clear performance standard. After drafting the statement, test it with other people to make sure it is clear, specific, observable/measurable, easy to understand, and so on.

5. **Validate the requirement.** Validation includes any step you can take to recheck the requirement to ensure it accurately reflects customer needs and expectations. One approach might be to give customers an example based on the requirement and then gauge their reaction to it, or just ask them! Requirement validation may also involve checking with the people in the process who will need to interpret and meet the requirement.

6. **Refine and finalize the requirement statement.** When you see a gap between what customers want and what you can actually *do*, the challenge is to *negotiate* a requirement that is feasible or, even better, improve the process. After the requirement has been finalized, distribute and/or communicate it to ensure that everyone is aware of the performance expectations and measurement.

Exhibit 12.1 provides a worksheet to help you through this process.

Requirements Definition Worksheet

1. Identify the Output or Service encounter (Moment of Truth).

   _____

2. Define the Customer or Customer segment for whom the Requirement will apply.

   _____

3. Note sources of data for "Voice of the Customer" input. (Attach relevant data as needed.)

   _____

   _____

4. Draft Requirement Statement (should include observable, objective factors for verification that requirement has been met).

   _____

   _____

   _____

   Check draft Requirement Statement for clarity, specifics, etc.

5. Note methods for Requirement Statement validation. (Attach validation findings as needed.)

   _____

   _____

6. Final Requirements Statement:

   _____

   _____

   _____

Exhibit 12.1   REQUIREMENTS DEFINITION WORKSHEET

If you end up feeling that your initial requirement statements are closer to conjecture than to hard reality, you are not alone. Vague requirements—due to weak knowledge of the customer or of one's process capabilities—are the rule in many processes. It will take time to build up your understanding and solidify your performance standards.

A couple of situational examples will help us to illustrate the issues and effort that go into creating a good requirement statement.

Case Study #8: Attention to the Customer

In the hotel business, one of the more important factors in customer satisfaction is how attentive and responsive staff are to the needs of their guests. Creating a performance standard along the lines of "Be attentive to customers" is not especially helpful. Over the years in evaluating keys to satisfying guests, the hotel industry has developed a way to make attentiveness measurable, by defining a service requirement for all chance encounters between a guest and staff member.

Called "10, 5, First and Last," the requirement stipulates that hotel personnel: (a) make eye contact with a guest by the time they are 10 feet away; (b) greet the guest no less than 5 feet away; and (c) be the first person to speak and the last person to speak in the conversation. It may not be perfect for every guest, but this standard is a good reflection of the kind of attention that most customers at a high-quality hotel would want and expect.[4]

Case Study #9: Designing Packages

Let's say that you manufacture and market disinfecting solutions for contact lenses. It is especially important that your packages be clear and easy for consumers to read for their convenience, of course, but also with respect to the safety and marketability of your product. Customer data tell you that contact wearers want to be able to find a product easily and to understand quickly what it does for them. Your first draft of a package design requirement statement might be "Easy to read." Yet you know that description is not nearly concrete enough to be observed and measured.

In this and similar cases, you will almost certainly want to test how far away customers stand when they are searching for contact solutions on the shelf. Following that research, your requirement might state: "Labels must be legible by persons with normal 20/20 vision no less than 6 feet from the package."

Note that this requirement statement does not describe the actual design of the label; it simply establishes a performance standard or specification that any design should meet. One of the advanced Six Sigma methods covered in Chapter 17, quality function deployment, is commonly used to help balance the trade-offs and relationships between multiple requirements, particularly in the design of products and services.

A variety of other tools and data-organizing techniques can help get you through the sometimes arduous process of distilling various customer inputs into tangible performance standards. For example, an affinity diagram can be used to organize a variety of customer issues or comments into logical groupings, and the latter can help you to pick the meaningful requirements out of a sea of customer feedback data. A tree diagram helps to link broad features and satisfaction components to specific characteristics and requirements.

Step 2C: Analyzing and Prioritizing Customer Requirements; Linking Requirements to Strategy

We began this chapter by looking at the broad objective of creating an effective system for gathering voice of the customer input. We also have examined the more concrete activity of attaching specific performance standards to outputs and customer encounters. In this final section we review some of the issues and decisions that arise as you begin to create a more detailed description of what customers want.

All customer requirements clearly are not created equal, nor will customer reactions to a defect (i.e., a case where a requirement is not met) be the same for every requirement. We may be upset over having to wait in a long line to check in at the airport gate, but we will certainly be even *more* upset if the plane lands at the wrong airport (hey, it's happened!). Another dimension of defining customer requirements, then, is to categorize and prioritize performance standards and their impact on customer satisfaction. This review can also help your business anticipate how customer expectations will *evolve*, giving you a chance to stay ahead of their needs and your competitors.

A model being used at a growing number of companies to analyze requirements is based on the work of Noriaki Kano, a Japanese engineer and consultant. In the most common application of Kano analysis, customer requirements are grouped into three categories:

1. **Dissatisfiers, or basic requirements.** These factors, features, or performance standards are what customers absolutely expect to be met. If you achieve these requirements, you do not get any extra credit, but if you miss them, you are guaranteed to have an unhappy customer. When you tune in a TV channel and see a picture, you don't say, "Wow! Great channel!" Getting a picture of some kind is your minimum expectation; you will really judge the channel on something more.

2. **Satisfiers, or variable requirements.** The better or worse you perform on these requirements, the higher or lower will be your rating from customers. Price certainly is the most prevalent satisfier; in most cases, the less expensive the price, the happier the customer. Most day-to-day competition takes place over these factors. Assuming that your organization is meeting the basic needs, many of your process improvement priorities are likely to concentrate on boosting your capacity or performance vis-à-vis these requirements.

3. **Delighters, or latent requirements.** These features or factors go beyond what customers expect or target needs no one else has addressed. We could provide you with some examples of delighters, of course, but we don't want to give away any of our big-money ideas. Actually, you can easily come up with your own. If you imagine something that you *wish* a vendor would offer you (delighters do not have to be free, but often they are), most likely you are thinking of a delighter.

The Kano analysis involves quite a few nuances, the most important of them being that features or requirements will change categories, sometimes quickly. For example, meals on coach airline flights used to be satisfiers: you expected a meal and rated the airline on the quality and quantity of the food. Now, many people would be delighted just to *get* a meal on a flight.

Most of the time, of course, it works the other way; as customers get used to what they initially view as being special or superior, that requirement moves toward the dissatisfier category. Ford's highly successful Taurus was a hit in part because of many surprise features it included. Sales slumped in later years, however, when these once-delighters were dropped to cut costs.

This push to offer more—and the tendency of customers to *expect* more—is one of the major drivers of competition and improvement. As your business develops a more objective and complete picture of customer requirements, you can also apply a concept such as Kano analysis to get a better idea of what the various features and capabilities mean in terms of your customers' satisfaction and your competitive edge.

Conclusion

Throughout this chapter, we tread close to those concepts and analyses that directly impact strategic issues (e.g., target markets and customer value propositions). That proximity shouldn't be a surprise; Six Sigma methods can and should drive strategic decisions or at least provide information that allows you or other company leaders to make better decisions. It would be premature, however, to begin basing key strategy choices simply on an initial inventory of customer requirements.

First, you need valid facts and data to gauge how well your processes are delivering requirements to customers. Using those measures will help you make better choices about top-priority improvements for your business and allow you to begin testing the accuracy of your current company strategies. Exhibit 12.2 is a list of "dos and don'ts" for defining your customer requirements; applying effective measures is our focus in Chapter 13.

Exhibit 12.2

"DOS & DON'TS" FOR DEFINING CUSTOMER REQUIREMENTS

- Do—*Have a broad-based system to collect and use customer and market input.*
  - External data are key to meeting today's customer needs and to getting new customers, as well as to your ability to see change coming. Tune your ear to the voice of the customer!
- Do—*Pay equal attention to service and output requirements.*
  - A company with Six Sigma products but lousy service and customer relations may survive, but only until customers find an alternative.

- Do—*Make the effort to create clear, observable, and relevant requirement statements.*
  - Even if your requirements are fuzzy at first, the learning and discipline that come through building clear, measurable requirements are essential to really understanding your customers and evaluating your own performance.

- Don't—*Close your mind to new information on what customers really want.*
  - Customer data can bring you messages that contradict what you always believed. At that point, individuals and companies often go into denial, refusing to accept that their assumptions are wrong or no longer valid. It is okay to question the data, but do not ignore information simply because it conflicts with your assumptions.

- Don't—*Hold people suddenly responsible for the newly defined requirements.*
  - If new insights into customer needs reveal a gap between what they want and what you are offering, avoid pushing people to "do better!" without looking at ways to change the process, too.

- Don't—*Turn new requirements into new paradigms.*
  - Be prepared to see customer requirements change, and soon. Plan to conduct reviews and mechanisms to redefine performance standards as new voice of the customer data warrant.

- Don't—*Fail to measure and track performance to requirements.*
  - Gaining a better understanding and definition of customer requirements is an essential prelude to asking the next big question (the topic of Chapter 13): "How well are we *meeting* these requirements?"

CHAPTER 13

Measuring Current Performance
(Roadmap Step 3)

The focus of this chapter is *measurement*. We will spend most of the time reviewing the "nuts and bolts" of understanding and carrying out good measures, but the underlying objective is for you to acquire good data that you can use to plan and track your Six Sigma improvement efforts. Unfortunately, you cannot do that well unless you begin with some solid measures.

Depending on your purpose, measures can be easy or a major effort. For example, gathering data on specific problems can be fairly quick: If the data are already available, the gathering may take as little as a few hours. On the other hand, getting enough data to comparatively measure core business processes can take weeks or even months of effort. An effective measurement infrastructure is a key ingredient of a successful continuous improvement culture and capability. Yet once it is developed, it is always in need of refinement and improvement.

The two major tasks in this measurement step involve:

▶ Planning and executing measures of your organization's performance against your customer requirements (covered in Step 3A in this chapter).
▶ Developing baseline measures and identifying improvement opportunities (covered in Step 3B in this chapter).

In addition, to recap, key deliverables include:

▶ Data to assess current performance of your process(es) against customers' output and/or service requirements.
▶ Valid measures derived from the data that identify relative strengths and weaknesses in and between your processes—a key input to good project selection in Step 4.

The techniques covered in the chapter—building as they do on some of the foundational concepts introduced in Chapter 2—may be some of the most vital to the Six Sigma Way. We start with a look at four of the foundational concepts of business measures, and then move on to Step 3A.

Measurement Concept #1: Observe, Then Measure

A lot of people, when facing the mere *thought* of measurement, claim, "You can't measure what we do!" Our response is that even though it may take a little work, most things that go on in a business *can* be measured. The number-one requirement for measurement is an ability to observe. In fact *observation* is a technical term in measurement and statistics, referring to an event or a count.

In Chapter 12, we introduced a performance standard used in the hotel industry: "10, 5, First and Last" (make eye contact with a guest at 10 feet; greet them at 5 feet; and be the first and last person to speak). With that clear standard defined, it is fairly easy to observe hotel staff and measure how well this standard is being met. At Loews Hotels, where we learned of this standard, the requirement has become a key to their customer and self-evaluations. Spotters and designated shoppers actually roam Loews hallways and record how they are acknowledged. Gathering specific data on eye contact, greeting distance, and who spoke first and last, the hotel can even break down measures to note which of the four factors is being missed or met most often. Bear in mind, this measurement of *attentiveness to customers* in a hotel would initially seem to be one of the "fuzzier" things you might want to measure.

One of the easiest things to measure, and also one of the most important in today's business world, is time. If you can read a calendar or start and stop a timer, you can gather time-related data. Obviously, dollars are an essential measurable element. Our understanding of how to accurately track costs has been enhanced through better information systems and by paying more attention to costs of poor quality and activity-based costing. The most important step is to get the "thing" being measured boiled down to an objectively observable event or behavior. In Chapter 12, we introduced the need to make customer requirements observable and measurable, and we return to this concept later when we discuss operational definitions.

Measurement Concept #2: Continuous versus Discrete Measures

Understanding the difference between *continuous* and *discrete* (or "attribute") measures is important, because it can affect not only how you define your measures but also how you collect data and what you can learn from them. We encounter these concepts in sampling and also later, when we look at data analysis and advanced tools.

At times the difference can seem confusing, so we are going to lay down the rule as explicitly as possible:

Continuous measures are only those factors that can be measured on an infinitely divisible scale or continuum (e.g., weight, height, time, decibels, temperature, ohms, money, etc.).

A discrete measure is anything else that doesn't fit the criteria for *continuous*. Discrete items might include the following:

► Characteristics or attributes, such as level of education (high school, bachelor's degree, etc.) or type (e.g., an airliner might be a Boeing 737, Boeing 747, or Airbus 300)
► Counts of individual items (e.g., numbers of credit cards, numbers of orders processed)
► Artificial scales, such as rating a song from 1 to 5 (good beat, easy to dance to) or describing your level of satisfaction with service

Discrete measures can appear deceptively continuous, especially counts or attributes that are converted to percentages. For example, gender is a discrete characteristic in most species; an individual will be either female or male (you can add an "undetermined" category if you like). If, however, you take some gender data and say that a group is 72.3334 percent female, that doesn't make that measure continuous; the source is still discrete. Scaled surveys can also *look* continuous; but again, really they are discrete.

For convenience, continuous measures often are converted into discrete measures, too. For example: Delivery times are recorded as "on-time" or "late" rather than in days and minutes. On car dashboards, oil pressure gauges (continuous) often have given way to warning lights (discrete). If you don't see a *number* on some kind of measurement *scale* like temperature or time, you know you are dealing with a discrete measure—period. Figure 13.1 provides some examples of common discrete and continuous measures, and continuous measures converted to discrete.

The Pros of Discrete Measures

The most obvious benefit of discrete measures, of course, is that many factors can be defined only as discrete or attribute data. Examples include location (state, city, street), customer type (new or repeat, business versus home user), product number, damaged versus undamaged, and so on.

Discrete and Continuous Measure Examples

DISCRETE	CONTINUOUS	→ DISCRETE
• Number of typographical errors	• Hold time per incoming call	• Number of calls on hold past 30 seconds
• Rating of service	• Average temperature per hour	• Hours with temperature over 85 degrees
• Units delivered/day		
• Percent of calls on new service program	• Minutes to board plane	• Delayed boarding incidents
• Number of claims in dispute	• Quantity of gas in tank	• Tank empty/full
• Fill rate (percent of on-time, complete deliveries)	• Width of chip (microns)	• Out-of-spec chips
	• Cost per unit	• Units exceeding target cost

FIGURE 13.1   MEASURE EXAMPLES: DISCRETE, CONTINUOUS, AND CONTINUOUS CONVERTED TO DISCRETE

Intangible factors can often be converted into measurable discrete characteristics. For example, to measure customer perceptions or satisfaction, researchers often use a rating scale that is really a discrete measure. If you wanted to gauge the effectiveness of an advertisement, you could ask customers whether they recall having seen it. The possible answers—yes, no, not sure—are discrete categories.

Generally, it is faster and easier to capture discrete data observations. Noting whether something "is" or "isn't" can be done more quickly (and less intrusively) than measuring it on a scale.

One of the most important observations (a defect) that we all make in the course of Six Sigma and business process improvement is a discrete factor. Thus if you are going to reduce defects, you must affect a discrete measure.

The Cons of Discrete Measures

Discrete measures do, unfortunately, have their drawbacks, too. When you have a choice and can afford the time, resources, and possible disruption, you will want to capture continuous data whenever possible.

You have to make more observations (i.e., do more measuring) with discrete data to get valid information. And the closer your performance is to "perfect," the more items you need to count to get accurate data because defects become so rare. Some statisticians note that continuous data can be accurate with a sample of just 200 items, no matter how high the volume of the process or how few the number of defects.[1] So discrete data can be more expensive to collect. (More discussion follows later in the chapter on determining sample size.)

Discrete measures can bury important information. If you are coaching a team and you note whether players' weights are "acceptable" or "too heavy," it will be hard to analyze later. How *much* overweight are they? What kinds of changes might get the results you need? It is a longer road to a more svelte team without specific, continuous measures. (And we haven't even considered whether a player might be too *light*. . . .)

Statistically speaking, you can do many more potentially useful forms of analysis with continuous data versus discrete. For example, many of the more advanced Six Sigma techniques are usable only with continuous measures.

All this is not to say that you shouldn't use discrete data. As noted, in many cases you will not have a choice; in others, you may not have the resources or capability to "go continuous." Fortunately, as we see a bit later, plenty of tools are available to help you use discrete data when they are all you have.

Measurement Concept #3: Measure for a Reason

Measurement consumes resources, attention, and energy, and that means you do not want to perform any measures you don't *have* to. Unless a measure has a clear purpose—a key question you need to answer or factor you want to track—it may not be valuable or relevant.

You can ensure a better choice and balance of measures when you keep in mind the different categories available to you. Next we look at two ways to define measures.

Predictor and Results Measures

We noted the tenet of Six Sigma measurement that is all about understanding relationships between changes in upstream factors (Xs: suppliers, raw materials, processes, procedures) and their impact on customer satisfaction, loyalty, and profitability (Ys). Another way to describe the X-Y concept (using more common language) is to consider the following two measure categories.

▶ **Predictors.** Similar to Xs, predictors are factors we can measure to forecast or anticipate events downstream in the process. For example, if we see an increase in cycle time in ordering raw materials, we might *predict* an increase in late deliveries.

▶ **Results.** They are similar to Ys in focusing on the outcomes of the process. Results can be immediate (e.g., on-time delivery) or longer term (e.g., customer retention).

Efficiency and Effectiveness Measures

This approach to categorizing measures looks closely at who gets the immediate benefit from the performance: you, the customer, or both.

▶ **Efficiency.** These measures track the volume of resources consumed in producing products and services. More efficient processes use less money, time, and materials. Efficiency has a significant bearing on the budget performance of your organization and eventually on profitability. Although you might pass along efficiency improvements to customers through lower prices, efficiency is primarily an internally focused measurement.

▶ **Effectiveness.** On the other hand, effectiveness looks at your work through the eyes of customers: How closely did you meet their needs and requirements? What defects did they receive? How happy and loyal have they become, based on your performance?

In a full-blown organizational measurement system, you should have a mix of all types: predictors and results, efficiency and effectiveness. A traditional business blind spot has been to look only at results measures. In improvement efforts, the temptation is to boost efficiency (with its quick potential bottom-line impact), without sufficient regard for how it will shake up effectiveness in delivering value to customers.

Measurement Concept #4: A Process for Measurement

Measures can and should be continuously improved, just as you would regular work processes. The basic steps for implementing any measure are straightforward as you can see in Figure 13.2. Then Exhibit 13.1 lists some of the key questions/actions you should ask/take at each of these measurement steps.

Exhibit 13.1

KEY QUESTIONS TO ASK WHEN MEASURING YOUR ORGANIZATION'S PERFORMANCE AGAINST YOUR CUSTOMER REQUIREMENTS

■ *Select What to Measure:*
- What key questions are we trying to answer?
- What data will give us the answer?
- What output or service requirement(s) will best help us gauge performance to customer needs?
- What upstream factors might help alert us to problems later on?
- How will we display, analyze, and use the measure?

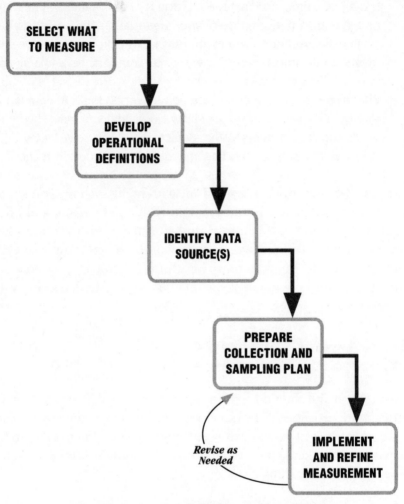

FIGURE 13.2   A FIVE-STEP MEASUREMENT
IMPLEMENTATION MODEL

■ *Develop Operational Definitions:*
   • How can we clearly describe the factor/thing we are trying to track or count?
   • If different people gather the data, will they interpret things in the same way?
   • How can we test our definitions to make sure they're air-tight?

■ *Identify Data Source(s):*
  • Where can we find or observe data to provide the measure?
  • Is past experience (or historical data) valid?
  • Are the data in our information systems accessible and in a usable format?
  • Can we afford (the time, money, disruption) to gather new data?
■ *Prepare Collection and Sampling Plan:*
  • Who will gather or compile the data?
  • What forms or tools will they need to capture and organize the data?
  • What other information will we need to be able to analyze the data effectively?
  • How many observations or items will we need to count to get an accurate measure?
  • How often will we need to do measures?
  • How can we best ensure that the data we get are representative?
■ *Implement and Refine Measurement:*
  • Can we test our measures before going into full-fledged implementation?
  • How will we train the data collectors?
  • How will we monitor the data gathering?
  • What issues may arise (or have arisen), and what can we do about them?
  • What will we change next time?

Next we cover some of the most important steps and concepts associated with this measurement process to help you select and execute your measures more smoothly. As we do so, we concentrate on the first priority of an initial Six Sigma effort: evaluating the company's success in meeting customer requirements.

Measuring Rare or Low-Volume Activities

Airliner crashes, fortunately, are quite rare. Then too, the measures that have been gathered on them have taken many years to collect. But imagine if a plane were to crash tomorrow and no past data existed.

You certainly wouldn't expect officials to say, "We are going to have to let a few more planes crash, so we can get enough data points to start our investigation."

That comment, however, sounds similar to the excuse we often hear: "This happens too rarely for us to measure it." If you never *try* to gather data from your process, of course you won't learn much.

Part of the problem here is the exclusive emphasis on *quantitative* data. Although rare events or low-volume operations offer less opportunity for numbers-based measures, it is a mistake to believe that acquiring quantitative data is the only worthy objective. Asking questions and getting factual information, even for a rare or one-time event, are still critical. Statisticians may rightly assert that danger comes with drawing conclusions from one-time events, but you still have to play the cards you are dealt.

Remember, too, that gathering facts is the starting point for measurement. Over time, isolated facts can become meaningful measures.

With these goals and guidelines in mind, we can now turn to the process of building good measures and measurement systems.

Step 3A. Plan and Measure Performance Against Customer Requirements

The next sections describe the tasks listed in brief in Exhibit 13.1:

- ▶ Select what to measure.
- ▶ Develop operational definitions.
- ▶ Identify data source(s).
- ▶ Prepare collection and sampling plan.
- ▶ Implement and refine measurement.

Select What to Measure

In an ideal world, you would begin this measurement fully equipped with a complete description of how customers evaluate your service or products. If your voice of the customer data and requirements are not yet somewhat sophisticated, you can still start measurement, but with a greater risk of using measures that do not pan out.

Selecting just your optimal performance measures (because you cannot measure everything) means balancing two major elements:

(1) what is *feasible,* and (2) what is most useful or *valuable.* Prioritizing customer requirements provides a good starting point for determining value. Areas in which you suspect performance gaps can also be good places to begin measures. Figure 13.3 provides you with a partial list of criteria to consider—in the feasibility and value categories—as you choose what to measure.

Develop Operational Definitions

If we asked you and a friend to run outside right now and count all the red cars you see—but not to talk to one another, how similar would your answers be? We think it is likely they would be fairly different, for some of the following reasons:

▶ What do you do about pickups and SUVs? Are they "cars"? (They seem to outnumber "cars" these days.)

▶ What is "red"? Some cars that you consider to be red your friend might call "rust" (not *really* red).

▶ Are you to count only moving vehicles or parked ones as well? Any variation in that choice is sure to affect the numbers a lot.

▶ If you jumped in your car (or pickup or SUV) and drove around *looking* for red whatevers, you obviously would get a different count. (And we didn't say you had to stick together!)

Criteria for Selecting Measures

Value/Usefulness	Feasibility
• Link to high-priority customer requirements	• Availability of data
• Accuracy of data	• Lead time required
• Area of concern or potential opportunity	• Cost of getting data
• Can be benchmarked to other organizations	• Complexity
• Can be helpful ongoing measure	• Likely resistance or "fear factor"

FIGURE 13.3   MEASUREMENT SELECTION CRITERIA

As that example illustrates, one of the biggest pitfalls associated with the quest for effective business process measurement is the failure to create good operational definitions and the data collection procedures to go with them. By *operational definition*, we mean a clear, understandable, and unambiguous description of what is to be measured or observed, so that everyone can operate, or measure, consistently on the basis of the definition.

Here is a real-world example of the challenge posed by trying to measure without good "op defs." We were working with the publicity group of a large company that was holding a major press event. The goal was to improve the processes of setting up and managing the event in order to increase the probability of favorable press coverage. The client decided (at the last minute) to track questions posed to speakers on a variety of factors (e.g., "tone," whether positive, neutral, or negative, and "topic") and then to track the answers to the questions. Two or three people were assigned to record the data, using a checksheet with 30 or so options to choose from.

The results, as you might imagine, were more than a bit of a mess. Even the number of questions counted by the data collectors differed, because the reporters often linked several questions together. Defining the tone of a question was especially subjective, and recording the content of answers was a hit-or-miss proposition.

Fortunately, the data gathering was not a total loss; enough broad trends were observable that some benefits were indeed gleaned through this tracking of questions and answers. The client learned a valuable lesson about the process (we found that executives ended up answering many more questions in informal hallway conversations than in the press conference per se) and about realistic objectives for measurement. But the "hard data" were not really usable, and future measurement activities clearly would demand much tighter operational definitions if they were to get some solid quantitative input.

Misunderstood measurement definitions can even have drastic consequences. It was a shock to the U.S. space exploration program when the Mars Polar Orbiter was incinerated in the Martian atmosphere in September 1999. It turned out that the spacecraft flew too low because one group of engineers had calculated course instructions in pounds per second, while a computer interpreted the data in *grams* per second. As Six Sigma experts might say: "Oops!"

When you are creating operational definitions for your measures, you simply have no substitute for focused work and a close scrutiny of your chosen terms.

Identify Data Source(s)

Data in an organization come from many possible sources. Your most important considerations are to ensure that the source you choose— or can get a hold of—has accurate data and represents the process, product, or service you want to measure. Ideally, you target measures for which you have good sources.

We will venture to offer just a few tips on a common source of data: the people working in the process. Even though many managers or teams starting out on measurement these days expect to get data from information systems, it frequently turns out that what you really need to know is not captured by the system. Or if it is, it can require a lot of work to extract it from other data. A better option in these cases is to gather data manually, from the people and the process. When you rely on people as your data source, especially individuals measuring their own work, however, you face obvious risks. Inattention and human error are most common; suspicion and paranoia are forces to be respected and reckoned with, too. If you keep the following pieces of advice in mind, you will ensure that your data are complete and accurate:

- ► Explain clearly why you are gathering the data.
- ► Describe what you plan to do with the data, including your plans to share findings with the collectors, keep individuals' identities confidential, and so on.
- ► Be careful whom you choose to participate; avoid making data collection either a reward or a punishment.
- ► Make the process as easy as it can be.
- ► Give data collectors the opportunity to provide input on the data collection process.

Prepare Collection and Sampling Plan

The ins and outs of executing measures could fill an entire book, so we limit our overview of this step to three major elements: forms, stratification, and sampling.

Data Collection Forms. Well-designed spreadsheets and check-sheets are the workhorses of data gathering. Even though some standard types of forms are available, you really should tailor each form to fit the actual data collection you want to do. The following guidelines will help you to create a data collection form:

- ▶ **Keep it simple.** Simplicity and clarity will affect how much data you effectively capture. If it is hard to difficult or crowded, you risk mistakes or noncompliance.
- ▶ **Label it well.** Make sure no one has questions as to what piece of data "belongs" where.
- ▶ **Include space for date (and time) and collector's name.** These obvious things tend to get left off, causing headaches later.
- ▶ **Organize the data collection form and the compiling sheet (the form or spreadsheet you use to pull together the data) consistently.** If these two work together, it can make entering raw data much easier and much less prone to mistakes.
- ▶ **Include key factors to stratify the data.** More on this guideline in a moment.

Some common types of checksheets are listed in Table 13.1.

The traveler checksheet listed at the end of Table 13.1 gives us a good opportunity to point out an important factor in collecting data: In process measures, you usually will want to gather various pieces of information about *one thing at a time* as it moves through the process. The temptation can be to grab a bunch of items (parts, forms, orders) at Point A in the process and record data about them, then move to Point B in the process, grab another bunch and record data about *them*. The problem arises when the items you count at Point B may not be related to those counted at Point A. This issue becomes especially critical when you are trying to identify root causes or determine the impact of upstream variables (predictors, or Xs) on downstream results (Ys).

A traveler is one good way of ensuring that you have data that can be correlated at each step in the process.

Stratification. Getting a baseline measure of performance against customer requirements is a key objective in Step 3 of the Six Sigma roadmap. At some point, however, you are likely to want to know

TABLE 13.1 COMMON TYPES OF CHECKSHEETS

Defect or Cause Checksheet	Used to record types of defects or causes of defects	• Reasons for field repair calls • Types of operating-log discrepancies • Causes of late shipments
Data Sheet	Captures readings, measures, or counts quantities	• Transmitter power level • Number of people in line • Temperature
Frequency Plot Checksheet	Records a characteristic of an item along a counted scale or continuum	• Gross income of applicants for a loan • Cycle time from order to shipment for each order • Weight of a package
Concentration Diagram Checksheet	Features a picture of the item or document being observed; data collectors then mark where problems, defects, or damage are seen on the item	• Damage diagram used by car rental agencies • Noting errors on invoices
Traveler Checksheet	Any kind of checksheet that "moves" with the product or service through the process; data about that item then are recorded in appropriate places on the form (see Figure 13.4)	• Capturing cycle-time data for each step of an engineering change order • Noting number of people handling a part as it moves through an assembly facility • Tracking rework on an insurance claim

more about those data, which is where stratification comes in. The word itself denotes layers (or "strata") of data; we prefer to equate it to "slicing and dicing" your measures. Stratification helps you to exercise your curiosity and to clarify what is really happening.

For example, if you make computer systems and you have data showing a high rate of returned systems, you will naturally ask: Where are the returns coming from? Which systems have the problems?

Traveler Checksheet
Loan Application - Underwriting

Loan # __3256-879__

Loan Type: ☒ Conventional ☐ Jumbo ☐ VA/FHA

Amount Requested __194,000__

Customer Location ☐ NW ☐ W ☒ SW ☐ E

Process Step	Date/Hour Received	Defects Found
Application Completion	0623/13:42	|||
Packet Preparation	0626/09:00	||||
Underwriting	0715/16:30	⊮ |

FIGURE 13.4   EXAMPLE: TRAVELER CHECKSHEET

Which customers are affected? But if your initial data collection has not captured those elements, you are not able to answer such questions. For that reason, you need to think through in advance, as best you can, what stratification factors you are likely to need later. (See Figure 13.5.)

Sampling Overview. To many people these days, *sampling* means taking other artist's music recordings—like a great bass line—and building a whole new creation. *That* isn't our subject here, but you will find parallels.

In the sphere of data collecting, sampling of course means using *some* of the items in a group or process to represent them *all*. The entire discipline of statistics is based on sampling, being able to draw conclusions based on looking at a part of the whole. Six Sigma measures tend to offer you more options about how to sample than you are likely to have encountered back in college statistics courses. If you are to understand why, we need to briefly explain the distinction between population statistics and process statistics.

Data Stratification

Factors	Examples (Slice the data by . . .)
Who	• Department • Individual • Customer type
What	• Type of complaint • Defect category • Reason for incoming call
When	• Month, quarter • Day of week • Time of day
Where	• Region • City • Specific location on product *(top right corner, on/off switch, etc.)*

FIGURE 13.5   MEASUREMENT AND DATA STRATIFICATION FACTORS

▶ **Population statistics.** Most textbook statistics courses focus on various methods of sampling and testing relationships between two or more groups (consumers, companies, products, voters, baseball teams, etc.). Population sampling is like dipping into a standing pool of water: As long as we know that the water in the dipper is like the rest of the water, we can rest easy that we have a good sample.

▶ **Process statistics.** Business measures often pose a different challenge, for here, taking a sample from a process is like testing a running stream of water. Besides having fewer frogs, a stream is different from a pool or pond because it changes from moment to moment. The sample I am taking at one moment could be different from the one I may take a few moments later; and it could be different again a few moments later. Things in the stream that may change include water temperature, oxygen content, number of fish, rate of flow, and so on. Then too, if two of us took samples at the same time but at different places in the stream, they would likely be different as well.

It is possible to do either kind of sampling—population or process—in a business environment. When you draw data from a group of people or items that are just "sitting there"—including a pool of items in a process—you can consider it a population sample. If however you are trying to track changes over time in order to understand the degree and type of variation in the process, you require a process sample. Table 13.2 provides some comparative examples of both types.

Getting a *valid* sample—one that represents the whole—can be a significant challenge in either case. The science (sometimes art) of sampling is a big topic. Thus our goal in the next few pages is just to give you some background and a few rough steps to help you understand the kinds of decisions that go into devising a sampling plan. Even after in-depth instruction it can still be challenging, so we recommend you consult an expert before you start collecting a lot of data, if your situation looks complicated.

Let's turn now to a hypothetical scenario, as a way of introducing some of the key concepts of sampling. Watch for the terms in italics; we will review them next.

Case Study #10: How Pivotal Logistics Handled Sampling

At Pivotal Logistics, a company that provides warehousing and distribution services to a variety of parts and raw-materials firms, a process management team was working on an apparent issue with errors in incoming bills of lading. Somehow, the paper documents accompanying

TABLE 13.2   SOME EXAMPLES OF POPULATION SAMPLING AND PROCESS SAMPLING

• Tallying the average loan amount from a group of applications.	• Capturing the average loan amounts requested by day, week, month
• Recording the age of all parts of inventory currently in stock.	• Tracking the average age of parts inventory by week.
• Conducting a survey of customer perceptions.	• Polling every tenth customer on his/her service experience each day.
• Compiling the reasons for inbound calls among all calls over the past six months.	• Recording inbound call volume every quarter-hour.

shipments seemed to have different data from those shown in the logistics tracking system. If true, the problem would create inventory inaccuracies, misbillings, and a variety of other defects directly affecting Pivotal's customers.

So they could understand the extent and impact of the possible paperwork discrepancies, the group wanted to capture data about the bills of lading from the receiving process. With more than 1,500 deliveries per day, however, it would be impossible to check every shipment. On the other hand, the process team was concerned about avoiding bias in the data. For example, gathering data from only a few key customers might not reflect what was really happening with the paperwork, or taking information at the wrong time might affect the accuracy of the results. "What we need," said process owner Les Lomas, "is a good sampling plan."

As the group sought to come up with a plan to collect a good, representative sample, it considered the following options:

Option #1. Have dock clerks take a look at delivered shipments when they are less busy, which seemed like a good way to avoid having the measurement disrupt the work and frustrate people in the warehouse. But as Monty Vista, the IT member of the process team, noted, "That's no good—it's a convenience sample!"

Option #2. Pick the shipments that seem to most resemble the traffic for a particular day, which would mean that dock clerks would look at the day's schedule and select a few deliveries that represented the mix for the day. It was Mark De la Salle of the scheduling group who objected: "How can they make that kind of judgment and still get us an accurate sample?"

Option #3. Have the dock clerks check every-so-many deliveries for bill of lading defects. "This option makes more sense," said Les Lomas. "It's a lot more systematic, and it seems to me like we can have more confidence in the results."

"Isn't it better," asked De la Salle, "to do a *random* sample?"

"I think we'd have a tough time doing this randomly," Lomas answered. "There's no way to pick the shipments without some guesswork, and this way we can keep the data in sequence so we can see whether patterns develop during the day."

The Pivotal group felt they were getting closer to a decent plan for sampling, but they still had some work to do.

Key Sampling Concepts. As the Pivotal Logistics group noted so far, some ways to sample are better than others. Some of the issues they encountered included the following:

▶ **Bias.** It is the iceberg in the shipping lanes of sampling. Having a biased sample means that your data are not completely valid and that any conclusions you draw from them are likely to be wrong. Some bias is almost always present; the trick is to keep it to a minimum.

▶ **Convenience sampling.** Collecting the items that are easiest to get is not just lazy, it is also a good way to *create* bias in your data.

▶ **Judgment sampling.** Almost as bad—though it may seem better—is to try to make "educated guesses" about which items or people are representative. Your guess is itself a bias.

▶ **Systematic sampling.** This method is recommended for many business measurement activities. In a process, systematic sampling might mean taking samples at certain intervals (e.g., every half-hour, every twentieth item, etc.). A systematic population example would be to check every tenth record in a database. The caveat with systematic sampling is to make sure the frequency of sampling does not correspond to some pattern that will bias the data.

▶ **Random sampling.** Although you hear that this method is best, in the real world it is harder than you might think to be *truly* random. Most business applications of random sampling involve computer-based random selections.

Some other relevant sampling concepts include the following:

▶ **Stratified sampling.** Stratifying your sample helps to ensure that all key groups are represented in the data. If Pivotal Logistics has two major types of shipment, they may want to sample each separately to ensure adequate data for each.

▶ **Confidence level.** The term *confidence level* refers to the issue of how certain you want to be that the data you gather and the conclusions you draw reflect the population or process (aka "reality"). Confidence usually is expressed in percentages, and a 95 percent confidence level is pretty standard in business process measures.

▶ **Precision.** The accuracy of the measure you plan to do actually links to the type of scale or amount of detail of your operational definition, but it can also have an impact on your sample size. For example, if you want to measure cycle times down to the second, you will need to ensure that your timer is especially accurate.

Sampling Prerequisites. The "Catch-22" in developing a solid sampling plan is that you have to *know something* about the data you are gathering. As a result, early measures often are less reliable because they are based on a best-guess sampling plan. The more you measure, and the better you get to know the characteristics of what you are measuring, the better your sample decisions can be.

Here are some of the most common things you need to know:

- ▶ Is it a continuous or discrete measure?
- ▶ If it is continuous, what is the degree of variation (standard deviation) of the process?
- ▶ If it is discrete, how often does the thing we are looking for (usually the "proportion defective" in the population or process) occur?
- ▶ How many items move through the process each day? Each week? *Or:* How large is the total population?
- ▶ What confidence level do we hope to reach through our measure?
- ▶ For continuous data, what is the desired precision of our measure?

Other important terms/concepts in sampling are shown in Table 13.3.

TABLE 13.3   OTHER IMPORTANT TERMS IN SAMPLING

Sampling event	The act of extracting items from the process or population to be measured.
Subgroup	The number of consecutive units extracted for measurement at each sampling event. A subgroup can be just one item, or several.
Sampling frequency	The number of times per day or week a sample is taken; sampling events per period of time. Sampling frequency tends to increase as the number of cycles or changes in a process increase.

Remember that getting your sample will often involve guesswork at the start (until you get some early readings of the data), and unfortunately will be affected by the feasibility of getting at the things you want to observe. Overall, keep in mind the rule of thumb that (as long as you do not bias your data) the larger your sample, the better your accuracy.

Implement and Refine Measurement

You are always better off if you can run a test of your data collection so as to ensure that forms, sampling plans, and definitions work as planned. If you cannot do a trial of the data collection, at least pay careful attention to how it works as you begin to gather the data. If you plan to use many different people to gather or compile data, some kind of training, whether formal or informal, is going to be essential.

Testing Measurement Accuracy and Value. There are various ways to check how accurate your measures are and to ensure that they stay accurate. In the manufacturing arena, the most common test of the effectiveness of a measure is known as "Gage R&R." It involves repeating a measure in various environments to test against four important criteria:

1. **Accuracy.** How precise is the measurement or observation?
2. **Repeatability.** If one person or piece of measuring equipment measures or observes the same item more than once, will s/he or it get the same results each time?
3. **Reproducibility.** If two or more people or machines measure the same thing, will they get the same results?
4. **Stability.** Over time, will accuracy or repeatability deteriorate or shift?

While Gage R&R is most commonly done with continuous data measures—and often with measurement instruments (e.g., scales, meters), similar methods can be used to test discrete data measures. Some form of measurement accuracy check can be used as a test before you implement a measure and as a check if you gather the data over a long period of time.

Step 3B: Develop Baseline Measures and Identify Improvement Opportunities

Developing effective data collection processes is important in any type of business and performance measurement. At this point, though, our objective is focused on establishing performance baselines to determine how well processes are working *today*. Then, you can decide where to focus the improvement work and, later on, gauge how well solutions have worked. We look first at output or end-result measures and then at measures that take into account internal performance.

Output Performance Measures

As we discussed in Chapter 2, Six Sigma measurement traditionally focuses on tracking and reducing *defects* in a process. In this review of comparative measurement, we again pick up the theme of defect measures and explain the various options and concepts you should be aware of as you go about choosing and implementing your own. The use of defect-related measures has several advantages:

1. **Simplicity.** Everyone can understand "good" and "bad." The calculations of the various types of defect-based measures can be made with basic math skills.
2. **Consistency.** Defect measures can be applied to any process that has a performance standard or requirement, whether for continuous or discrete data or a manufacturing or service process.
3. **Comparability.** Six Sigma measures can track rates of improvement on processes of all types and can compare the performance of efforts in different areas of the business.

This Six Sigma approach to measuring results is also fully aligned with Lean principles. Because delivery time (speed and/or accuracy) is nearly always a customer requirement, measuring on-time performance gives a good overall view of a cycle time. And delivering defective products and services to customers is certainly a key source of waste.

Defect measures have drawbacks, too. For one thing, by looking *only* at good and bad, they may hide key information or subtleties in the data, especially with continuous data measures. Our purpose here, however, is to help you build a foundation for measurement that can then be used as a base for evaluating the overall effectiveness of a process. When we get into data analysis in Chapter 14, we look at other measurement methods that can provide a more detailed picture of process performance and help you to determine root causes.

Key Concepts of Defect-Based Measurement

A few simple terms need to be reviewed or clarified if we are going to understand defect measures:

- ▶ **Unit.** An item being processed, or the final product or service being delivered to the customer (a car, a mortgage loan, a hotel stay, a bank statement, etc.)
- ▶ **Defect.** A failure to meet a customer requirement/performance standard (a leaky crankcase, a delay in closing the mortgage loan, a lost reservation, a statement error, etc.)
- ▶ **Defective.** Any unit that contains a defect (Hence, a car with any defect is, technically, just as defective as a car with 15 defects.)
- ▶ **Defect opportunity.** Because most products or services have multiple customer requirements, they also include several chances or opportunities to have a defect (e.g., the number of defect opportunities on a car might be well more than 100)

One final essential: Remember that your data must include information on performance against customer requirements. Thus if a key requirement is on-time delivery, and your data capture only cost per order, you need to get more data.

Defective and Yield Measures. We start with measures that focus on defectives, units that contain one defect or ten. Defective measures are especially important in businesses or with products for which *any* defect is serious. For example, any typographical error in a magazine ad is going to hurt its credibility. Any flaw in the stitching of a dress will make it unsellable at full price.

The following are two measurement expressions for defectives:

- ▶ **Proportion defective.** The fraction or percentage of item samples with one or more defects. The formula for, and some examples of, proportion defective are shown in Figure 13.6. We use these same examples for each type of defect measure.

▶ **Final yield.** Noted as Y_{FINAL}, this calculation is 1 *minus* the proportion defective. It tells you what fraction of the total units produced and/or delivered was defect-free. (Multiplying final yield by 100 gives you the percentage good products.) Figure 13.7 shows some examples of final yield.

Defect Measures. Defects per unit (DPU) reflects the average number of defects of all types over the *total* number of units sampled. (See the formula and examples in Figure 13.8.) For example, if you calculated a DPU of 1.0, it would indicate a likelihood that every unit will have one defect, though some items may have more than one, and others, no defects. A DPU of .25 shows a probability that one in four units will have a defect.

These first three measures help you to see both how well or poorly your process is performing and how defects are distributed in your work efforts.

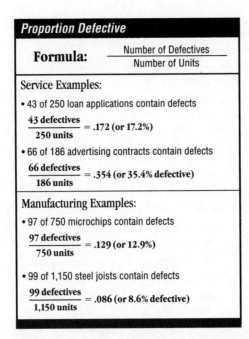

Proportion Defective

Formula: $\dfrac{\text{Number of Defectives}}{\text{Number of Units}}$

Service Examples:

• 43 of 250 loan applications contain defects

$\dfrac{43 \text{ defectives}}{250 \text{ units}} = .172 \text{ (or 17.2\%)}$

• 66 of 186 advertising contracts contain defects

$\dfrac{66 \text{ defectives}}{186 \text{ units}} = .354 \text{ (or 35.4\% defective)}$

Manufacturing Examples:

• 97 of 750 microchips contain defects

$\dfrac{97 \text{ defectives}}{750 \text{ units}} = .129 \text{ (or 12.9\%)}$

• 99 of 1,150 steel joists contain defects

$\dfrac{99 \text{ defectives}}{1,150 \text{ units}} = .086 \text{ (or 8.6\% defective)}$

FIGURE 13.6 FORMULA AND EXAMPLES: PROPORTION DEFECTIVE

Final Yield

Formula: 1 - Proportion Defective

Service Examples:
- 43 of 250 loan applications contain defects
  1 − .172 = .828 or 82.8% yield
- 66 of 186 advertising contracts contain defects
  1 − .354 = .646 or 64.6% yield

Manufacturing Examples:
- 97 of 750 microchips contain defects
  1 − .129 = .871 or 87.1% yield
- 99 of 1,150 steel joists contain defects
  1 − .086 = .914 or 91.4% yield

FIGURE 13.7   FORMULA AND EXAMPLES: FINAL YIELD

Defects/Unit or DPU

Formula: $\dfrac{\text{Number of Defects}}{\text{Number of Units}}$

Service Examples:
- 52 defects on 250 loan applications (43 defective)
  $\dfrac{52 \text{ defects}}{250 \text{ applications}} = .208 \text{ (or 20.8\%) DPU}$
- 321 defects on 186 advertising contracts (66 defective)
  $\dfrac{321 \text{ defects}}{186 \text{ contracts}} = 1.73 \text{ (or 172\%) DPU}$

Manufacturing Examples:
- 99 defects on 750 microchips (97 defective)
  $\dfrac{99 \text{ defects}}{750 \text{ microchips}} = .132 \text{ (or 13.2\%) DPU}$
- 233 defects on 1,150 steel joists (99 defective)
  $\dfrac{233 \text{ defects}}{1,150 \text{ joists}} = .202 \text{ (or 20.2\%) DPU}$

FIGURE 13.8   FORMULA AND EXAMPLES: DEFECTS PER UNIT

Determining Defect Opportunities. One of the innovations of Six Sigma measurement noted in Chapter 2 is to adjust measures according to the complexity or number of opportunities for defects. The purpose is to level the playing field, so that a complex service or product can be compared in performance to a simpler one. First we look at the steps to get to opportunity-based measures, and then at how these measures can be expressed.

Judging from the looks of a coffee mug, you would probably not view it as a terribly complicated product. But open up a couple's mortgage application for the new home they hope to buy and—though it is apples-and-oranges-different from the mug—it is easy to tell it is a lot more complicated. And even if the calculator in your briefcase is harder to peer inside, chances are it is more complex than the mortgage application. Thus in Six Sigma measures, the word *complex* translates into more opportunities for defects. The challenge is to identify a realistic number of defect opportunities for each product or service. In many cases it is a judgment call, but we can identify three main steps in defining the number of opportunities:

Step 1. Develop a preliminary list of defect types. Let's take the coffee mug as our example here (we look at a service example next). How many types of defects might there be? Here's an initial list of possibilities:

- ▶ Leaks
- ▶ Glazing/finish blemishes
- ▶ Misshapen container
- ▶ Misshapen handle
- ▶ Broken

Step 2. Determine which are the actual, customer-critical, specific defects. We could just make do with our first list, and say it has five defect opportunities, period. But some defects may not actually happen, or two types of the same defect may occur. So it is a good idea to scrutinize your first draft list. Also, as we will see when we calculate Sigma measures, including more opportunities will make our *Sigma performance look better.* Being of high integrity, we don't want to pad our opportunities just to boost our score; plus, painting an overly positive picture initially would make it harder to show improvement later. With that attitude, and a little common sense, we propose defining just three opportunities for error on a mug, as follows:

- ▶ Glazing/finish blemishes
- ▶ Misshapen (container or handle)
- ▶ Broken

We have taken leaks off our list, because they are so rare and not a realistic consideration in terms of day-to-day measuring of our performance. It is both simple and realistic to consider all malformed mugs as falling under one opportunity.

Of course, it would not be *wrong* to say five opportunities are possible. The number of opportunities will fall within a range of "right" answers. We suggest you adopt such criteria as reasonable, realistic, practical, and most importantly *consistent*, when you determine numbers of opportunities.

Step 3. Check the proposed number of opportunities against other standards. If your company makes coffee mugs, over time guidelines or conventions for opportunities of coffee-mug defects most likely would emerge. As noted earlier, some companies have a committee set standards for opportunity calculation, so that they can be sure of a consistent comparison of processes.

Having walked through opportunity-counting for coffee mugs, let's take another example: that all-important document, the invoice. Each keystroke in a document like an invoice could technically be considered a defect opportunity, but to count each one would be neither practical nor consistent. Also, some parts of an invoice will be standard or done from a template, which makes them fixed. We want our search for defects to focus on elements of the invoice that change each time one is issued.

On a generic invoice, you *could* have as many as 17 opportunities, if not more, including:

- ▶ Customer name
- ▶ Contact name
- ▶ Customer address: street and number, city, state, zip code, mail stop
- ▶ Account or customer number
- ▶ Purchase order number
- ▶ Items ordered

- Quantity ordered
- Unit price
- Discounts
- Total price
- Tax
- Shipping costs
- Payment due date
- Remittance address
- Printing errors
- Folding/stuffing errors
- Timeliness

This list is, arguably, long. It would be a challenge to track each defect type individually. Also, having many opportunities would make for an overly good-looking Sigma score. So another option might be *four* opportunities, as follows:

1. Customer data (including name, address, and P.O. number)
2. Order information (items, quantity, ship-to address)
3. Pricing (unit price, discounts, taxes, etc.)
4. Production (print quality)

So, trimming down from a starting total of 17 defect types, we could arrive at just *four* opportunities. But in fact, as long as we are consistent and our reasoning is sound, either of these numbers—or something in between—could work.

Really complex products can have many more opportunities. An example done at Texas Instruments for an electronic component showed more than 4,000 opportunities, which is understandable when you think of the numbers of individual items (each of which can have defects) and requirements for such a complex piece of equipment.

We can summarize by giving you some guidelines for figuring opportunities for your products or services:

- **Focus on "standard" problem areas.** Defects that are rare should not be considered opportunities.
- **Group closely related defects into one opportunity.** This approach both simplifies your work and ensures against any inflating of opportunities.

- ▶ **Make sure the defect is important to the customer.** If you focus on validated requirements/performance standards, following this guideline will be easier.
- ▶ **Be consistent.** If your business plans to use opportunity-based measures, you should consider setting standards for defining opportunities.
- ▶ **Change only when needed.** Each time you change the number of opportunities, you shift the denominator for your Sigma measure—meaning that your comparison with earlier results is less valid. You should change the rules only when really necessary.

Some organizations we worked with (e.g., an aerospace parts logistics group and an equipment-leasing company) have simplified the issue by defining just *one* opportunity, in essence focusing on *defectives.* The argument in these cases is that customers want *no* defects and that opportunity calculations can make things appear better than they are. On the other hand, the one-opportunity choice makes cross-process comparisons less effective.

Calculating Opportunity-Based Measures

Calculating and expressing measures based on defect opportunities can be done in several ways:

- ▶ **Defects per opportunity (DPO).** This measure expresses the proportion of defects over the total number of opportunities in a group. For example, if DPO were .05, it would signify a 5 percent chance of having a defect in one category. Figure 13.9 illustrates this formula and shows some examples.
- ▶ **Defects per million opportunities (DPMO).** Most defect opportunity measures are translated into the DPMO format, which indicates how many defects would arise in 1 million opportunities. In manufacturing environments especially, DPMO often is called *PPM*, from parts per million.[2] Figure 13.10 illustrates this formula and shows some examples.
- ▶ **Sigma measure.** Getting to Sigma performance equivalents now is a piece of cake. As we showed you in Chapter 2, the easy way to get your number is to translate your defect measure—usually DPMO—by using a conversion table. The numbers for our examples shown in

Defects/Unit or DPU

Formula: $\dfrac{\text{Number of Defects}}{\text{\# of Units} \times \text{\# of Opportunities}}$

Service Examples:

• 52 defects, 250 loan applications, 4 defect opportunities

$$\frac{52 \text{ defects on applications}}{250 \text{ applications} \times 4 \text{ opportunities/application}} = .052 \text{ DPO}$$

• 321 defects, 186 ad contracts, 8 defect opportunities

$$\frac{321 \text{ defects on contracts}}{186 \text{ contracts} \times 8 \text{ opportunities/contract}} = .216 \text{ DPO}$$

Manufacturing Examples:

• 99 defects, 750 microchips, 150 defect opportunities

$$\frac{52 \text{ defects on microchips}}{750 \text{ chips} \times 150 \text{ opportunities/chip}} = .00046 \text{ DPO}$$

• 319 defects, 1,150 steel joists, 15 defect opportunities

$$\frac{319 \text{ defects on joists}}{1,150 \text{ chips} \times 15 \text{ opportunities/joist}} = .018 \text{ DPO}$$

**FIGURE 13.9   FORMULA AND EXAMPLES:
DEFECTS PER OPPORTUNITY (DPO)**

Figure 13.11 were derived from the Sigma conversion table shown in Figure 13.12. If in each example the data are accurate and the opportunity guidelines are consistent, we would conclude the microchip manufacturing process as the one functioning most effectively and the advertising contract process as the worst. In the real world, these results would be typical.

The Difference Between Sigma and Standard Deviation. An anomaly to the Sigma Conversion table may be of interest here, especially to the statistically savvy or just plain curious. We will try to explain it briefly in layperson's language, though if you plan to use a table to get a Sigma performance score, you may find this explanation more than you *need* to know.

The convention in Six Sigma is to use a scoring system that accounts for more variation in a process than will typically be found in a few weeks or even a couple of months of data gathering. As an

Defects/Million Opportunities (DPMO)

Formula: DPO x 1,000,000 (10^6)

Service Examples:
• Loan Applications
    $.052 \times 10^6 = 52,000$ **DPMO**

• Advertising Contracts
    $.216 \times 10^6 = 216,000$ **DPMO**

Manufacturing Examples:
• Microchips
    $.00046 \times 10^6 = 460$ **DPMO**

• Steel Joists
    $.018 \times 10^6 = 18,000$ **DPMO**

FIGURE 13.10   FORMULA AND EXAMPLES:
DEFECTS PER MILLION OPPORTUNITIES (DPMO)

example, let's say we work in a customer service call center and find that for one quarter we hit a "first-call resolution" rate of 95.44 percent. Out of 1 million calls, about 45,600 would be considered defects, or calls not resolved in the first conversation.

However, what we see in a single month is usually not representative of what would happen over, say, a year or two. Over the longer term we probably find that our performance is more variable and perhaps not quite as good. A more realistic yield, based on assumptions drawn from electronics manufacturing but now applied to the rest of us, would be about 69.2 percent or 308,000 defects per million calls. Ouch!

Fortunately, the way this convention is applied is less depressing. Instead of lowering the Sigma score, the scoring itself has been shifted so that for our one-month's data of 95.44 percent we consider our *short-term* Sigma level to be about 3.2σ (technically noted σ_{ST}). This score reflects a more realistic expectation of your likely defect levels; if we were to perform at 3.2σ over the long term (i.e., without this shift in the scoring), normal statistical tables would tell you to expect fewer

Sigma

Calculate DPMO, Consult Table

Service Examples:

• Loan Applications
   52,000 DPMO = 3.1 Sigma

• Advertising Contracts
   216,000 DPMO = 2.3 Sigma

Manufacturing Examples:

• Microchips
   460 DPMO = 4.8 Sigma

• Steel Joists
   18,000 DPMO = 3.6 Sigma

FIGURE 13.11   SIGMA MEASURE EXAMPLES

than 3,000 defects; whereas this table says that if you think you are at 3.2σ now, you should figure on getting more than *45,000* defects.

If you think this calculation is enough to make your head swim, we are right in the water with you. This so-called "1.5 Sigma shift" is one of the key bones of contention among statistical experts about how Six Sigma measures are defined. The lucky thing is that when a convention is adopted and applied consistently, it is still valid. Because every company we know of prepares their Sigma scores this way, we can assure you that it works just fine. The only challenge comes if you try to equate the accepted Six Sigma scoring system to strict standard deviations under a normal curve.

Internal or Process/Input Measures

The baseline measures we have reviewed so far address the overall or end-of-the-line performance of a process or system: "How good was the final product or service we delivered to the customer?" But that may not tell the whole story. You may have perfect output, but

Six Sigma Conversion Table

YIELD (%)	DPMO	SIGMA
6.68	933200	0
8.455	915450	0.125
10.56	894400	0.25
13.03	869700	0.375
15.87	841300	0.5
19.08	809200	0.625
22.66	773400	0.75
26.595	734050	0.875
30.85	**691500**	**1**
35.435	645650	1.125
40.13	598700	1.25
45.025	549750	1.375
50	500000	1.5
54.975	450250	1.625
59.87	401300	1.75
64.565	354350	1.875
69.15	**308500**	**2**
73.405	265950	2.125
77.34	226600	2.25
80.92	190800	2.375
84.13	158700	2.5
86.97	130300	2.625
89.44	105600	2.75
91.545	84550	2.875
93.32	**66800**	**3**
94.79	52100	3.125
95.99	40100	3.25
96.96	30400	3.375
97.73	22700	3.5
98.32	16800	3.625
98.78	12200	3.75
99.12	8800	3.875
99.38	**6200**	**4**
99.565	4350	4.125
99.7	3000	4.25
99.795	2050	4.375
99.87	1300	4.5
99.91	900	4.625
99.94	600	4.75
99.96	400	4.875
99.977	**230**	**5**
99.982	180	5.125
99.987	130	5.25
99.992	80	5.375
99.997	30	5.5
99.99767	23.35	5.625
99.99833	16.7	5.75
99.999	10.05	5.875
99.99966	**3.4**	**6**

FIGURE 13.12   SIX SIGMA CONVERSION TABLE

an *inefficient* operation that survives only by significant, heroic effort. Or you may be squandering a big portion of your profits on wasteful activities that the customer never sees. So now let's look at some ways of baselining the *internal* performance of your process.

Identifying and Quantifying Waste and Cycle Time

One common distinction made in the debate over Six Sigma and Lean is that Six Sigma looks at *defects*, whereas Lean looks at *waste*. Although that distinction is somewhat of an exaggeration, because both are concerned with boosting efficiency and effectiveness of a business, bringing Lean Six Sigma into a single system has been overall a positive development.

Finding and Measuring the Eight Wastes. Waste is simply time, effort, or material that is not contributing value to the organization or the customer. (In Chapter 15, we talk more about how to distinguish value-adding from non-value-adding work.) Even though you might think identifying and getting rid of waste would be easy and obvious, the truth is it is often ignored and hard to get rid of. For various reasons, waste goes undetected, but certainly the most common reason is that we just *get used to it* and fail to think of it as a bad thing.

For example, we have done work in health care organizations where for years, nurses (as well as other professionals) have had to walk long distances from one patient to another, to get supplies and medication, to pick up test results, and so on. Obviously, when a nurse is walking from one place to another, he or she is not doing the valuable work of providing care: it is waste. Only when looking more closely, with a waste-focused mindset and literally measuring and mapping the distances walked, does the level of lost value become clear.

Exhibit 13.2 provides an overview of what are called the "eight wastes," categories that help people examining their work space, supply chain, process, or other environment to find waste that they would otherwise miss (and may have lived with, like the long-distance-walking nurses, for years). Often, you will find plenty of overlap between the waste categories (e.g., overproduction leads to excess inventory), but the benefit of the different types of waste is to help find *all* waste that exists.

Exhibit 13.2 The Eight Wastes

1. *Overproduction*—Making goods or preparing service capacity in excess of what the internal or external customer(s) actually will use.
2. *Time*—Delays or waiting resulting in idle people or assets.

3. *Defects*—A product or service that fails to meet customer requirements, resulting in scrap, rework, and/or dissatisfaction.
4. *Process Inefficiency*—Excess complexity, lack of standardization, unnecessary reviews or inspection, redundant activities, and other factors that add to costs and disrupt smooth operation of the process.
5. *Transportation*—Unnecessary, non-value-adding movement of product, material, information, or people.
6. *Inventory*—Inappropriate levels (high or low) of material, goods, work in process (including paperwork), or information.
7. *Motion*—Excessive people movements, actions, and effort driven by poor ergonomic, workspace layouts, or organizational configurations.
8. *Misuse of Talent*—Tasks assigned to or executed by individuals who are not the best fit in terms of ability and knowledge; includes gaps created by poor training/preparation of staff for their jobs.

Developing a baseline measure of waste is often a fairly easy calculation, connecting the volume of time, material, or other waste to money (e.g., hours nurses spend walking × pay/hour). (See more in the section Cost of Poor Quality.) The real key is doing the work to detect the waste and add it up, which often turns out to be an appallingly high number. But, once you see it, you can start to eliminate it!

Takt: Measuring Speed Against Customer Demand. Another measure associated with Lean improvement examines the ability of an operation to respond to the level of customer demand. The term *takt* means "beat" in German, and is usually calculated in two ways:

Takt rate: The number of units requested or inquiries from a customer in a given period. For example, if 900 customers call a service center with questions during the 12-hour period the center is open each day, the takt rate is 75 per hour (900 ÷ 12).

Takt time: The average time between each customer for a product or service (internal rate at which "units" must be processed to keep up with demand). Using the same example, and converting the 12 hours the service center is open, the takt time is .8 minutes; meaning the center must be able to handle customer calls at the rate of one every .8 minutes (720 minutes ÷ 900 calls).

Of course, the actual rate of calls in this example may vary over the 12-hour period, so takt rate and time may need to be calculated for segments of the day to be more accurate.

Takt measures can provide a useful insight into how quickly an operation must be able to operate in order to avoid a bottleneck, and when an opportunity to adjust to avoid *excess* capacity (a form of waste) occurs.

Internal Yield Measures

Another measure of internal process performance looks at the percentage of "good" product or service (yield) produced during *substeps* of the process. Because poor internal yield is often covered up by rework, these measures may be revealing, if not shocking. We start with an imaginary process (it could be in a service or manufacturing business). As shown in Figure 13.13, data collected at the process output point showed a final yield of .985 (98.5 percent) and a Sigma of 3.7.[3] Of 1,500 units (orders, parts, etc.), 1,477 were delivered at the end of the process defect-free.

Now let's look inside the process. We can see in Figure 13.13 that among the three major "subprocesses," each operates with a yield in the upper 90 percent range. The company has caught the defects and can rework them, but over the course of the process, 89 items have to be reworked. So at the end of the internal data gathering, only 1,411 items have *really* gotten through defect-free, with 89 undergoing some rework.

In Figure 13.14, we included the calculation of what is called "first-pass yield" based on the total number of reworked items and the total input. Noted Y_{NORM}, which shows a yield in this example quite a bit

Final/Output Data:

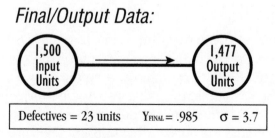

FIGURE 13.13   YIELD EXAMPLE 1: FINAL YIELD

First Pass Yield:

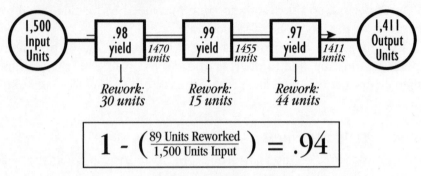

$$1 - \left(\frac{89 \text{ Units Reworked}}{1,500 \text{ Units Input}}\right) = .94$$

FIGURE 13.14   YIELD EXAMPLE 3: FIRST-PASS YIELD

Subprocess Sigma Scores:

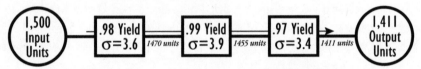

FIGURE 13.15   YIELD EXAMPLE 4:
SUBPROCESS YIELD AND SIGMA SCORES

worse than the Y_{FINAL}: .94 compared to .985. In other words, the final yield numbers are hiding defects being fixed in the process.[4]

Lastly, we can develop Sigma performance figures for each substep in the process, based on the defect data we have been examining. As we can see, based both on the yield and on the Sigma numbers shown in Figure 13.15, the third step in the process shows the most need of attention.

Including Cost of Poor Quality

An important performance dimension not captured by defect or Sigma measures is the dollar impact of defects, often called cost of poor quality (COPQ).[5] For example, if you have two processes both performing at 3.5 Sigma, their defect-based performance seemingly is equal. However, adding up the dollars lost to defects in both processes, you may find the bottom-line impact of one process far higher than the other.

For this reason, we urge teams and Six Sigma implementers to make COPQ a key part of their measurement efforts early on. This approach entails some work in translating problems or defects into dollar costs per incident, including labor and materials for rework or customer hand-holding, as well as opportunity or lost business costs. COPQ numbers are often *more* meaningful to the business leaders or others having no Six Sigma background, because unlike Sigma or DPMO, they speak a language almost anyone understands: *money.* COPQ measures can represent a useful way of strengthening consensus for improvement and of helping you to select problems with clear bottom-line benefits. If you can include reasonable dollar estimates on the *external* impact of problems (e.g., quantify the volume of business lost for every point decrease in a customer satisfaction rating) COPQ can make an even stronger case for customer-directed improvement.

Using Baseline Measures

The immediate rationale for exploring these various process measures is to give you and your leaders better input as you go about setting priorities for improvement. With good data and process performance measures such as Yield, DPMO, Sigma, or COPQ—especially if the measures cover most of your key customer-focused processes—the organization can look for areas of greatest gap or concern. Also, you have a head start on getting projects started more quickly, because current performance data already are available. Finally, these measures are a great starting point to track improvement down the road, allowing you to document gains and performance enhancements based on hard data versus anecdotes.

Exhibit 13.3 summarizes the "dos and don'ts" for the measurement phase of Six Sigma. Your new measures and measurement skills also lay the foundation for those ongoing measurement systems that can do so much to create a more responsive company. Learning from your mistakes and applying good data collection and measurement habits will make the long-term goal of measurement systems that much more achievable. We pick up the theme of measurement systems in Step 5 (Chapter 16), where we review how to combine all the key elements of the Six Sigma methodology and system to drive sustained success and continuous improvement.

We've laid the groundwork for *real* improvement by taking a careful look processes, customers and measures. In Chapter 14, we turn to the execution of a meaningful improvement effort.

Exhibit 13.3

"DOS AND DON'TS" FOR THE MEASURE PHASE OF SIX SIGMA

■ Do—*Set measurement priorities that match your resources.*
  • If you can afford and have the knowhow to begin measuring all core processes, go for it. Most companies have more limited resources, though, and in the majority of cases you should target measurement where the knowledge gained will be most helpful and is feasible to obtain.
■ Do—*Consider ways to measure service as well as output factors.*
  • For simplicity's sake, we focused our examples and discussion on the more concrete output requirement measures. Measuring performance and defects on key service dimensions may be just as useful however, in helping you to identify improvement projects.
■ Do—*Practice continuous improvement of your measurement.*
  • Good business measurement is not easy. The people aspects of measures can be just as important and challenging as the technical side. Expect to make mistakes and to learn as you and your organization become more measurement-savvy.
■ Do—*Stop measures that are not needed or useful.*
  • If a good reason to keep up with a measure cannot be given, abandon it. If you are not on your toes, a measurement bureaucracy can arise that protects *all* measures, and then the objective becomes "measure for measurement's sake."

■ Don't—*Use Sigma or Lean measures if they are not going to add value.*
  • Some organizations adopt and continue to apply Six Sigma measures as a good way of building consistency and readily understood indicators of performance. But many just did it because it was supposedly a *requirement* for success, which it is not. Adopt new measurement approaches carefully and if they are really needed.

- Don't—*Expect the data to confirm your assumptions.*
    - Often, people will find that the baseline data they gather is right in line with what they thought. It seems to be just as often, though, that measures bring a big surprise. When that happens: pay attention. Dig deeper if you have to, but do not dismiss the data as "Impossible!"

CHAPTER 14

Six Sigma Process Improvement
(Roadmap Step 4A)

In this chapter, the Six Sigma engine really gets revved up. As we take you through the process improvement steps, both here and in Chapter 15, the goal is to help you match or exceed the gains described back in Chapter 1. In this chapter, we focus on analyzing, developing, and implementing root cause–focused solutions. Our plan is to illustrate the paths that go through the define, measure, analyze, and improve phases of DMAIC by telling you a story, one that reveals how a typical team tends to work through a typical project. We mix the story with fascinating interludes in which we explain actions and tools. Of course, no team or project is really "typical"; each is unique and poses special challenges. Still, an example will give you a better feel for the work that needs to be done and for how to do it well.

By the way, you may notice that we left off the *C* in DMAIC. Control is the end of DMAIC, but really the *beginning* of the sustained improvement and integration of the Six Sigma system. So, we tie Control tools and concepts into our discussion of Step 5 in Chapter 16, Expanding and Integrating the Six Sigma System.

This chapter also focuses on many of the basics of DMAIC (e.g., the elements of a project charter); then Chapter 15 focuses on variations for design/redesign projects. If you expect to be involved in process design/redesign, you will want to review both chapters. If your only interest, for now, is in process improvement (i.e., incremental change), you can concentrate on this chapter. Also, because we covered many of the basics of measurement in Chapter 13, our review of the Measure phase will cover how a team might apply the concepts (e.g., by selecting measures and developing baseline data). In the Analyze step, we get into how to *use* measures to find out why things are happening in the process.

We will be describing and giving examples of a number of common and/or valuable improvement tools and techniques that support the DMAIC process. Our emphasis will be on which tools to use, when, and why, which is one of the biggest challenges for organizations and teams embarking on a Six Sigma effort. The References section at the end of the book lists other resources where you can get more details on the techniques.

Whenever we teach improvement tools, the worry is that people will misuse or abuse them. Having a variety of tools to apply to different business problems is important, but people can become tool-happy. Here are some tool guidelines to keep in mind:

1. **Have a clear objective whenever you decide to use a tool.** Never use a tool just because "it's in the book" or "we haven't done that one yet." Only pull out a hammer if a nail needs pounding.

2. **Consider your options, and select the technique that looks most likely to meet your needs.** With the variety of techniques in the Six Sigma toolkit, often more than one method *might* be of help. Be careful of which one you try.

3. **Keep it simple; match the detail and complexity of the tool to the situation.** The most basic tools should be used the most often. If you are using detailed statistics for every problem or project, you are more than likely overcomplicating things.

4. **Adapt the method to your needs.** Even though some organizations or consultants like to play "tool police," it is okay to create your own variations on a method *if*, that is, (a) you do not make a change that no one else can understand, and (b) you avoid drawing faulty conclusions from it.

5. **If a tool is not working, stop.** Consider every tool you use a trial. If you do not get the answer you need or if it is not working, try something else.

Now let's see how process improvement can actually work, by introducing the company we will use for our case study throughout this chapter.

Case Study #11: AutoRec Tries Six Sigma to Heal Its Growing Pains*

The market for handheld dictation and note recorders has been growing like gangbusters. People have gotten so used to talking into their cell phones while in the car, walking down the street, in restaurants, and so on, that apparently when no one is left to call, they still like to chat away to themselves. A new array of devices has been introduced that take advantage of digital memory and minidiscs. As a result, consumers have a variety of types of recorders to choose from, all of them lumped into a product category called "auto-talk devices."

In the past 18 months, one of the auto-talk leaders, AutoRec, Inc., made a breakthrough by linking various dictation format devices with voice-recognition technology. Now, people can actually have their utterings converted into text automatically. A new market has opened up for AutoRec in the sales force automation arena, meaning for instance that account executives can more easily keep notes on their clients and prospects, as well as dictate letters and proposals without the need for administrative support.

The challenge, however, is to meet the specific requirements of AutoRec's growing group of corporate accounts. Because the auto-talk devices have to interface with a client's existing technology (i.e., laptops, networks, word-processing and contact-list applications, etc.), each large order for a sales group needs to be specially designed and produced. Unfortunately, the number of deliveries that fail to meet client specifications has always been high, and it is growing. AutoRec's leadership group, having heard about the big impact of Six Sigma improvement efforts at other companies, decided to see whether the methods would help them to address their problems.

---

* When the first edition of the book was done, the vision of voice-to-text productivity enhancement was pretty "out there." Today, AutoRec's technology seems quaint in light of huge strides in software and new tools like smart phones. But the original story is still quite relevant to illustrate and understand how continuous improvement works!

"We only have a few months," said AutoRec's CEO, "before some-one matches our technology and clients start looking elsewhere. We've got to get our [censored] act together, or we'll be called Auto *Wreck!*" (Which, in fact, they already were.)

The leadership team put together a project rationale statement:

> Mistakes in deliveries to customers are affecting almost 40 percent of our shipments. Rework costs are up to $300,000 per month, and 2 of the top 25 companies in the country who were considering major orders now say they need assurances we can deliver. If we don't improve our effectiveness in meeting customer requirements, we risk slipping behind TalkNBox [key competitor] when they introduce their voice integration system in the Fall. This team is charged to find out why we are making so many out-of-spec deliveries—and to get results fast.

A team consisting of seven people was chosen from different functions within AutoRec, including two from assembly (manufacturing), and one each from order administration, procurement, product design, shipping, and sales. Initially the team was going to number only six, but the vice president of sales insisted on having a representative. (For guidelines on project team selection, see Chapter 8.) The director of product design was selected to be team leader. The leader and team members attended a one-week workshop that gave them an overview and key methods for executing a Six Sigma–focused process improvement project. The CEO visited each team member personally, to pledge support for the project.

In the AutoRec team's training, they were given an overview of the five phases of the DMAIC model. Because the team knew that time was of the essence, they realized they would have to focus on *fixing* the problems in their current processes: no time was available to attempt to redesign their workflows.

Before we take the AutoRec story any further, we should emphasize an important fact: the DMAIC cycle is *not a purely linear activity.* As any team begins probing, gathering data, and so on, they almost invariably make discoveries about the problem and process. For example, these revelations mean that the project goal can be revised even up to the point of implementing solutions. Or after testing a solution, a team may need to do more "Analyze" work. In general, improvement teams can plot their progress using the D-M-A-I-C phases, but overall it is an *iterative* activity.

The "Define" Phase of DMAIC: Clarify the Problem, Goal, and Process

The Define phase sets the stage for a successful Six Sigma project by helping you to answer four critical questions:

1. What is the *problem* or opportunity on which we will focus?
2. What is our *goal*? (i.e., What results do we want to accomplish, and by when?)
3. Who is the *customer* served and/or affected by this process and problem?
4. What is the *process* we are investigating?

In documenting project goals and parameters at the outset—in what is usually called the *project charter*—improvement teams can help ensure that their work meets with the expectations of organization leaders and project sponsor. Let's see how this works in our case study example.

Case Study #11 Continued: AutoRec Gets Started on the Project Charter

At the AutoRec group's first meeting, the agenda contained one item: "Define the problem." A couple of team members questioned why that would take an entire meeting, since the project rationale given to them by the executive team stated the situation pretty clearly. In the first five minutes of discussion, though, several different perspectives on the issue were identified, including the following:

- ► Customer expectations for the AutoRec units are too high.
- ► People on the assembly floor are making mistakes that lead to product errors getting to customers.

▶ Order specifications somehow are not being followed properly, meaning that products are not configured to customer requirements when shipped.

▶ Late deliveries are creating angry customers, who take it out on AutoRec when they find the slightest thing wrong with the units.

▶ Clients' sales staff (i.e., end users of AutoRec's products) do not understand how to use the units.

With such a wide range of notions about the problem, the team decided to write a general problem statement, which they would refine as more data were gathered.

The team also prepared an initial goal statement, which identified the results they would work to achieve. Some of the members were uncomfortable with the deadline they set, but they agreed that they did need to aim for early successes.

"Well," concluded the sales department member, "these are pretty general statements. We're going to have to get some more specifics pretty quick."

Develop Your Six Sigma Project Charter

Each business faces many options for developing and formatting a charter. The AutoRec team has so far done only the two most essential charter elements. Here's a rundown of many of the most common items included in a project charter, as well as some guidelines for producing your own project document.

Write a Problem Statement. This concise and focused description of "what's wrong" evolves from either the pain arising from the problem or the opportunity that needs to be addressed. In some cases the problem statement can be a distilled version of the project rationale; but usually a team will need to define the issue much more specifically, because even the best project rationale statements will be fairly broad.

A problem statement and the process of writing it serve to do the following:

1. Validate that the project rationale has been clearly understood by the improvement team.
2. Solidify consensus and ownership of team members around the problem to be addressed.

3. Ensure that the team is beginning to focus on a problem that is neither too narrow nor too broad.
4. Assess the clarity of the data supporting and helping to define the problem
5. Establish a baseline measure against which progress and results can be tracked

This last benefit, the baseline measure, may not exist when the team first meets, so it is an example of one of the elements of the problem statement that would need to be clarified over time. Figure 14.1 summarizes the four key questions you should pose as you develop a problem statement.

Write a Goal Statement. Problem statements and goal statements are a matched pair. Although the problem statement describes the

Problem Statement Structure	
What?	• Which process is involved? • What is wrong? • What is the gap or opportunity?

Where?/ When?	• Where do we observe the problem/gap?
	  ✓ department
	  ✓ region
	  ✓ etc.
	• When do we observe the problem/gap?
	  ✓ time of day/month/year
	  ✓ before/after X
	  ✓ etc.

How big?	• How big is the problem/gap/ opportunity? • How will we measure it?
Impact?	• What's the impact of the problem/opportunity? • What are the benefits of action/ consequences of inaction?

FIGURE 14.1   ELEMENTS OF A PROBLEM STATEMENT

pain or symptoms, a goal statement defines "relief" in terms of concrete results. Goal statement structure can be standardized into three elements:

1. **A description of what is to be accomplished.** The goal statement should start with a verb: "Reduce . . ."; "Increase . . ."; "Eliminate . . ." (but try to avoid "Improve" as too vague).
2. **A measurable target for desired results.** The target should quantify the desired cost saving, defect elimination, or time reduction, and so on, in percentages or actual numbers. If it is too soon to even guess, leave a "placeholder" to indicate where you plan to add the target later. The measurable target is what your team and business leaders will use to gauge the project's success.
3. **A project deadline and/or timeframe for results.** The date set in the early part of the project may need to be revised later, but establishing a deadline helps to rally resources and commitment and shorten project cycle times.

A suggestion: For clarity, you may want to include *two* deadlines in a goal statement—one date for implementing solutions and the second for when you expect to show measurable results.

Many teams say that agreeing on the problem and goal is one of the most challenging aspects of their Six Sigma project. Individuals from different parts of your company may see the issue differently, making consensus hard to come by. Moreover, the initial drafts tend to be based more on guesses than on hard data, allowing more room for disagreement. One way to avoid problem and goal wheel-spinning is to remember that these statements will *evolve* as you gain more knowledge about the process and data. (It is common to describe a project charter as a "living document," which somehow suggests to us a B-movie scene: "Look, Professor, it's *breathing*!")

Document Your Constraints and Assumptions. This section of a charter, which might also be called "resources and expectations," helps you to clarify and document the limitations and other relevant factors that may affect your team's efforts. One common example is time availability: Are improvement team members expected to spend 100 percent of their time on the project? Will there be sufficient resources to cover their "regular" jobs? Some possible solutions may be "out of bounds" (e.g., you may decide that a major information technology upgrade just is not feasible for the time being). These types of realities are best clarified upfront, so that teams can avoid going down the wrong path or holding any false expectations.

Not all the elements noted in this category are necessarily limiting, either. An assumption may be that "The team will make all key decisions about the solutions to be implemented" or "The finance department will provide one full-time person to help the team gather cost of poor quality data." Other assumptions may define the anticipated frequency of team meetings, contributions of the sponsor, and so on. Even if constraints and assumptions are not made formal elements of the project charter, just asking the questions around them is a good idea.

Summarize Your Initial Problem or Opportunity Data. Because you don't want the problem statement to run longer than two or three brief sentences, any measures or facts that you feel are relevant to identifying or understanding the problem can be summarized in a separate section of the Charter. You can update these data as you go, or just leave them "as is" as a record of the facts you had available at the outset of the project.

Identify Team Members and Responsibilities. A project charter may also list the people who are involved in the Six Sigma project, including team members, support people, coach or consulting staff, and project sponsor or champion.

Set Team Guidelines. Expectations as to how the team will collaborate can also be incorporated into the charter. These may include team ground rules, roles for managing meetings, decision processes, or other aspects of teamwork.

Create a Preliminary Project Plan. Final deadlines alone cannot keep most teams on track throughout the course of a Six Sigma project. Identifying and setting dates for key milestones helps keep energy levels higher and creates a sense of urgency. Having team members commit voluntarily to the milestone dates, rather than imposing them, usually is preferred, but sometimes a little pushing is needed, especially if all team members continue to work at their "regular" jobs.

Note that an additional element of a project charter often included in some organizations is known as the *scope*. We will wait till we look at process design/redesign in Chapter 15 to discuss scope, because it is more relevant to those projects.

Let's see how the project charter process is unfolding at AutoRec.

Case Study #11 Continued: AutoRec Completes Its Project Charter

It took the AutoRec team an entire two-hour meeting just to prepare their initial problem and goal statements. Prior to the second meeting a couple of days later, the team leader drafted several other pieces of the charter, including a list of team and project participants and constraints and assumptions.

A heated discussion arose about the expectations swirling around how much time team members were to devote to the project: the draft charter indicated that each member of the team would carve out 25 to 50 percent of his or her schedule for the project. "I've got work stacked on my desk," said the procurement group member. "I can't be in meetings for two hours every other day without some relief." Others had similar complaints. The team leader agreed to talk to their sponsor to ensure that people would have time freed up for the project.

So far, the problem statement was vague on the size of the problem. Then the shipping department team member spoke up: "I finally found some figures on the bad deliveries," she explained. "It turns out about 8 percent of orders are arriving late, and 30 percent are not configured properly, with a few miscellaneous problems here and there."

Based on the new data, the team revised the problem statement and completed their initial charter (shown in Figures 14.2 and 14.3).

Identifying and Listening to the Customer

Here are some of the practical benefits of using a voice of the customer (VOC) assessment in the define phase:

1. Ensuring that the problem and goal are defined in terms that truly relate to key customer requirements
2. Avoiding cost- and time-cutting solutions that actually hurt service to or relations with customers

Six Sigma Customer Delivery Team:
Project Charter

Problem Statement
Forty percent of orders delivered to AutoRec corporate clients are not meeting customer requirements, including 30% rejected for out-of-spec units and 8% noted as late deliveries. These defects are hurting our image, creating customer dissatisfaction, and costing us roughly $350,000 per month to rework rejected orders. Continued high levels of delivery errors threaten our position as leader in this growing industry.

Goal Statement
Reduce delivery errors by 70% (to less than 12%) and cut rework costs by 50% by the end of Q3 of this year.

Constraints
Team members will be expected to devote 25% to 50% of their time to the project. Backup support for their existing jobs will be . . . [*to be reviewed with sponsor*].

Assumptions
No reasonable solutions will be considered "out of bounds," however, the focus of the team will be on improving existing processes, not on designing or redesigning processes.

Team Guidelines
The team will meet at least once a week. Tuesday mornings from 9 a.m. to 10 a.m. Decisions will be made by consensus, guided by criteria analysis where needed. If consensus cannot be reached, the team leader will make the final call.

CHAPTER: Draft One, Page 1

AutoRec

FIGURE 14.2   AUTOREC TEAM PROJECT CHARTER (PAGE 1)

3. Providing information on possible output measures that may need to be tracked as solutions are implemented
4. Giving team members practice in, and reinforcing the importance of, focusing work on the *customer*

If your organization already has an effective VOC strategy and the data are accessible (as described in Chapter 12), it may be easy for a DMAIC team to validate customer needs and specifications. Without

---

Project Charter, continued

Team Members
The team is comprised of the following members:
- – Ravi Gosai, Order Administration
- – Al Johnson, Product Design (Team Leader)
- – Daphne Martin, Assembly
- – Mike Moshivitz, Assembly
- – May Yamamoto, Sales
- – Elena Zarzuela, Procurement
- – Arnold Ziffle, Shipping

Other key players include:
- – Pat DeLia, VP of Customer Satisfaction (Sponsor)
- – Martin Wyck, Six Sigma Coach
- – Eleanor Carajota, Finance liaison/support
- – Bob Megabyte, IT liaison/support

Preliminary Project Plan
To achieve our goal and results by our target date, the team will have to work aggressively and rapidly. The following are milestones for completing each phase of the DMAIC process:

> *DEFINE* – March 15
>
> *MEASURE* – April 15
>
> *ANALYZE* – May 15
>
> *IMPROVE* – June 15
>
> *CONTROL* – July 15

CHARTER: Draft One, Page 2

FIGURE 14.3   AUTOREC TEAM PROJECT CHARTER (PAGE 2)

good upfront sources, however, getting the relevant customer input may take time and money. Under pressure to get results, your process improvement teams will have to balance the *ideal* of having a thorough understanding of customer requirements with the need to keep the DMAIC project moving.

Case Study #11 Continued: AutoRec Gets in Touch with Its Customers

At the end of their meeting to finalize the project charter, the AutoRec "We Deliver" team (their new name) agreed that May from sales and Arnold from shipping would make contact with several sources to get

a better idea of how the delivery problems were affecting corporate account customers.

Because of the need for speed they decided to divide the work, with each focusing on one source of customer data:

1. May would put together a brief phone survey, and phone about 10 sales managers and 10 IT managers to develop a detailed list of customer requirements and priorities.
2. Arnold meanwhile would review letters and complaint forms from corporate customers to see what patterns emerged or conclusions could be drawn from it.

After a week, May and Arnold got together to compare findings. What they learned was a bit of a surprise: Corporate clients were not nearly as concerned about quick delivery of orders of auto-talk devices as they had thought.

"All the customers told me they are eager to have the systems to boost their groups' productivity," May noted. "But if they had to wait a few weeks or a month, it wouldn't be a huge issue."

The data Arnold culled from complaint forms and letters was indicative, too. "It took me about three hours just to separate the corporate account items from the rest; they were all mixed together! But I could only find six forms or letters that had anything to do with late deliveries, and they were pretty mild. The clients whose systems could not be used right away were almost unanimously livid—there were more than 150 of those."

May and Arnold prepared a one-page summary of their findings for the team (see Figure 14.4).

When the other team members saw the list and the data, their jaws dropped and eyes widened (it is an expressive group). The top priority for everyone at AutoRec had been to ship the systems *as soon as possible*. The rationale was that, as the "only game in town," AutoRec needed to get its products to customers fast.

"The customer's sense of urgency doesn't seem to be nearly as intense as ours is," May explained. "Fast is fine, but not a big deal. Wrong is, however, a big deal."

The team left the meeting with some things to think about.

Customer: Corporate Sales Department

Output: "AutoText" Devices and Support Materials

Weight	Customer Requirement	Type
10	Compatible with existing hardware	DI
10	Compatible with existing software	DI
8	Accuracy of voice translation to text (at least 95 percent accurate)	SA
5	Usable by reading instructions in 5 minutes or less	SA
5	Correct quantity	DI
3	Delivered on date noted on purchase order	SA

SA = Satisfier
DI = Dissatisfier (minimum requirement)
DE = Delighter

AutoRec

FIGURE 14.4 AUTOREC CUSTOMER
REQUIREMENTS WEIGHTING AND TYPE

Identifying and Documenting the Process

A final, essential define activity is to develop a "picture" of the process involved in the project. Some groups are tempted to skip this step, but several strong reasons make it a must at the outset of any DMAIC project.

▶ **Putting the problem in context.** Understanding how the work flows in and around the problem will help clarify the various factors that may influence performance.

▶ **Refining the scope of the project, or focusing analysis.** A quick way to help a team concentrate its attention is to create a diagram of

its process. It is typical to recognize that the process described is so huge that some immediate narrowing of focus is needed.

▶ **Revealing possible obvious root causes.** We don't advocate conclusion-jumping, but sometimes just documenting how the process is working (or *not* working) will help a team see the cause of the problem.

▶ **Clarifying inputs, roles, and supplier/customer relationships.** Such clarification can help team members to better understand one another's role in the process and to see how they contribute to the project. It also can help to determine whether the team has the right mix of members.

▶ **Helping to target what and where to measure.** Having a broad view of the process makes tangible where key data may be needed and/ or available.

An important question to raise with respect to documenting a process early in a DMAIC project is "How much detail do we need?" As usual, the answer is, "It depends." In general we suggest that you begin with a SIPOC diagram, as introduced in Chapter 11. Once that diagram is completed, you can decide whether a more detailed process map is needed. The AutoRec team elected to do a high-level SIPOC map, shown in Figure 14.5.

With a SIPOC diagram, customer requirements, and project charter completed, a team may be ready to move into the measure phase of DMAIC. An optional final task would be to create a detailed process map to use in helping to identify where to implement measures, but only when and where it is really needed. It is best to avoid too much detail too soon.

Before we move on to the next phase of DMAIC (measuring), Exhibit 14.1 provides a list of "dos and don'ts" to keep in mind during the define phase, and Exhibit 14.2 provides a checklist you can use during your own define phase.

Exhibit 14.1

"DOS AND DON'TS" FOR THE DEFINE PHASE OF SIX SIGMA

■ Do—*Make problem statements as specific and fact-based as they can be.*
  • Focus on what is observable and confirmed, not on suspicion or assumptions.

AutoRec Order-to-Delivery SIPOC Diagram

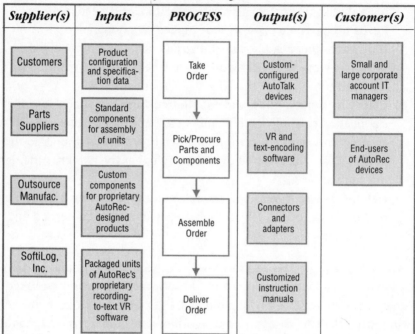

Supplier(s)	Inputs	PROCESS	Output(s)	Customer(s)
Customers	Product configuration and specification data	Take Order	Custom-configured AutoTalk devices	Small and large corporate account IT managers
Parts Suppliers	Standard components for assembly of units	Pick/Procure Parts and Components	VR and text-encoding software	End-users of AutoRec devices
Outsource Manufac.	Custom components for proprietary AutoRec-designed products	Assemble Order	Connectors and adapters	
SoftiLog, Inc.	Packaged units of AutoRec's proprietary recording-to-text VR software	Deliver Order	Customized instruction manuals	

FIGURE 14.5   AUTOREC ORDER-TO-DELIVERY SIPOC DIAGRAM

■ Do—*Use the charter to set direction and to gain agreement on the problem, goal, and project parameters.*
  • Take the time to address questions or uncertainties with the team and sponsors *early* to help smooth the path for the project.
■ Do—*Keep the charter "visible" and revise it as needed.*
  • It is a tool to keep things focused, and maintain a "living document."
■ Do—*Listen to the voice of the customer.*
  • Six Sigma is all about customer-focused improvement. Even efficiency-enhancing projects need to pay close attention to value and impact on customers.

■ Don't—*Describe suspected causes or assign blame for the problem.*
  • A key to Six Sigma improvement is the assumption that you do not know the cause of the problem, even if you have some guesses.

Define Checklist ✓

1. Define

Instructions:

If you can respond "yes" to each statement, you are off to a good start with your project and are ready to move into the measure phase of DMAIC.

For our project we have ...

1. Confirmed that our project is a worthwhile improvement priority for our organization and is supported by business leaders.   YES   NO

2. Been given (or written) a brief project rationale explaining the potential impact of our project on customers, profits, and its relationship on the company's business strengths.   YES   NO

3. Composed and agreed to a two- to three-sentence description of the problem as we see it (the problem statement), focusing on symptoms only (not causes or solutions).   YES   NO

4. Prepared a goal statement defining the results we are seeking from our project, with a measurable target (or placeholder to add one). No solutions are proposed in the goal statement.   YES   NO

5. Prepared other key elements of a DMAIC team charter, including a list of constraints and assumptions, a review of players and roles, a preliminary plan and schedule, and a process scope.   YES   NO

6. Reviewed your charter with our sponsor for this project and confirmed his/her support.   YES   NO

7. Identified the primary customer and key requirements of the process being improved and created a SIPOC diagram of the areas of concern.   YES   NO

8. Prepared a detailed process map of areas of the process where we expect to focus our initial measurement.   YES   NO

Exhibit 14.2   **DEFINE CHECKLIST**

■ Don't—*Overpublicize preliminary goals.*
- It is okay to set ambitious targets as long as they do not lead to false expectations.

■ Don't—*Over-"wordsmith" the charter.*
- Easier said than done, because people like to get the wording of these statements "just right." Taking a long time, however, can kill enthusiasm and commitment.

- Don't—*Get mired in process detail.*
  - A basic high-level view of the process is essential, but usually is enough at the beginning of the project. Create detailed process maps only where that extra information will be immediately useful.

The "Measure" Phase of DMAIC: Baselining and Refining the Problem

Measurement is a key transitional phase, one that serves to validate or refine the problem and to begin the search for root causes, which is the objective of the analyze phase. Measure addresses two key questions:

1. What are the focus and extent of the problem, based on measures of the process and/or outputs (commonly called the "baseline measure")?
2. What key data may help to narrow the problem to its major factors or "vital few" root causes? (*Note:* For some background information on how to execute measurement, see Chapter 13.)

Let's begin by seeing how AutoRec plans to measure its problem.

Case Study #11 Continued: AutoRec Plans for Measurement

Prior to their next meeting, Al, the AutoRec team leader, sent an e-mail asking each member to bring along some ideas as to what measures would best build understanding of the delivery problems. The team posted and grouped the measures into two broad categories: Output and Input/Process. After eliminating duplicates, their list looked like this:

Output Measures:
- Number of defects by type of defect
- Proportion defective and yield (overall, and by customer type)
- Output Sigma

Input/Process Measures:
- ▶ Discrepancies between order form and final shipment
- ▶ Cycle time per major process phase
- ▶ Pulse rate of shipping staff on last day of the quarter
- ▶ Time between ordering and receipt of parts
- ▶ Average days that parts inventory are on hand

Unfortunately, the team realized, existing data on defective deliveries and the customer complaint forms did not have enough detail to really help them narrow the problem. They therefore had to develop a new data collection plan.

"If we can see whether the specs on the order forms are the same as what's shipped," noted Daphne from assembly, "we'll know if it's a mistake in the order-taking or somewhere later in the process."

By the end of the meeting the group decided to focus on three measures. Over the next few days, subgroups of the team developed a description of the purpose and operational definitions for each:

- ▶ Delivery Defects: This measure actually would identify a variety of factors, including date of delivery, type of delivery defect (four categories or opportunities), product type (e.g., microcassette or digital memory), customer type, and salesperson.
- ▶ Process Cycle Time: The team decided to follow a sampling of orders through the entire process and to gather cycle time data for each phase. For this task, they created a simple "traveler" check-sheet to be attached to the documentation that followed each job from order entry to shipment.
- ▶ Order/Shipment Discrepancy: For this measure, the team was able to use existing ("historical") data from bad deliveries. They were checking to see, as Daphne had suggested, if the orders were wrong or if somehow the problems were arising during the process.

Measurement Choices

Decisions on what to measure are often difficult, both because of the many options available as well as the challenge of collecting data. In process improvement efforts, the need to collect data in several phases is one of the main reasons that projects can often take months to complete. Every team needs to make its measurement choices carefully. Sometimes it is not possible to do the measures you would *like* to do, so the ability to find alternatives or else make the best use of the data you *can* gather is important. Over time, improvement projects will tend to go faster as measurement choices and resources improve. Part of the art of Six Sigma is to base decisions and solutions on enough facts to be effective and to learn how to better use data over time.

Let's see how AutoRec handled data gathering and interpretation.

Case Study #11 Continued: Gathering and Interpreting AutoRec Data

It took the full month allotted in their preliminary plan for the team to gather data on their three targeted measures. They were fortunate, because the data collection period covered the end of the first quarter of the year, so they could see how the process performed during both calm and busy cycles. (They knew it was important for data to be representative of how work levels and other factors vary over time.)

Here are the conclusions they drew from each of the measures:

▶ Delivery Defects: The data gathered on this key output measure (actually, several measures) was compiled in a spreadsheet. As Elena from procurement noted, "There are lots of things we could look at in this data!" For the time being, though, they developed two views of the data:

1. The performance of the process was determined to be a DPMO of 122,800, or 2.7 sigma.
2. Defect data was broken down by type and displayed on a Pareto chart. This chart revealed that most of the problems were related to incompatibility, with hardware problems showing the most incidents.

▶ Process Cycle Time: Average cycle time, from order entry to delivery, was found to be 17.3 days. A breakdown of the time involved in the major process steps (from the SIPOC diagram) showed that the largest amount of that time was devoted to order assembly: 11.6 days.

► Order/Shipment Discrepancy: For this measure, the team was able to make use of existing data on defective deliveries. They checked to see whether the orders themselves had been done incorrectly or if the problems were arising somewhere later in the process. The data were conclusive: For about 93 percent of the defective orders they examined from the previous four months, the order specification sheets (OPS forms) were different from what was actually shipped to the customer. They also checked a significant proportion of those to find that the OPS forms were accurate—that is, the information did reflect the proper customer configuration.

Altogether, the data gave the AutoRec team a much clearer picture of the problem and helped them to narrow their focus as they begin the search for root causes of the defective deliveries. They were able to update their problem statement based on the findings in measure:

Forty percent of orders delivered to AutoRec corporate clients are not meeting customer requirements, including 30 percent for hardware and software incompatibility problems. These defects hurt our image, create customer dissatisfaction, and cost us roughly $350,000 per month to rework rejected orders. Continued high levels of delivery errors threaten our position as a leader in this growing industry."

The Transition from Measure to Analyze

The main requirement, before declaring yourselves ready to begin the analyze phase of DMAIC (described in the next section of this chapter), is to have at least one solid, repeatable measure confirming and often clarifying the problem or opportunity. This measure should be the one you repeat during and after solutions are implemented to track the effects of your improvement. Another common result of measure is a new, more sophisticated set of questions about your problem. Those questions are a good sign: They show you are thinking about how you can *investigate* the problem, versus just coming up with off-the-cuff solutions.

Before we move on to the next phase (analyze), Exhibit 14.3 recaps the essential "dos and don'ts" of the Measure phase, and Exhibit 14.4 provides a checklist you can use to help you through this phase of DMAIC.

Exhibit 14.3

"DOS AND DON'TS" FOR THE MEASURE PHASE OF SIX SIGMA

■ Do—*Balance output with process/input measures.*
 • Make sure you are tracking impact on the customer and end product/service, even if your focus is on boosting efficiency.
■ Do—*Use measures to narrow the problem.*
 • Try to find the most significant components of or contributors to the problem, so that your analysis and solutions will be well targeted.
■ Do—*Anticipate what you will want to analyze later.*
 • Try to reduce the cycles of data collection by gathering facts that will help you to find the root cause.

■ Don't—*Try to do too much.*
 • Even though you want to get a jump on analyze, don't get greedy and try to measure too many things at once. Focus on the measures that you are pretty sure you will use and that you can complete in a reasonable time frame (one week to a month is a good rule of thumb).
■ Don't—*Skip the key steps in measurement.*
 • Taking the time to create good operational definitions, collection forms, sampling plans, and so on, and testing your measures before launching them avoid worthless data and frustrating remeasures.

The "Analyze" Phase of DMAIC: Becoming a Process Detective

Analyze is the most unpredictable of the DMAIC phases. The tools you use and the order in which you apply them will depend a lot on your problem and process and on how you approach the problem. Like

Measure Checklist

2. Measure

Instructions:

If you can respond "yes" to each statement, you are doing well with measurement and are ready to move into the analyze phase of DMAIC.

For our project we have ...

1. Determined what we want to learn about our problem and process and where in the process we can go to get the answer. **YES** **NO**

2. Identified the types of measures we want to collect and have a balance between effectiveness/efficiency and input/process/output. **YES** **NO**

3. Developed clear, unambiguous operational definitions of the things or attributes we want to measure. **YES** **NO**

4. Tested our operational definitions with others to ensure their clarity and consistent interpretation. **YES** **NO**

5. Made a clear, reasonable choice between gathering new data or taking advantage of existing data collected in the organization. **YES** **NO**

6. Clarified the stratification factors we need to identify to facilitate analysis of our data. **YES** **NO**

7. Developed and tested data collection forms or checksheets that are easy to use and provide consistent, complete data. **YES** **NO**

8. Identified an appropriate sample size, subgroup quantity, and sampling frequency to ensure valid representation of the process we are measuring. **YES** **NO**

9. Prepared and tested our measurement system, including training of collectors and assessment of data collection stability. **YES** **NO**

10. Used data to prepare baseline process performance measures, including proportion defective and yield. **YES** **NO**

Exhibit 14.4 **MEASURE CHECKLIST**

a detective story, you can try to anticipate what will happen next, but often as not you will be surprised. One of the most valuable lessons of the Six Sigma approach, in fact, is that the "usual suspects" (the causes you *think* are at the root of the problem) often turn out not to be "not guilty," or else just accomplices to the *real* culprit. (Hey, we're on a roll with this detective thing!)

When your teams and business leaders see their hunches go wrong a time or two, it teaches everyone to be wary of assumptions and educated guesses. Do not *ignore* past experience or intuition, but to rely on them alone can let the real criminals go free to cause further problems. (End of detective analogy.)

The Root Cause Analysis Cycle

We can represent Analyze, as applied in process improvement, as a *cycle* (see Figure 14.6). The cycle is driven by generating and evaluating hypotheses (or educated guesses) as to the cause of the problem. You can enter the cycle either at point (a) by looking at the process and the data to identify possible causes, or point (b) where you *start* with a suspected cause and seek to validate or refute it through analysis. When you find a hypothesis is not correct, you may have to go back to the beginning of the cycle to come up with a whole new explanation. But even "incorrect" causes are actually opportunities to refine and narrow your explanation of the problem.

As the analysis cycle diagram in Figure 14.6 indicates, two key sources of input determine the true cause of your targeted problem:

▶ **Data Analysis.** Use of measures and data—those already collected or new data gathered in the Analyze phase—to discern patterns, tendencies, or other factors about the problem that either suggest or prove/disprove possible causes.

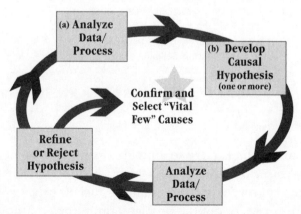

FIGURE 14.6 THE ROOT CAUSE HYPOTHESIS/ANALYSIS CYCLE

▶ **Process Analysis.** Deeper investigation into and understanding of how work is being done to identify inconsistencies, disconnects, or problem areas that might cause or contribute to the problem.

These two strategies, combined, produce the real power of Six Sigma analysis. Independently, either can give you a pretty good idea of a likely root cause, but your knowledge will always be lacking unless you can bring data and process findings together.

The two biggest mistakes in analyze, for process improvement teams, are the following:

1. To shortcut the cycle prematurely, declaring the suspected cause "guilty" and moving to solutions without sufficient evidence, much like convicting the wrong person.
2. To get stuck on the cycle, never being convinced you have sufficient data and never mustering the confidence to apply solutions to the most probable cause.

It is especially important at the early stages of Six Sigma to avoid these two extremes. With practice, a team can develop good habits and a good sense of what is enough, but not *too much*, analyzing of the problem. As we work through analyze and look at the AutoRec team's story, we will explain how you and your teams can try to avoid these pitfalls.

Case Study #11 Continued: AutoRec Prepares Its Initial Line-Up of Causes

"In our Six Sigma workbook," Ravi, from order administration, reminded the team at their next meeting, "it says there are two major strategies in analyzing a problem: examining the process or examining the data. Which should we use?"

"That's not an either/or question" was the response. It came from Martin Wyck, the coach working with the team who was sitting in on the meeting. "It's usually better to look closely at both the data and the process," he added. "You can get clues from both sources, and when the clues match up you really learn about the problem."

"I'll buy that," Ravi agreed, and the rest of the team concurred. They had trouble, however, agreeing which to do first: delve into the data or look at the process in more detail.

However, at the suggestion of Elena from procurement, they decided to start not with data or process analysis, but with a list of possible root causes to consider. Using a cause-and-effect diagram, the team brainstormed all the possible causes that might create the high level of bad deliveries. They then narrowed the list down to several prime suspects or, more technically, causal hypotheses. Perhaps:

▶ Order specification forms were being entered incorrectly into the procurement system.
▶ Parts vendors were mislabeling items, so that the wrong connectors and adapters were being packed into the shipments.
▶ Errors were being made when shipments were rushed out to meet delivery deadlines.
▶ Assembly staff, being hired at a rate of several dozen per month, were not adequately trained and were mixing up digital and tape-recording devices.
▶ Shipments were being mixed up at the dock, mislabeled, and sent to the wrong customer.

"But these are just guesses!" commented May from sales.

"That's true," responded Coach Martin. "What you've done is put some of your hunches down on paper. So now, you can look at the data and the process to see whether those hunches make sense. But the real cause might be something not even on this list."

To take their analysis further, the team divided up their assignments: three of the members would work on a more detailed process map of the procurement, assembly, and shipping activities, while the other four looked more deeply into the data they had already collected.

A Starting Point for the Root Cause Cycle: The Cause-and-Effect Diagram

The AutoRec team chose a common way to begin their analysis: by developing a list of potential causes or causal hypotheses. The tool they chose—the cause-and-effect or fishbone diagram—has for years been one of the favorites for quality teams, and still is used by Six Sigma improvement teams. Cause-and-effect analysis lets a group start with an effect—a problem, or in some cases a desired effect or result—and create a structured list of possible causes for it. Benefits of the cause-and-effect diagram include the following:

▶ It is a great tool for gathering group ideas and input, being basically a structured brainstorming method.
▶ By establishing categories of potential causes, it helps ensure that a group thinks of many possibilities, rather than just focusing on a few typical areas (e.g., people, bad materials).
▶ It helps get the Analyze phase started. Using a cause-and-effect diagram to identify some "prime suspect" causes, as the AutoRec team has done, provides the focus to help begin process and data analysis.

The cause-and-effect diagram also brings us back to the issue of *variation* that we introduced back in Chapter 2. We noted that a business process has variation of two types. Upstream from the customer (in the inputs or process), we call factors of variation "the Xs." The downstream or output variation that is the result of the changes in the Xs we call "the Ys." We can apply the same principle of X and Y to the cause-and-effect model: the "effect" or problem is the Y, and the possible root causes that appear are the Xs.

As shown in Figure 14.7, six major factors typically cause variation in a business process, sometimes called the "5Ms and 1P":

▶ *Material*—the consumables or raw inputs that are used in the process
▶ *Method*—procedures, processes, work instructions
▶ *Machine*—equipment, including computers and nonconsumable tools
▶ *Measures*—techniques used for assessing the quality/quantity of the work, including inspection
▶ *Mother Nature*—the environment in which the work is done or that affects any of the other variables; may include facilities, not just the natural environment
▶ *People*—bipedal primates native to most continents on earth; reportedly show signs of intelligence

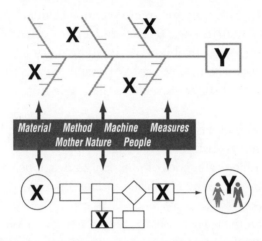

FIGURE 14.7   PROCESS MAP AND CAUSE-AND-EFFECT
DIAGRAM SHOWING CAUSES OF VARIATION
IN UPSTREAM (X) AND DOWNSTREAM (Y) FACTORS

As we move deeper into root cause analysis, we will likely be examining all of these potential causes of variation so as to target the so-called vital few Xs, or causes, that contribute most to the problem. Before we do that, though, let's take a closer look at AutoRec's process, from procurement through shipping.

Case Study #11 Continued: The AutoRec Process, Defined

Nine people were in the conference room on the morning set aside to build a complete process map of the AutoRec process from procurement through shipment. One or two representatives from each area involved in the process had been invited to attend, to ensure broad input into the map.

"We want to look at the process 'as is,'" explained team leader Al of product design. "We'll be checking this with other people, so it doesn't have to be perfect, but we definitely do not want to describe the process the way it ought to be done, or the way the execs think it's being done."

It actually took two two-hour meetings to create the full map of the process. Between the sessions a preliminary draft was created (using a process-mapping software program) and circulated for feedback, which led to some corrections.

One interesting part of the process involved the links between procurement and assembly. Procurement's strategy has been to keep a month or more of stock on hand in the case of small items like connectors and adapters as well as software packets, because they are not expensive and do not tie up a lot of capital in inventory, which leaves them time to focus on ordering more complex custom parts like recording-device components.

In assembly, for each order received, a "kit cart" is prepared with bins for all the items needed, based on a bill of materials generated by the computerized configuration software. For each order, a "twosome" is assigned primary responsibility for ensuring that the materials get delivered on time. After the kit cart is ready, the twosome pulls all available inventory of key components for the recording devices and submits an order to procurement for any items not available. Because volume has grown so dramatically and continues to increase, almost every order requires a special purchase of items for the recorders.

For the smaller items such as connectors and adapters that are kept in quantity, supervisors in the assembly storeroom check stock levels every week to see what is needed. When pieces are low, they e-mail a list of low inventory items to the procurement department for reorder.

Looking at the process, the group took note of the difference in how the two types of parts were being ordered, as something to look into further. One of the people from assembly in the meeting commented that some of the adapter and connector parts are always "on order," while others run out only rarely.

The other discovery from the meeting involved responsibility for and participation in getting shipments made on time. Although everyone at AutoRec knows the high priority the company has placed on on-time delivery, the folks in shipping seem to be most attentive to dates, and will check with assembly on orders when deadlines are getting close. "We go in and help them complete the kit carts pretty often," explained one of the shipping people. "We get a bonus every month based on the number of on-time deliveries, so we probably take it a little more seriously."

The We Deliver team members exchanged looks when they heard that comment, and after the meeting agreed that here might be a clue to the problem: Shipping people were involved in doing assembly's job.

A segment of the process map is shown in Figure 14.8.

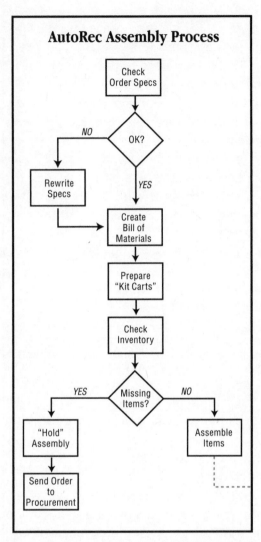

FIGURE 14.8   AUTOREC ASSEMBLY PROCESS MAP (PARTIAL)

Process Mapping and Analysis

Process maps are among the most essential tools of Six Sigma, in which improving, designing, measuring, and managing processes are the primary focus. The basics of a process map are simple: a series of tasks (rectangles) and decisions/reviews (diamonds), connected by arrows to show the flow of work. The AutoRec example is a standard business process map; later we will see some variations on the process map theme.

As you build process maps for your Six Sigma projects, you are likely to find that some of the most enlightening information comes right in the actual map creation sessions, as people start to hear about how work is done and processes managed in other parts of the business. When a process is documented and validated (i.e., checked with others who do the work to see if the map matches reality), you can analyze it for some of the following specific problem areas:

▶ **Disconnects.** Points where handoffs from one group to another are poorly handled, or where a supplier and customer have not communicated clearly on one another's requirements.
▶ **Bottlenecks.** Points in the process where volume overwhelms capacity, slowing the entire flow of work. Bottlenecks are the weak link in getting products and services to customers on time and in adequate quantities.
▶ **Redundancies.** Activities that are repeated at two points in the process; also can be parallel activities that duplicate the same result (e.g., entry of the same data into different departments' systems).
▶ **Rework loops.** Places where a high volume of work is passed back up the process to be fixed, corrected, or repaired.
▶ **Decisions/Inspections.** Points in the process where choices, evaluation, checks, or appraisal intervene, creating potential delays. These activities tend to multiply over the life of a business and/or process.

Let's see how AutoRec analyzed the data it gathered.

Case Study #11 Continued: Fun with Data Analysis at AutoRec

When the We Deliver subteam working on data analysis met to plan their approach, they started by looking at the list of possible causes to see how data might support or refute them. As a reminder, the initial hypotheses were these:

▶ Incorrectly entered order specification forms
▶ Mislabeled connectors and adapters being packed into the shipments
▶ Errors made due to the rush to meet delivery dates

► Untrained assembly staff, hired at a rate of several dozen per month, were mixing up digital and tape-recording devices

► Shipments being mislabeled at the dock and sent to the wrong customer

Because quantities shipped usually were accurate, the team ruled out mislabeled shipments as the root cause. "You'd expect to see the quantities to be all wrong," noted Ravi from order administration. "I don't think I've ever had two orders that wanted the exact same number of units."

The group agreed to look more closely at the largest category of defect from the initial breakdown: hardware incompatibilities. The team was able to construct a second-level Pareto chart focusing on the hardware incompatibilities, shown with the first-level, which showed the major issues involved incompatible connectors and adaptors (see Figure 14.9).

"But I know we're sending adapters and connectors," said Arnold from shipping. "This still doesn't explain why they're wrong."

One issue they investigated required some statistical analysis. A hypothesis suggested that the rush to get orders out was causing the problem. They first developed a histogram showing distribution of defective shipments, based on how many days before or after a scheduled delivery date the order was shipped to the customer (see Figure 14.10). Clearly, rushing seemed to be an issue. However, when they stratified the defective data by *type* of defect they found—using analysis of variance or ANOVA (see Chapter 17, page 368)—that the pattern for rushing was no different for hardware incompatibility than for any other type of defect. So, while "rushing" seemed to be a *general* cause of defects, it was not specific to the main problem they were addressing.

Logical Cause Analysis

Investigating the data surrounding a process improvement problem requires discipline, an open mind, and a mix (strange as it may seem) of logical and creative thinking. Armed with a pool of (accurate) data of the kind the AutoRec team has collected, you want to use the data, and other available facts, to surface new cause hypotheses or to objectively test existing hypotheses to see whether they fit the data.

Level One Pareto

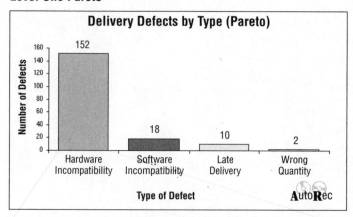

Level Two Pareto

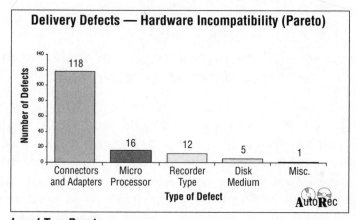

FIGURE 14.9   AUTOREC LEVEL 1 AND LEVEL 2 PARETO CHARTS

The method of logical cause analysis is an approach that all of us use intuitively, at least some of the time. For example, if a small child tells you, "Doggie ate cookies," yet you see crumbs all over his or her face, you are skeptical of the child's "hypothesis." Or if your car (SUV) won't start and the motor doesn't make a sound, but the lights, radio, wipers, power windows, and so on all work as usual, the evidence shows that the battery is *not* the problem. In both these cases what you *observe* (the facts) does not fit the hypothesis.

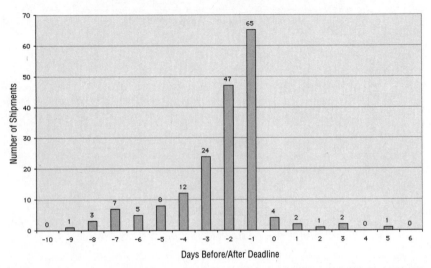

FIGURE 14.10 AUTOREC DISTRIBUTION OF DEFECTIVE DELIVERIES BY DAYS BEFORE OR AFTER DELIVERY DATE

The beauty of the logic-based approach (technically, deductive logic) is that you need not be an expert in a subject or technology to contribute to the narrowing down of possible causes. Another benefit of this logical cause analysis is its objectivity and emphasis on facts. The technique (it is also an attitude) is driven by questions and supported in most cases by stratified data about the process, problem, or product. (We already talked about gathering stratified data in Chapter 13—now we can see how to use it.) Typical logical analysis questions for you to pose when involved in a DMAIC project include the following:

► What types or categories of problems are more common? What is different about the most common types?
► Is the problem greater in specific locations (regions, places on the item itself)? How are those places where the problem occurs more unusual?
► What are the times, days, weeks, or conditions when the problem is most prevalent? During those times, what unique events were happening?
► What factors or variables change as the problem changes (or "correlate" with the problem)?

These and other questions support the analysis cycle by narrowing the problem, eliminating possible causes (an important step in finding the real cause), and/or validating hypotheses. If your team has not included stratification factors in your initial data collection, the ability to do this analysis will be more limited; as we noted, however, more than one round of data collection is not uncommon.

Visual Tools for Data Analysis

Often, the best way to learn from your data is to literally "see" the answers to the questions you pose. We already saw a couple of these visual data analysis tools in the AutoRec case; here we provide background and examples of four of the most common techniques and how they can be used: Pareto charts, histograms, run charts, and scatter plots.

Pareto Chart or Pareto Analysis. The Pareto chart is used to stratify data into groups from largest to smallest. A specialized form of bar chart, the Pareto chart helps you identify the most common occurrences or causes of a problem. To use a Pareto chart, however, you need to make sure you have discrete or category data; it does not work with measures such as weight or temperature (i.e., continuous data). Pareto analysis is based on the "80/20 rule"—the notion that 80 percent of the costs or pain in an organization are created by just 20 percent of the problems. The numbers are not always exactly 80 and 20, but the effect is often the same. You can use a Pareto chart in the following ways:

▶ Sort problem data by region, and find which region has the most problems.
▶ Compare defect data by type, and see which defect is most common.
▶ Compare problems by day of the week (or month, or time of day), to see during which period the problems occur most often.
▶ Sort customer complaints by type, to see what the most common complaints are.

Histogram or Frequency Plot. Histograms are used to show the range and depth of variation in a group of data (aka "population"). A histogram technically shows continuous data only, while a frequency plot can display discrete counted data (e.g., numbers of defects). Both show data along a continuum or increasing quantity on the horizontal

(x) axis and the number of occurrences/observations on the vertical (y) axis. In process improvement, groups of data on the continuum are displayed as a bar chart; the more classic view of a histogram, though, is the bell-shaped curve. You can use a histogram or frequency plot to:

▶ See the range and distribution of continuous factors (e.g., weights for each shipment; dollars spent per purchase; size of each hole; reboot time for each computer).

▶ See the variation and performance around a customer specification/requirement (e.g., size, cycle time, temperature, cost; *note:* continuous factors only).

▶ See how many defects occur on each unit in a group of defective items (when there are multiple opportunities for error; may include discrete characteristics).

▶ See how key "count" characteristics in a group or population are distributed (e.g., customers by number of purchases per year, suppliers by score on our quality audit).

Run Chart or Time Series Plot. A run chart shows the variation in a process, product, or other factor *over time*, which is a valuable tool for understanding processes that are, by nature, ever-changing. The run chart (also called a "trend chart" or "line graph") and its cousin the control chart show how things change from moment to moment, day to day, and so on, making them the best tools to track ongoing activity or performance. In structuring a run chart, the horizontal or x axis is *always* the time or sequence of occurrence moving from left to right. The vertical (y) axis can represent any continuous or count measure, including percentage, number of defects, and temperature. As each observation, or sample of observations, is made, it is noted in the proper time-order at the value observed.

You can use a run chart or time plot to:

▶ See the degree and pattern of variation in a process or product over time (e.g., how much difference there is in test data from day to day; or how much variation occurs in process cycle time from item to item).

▶ Identify possible timing patterns in variation (e.g., Is there a weekly cycle? Do certain events seem to match changes in the process?).

▶ See how a process or key factor is responding to change (e.g., how process improvements are impacting performance; how the new phone system is affecting caller hold times).

Scatter Plot or Correlation Diagram. The scatter plot shows the link or "correlation" between two factors that vary by count or on a continuum. Scatter plots show potential causal relationships between one factor and another. As a simple example, daily high temperatures and ice cream sales would tend to be correlated: It is reasonable to conclude that hotter weather causes people to buy more ice cream. It can be dangerous, however, to assume that a correlation guarantees that one factor causes the other. For example, chlorine sales at pool supply stores may increase as ice cream sales do (i.e., they are positively correlated); but we're pretty sure one doesn't cause the other. Another cause—hotter weather, perhaps?—happens to affect both.

Nevertheless, scatter plots can be a great tool for you to use to test the links between the suspected causes of a problem. A strong correlation can be a good indicator that your hypothesis is valid, as long as you apply common sense when drawing your conclusions.

You may find several types of correlation:

▶ **Positive correlation.** Mentioned already, in this relationship an *increase* in one factor tracks with an *increase* in the other.
▶ **Negative correlation.** In this case, an increase or decrease in one factor matches the *opposite* effect in the other.
▶ **Curvilinear correlation.** This scatter plot version of "what goes up, must come down" means that for some factors a positive or negative correlation may exist up to a certain point, at which it actually turns into the opposite.

In cases of *no* correlation, the points will literally be scattered all around the chart like a cloud, and a change in one factor has nothing to do with a change in the other. You can easily measure the strength of the link between two factors statistically with the formulas built into most spreadsheet programs.

You can use a scatter plot or correlation diagram to:

▶ See the degree to which one factor's increase in value or performance is linked to the increase or decrease in another.
▶ Test the relationship between a suspected root cause of a problem and the level of the problem (defects, costs, etc.).

Let's see how AutoRec is doing with its data and process analyses.

Case Study #11 Continued: AutoRec Brings Together Data and Process Knowledge

Back at AutoRec, two subteams had been working on process analysis and data analysis for the delivery defects problem. The full team then convened to share the subteams' findings. They realized they had not yet gotten to the true root cause of the problem, but they were ready to formulate some more refined hypotheses. They noted the most revealing facts so far:

1. The most common defects in deliveries were due to incompatible connectors and adapters, accounting for about 60 percent of the bad deliveries.
2. Connectors and adapters were being carried in inventory, not ordered on a just-in-time basis. Ordering for those parts was triggered when the storeroom in assembly noticed that stock was low.
3. Defective orders tend to be those shipped just before the due date; however, all types of defects occur in the same pattern, indicating that rushing alone is not the reason for the high level of adapter/connector incompatibilities.

A couple of suspected causes—order entry mistakes and mislabeled shipments—had been eliminated. Inadequate training of the assembly staff did not appear a strong possibility, and the team felt that other problems would be found that were not seen in any of the data.

A heated discussion about what to do next ensued. A couple of members wanted to simply tell customers they would get their orders a little later, and lengthen the lead time that sales promised for delivery.

The other view was expressed by Al, the team leader. He noted that the company might be hurt even more in the long run if it slowed delivery time just to cut defects. "If TalkNBox can fill orders faster than we can when their products come out, it will become important to customers, and we'll be left in their dust."

Finally, two "next steps" were agreed to:

1. Al would confer with Pat DeLia, the team's sponsor, to get an executive perspective on the problem and on the issue of delivery cycle times.
2. The team would think about the problem and bring other ideas on where to go next with their analysis to a half-hour update meeting the following day.

Narrowing Down the Root Causes

The next day, Al brought feedback from the team's sponsor to the group. "Pat was pretty adamant that we not lengthen delivery commitments," he said. "It'll reduce our capacity in the long run, and we're still looking at significant growth if we can keep our edge on TalkNBox. So we really need to figure out why the connectors and adapters are wrong so often." The next person to speak up was Elena from procurement: "I've been thinking a lot about this. One thing we haven't thought about is that we never had this level of rejected deliveries a year and a half ago, when the AutoTalk systems first came out."

"So what's different now from back then?" Al asked. "I mean, other than we have more people and more customers and might be out of business in six months if we don't figure out this problem."

"That's easy," said May from sales. "The product mix."

"Right!" said several people at once. May pulled out a brochure and opened it to a chart that broke down AutoRec sales between tape and digital memory recording devices. It showed that as sales had grown, tape devices had slipped from being almost 80 percent to now being about 30 percent of total units shipped (see Figure 14.11).

"So if the mix has changed," asked Ravi from order administration, "how would it cause our problem?"

Daphne and Mike from assembly explained that the connectors and adapters for the two types of products are different, though in a plastic bag it can be hard to tell them apart. After some more discussion, they came up with a new root cause hypothesis:

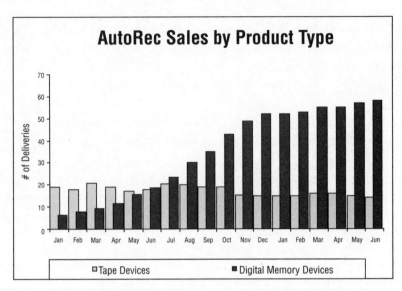

FIGURE 14.11 AUTOREC TREND CHART OF TOTAL SALES STRATIFIED BY PRODUCT TYPE

Connectors and adapters for tape media recording devices are being mistakenly shipped with digital memory devices, making them incompatible with the recorders and causing customers to report unusable deliveries.

"But wouldn't we know that?" asked Ravi, a little incredulously.

Daphne and Mike again explained to the team that when a shipment is reported "defective," they immediately go to work to reassemble and ship it correctly. "To be honest, we haven't had time to do a postmortem to figure out what the real problem was," Mike explained. "When the returned items come back from the customer, the returns groups just puts anything that is still usable back in inventory."

"How can we test this cause?" Al asked the group.

"Easy," said Arnold, "if the wrong connectors are going in with digital memory units, those are the ones that should be involved in the bad deliveries." Arnold volunteered to use their spreadsheet to do a comparison by product type. Meanwhile, Elena from procurement, who had been quiet for a while, said she was going to check out another hunch.

The End of the Detective Trail

Arnold's chart brought applause from the team (see Figure 14.12). "I guess that settles it," said Al. "Or does it? I'm still not clear on why the wrong cables are going into the shipments."

"I told you I had a hunch," Elena from procurement spoke up, "and I was right. We place orders for connectors and adapters with our MRP [Materials Resource Planning] system based on a usage forecast. Turns out the forecast is only updated every four months, so we always order a lot more tape device parts than digital."

After more discussion, all of the pieces fell into place; it turned out many digital unit orders were being held up in assembly because of the shortage of correct connectors and adapters. As the delivery deadline approached, and shipping became more insistent about getting the orders ready, they would "help" in assembly and—innocently, but ignorantly—include the wrong parts to complete the shipment. Out the shipments would go—on time, but destined to be rejected because the connectors and adapters would not work.

"This is a great example," someone commented, "of how when a problem is big enough, there's plenty of blame for everyone."

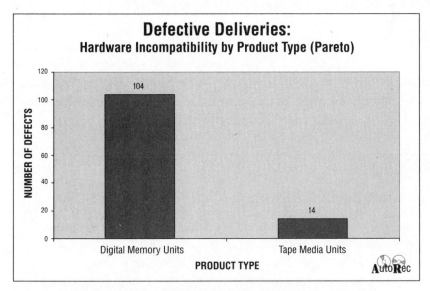

**FIGURE 14.12   AUTOREC DEFECTIVE DELIVERIES
BY PRODUCT TYPE (PARETO)**

Completing the Analyze Phase

It is impossible to be absolutely certain about a root cause. Here are some final steps that will help you to confirm your causal hypothesis and move into the improve phase:

1. **Verify the cause through logical analysis.** Test the cause against the data you have gathered and ask: "Does this explanation fit the facts, including both what we see *and* what we don't see happening?"
2. **Check the cause through observation.** Visit the process or the place where the cause is suspected to be happening to see whether you can watch it in action.
3. **Confirm your suspicions with people who know.** Talk to people involved in the work—customers, suppliers, or subject matter experts—to get their validation or refinement or rejection of your hypothesis.
4. **Apply the confidence test.** As a team, see whether you can reach consensus on the following questions:

   ▶ Are we comfortable that we understand enough about the process or problem and its root cause(s) to develop effective solutions?
   ▶ Is the value of further confirmation of our conclusions worth the additional time, resources, and momentum?

If your answers are "Yes" and "No," respectively, you are ready to move on to the Improve phrase, discussed in the next section of this chapter. But first, Exhibit 14.5 lists the "dos and don'ts" to keep in mind during the analyze phase, and Exhibit 14.6 provides a checklist you can use to help you through that phase.

Exhibit 14.5

"DOS AND DON'TS" FOR THE ANALYZE PHASE OF SIX SIGMA

■ Do—*Carefully state your suspected causes (i.e., hypotheses).*
  • Avoid the tendency to describe suspected causes vaguely or too briefly (e.g., "Bad training," "Defective parts"). General cause statements are not only hard for people to understand, they are difficult to disprove. Rather, create a clear *explanation*

of the factors you suspect, and how you think they cause the problem.

- Do—*Be skeptical about your hypotheses.*
  - The real cause should fit with the data and the process. If it does not, resist the temptation to bend the data to fit; instead, consider what other causes or other facts may be involved.
- Do—*Apply common sense and creativity.*
  - Statistical techniques have their role, but not as big a role as the ability to ask good questions, recognize patterns and trends, and challenge cause assumptions by setting up logical tests, which can take some creative thinking.

- Don't—*Overanalyze.*
  - The degree and depth of analysis should be adjusted based on benefits and risks.
- Don't—*Underanalyze.*
  - Too many shortcuts, or failure to understand the process, can lead to solutions that either *miss* the root cause or solve one problem while creating others. If you really understand the process and problem, you can move to solutions. If not, consider more investigation.

The "Improve" Phase of DMAIC: Generating, Selecting, and Implementing Solutions

All the work of defining, measuring, and analyzing problems pays off in the improve phase, *if* your team and organization handle it well. Lack of creativity, failure to think solutions through carefully, haphazard implementation, organizational resistance are all factors that can squelch the benefits of a well-intentioned improvement project. Fortunately, after the "spade work" of investigating a problem is through, most teams find new energy when they begin to ask the questions that drive the Improve phase:

- ▶ What possible actions or ideas will help us address the root cause of the problem and achieve our goal?
- ▶ Which of these ideas form workable potential solutions?

► Which solution will most likely achieve our goal with the least cost and disruption?

► How do we test our chosen solution to ensure its effectiveness and then implement it permanently?

Analyze Checklist

3. Analyze

Instructions:

If you can respond "yes" to statements 5 or 7 and have done many of the tasks described in the other statements, chances are good you are ready to begin developing solutions in the improve phase of DMAIC.

For our project we have ...

1. Examined our process and identified potential bottlenecks, disconnects, and redundancies that could contribute to the problem on which we are focusing.   YES   NO

2. Conducted a value and cycle time analysis, locating areas where time and resources are devoted to tasks not critical to the customer.   YES   NO

3. Analyzed data about the process and its performance to help stratify the problem, understand reasons for variation in the process, and identify potential root causes.   YES   NO

4. Evaluated whether our project should focus on process design or redesign, as opposed to process improvement, and confirmed our decision with the project sponsor.   YES   NO

For Process Design/Redesign:

5. Ensured that we understand the key workings of the process so we can begin creating a new process to meet the needs of the customer efficiently and effectively.   YES   NO

6. Developed root cause hypotheses to explain the problem we are solving.   YES   NO

7. Investigated and verified our root cause hypotheses, so that we are confident we have uncovered one or more vital few root causes that create our problem.   YES   NO

Exhibit 14.6 **ANALYZE CHECKLIST**

We suggest it is important during the Improve phase to look for ways to *maximize* the benefits of your efforts. If your limited solution can help remedy other issues, you should take that advantage, as long as the risks are acceptable. Too often, teams apply *narrow* solutions when they might have achieved more with just somewhat greater creativity and a broader perspective. Let's see how AutoRec addressed this problem.

Case Study #11 Continued: AutoRec Generates Ideas for Improvement by Brainstorming

"In our workbook," Ravi of order administration spoke up at the team's next meeting "it says the best way to start the Improve phase is to come up with a lot of ideas of how to solve the problem, and then use those to develop workable solutions." (Ravi had become something of a DMAIC process expert and several times had helped keep the team on-track by reminding them of key steps.)

After a 20-minute brainstorming session, the team had about 40 ideas, including some pretty good possibilities. But they wanted more input. Daphne from assembly recommended they try a billboard approach to get other people's input. "We've been so close to this problem for a while, I'm not sure my creativity is really good."

Martin the coach offered to post flipchart paper in strategic spots around the three AutoRec buildings to get ideas from other AutoReckers (what employees call themselves). At the top of each poster he wrote: "How do we stop shipping the wrong connectors and adapters in customer deliveries? Give us your ideas!" It worked. After three days they had 40 more suggestions.

Idea Generation, Objectives, and Methods

A Six Sigma organization, empowered with systems to understand customers and measure processes, can be a great place for creative thinking. Ideally, new ideas stretch the envelope, provide new perspectives on how we work, and pose challenges—and they can be a lot of fun.

Unfortunately, people at work are used to being rather practical, which is okay when you are implementing a solution, but not so cool when you are trying to think "outside the box." Here are some of the basics of effective idea generation and ways to help you broaden your thinking, even in the practical environment of a DMAIC project.

Keys to Brainstorming Success

1. **Clarify the objective of your brainstorming.** Unless everyone has the same purpose in mind, ideas will be a jumble. Another important objective is quantity, as well as quality. Setting number targets (e.g., "let's generate 30 ideas in the next five minutes") can help boost the numbers of ideas and raise the odds of a breakthrough.
2. **Listen to and build on the ideas of others.** Brainstormers need to pay attention to other people's ideas and not get totally wrapped up in their own thought processes. The spark of one person's suggestion may light a larger creative flame in another's brain, but not if no one is listening.
3. **Prohibit judging, criticizing, or commenting on ideas.** This key to success may be the one most frequently missed. However, the typical brainstorming session—one idea, followed by five minutes of discussion—tends to keep the really new ideas at bay.
4. **Avoid self-censorship.** The most insidious, evil form of judging ideas happens in *your own head*! Most of us are conscious of how our ideas make us appear to others. Remember, however, that your "goofy" idea may be the spark for another person's genius. (In brainstorming statistics, we call that "an assist.")
5. **Abandon assumptions and be wild.** Being completely uninhibited is easier said than done, of course. Remember, though, that you can take time for the practical and analytical considerations later in the Improve phase. Doing the same old thing will not get you to Six Sigma.

Other practical considerations for idea generation include the following:

▶ **Time and place.** Avoid times of low energy or high distraction, or places where people will tend to think more practically.
▶ **Participation.** Usually more is better (up to a point, of course), so expanding to include other groups and individuals is quite common.

On the other hand, people may be less free with their ideas when the boss is in the room.

▶ **Understanding of the idea development process.** People will be more comfortable if they understand how you plan to narrow and synthesize the ideas into workable solutions.

Once you are loaded with ideas, great and not-so-great, the next challenge is to turn them into real *solutions*. Let's see what AutoRec did with its new ideas.

Case Study #11 Continued: AutoRec Narrows Down Its List of Improvement Ideas

A veritable blizzard of sticky notes was plastered across the We Deliver team's meeting room—ideas from their brainstorming session and the billboards they had posted around the hallways. The team first eliminated redundant ideas, then used the affinity method to silently organize the remaining ones.

What emerged were five broad categories of ideas:

1. Changing frequency of updating the MRP system (This one, everyone agreed, was a no-brainer.)
2. Changing the performance incentives for on-time delivery
3　Broadening the responsibility for preparing shipments
4. Reorganizing the assembly storeroom
5. Improving the ease of telling tape media parts from digital memory parts

Through a round of "multivoting," in which each person voted for several of his or her preferred ideas, the list was narrowed to about 12 ideas.

"I don't think we can do all of these," said May from sales.

"Absolutely not," agreed Al. "If we go to the leadership team with a laundry list like this, we'll get tossed out." Ravi, ever-watchful of the DMAIC process, suggested they try combining ideas into some more coherent solutions. The group agreed to think and confer informally for a couple of days, and then get back together to try to hash out a final solution on Thursday.

AutoRec's Improvement Plan Comes Together

At their next session, all of the team members had fresh input on the various ideas still under consideration. Eventually those were boiled down to two main options, which they called their "solution statements."

Option 1. To eliminate hardware incompatibilities in shipments to corporate clients, change the MRP formula for reorder quantities of connectors and adapters to match the current product mix. Also, change the labeling on connector and adapter packaging to make them easier to identify.

Option 2. To eliminate hardware incompatibilities in shipments to corporate clients, include all parts—including connectors and adapters—in the just-in-time ordering system, eliminating all product parts from the assembly storeroom. Change performance criteria so that procurement, assembly, and shipping personnel are all evaluated on meeting delivery schedule correctly.

The team soon began calling the two solutions the "safe option" and the "risky option," as the second choice clearly involved more substantial changes. They set up the following list of selection criteria, to help them choose the most appropriate solution:

- ► Cost to implement
- ► Cost to operate
- ► Ease of implementation
- ► Likelihood of achieving project goal
- ► Additional/long-term benefits
- ► Buy-in from the organization

Setting up a criteria matrix, the team compared their two options. The implementation and operating costs between the two were about the same. While Solution 1—the safe option—was clearly easier to implement, the team was not convinced it would achieve its goal or offer the benefit of addressing some of the other defective delivery issues, such as software incompatibility. And although changing performance criteria was a potential area to meet some resistance, they felt they could get people in procurement, assembly, and shipping to understand the need for the changes.

"We're going to have to work a lot harder to make Solution 2 work," Elena from procurement said, "but it is basically a much better solution. Option 1 is more of a Band-Aid."

Because AutoRec's leadership team was meeting the following day, most of the team members stayed late that night, preparing an initial implementation plan while Al finished work on a presentation of their recommended solution to the senior managers. By 10 a.m. the next day, they had the go-ahead to convert to the just-in-time ordering and work out new performance criteria across the three key order fulfillment functions.

Synthesizing and Selecting Solutions

Ideas generated in the Improve phase are like raw material: They need to be refined to have real value to the organization. Usually, Six Sigma solutions will be combinations of ideas that together make up a plan for results, whether it is reduced defects, faster cycle times, or enhanced value for customers. It is important to recognize that solution selection may not be an either/or choice. Combining several actions into one plan is okay. On the other hand, a "shotgun" solution that sprays many different mini-fixes at the problem can be a big waste of resources.

The *solution statement* provides a clear description of a proposed improvement. The value of the solution statement is that it ensures a thorough definition and understanding of the idea under consideration. We recommend that your teams consistently create these statements to ensure that solutions have been well thought through. The solution statement becomes the project objective once you choose a solution to be implemented. It also becomes the last of the four key statements a DMAIC team should create in the course of a process improvement project (problem statement, goal statement, hypothesis statement, and solution statement).

A criteria-based choice is a way to show the rationale behind a recommended solution, which is why Al of AutoRec was able to get the senior managers' approval so quickly. A cost/benefit analysis can be incorporated into the decision process as well.

Now let's take a moment to summarize the key steps leading up to a final DMAIC solution:

1. **Generate solution ideas.** Use brainstorming, common sense, and other techniques (i.e., best practices analysis, expert input, etc.) to create a broad array of possibilities to deal with the root cause.
2. **Narrow options and create solution statements.** Refine the ideas into workable approaches that can be implemented in the process/ business. Describe them in a formal statement.
3. **Select the solution to be recommended/implemented.** Review your short list of options and identify the solution to be implemented to achieve your goal. Be aware that other potentially terrific solutions *may* be put on a plan for later implementation.

Implementing Improvements

This midpoint in the Improve phase is a major threshold for a team. After what are usually weeks of talking, measuring, and analyzing, they are finally going to *do* something. Depending on the nature of the solution, a team may need other knowledge and resources. The atmosphere changes from one of reflection to one of action.

Even though the potential benefits increase as actual improvement gets closer, the risks increase as well. To launch solutions successfully, you should focus on planning, piloting, and problem prevention:

▶ **Planning.** Changing or fixing a process demands strong project management skills. Having a solid implementation plan that covers actions, resources, and communication is key, and more critical as the complexity of the solution increases.
▶ **Piloting.** Trying solutions on a limited scale is a must. The chances of unforeseen problems are high, and the learning curve can be steep when changing to a new way of doing things.
▶ **Problem prevention.** Asking tough questions such as "How could this thing crash and burn?" can seem like negative thinking when you are in the midst of an exciting improvement project, but it is key to ensuring that your team has thought through as many

possible difficulties as it can and is prepared to deal with them proactively.

Let's see what AutoRec did to implement effective improvement.

Case Study #11 Continued: AutoRec Puts the Solutions in Place

The AutoRec team got busy right away on planning for their solution. Realizing that their proposal had two major elements—switching to just-in-time inventory (JIT) and developing the new performance criteria—they set up two parallel implementation teams. The original project charter had included an IT support liaison person, Bob Megabyte, but the performance criteria changes clearly would call for some help from human resources. Thus the vice president of HR agreed to let Bonnie Fitz, one of the most experienced people in the HR group, become part of the implementation team.

Each implementation team put together a plan to pilot its solution. For the JIT effort, one vendor of adapters was chosen to try out the new ordering and delivery procedure for a two-week trial. After addressing the initial bugs, the procedure was working well. The main challenge was getting people in assembly and procurement, and the vendors, to get used to a new way of handling the adapters. Once AutoRec's people had gone through the change with one vendor, though, they were more comfortable with making the switch for other vendors.

Because their biggest fear was that a vendor would not meet AutoRec's short-turnaround delivery commitments, procurement and assembly agreed to have a backup supply on hand so the new system would not cause even more late or bad deliveries if it did not work. (They only had to use the backup connectors for one shipment, and after a while were able to eliminate the spare supply.)

For the new performance criteria, one of the problem prevention techniques chosen was to let AutoReckers have input into the new system. Because many of the people already knew of the havoc created by bad deliveries, they were open to change. In fact, one of the suggestions was to measure not just on on-time delivery but actual speed of order fulfillment. The plan was begun first in assembly, where it went well. Within a month the new guidelines and performance criteria were in effect for all three groups.

Measuring Results at AutoRec

The We Deliver team continued to measure delivery defects during the planning and piloting effort. It was interesting to see that, once the cause of the problem had been uncovered, some improvement happened right away. As each element of the solution was rolled out, the level of defective deliveries dropped sharply, as the team's run chart showed (see Figure 14.13).

Other reasons for defective deliveries were reduced, too. The level of coordination between procurement, assembly, and shipping increased substantially as they were all given a clear, common performance standard: Get orders out as early as possible, but get them done right. Informal teams—helped by the data the We Deliver team had developed—started to look into other causes of bad shipments. They were able to change some of their procedures to avoid those issues, and rush shipments eased up somewhat as well. With the reduction in incompatibility defects and other benefits, the DPMO for the process was cut from 122,000 to 39,000—a Sigma level of about 3.3.

Concluding the Project

With results beyond even their ambitious goal, the We Deliver team was a proud group. They worked with managers in the key functions affected by the project to transition the improvements to their responsibility. However, because we will be talking about the Control phase later, we leave the AutoRec group to enjoy their postproject party (complete with DJ) and their new commitment to Six Sigma improvement.

Completing the Improve Phase

It can take a while to test solutions, measure results, and ensure the success of a DMAIC project. A final, critical element of the implementation is to capture data to track the impact of the changes as they take effect, both to tally the results and to look for and respond to any possible glitches. Before we move on to the next chapter, Exhibit 14.7

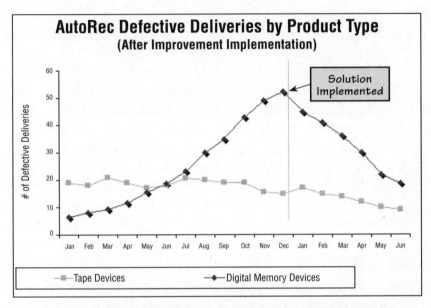

**FIGURE 14.13   AUTOREC RUN CHART SHOWING DEFECT
LEVELS BEFORE/AFTER DMAIC SOLUTION**

lists the "dos and don'ts" you should keep in mind during the improve
phase of DMAIC, and Exhibit 14.8 provides a checklist to help you
through this phase.

Exhibit 14.7

"DOS AND DON'TS" FOR THE IMPROVE PHASE OF SIX SIGMA

■ Do—*Look for really innovative solutions.*
- Every Six Sigma project is an opportunity to take your business performance to a new level. Even though process design/ redesign is usually the approach that yields exponential improvement, any solution can be a home run.
■ Do—*Target your solutions.*
- Keep your goal in mind at all times. Guard against let the thrill of brainstorming and developing solutions lead you into other changes that do not directly impact the problem you have been assigned to address.

- Do—*Plan carefully and proactively.*
  - Rushing to implement a solution can undermine all your efforts. Processes are stubborn, and people are creatures of habit. You have to approach any solution with the realization that it will work only if you do it right the first time.
- Do—*Pay close attention to change management.*
  - By the time the improvement team and leaders are ready to implement a solution, everyone will be fully familiar with or even tired of the problem and process. But remember that for many others, the need to change is often just *beginning* to be understood. You should be working to build support well before implementation, but now is when you often need to be more focused on gaining buy-in and helping people through the transition.

- Don't—*Move to full-scale implementation too fast.*
  - Failure to manage risks and build learning opportunities into your implementation can lead to disaster. Find ways to test or pilot your change so you can assess results, identify and work out bugs, and build confidence in the people doing and managing the work. You can recover from small setbacks and manage limited problems; you may *not* recover if your solution backfires on the organization.
- Don't—*Forget to measure.*
  - Measures help you see what is working and what is not; they prove your results, and they convince others that this improvement stuff, well, it's okay! Without measures, your results are only anecdotes and your successes a matter of opinion.
- Don't—*Forget to celebrate successes.*
  - Successful improvement can be a thrill. Share it and enjoy it when it works. And remember: Small wins count, too!

If Your Company Isn't AutoRec

And of course, it isn't. The story we told and the one on process design/redesign found in Chapter 15 reflect just some of what an improvement project is like. Most projects are likely to encounter a few more bumps along the way than the We Deliver team did. On

Improve Checklist

Instructions:

4. Improve

If you can respond "yes" to each statement, you have achieved success with your improvement and are ready to plan to "control" your process/solution.

For our project we have ...

1. Created a list of innovative ideas for potential solutions.   YES   NO

2. Used the narrowing and screening techniques to further develop and qualify potential solutions.   YES   NO

3. Created a solution statement for at least two possible proposed improvements.   YES   NO

4. Made a final choice of our solution based on success criteria.   YES   NO

5. Verified our solution with our sponsor and received buy-in and the go-ahead.   YES   NO

6. Developed a plan for piloting and testing the solution, including a pilot strategy, action plan, results assessment, schedule, etc.   YES   NO

7. Evaluated pilot results and confirmed that we can achieve the results defined in our goal statement.   YES   NO

8. Identified and implemented refinements to the solution based on lessons from the pilot.   YES   NO

9. Created and put in place a plan to expand the solution, refinements, to a complete implementation.   YES   NO

10. Considered potential problems and unintended consequences of the solution and developed preventive and contingent actions to address them.   YES   NO

Exhibit 14.8   **IMPROVE CHECKLIST**

the other hand, many projects are simpler than theirs was, but just as many are more complicated. But more than on the details of this project, we hope you will focus on the *process* the team followed:

1. They encountered a problem and clarified it. *Define!*
2. They measured the problem and narrowed it. *Measure!*

3. They delved into data and the process, learned about the problem, and figured out what was causing it. *Analyze!*
4. They considered the cause and targeted solutions to eliminate the cause and achieve the improvement they committed to. *Improve!*

Amidst the plethora of tools, questions, and challenges, it really is as simple as that.

CHAPTER 15

Six Sigma Process Design/Redesign (Roadmap Step 4B)

The ability to create a new or wholly renewed process was described in Chapter 2 as a critical core competency for twenty-first-century organizations. To achieve world-class levels of performance and keep pace with market and technology changes, a range of change/improvement approaches, including thorough design/redesign, will be needed. This reinventing activity, which is focused on *exponential* versus incremental improvement, is our focus in this chapter.

The DMAIC process, applied to designing or redesigning a business process, can be revealed to you by asking a few key questions, listed in Exhibit 15.1.

Exhibit 15.1

KEY QUESTIONS TO ASK WHEN DESIGNING OR REDESIGNING A BUSINESS PROCESS

- *What is the extent or scope of activities that will be subject to our process design?*
- *What are the critical outputs, output requirements, and service requirements that the new process must be able to achieve? What new standards should the process be able to meet in the future?*

- *What internal performance goals are key to the success of the new process (e.g., speed, cost, ease of use, flexibility, etc.)?*
- *What will the new flow of work and assignment of responsibilities look like? How can we improve on our first-pass redesign?*
- *How will we test, refine, and transition to the new work process?*
- *How will we manage the organizational impact of a substantial change in how we accomplish this work?*

Before we look at how to answer the questions in Exhibit 15.1, though, let's explore some of the key issues relating to *why* and *when* process design/redesign is needed.

Benefits of Six Sigma Design

Six Sigma design includes tools to create new products and services, not just processes. In fact, several of the advanced Six Sigma techniques covered in Chapter 17 are commonly applied to creating high-performing, low-defect new products. For *process* design and redesign, our focus in this chapter, Six Sigma offers many of the following benefits:

- ▶ **Emphasis on value and customer.** Six Sigma process design/redesign emphasizes enhancing value to customers and making major strides in productivity, speed, and efficiency.
- ▶ **A scalable, focused method.** Redesign efforts under Six Sigma focus on specific segments of a business or on critical change opportunities, resulting in a smaller, more manageable design and redesign projects, rather than a sweeping overhaul of an entire organization. Also, more-focused design projects are easier to manage and faster to complete, though they almost always will be longer than process improvement projects.
- ▶ **Broader application of design/redesign efforts.** Making process design/redesign a standard part of the Six Sigma system allows for broader participation and a better range of ideas and skills. Again, organization-wide overhauls may look terrific at the 30,000-foot level but may not be practical when implemented. At the same time, people who are close to the process and accustomed to doing things a certain way may be unable to "think outside the box" in seeking new ways to design their work.

Process design/redesign success depends on a balance between break-the-mold creativity and practical implementation. Involving a broader range of people in your design/redesign efforts will help your business to learn that it must not just *fix* problems, but also *design* processes that work.

► **Applying technology wisely.** One of the often-cited drivers of an organization's performance improvement is information technology (IT). But IT change has proven to be a sharp double-edged sword, when it comes to streamlining processes and improving service to customers. The Internet, database technology, customer relationship management (CRM) systems, and the increasing processing power of computers have enabled many companies to better manage inventories, respond faster, tailor their offerings, and so on. In many cases, business processes have been completely redesigned so as to take advantage of technological capabilities.

The other edge of the technology sword, however, has been the tendency to take on huge systems-upgrade projects and to expect them to magically produce dramatically better business processes, a notion now proven to be overly optimistic. Complicated, corporate-wide IT solutions are, if nothing else, complicated (also expensive, risky, and challenging). The many stories of delays, frustration, patched-together fixes, and unmet needs in major IT projects signal that systems changes may be better off scaled down.

The link between Six Sigma process design and IT change is getting stronger, as companies find the two coming together naturally. At General Electric, Six Sigma design is now part-and-parcel of many IT efforts: any significant system or software implementation must be guided by GE's process design/redesign model. In fact, the corporate leader of GE's Six Sigma initiative in its first two years, Gary Reiner, was also the company's chief information officer.[1]

Getting Started on Process Design/Redesign

The decision as to when to take on a process design or redesign is usually not black and white. In the process redesign case study to be introduced in a moment, the team decides early on that they need to redesign an inadequate process. In other instances, however, it will be *during* the DMAIC effort that a team will decide (with sponsor approval) that a design or redesign is needed. Let's get the background on the case example, and then explore when to take up the banner for design/redesign.

Case Study #12: An Insurance Company Needs to Write Contracts Faster[2]

As companies have become more dependent on information technology, the risks of major system outages and crashes have become enormous. Previous Internet service disruptions show the potential liability for loss of service, not to mention potential lost information and revenue, and how they can threaten the very existence of companies in the technology business. Fortunately, a rule of the free market is: "Where there's risk, there's insurance."

In fact, fueled by demand from independent start-ups and new divisions of large insurance companies, IT outage and liability coverage has gradually grown into a big chunk of business for the insurance industry. One of the traditional insurance practices carried over into this new arena is the letter of agreement (LOA). When a large IT provider or major corporation is sold a policy for outage and liability insurance, the LOA is the document used to initiate coverage. It is not an official policy, but it lays out general guidelines for the insurance to be provided. Legally, after the LOA is complete, the insurance company has 12 weeks to complete the policy, which represents the formal, official contract.

The people at Computer Outage Liability Assurance (COLA) have been increasingly worried about the impact of the so-called 12-week limit. (COLA is an independently operated subsidiary of mammoth insurance leader, International Insurance and Indemnity [III], known in the trade as "Number Three.") A number of recognized issues pertain to the standard four-month policy-writing effort:

▶ The efficiencies of an 8- to 12-week contract-writing process are questionable. COLA CEO R. O. Biere (known as "Rute") has commented on a number of occasions: "My grandmother—may she rest in peace—could get a contract done in six weeks!"
▶ Legal issues that arise between the signing of the LOA and completion of the policy, including claims and disputes over coverage

terms, keep the COLA legal department on a permanent hiring binge and cost the company $2–$3 million per month.

▶ COLA customers are beginning to complain vehemently about the lag time between LOA and formal policy. Although some industries have not put up much fuss about the 12-week limit, in the IT business 12 weeks can cover two mergers and three product life cycles. Often, new LOAs are written for a client before the policy for a first one is ready. Even customers who filed no claims say they feel vulnerable with only semiofficial coverage.

▶ Insurance regulators are rumored to be considering cutting the 12-week limit, perhaps in half.

COLA's Process Improvement Projects

Over the past year and a half, COLA launched several projects in an effort to reduce the time it takes to get a policy completed. In each case, some progress was made: One project team, discovering that LOAs were being handled on a last-in, first-out basis, cut last-minute and late policy writing by about 20 percent. Another project changed the way its LOAs are written so that it will be easier to transfer basic terms to the formal policy.

Despite those efforts, the average time to complete a policy at COLA is still 10.4 weeks after the signing of the LOA, which is down from 11.2, but remains a long way from what customers are asking for.

Essential Conditions for Process Design/Redesign

The people at COLA face a dilemma that will become increasingly common for Six Sigma organizations: "Which approach to improving our business is best in this situation?" COLA's leaders *could* take an improvement-based approach; after all, they have been successful with earlier projects. On the other hand, the concern is that additional process improvement projects—even effective ones—will not be enough.

Business leaders often ask for a formula for deciding when to launch a redesign effort. Our honest answer is "Not available," because most often so many variables must be considered, from the scope of the process you want to change, to your willingness to undergo business upheaval,

298 THE SIX SIGMA WAY

to the urgency of the need for major performance gains. We can offer an assessment model, however, based on two major conditions—*both* of which must be met if process design/redesign is going to work. The next sections describe these conditions, then we look at how COLA, our case study company, deals with these conditions.

Condition #1: A Major Need, Threat, or Opportunity Exists

The benefit side of the design/redesign equation can emerge out of various sources or threats. Although some overlap occurs in the following sources of threats, these situations indicate a new process may be needed.

- ▶ **Shifts in customer needs/requirements.** Newly emerging needs, more stringent demands, and changes in the customer's market and industry all put pressure on your business to make dramatic changes in services, product features, delivery capability, and so on.
- ▶ **Demand for greater flexibility.** Increasingly segmented or individualized customer demands mean that your processes need to handle a wider range of needs and requirements. Your current processes may not be ready to meet a one-size-fits-one objective.
- ▶ **New technologies.** Whether they are perceived as a threat or an opportunity, your organization needs to accommodate those advances that affect your products and services. Note that new technologies may have nothing to do with your products or services themselves: Books are much the same as they ever were, but the Internet is demanding new processes among booksellers.
- ▶ **New or changed rules and regulations.** Deregulation played a huge role in processes in many industries over the past 20 years or so. New laws—the Americans with Disabilities Act, or the air and water pollution guidelines—had significant effects, too. Companies that respond to those changes quickly and decisively may gain a big edge.
- ▶ **Competitors are changing.** Others serving your market, or new entrants, may be tapping into needs or opportunities you missed. When the competition gains an edge, it may be time to look for ways to leap over them in terms of value, speed, or any other key competitive factor.
- ▶ **Old assumptions (or paradigms) are invalid.** This internal wake-up call draws attention to some of the elements noted already.

Sometimes the shifts in customer demands, markets, and technologies are observed by a business, but still not understood or heeded.

A sad anecdote will illustrate here. We worked with a once-successful high-tech firm that enjoyed a couple of years as the shining star in the technology universe before suffering a rapid and eventually fatal decline. One of the factors we observed just as the star began to fade: Their customer base had evolved from a self-sufficient, highly technical end-user to a more "average" nontechnical user. Despite that shift, the company had no dedicated customer support resources. The company's engineers, who were supposedly dedicated to all-important new-product design efforts, were constantly being pulled away to deal with existing customer issues. Meanwhile, a major new product was two years overdue. Yet no hint of an effort to change the situation was evident.

▶ **Process redesign is sometimes needed** to jolt the people and the assumptions that govern an organization out of their reverie or belief that things are just fine the way they are.

▶ **The current process is "a mess."** We like that phrase a lot more than a technical definition such as "The current process is not capable"—"capability" being a statistical definition—or "The process has reached its entitlement" (makes you want to respond: "Whatever!"). Statistical or technical assessments of a process alone cannot tell a business leader whether a process warrants redesign. For example, a woefully incapable process can in many cases be improved substantially through some well-executed improvements (i.e., not a redesign). Other processes—like the one at COLA—are so littered with problems or with old, ingrained ways of doing things that trying to just weed out root causes would be fruitless.

Condition #2: You Are Ready and Willing to Take on the Risk

The dangers of design/redesign are not trivial, but they can be managed. So the real question is "Are we ready and able to take this project to completion?" The following description indicates some of the requirements for taking on the added risk of a redesign effort.

▶ **Longer lead time for change is acceptable.** In many cases, designing or changing a process takes more time than you expect.

▶ **Resources and talent are available.** You cannot expect to just swap an old process for a new one. You need people on the redesign team who understand the customer, services/products, process, technology, and people. The chances of needing capital investment, new IT systems, and even the right new people increase whenever you take on a complete "rethinking" of your work.

▶ **Leaders and the organization as a whole will support the effort.** Consensus need not be total, because some resistance is guaranteed, but the ability to make a convincing case in favor of process redesign is a huge advantage. Leaders need to be ready to make painful choices, too, because new processes realistically may mean fewer people.

▶ **The risk profile is acceptable.** Significant change brings more chances for mistakes, opposition, technical problems, and so on. You should consider whether a more limited approach (e.g., a process improvement project) represents the safer bet.

Case Study #12 Continued: Moving to Redesign

COLA CEO Rute Biere and his top executives have been talking about the need to make more progress in shortening the policy completion process. "I think we have an opportunity," said marketing vice president Sal Sparilla. "Our latest voice of the customer data show a huge dissatisfaction among IT executives with our performance and with the way the whole outage liability sector is dealing with policy cycle time."

"I know there are a lot of problems in the policy-processing area," confessed the vice president of policy administration Di Edsota. "I can give you seven or eight projects we could launch today—but I still can't guarantee we'd achieve what we want. This 12-week limit is just ingrained in how this industry has been working for a long time."

The executive group was concerned, though, about the organizational trauma that might come from trying to remake the policy-writing process. The challenge of managing large-scale change was daunting, to say the least. Finally, though, the group agreed, or was compelled to agree by Rute Biere's strong insistence, to set up a team to explore a ground-up redesign. "It may be the only way," said Biere.

Since launching its process improvement effort a little over a year earlier, COLA had not done any process redesign projects. One new process had been created, to cross-market backup power systems as a joint venture with an equipment manufacturer. "That was easier, though," noted the director of the COLA Management Process (the name for their Six Sigma initiative), Juan Callorrí. "We weren't trying to replace an existing process with a new one."

At a meeting the following week, Callorrí brought a draft project rationale to the executive group.

Project Rationale

The information technology industry, our market, is driven by a need for speed. Unfortunately, the administrative activities at COLA and other insurers in the outage liability business have not yet responded to that critical need. Where our customers are asking for policies in days, we are taking over ten weeks. Even though that length is better than the industry average, we are vulnerable to either faster competitors or possible self-insurance by our customers.

We need to completely rethink and redesign our approach to getting policies completed and into the hands of our customers. In doing so, we can offer major benefits to our insureds and to prospective customers, improve our profitability, reduce frustration for our associates, and position COLA for faster growth.

In reviewing those words, several of the executives commented that the thought of cutting policy lead time dramatically was exciting.

"Yeah," said chief counsel Tom Collins, "but kind of scary, too."

The "Define" Phase: Defining the Redesign Goal, Scope, and Requirements

Case Study #12 Continued: COLA Forms a Redesign Team

When word got around that the policy development process was going to be redesigned, the reaction around COLA was mixed. Some people were pleased and felt it was an overdue decision; others either did not understand the reasoning or were just afraid of the change. Nevertheless a number of people came forward right away, to volunteer for the redesign team. The first choice was team leader: Toni Kwahter. Toni had been at COLA for two and a half years, and was well respected throughout the company. As a former underwriter, she had the core credentials for an insurance company, plus she had worked for several years at a network systems company and knew the mentality of COLA's customers. Her current position was as head of customer relations.

Working with Di Edsota, the vice president of policy administration, and with the consultant who would be advising the team, Art Glass, Toni selected a team that included a cross-section of the processes and functions in the company:

Bev Ehridge	Human Resources
Ike Scube	Underwriting
Bob Tull	Legal
Colleen Waters	IS (Information Systems)
Tye Neebublscz	Policy Administration

When the team met for the first time, Toni presented the project rationale and told the group they were in for a challenging effort. "There are a lot of people who'll say that what we want to accomplish—to get a contract completed fast—is either impossible or unnecessary. We're going to have to be change agents for the company, and as we put together our charter we want to be focusing on the opportunity we have to make a big impact on our company and especially on our customers."

The Design/Redesign Charter

The basic purpose of the project charter in a process redesign effort is the same as in an improvement project: to set direction and to define project parameters. The spirit of the design charter, however, should be somewhat different. Although the work of a process improvement team is to analyze and fix problems, in redesign the intent is more far-reaching: to design and bring to fruition a new way of doing key work in the organization. It may not be awe-inspiring to outsiders, but to people in the business, the sense of purpose should be strong. Without a vision, the level of creativity and energy the team exhibits may be weak and the new process only incrementally better than the old one.

Also, it is acceptable here for the problem and goal statements to be a little more vague, because the focus is often on more global rather than specific issues. Measures are still important, but a goal statement that is too concrete can actually *lower* the bar for the team. For example, to people with backgrounds in the technical side of quality, these ideas may seem to lack rigor. The rationale, though, is that the level of benefit being sought through Six Sigma design requires a sense of passion and purpose beyond what is typical for a process improvement project (though passion is a good thing for those teams, too).

Let's see how COLA began its define phase by crafting its problem and goal statements.

Case Study #12 Continued: The COLA Team Defines Its Problem, Goal, and Scope

The team at COLA decided they should give their project a name, to bring some focus to their activities. They agreed to "The Limit Busters" since they were trying to break away from the 12-week limit concept that had so upset their customers. It took longer to come up with problem and goal statements, but the final drafts were finished at the end of a tiring, day-long meeting:

Problem Statement

Completion of insurance policies for COLA clients takes an average of 10.4 weeks. While previous efforts to improve our turnaround have reduced the number of policies not meeting the industry-standard 12-week limit, we are still far short of the speed being demanded by our customers in the computer and networking industry. If we do not substantially reduce our policy completion time, we risk losing existing and potential customers to self-insurance or to faster competitors. Seeing a dramatic improvement in our processes is key to COLA's survival and growth.

Goal Statement

Our goal is to redesign COLA's policy completion process—from signing of the letter of agreement to execution of policy documents—to an average of 1.5 weeks by the end of the current fiscal year. In doing so, we will enhance COLA's competitive strength and profitability and set a new performance standard for our industry.

One of the initial decisions the Limit Busters team made in developing its charter was in relation to the project scope, which was incorporated into the goal statement in the form of the phrase "from signing of the letter of agreement to execution of policy documents," and quickly became one of the most controversial parts of the meeting.

"Can we really redesign that entire process?" asked Bev Ehridge from HR. "That's a huge amount of activity."

"No kidding," agreed attorney Bob Tull. "It seems like too much to get our arms around."

After several rounds of debate, Toni (team leader) asked the group's consultant, Art Glass, for his thoughts. "Well," he said, pausing reflectively and stroking his beard, "I'd say two things." He paused again. "Maybe three." (The team had been warned that Art was brilliant, but it took some time to get the brilliance out of him.)

"Number One, you may have to take on the entire process to meet your goal. After all, to cut four-fifths, or four-and-a-half-fifths, or even five-sixths of the time out of your process, you may need to look everywhere to cut time from the work. Number Two (he was picking up momentum now), you're right that it will be harder to manage a bigger scope—so you may want to narrow it some if you can. Number Three, which I guess I do have, you can adjust your scope later to meet the needs of your projects and according to the information gained through your further efforts.

"I'd recommend," he concluded, "that you leave it as is, and review or revise it as you get more data."

At that point the team felt much better about their draft and agreed to leave the scope as written for the time being. They also were glad to have had Art's input, though as one anonymous team member commented to another later: "We're lucky this is a nonsmoking building. Give that guy a pipe, and we'd be listening to him for hours."

The Project/Process Scope

The term *scope* generically describes the size of a problem or the breadth of a team's focus. In Six Sigma projects the term has a more specific definition; by "scope," we mean the *boundaries* of the process that the project team will seek to design or redesign. Thus the scope describes the playing field or the limits within which all process activities will be considered to be fair game for redesign. Defining scope can be useful in process improvement projects, too, because it can give a team guidelines on where their solutions can be implemented.

Selecting the *right* scope for a project can be the big challenge. As shown in the COLA team's goal statement, a scope is identified simply by naming the process(es) involved and specifying the *starting* and *ending* points of the steps to be redesigned:

▶ "We'll redesign the invoice payment process, from receipt of invoice through clearing of checks from our account."
▶ "Our scope for the new packing process will start with the labeling of filled product containers and end with palletizing for shipment."

Having a SIPOC diagram or a more detailed process map helps you to define the scope, because it allows a team to literally *draw* the process boundaries on the diagram.

The choice of scope is often a subjective judgment. Each of the preceding examples, for instance, could have been broader or narrower and still have been "correct." The debate that transpired among the Limit Busters team at COLA, then, is common; the scope can be and often is adjusted over the course of the design project.

The following paragraphs describe what steps to take and questions to ask, in order to help you clarify the scope of your project.

1. **Name the process.** It is better to *avoid* department names (e.g., "the sales process") so that you will clearly distinguish redesign (changing how work gets done) from reorganization (changing the reporting structure in a group or function). For instance, make it

    ▶ The "invoice payment process," not "accounts payable."
    ▶ The "service call dispatch process," not the "tech support process."

2. **Identify the end point.** The most important element of a process is its final product, service, or output. The best guideline is to define the end point where the "thing" being processed is passed on, completed, to the customer or next process. Ask the following questions:

   ▶ What is the key output of the process?
   ▶ Who is the customer?
   ▶ What is the best final step for us to consider within our scope?
   ▶ Can we realistically hope to redesign work activities up to that point?

3. **Define the starting point.** The next step is to clarify the upstream boundary of the process to be designed. If a clear trigger or initiating point for the process is clear (e.g., a customer call, a work order, receipt of raw materials or parts), the starting point can be easy to describe. In other cases, especially with internal process activities, it may be more subjective. Ask the following questions:

   ▶ At what point or with what action does the process begin?
   ▶ What key input or handoff would make a reasonable starting point?

4. **Test the scope.** As the boundaries of the process take shape, the team needs to be wary of describing an overly vast or too-narrow chunk of activities. The balance here goes back to our two generic criteria: meaningful and manageable. Ask the following questions:

   ▶ Do the boundaries as defined include the activities necessary to achieve our goal?
   ▶ Can we effectively design and manage all the activities within our current scope?
   ▶ If we change and improve these steps, will we truly be able to raise the bar of performance, efficiency, competitiveness, value, and so on?

Ensuring a Manageable Scope

One approach that fits well with today's need for speed and its constantly changing business environments is the staged redesign of a process. After establishing a vision and goals for the new-generation performance of an entire process, executives, process owners, and/or project teams can segment the design effort into stages in which a complete overhaul of the work process is undertaken in two or more successive (or, less often, concurrent) projects. For example, if your company needed to redesign its service delivery process so as to enhance global capability, the entire effort might be scoped into three stages: (1) service ordering, (2) order preparation, and (3) order delivery and completion.

Whenever you are tempted to take on a larger scope, remember the following rule: As the "width" of the process boundaries widens, complexity tends to grow geometrically. One of the challenges of Six Sigma design is that you are not changing *just* the process within the scope, but also potentially all the current inputs and interfaces in the project. A redesign project of fairly limited scope may have from two to eight key interfaces and various other minor ones. As you expand the boundaries, that number could grow dramatically. If input requirements change, you may need to renegotiate with many more suppliers, making the whole effort a lot more challenging.

Let's see what COLA's project scope looks like.

Case Study #12 Continued: Putting the Project Scope on Paper

The team at COLA reviewed their initial problem and goal statements with the company leadership group. They also included a SIPOC diagram of the policy completion process (Figure 15.1), which they were able to "borrow" from one of the teams that had completed one of the earlier process improvement projects.

Defining and Revising Process Outputs and Requirements

The most thrilling and inspiring process design/redesign stories come from the groups who took advantage of their projects to redefine their understanding of customer requirements—in some cases, even to change *customers'* understanding of their requirements. In this step, as in many of the activities of process design/redesign, a fundamental objective is to *question existing assumptions* about what's important, why it's needed, and how it can be accomplished. The trouble is, assumptions are hard to abandon.

COLA's Policy Completion Process

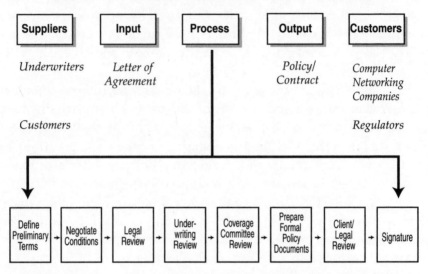

FIGURE 15.1   COLA'S POLICY COMPLETION SIPOC DIAGRAM

For example, we know of a training company that spent significant resources, including buying a printing operation, based on the assumption that customers "needed" high-quality, multicolor-printed training workbooks. In spite of an increased insistence on the part of clients for "custom" and "tailored" training, the firm kept printing materials in large quantities on traditional printing presses. A lot of the stuff ended up getting scrapped, because custom materials were usually used only in small volumes.

Finally, the company awoke to reality: Customers cared much less about color or fancy printing and much more about having training fit their specific needs. That delayed revelation enabled the training company to switch its production to demand publishing (printing small runs on black-and-white high-speed laser printers), close its warehouse, and sell the printing operation, all because what they had come to believe about what was important to training buyers was no longer valid.

Steps to Clarify the Output and Requirements

The output and requirements form the "reason for being" (or in the French, *raison d'être*) of the process. Over the course of the design effort, however, you will want to take the actions and ask the questions listed in Exhibit 15.2.

Exhibit 15.2

STEPS TO CLARIFY THE PROCESS'S OUTPUT AND REQUIREMENTS

1. Define and reexamine the process output. *Ask these questions:*
    - What is the current output or end product of the process?
    - Is this output still the best "thing" to fulfill the needs and objectives of the customer?
    - What other alternatives—products or services—might we offer instead, or how might the nature of the output be changed?
2. Clarify and scrutinize the key requirements of the output. *Ask these questions:*
    - What features or characteristics of the output make it usable by/effective for the customer?
    - What other features or characteristics are not being met?
    - What are the needs or changing requirements of our *customers'* customers that we can help them meet more effectively?
    - What other opportunities will make the product/service more valuable, usable, and convenient for the customer?
    - What lessons or other needs can we identify by understanding how the customer uses the output?
3. Review and retest output and requirements assumptions with customers. *Ask these questions:*
    - How can we check the validity of our, or the customers', assumptions about what is required?
    - What recent data confirm these requirements? Which pieces of data could be questioned?
    - Should different groups within the process "customer base" be addressed separately?

All of the questions in Exhibit 15.2 reflect our point that if you are going to break the paradigms on which your process is based, *now is the time to do it.* One of our colleagues has the groups involved in redesign efforts actually write out all their assumptions about a process on sheets of paper and then *tear them up*, to symbolize making a deliberate break with the past.

We wrap up this phase of DMAIC by looking at how COLA clarified the output and requirements for its processes. Exhibit 15.3 then provides a list of "dos and don'ts" to help you through your own process design/redesign work, so that we can move on to the Measure phase of DMAIC.

Case Study #12 Continued: The COLA Team Visits Customers to Learn How COLA Can Improve Its Processes

The Limit Busters team decided they would put some heavy emphasis, early in their project, on gaining a renewed understanding of their customers' computer system outage insurance and other areas where COLA could add value. They began by doing a thorough review of existing voice of the customer data, noting each key output and the requirements.

Next, the team scheduled a series of telephone and in-person meetings with the risk management staffs, senior managers, and legal departments of a cross-section of customers. Those discussions proved very enlightening. They began to realize that they might "delight" their customers not only by completing policies faster, but also by making the policy documents themselves easier to understand. They completed their define phase by creating a preliminary set of output design specifications for the policy completion process.

Exhibit 15.3

"DOS AND DON'TS" FOR THE PROCESS DESIGN/REDESIGN DEFINE PHASE OF SIX SIGMA

- Do—*Think* big *in terms of results, benefits, and scale of improvement.*
  - Inspired and enthusiastic people tend to be more creative and to persist in spite of resistance. The design team members need to view themselves as change agents.

■ Do—*Define a scope that balances opportunity with risk.*
  • You may gain more with a larger scope, but the complexity grows rapidly. Adjust the scope as needed during the project.

■ Don't—*Assume that the output and requirements are static.*
  • Use the design/redesign as an opportunity to establish new standards or even to change the solution delivered to customers.

■ Don't—*Wait to prepare the organization for change.*
  • A change management plan should be part of the initial work of a design/redesign team, in collaboration with the project sponsor and team leaders.

The "Measure" Phase: Establishing Performance Baselines

Few, if any, key differences separate the work of a team in the measure phase of process design/redesign from the process improvement projects. If anything, measurement can be simpler, because the objective of a process design is not to ferret out root causes but just to understand enough about the current process to ensure that the new one can achieve dramatically improved performance. As always, be sure any measure you decide to implement has clear objectives and value to the overall project goal.

Benchmarking and External Measures

External measures are one dimension of the Measure phase that can bring special benefits to a process design/redesign effort. (Process benchmarking is an option for improvement projects, too, but tends to have more applicability when the process itself is being revamped.) Benchmark measures help to establish a point of comparison between your performance and that of other comparable processes.

Often, the best candidates for benchmark measures are *not* your direct competitors. For obvious reasons, it can be hard to get them to share information. Moreover, industry "inbreeding" can see to it that the worst (not best) practices are replicated throughout a business sector. As you consider other places to gather data or conduct measures outside your organization, ask "Who does this *really* well, and how can we set a higher standard and learn *better* practices?" From an access and cooperation perspective, looking at other divisions, business units, or acquisitions *within* your overall organization may be a good source for benchmarking data, as well.

Defining Future Measures

One of the tasks of the Six Sigma design process that is often begun in the Measure phase is to establish measures to be used later in testing design options. Using requirements identified in the Define phase, you can develop specific measurable factors to be evaluated, using process simulation tools and/or methods such as design of experiments.

Setting up these measures early should not lock them in, but it helps to ensure that key requirements are met throughout the design effort.

Let's see how COLA tackled its Measure phase, then Exhibit 15.4 provides a list of "dos and don'ts" to help you through your own measurement work, before we move on to the Analyze phase of DMAIC.

Case Study #12 Continued: The COLA Team Measures Its Speed and Performance

The process redesign team at COLA already had good data on the overall output cycle time for the policy completion process. They realized, however, that if they were to gain a better understanding of the current process performance, it would help to have information on how that time was being used within the process. They also decided to add a new, previously missing measure, based on the new feedback from customers: length of policy documents.

The team formulated a data collection and sampling plan, using a traveler checksheet to get a view of how long each step in the process was taking. They hoped to be able to see whether document size had any impact on processing speed. With the data in hand, they were ready to push ahead into the Analyze phase.

Exhibit 15.4

**"DOS AND DON'TS" FOR THE PROCESS DESIGN/REDESIGN
MEASURE PHASE OF SIX SIGMA**

■ Do—*Ensure that you have solid baseline performance measures
for the process in all key requirements.*
  • As you confirm results and track performance of the new
    process, you will need to compare to the baseline data.
■ Do—*Look for information that will help you to identify
redesign opportunities, both inside the process and outside the
organization.*
  • The intent here is to find ways to build in those better
    performance practices that measures can help you to identify.

■ Don't—*Go on a hunt for root cause data when you plan to
redesign the process.*
  • Unnecessary measures not only can waste your time, but also
    can hamper creativity by burdening people with *too much* data
    about the current process.

The "Analyze" Phase: Building a Foundation for Redesign

In process *improvement*, the analyze or root-cause-finding stage is
pivotal. By contrast, once your organization or team has decided to
undertake the *redesign* of a process, root-cause analysis is no longer
critical. The objective instead is to create a new process that applies
new workflows, procedures, technologies, and so on to meet a significantly higher level of performance. Overanalysis can actually hamper
redesign by locking the current way of doing things into people's
heads. At the same time, as the COLA team discovered, some helpful lessons as to *how* a redesign might lead to a dramatic performance
improvement can arise during the Analyze phase. Let's take a look at
what the COLA team learned.

> ## Case Study #12 Continued: Dissecting the Baseline Data
>
> The measures the COLA team collected proved to be quite enlightening. As they suspected, the cycle time for most of the nine major steps in the policy completion process was in a tight range. They displayed the times per step on a bar chart (Figure 15.2). However, when they prepared a scatter plot diagram to look at the relationship between document length and total cycle time, the data were more revealing (see Figure 15.3).
>
> ### A Closer Look at the Process
>
> Despite the findings so far, a lot of skepticism remained among the team members who were not certain redesigning the process really could get them close to their goal of a one-and-a-half-week policy completion. After a longwinded preamble, consultant Art Glass suggested that the team do a "value and time analysis."
>
> "What's that?" asked Bob from legal, immediately regretting having tossed a question to Art.
>
> Fortunately, for Bob, Art's answer was surprisingly brief: "That's how you figure out how much of the work in the process is really important, and how much time you're spending on it."

Process Value Analysis

As processes get more complex, they tend to insulate people from the real reason that customers patronize a business. *Value analysis* is a way of reemphasizing the key *raison d'être* of a business or process by looking at work from the external customer's point of view. In the analysis, we assign each process step to one of three categories—value-adding, value-enabling, and non-value-adding activities—described in the following paragraphs.

1. **Value-adding activities.** These tasks or activities are valuable *from the external customer's point of view.* That last bit is critical, because almost any step can be justified in *someone's* eyes. "We do this because the boss wants it" does not mean that a task is adding value to the customer.

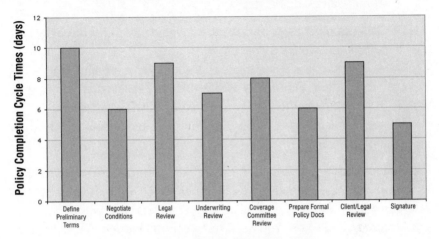

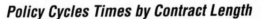

FIGURE 15.2   COLA POLICY COMPLETION
PROCESS CYCLE TIMES PER STEP

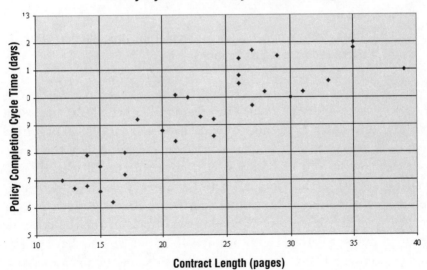

FIGURE 15.3   COLA SCATTER PLOT OF POLICY CYCLES
TIMES (Y) BY CONTRACT LENGTH (X)

Here are the three criteria you should consider in relation to taking customer-value-adding steps:

▶ The customer cares about and/or would pay us for this activity if s/he knew we were doing it.
▶ Some change is being made to the service or product. Hence, just moving things around is usually *not* value-adding.
▶ It is the first and only time we are doing it. (Fixes, rework, replacements, etc., only correct mistakes made before; they do not *add* value.)

2. **Value-enabling activities.** A class of activities that allow you to do work for the customer more quickly or effectively means that you can deliver products or services sooner, at less cost, with greater accuracy, and so on. You need to be careful, though, not to let all the steps that do not fit the value-adding category become value-enabling. The contents of this group are usually quite minimal.

3. **Non-value-adding activities.** These "rude awakening" aspects of a process add no value to the customer but seem to be numerous in most organizations. The kinds of activities that fit in this category include rework, as well as:

▶ Delays
▶ Inspections
▶ Reviews
▶ Transport (from one location or step in the process to another)
▶ Internal report and justifications
▶ Setup and preparation

The non-value-adding category can seem rather brutal. Because when you get right down to it, most of what happens in a typical organization does not, in the eyes of the customer, add value. You the reader (our customer) probably do not care that we purchased special book-writing software that sets off an alarm every-so-many-words to remind us it is time to say something witty. As far as you are concerned, you are paying for the value we offer, not for the costs we incur to make it better, right? It hurts to admit we may have wasted money on this software, but that is the harsh reality of non-value-adding activities. You can bet that a *lot* of things done in your company "in the interest of the customer" are things the customer really doesn't give a hoot about.

Balancing Value-Adding and Non-Value-Adding Tasks

Realistically, it would be a *bad* idea to eliminate every non-value-adding task. Filing tax returns, for example, or providing benefits to your employees, or backing up your computer files (all non-value-adding from the customer's point of view) is nonetheless in the best interest of your company if you want to stay in business.

As another example, take customer credit checks, which are a smart business practice to protect you from deadbeats and slow payers. They do not add value from the customer's point of view, but you probably will not want to abandon them. On the other hand, realizing that they really are *not* value-adding helps you to put those activities in perspective. You *could* speed up or even eliminate credit checks without much risk of customers complaining. And in fact, instant credit checks have become increasingly important in financial services, as companies look for ways to reduce a non-value-adding activity's impact on customers—while still, of course, limiting the business's risk.[3]

Value Analysis Steps

To do an effective value analysis, you need a detailed view of the process. Otherwise, the technique is fairly easy:

1. Identify and map the process to be analyzed.
2. Categorize each step, according to the criteria noted, as value-adding, non-value-adding, or value-enabling.
3. Compute the proportion of activities that falls in each of those categories, and review the balance between value- and non-value-adding work.

Let's see how our insurance company conducted a value analysis of its processes.

Case Study #12 Continued: The COLA Team Conducts a Value Analysis

It took the COLA team several days to prepare more detailed maps of the processes in the policy completion process. Next, they organized the process map into a deployment or cross-functional format, showing departments and the customer along the top, with process steps falling in the appropriate columns. At the right, they categorized each step as value-adding (VA), value-enabling (VE), or non-value-adding (NVA).

Their overall findings revealed that of 45 basic steps in the process, 4 were value-adding (8.9 percent), 2 were value-enabling (4.4 percent), and the remaining 39 steps (86.7 percent) of the tasks were non-value-adding. "I guess that makes sense," commented team leader Toni. "Insurance or risk protection is what we sell, not documents."

Colleen Waters from IS voiced the view that several of the non-value-adding steps were things they could not just eliminate without risk of prosecution under the law, and they still had not proved the process could be cut to 1.5 weeks.

"Well," agreed Toni, "we still need to factor in the time dimension."

Process Time Analysis

To the three categories of value analysis, we can add two aspects of time analysis to our understanding of the process:

1. **Work time.** The time actually spent *doing* something to the product or service as it flows on its way to the customer.
2. **Wait time.** The time the product or service spends waiting for something to be done. Imagine a bunch of parts, a stack of applications, or truckloads of product all sitting around twiddling their thumbs (if they had them) waiting for someone to come and work on or move them. This part of the process is also called "queue time," "staging time," or just "delay."

Time analysis can be another shocker if no one has paid attention to it before. It may not be news to you, but there is a *lot* of idle time in business processes. Where cycle-time improvement has been a priority, time analysis has been a tremendous benefit in cutting process turnaround to minutes instead of hours, days instead of months. The need for speed—from just-in-time delivery to rapid product cycles to time-based competition—has driven some of the most impressive improvements in corporations around the world over the past 15 years.

Let's see what our insurance company's time data analysis revealed.

Case Study #12 Continued: COLA's Time Data Analysis Reveals It Can Cut Its Policy Completion Process Dramatically

As the COLA process redesign group looked at time data from the perspective of the entire process, it became an even bigger revelation than the value analysis.

"Okay, I'm convinced," said Colleen of IS when she saw the figures. The team had done a ballpark estimate of the amount of actual work time needed for each step in the process, and then reviewed and revised their estimates by talking with people doing the work. When the team totaled all the possible time, they found that of the roughly 10.4 weeks (52 days) the average policy took to be finished, only about 8 days of that time was actual work time, or 15.4 percent of the total.

Factoring in the value analysis data was even more revealing: A big chunk of the work time was devoted to non-value-adding steps. Overall, they estimated that only 3 percent of the total time of the policy completion process was spent working on value-adding activities, or *less than two days*.

"Twelve-week limit, you are history!" exclaimed Ike from underwriting.

"Not so fast," cautioned consultant Art, in no danger of breaking any speed records himself. "You won't be able to just eliminate all the steps and idle time in the existing process and expect the current levels of performance to be maintained at an adequate level while keeping clear controls on the . . ." Anyway, the gist was that the real solution would come from rethinking how COLA could prepare policy documents, and find a way to do it under the new parameter of 1.5 weeks. The team agreed they were ready to start their design work.

Wrapping Up the Analyze Phase

Value and cycle time analyses are helpful tools you can use in process design projects to confirm or raise questions about the feasibility of achieving dramatic improvements in process efficiency and effectiveness. Some of the most powerful "*ahas*" we have witnessed arise when people see how much of their work and time actually is essential.

These techniques can also be useful in process improvement activities, or if a team is uncertain whether they should try to fix a process or redesign it.

As revealing as this kind of data can be, though, it needs to be used carefully. For one thing, you may not be ready to redesign the process; that means you cannot, as Art Glass said, just boot out all the non-value-adding work and declare wait time to be forbidden. Moreover, these non-value-adding tasks (some of which can be critical to the *company*) represent people's jobs. Telling a large percentage of the people working their tails off every day that their work is non-value-adding could create repercussions you would rather avoid—as we will see in what happened at COLA. Then Exhibit 15.5 lists the "dos and don'ts" to help you through your own analyze phase of Six Sigma, so that we can move on to the improve phase.

Case Study #12 Continued: Reducing Process Time Can Eliminate Jobs, and COLA Faces a Minor Revolt

"I'll just have to explain to people what's going on." COLA CEO Rute Biere was talking at an emergency meeting of the company's leadership group in the wake of sudden rumors of massive layoffs. "We won't gain anything by keeping quiet," he said.

Toni Kwahter, who was included at the meeting, spoke up: "It's possible we may have opportunities to reduce some head count, Rute. Isn't that still an option?"

"It may have to be, Toni," Biere agreed. "But I'm also expecting that the growth we can achieve, if you can come up with a faster process, will give everyone plenty of chances to stay on board. But we can't sugarcoat it, either: There may be some cuts—we can't have people sitting around doing nothing."

Policy administration VP Di Edsota (the redesign team sponsor), offered an apology: "Well, Rute, I have to confess that Toni and her team had asked me a couple of times to have you make a more direct announcement about the project and our possible plans. But I've not been as pushy as I should have been."

"You know," noted COLA management systems director Juan Callorrí, "I think lots of companies are going to have to deal with these kinds of issues more and more. When you become more proactive about improving your business—or staying abreast with customers and competitors—it means more change, more often. But we have to learn how to manage the implications better."

The following day, all associates at COLA received an e-mail from Rute Biere that read in part:

> To continue to grow our business and meet the increasing demands of our customers for fast response to their risk-management needs, COLA must solidify its policy agreements much more quickly, but with the same accuracy and professionalism on which our reputation has been based. The team now seeking to redesign our policy completion process has taken on the goal of cutting policy turnaround from more than 10 weeks to less than 2 weeks. Our intent is not to cut staff, but there is the possibility some positions will be eliminated in changing how we approach this important work. It is also possible we may add staff. I promise to do a better job than I have in keeping you all posted on this effort, and I ask for everyone's support on this initiative. If we succeed, it will mean significant new opportunities for COLA and all our associates.

Over the next few days, COLA senior leaders held a series of luncheon discussions with staff. Although some concern remained among the employees, the general mood became much more positive when the story behind the rumors was clearly explained.

Exhibit 15.5

"DOS AND DON'TS" FOR THE PROCESS DESIGN/REDESIGN ANALYZE PHASE OF SIX SIGMA

- Do—*Use process analysis to clarify the potential for redesign gains.*
  - Look for data to support your conclusion that redesign is necessary and for ways it can be done that will help you to achieve your goal.

■ Do—*Be ready to revise your plans based on what you learn.*
  • For example, if you find that a single solution will achieve big gains without the need for a complete redesign, change your focus. Don't redesign if you don't need to.

■ Don't—*Start analyzing every problem in detail.*
  • Keep a broad perspective on the process. The more you delve into specifics, the harder it may be to design without ingrained assumptions.

The "Improve" Phase: Designing and Implementing the New Process

Envisioning, designing, and then operationalizing a new work process can be an almost schizophrenic effort. The team needs to display different personalities as it tries to break down accepted norms and fears, identify new workflows and procedures, and then construct a new way of doing work that is practical, cost-effective, free of problems and rework, and shows quantum gains in performance. An extra challenge comes from the fact that your existing processes are comfortable to the people who work in them every day.

The best path for process design to follow, in light of these common fears and the multiple personalities required, is to alternate between the creative and the analytical, adding detail and refining the design as you go. The initial design phase is followed by the refinement phase during which more work is done to test, refine, and foolproof the process, and finally by the implementation phase where the process is put into full operation. Figure 15.4 presents a guide to the high-level set of steps for the improve phase, from design through implementation, then let's see how the insurance company in our case study developed its high-level map of the policy completion process that it wants to redesign.

Case Study #12 Continued: COLA Takes a High-Level View of the Process It Wants to Improve

A little shaken by the worries their project had aroused, the Limit Busters team spent the first part of their next meeting reviewing their project

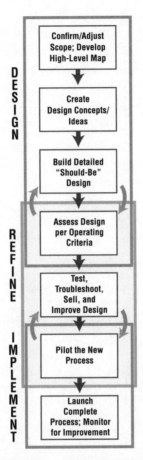

**FIGURE 15.4   PROCESS DESIGN/REDESIGN IMPROVE
PHASE HIGH-LEVEL STEPS**

charter and reaffirming the essential need to redesign the policy completion process from the ground up.

To begin rethinking the process, they decided to find an offsite location to help them get away from their thinking about how the process was done now. With the coaching of Art and Juan, they mapped out a process for their design work that included several rounds of creative design, followed by scrutiny and analysis, then implementation.

Early in the design discussions, the team agreed on one important feature of the streamlined process: the contract document itself would have to be dramatically simplified. "It wasn't part of our plan, but the effect of these 30-page contracts is pretty obvious. We can move things through faster and customers will be a lot happier with something they can maybe understand," said Tye from policy administration.

A shorter contract, of course, would have to be legally sound and acceptable under insurance regulations. The COLA legal department would have to be supportive, too, or the whole idea could be derailed. Bob Tull from legal volunteered to put together a separate contract redesign team; it was agreed he and Tony would meet with Di Edsota from policy administration and Bob's boss, chief counsel Tom Collins, to get their support for the contract revision subproject.

Other design principles or ideas the team discussed included:

- Limiting and/or eliminating reviews
- Creating more standard contract features as "building blocks" for policies
- Front-loading some decisions into the letter of agreement
- Taking wait time out of the process
- Electronic transmission of documents
- Assigning an "owner" or "coordinator" to each contract to be responsible for its timely completion

The final action in the offsite meeting was development of the high-level process diagram (see Figure 15.5). "We had eight steps and now we have four, so that's a start," noted Bev.

Essential Ingredients for Process Design

As a team begins to build the new process, it is important to check that all the right ingredients are in place. These elements are described in the following paragraphs, and although some of these are common sense, others may not be so obvious.

- **Clear goal, objectives, and/or vision.** These help the team see where you want the new process to be. They serve as a beacon, like the green-and-white signal light of a distant airport.
- **A well-defined process scope.** Any significant refinement in process/project scope should be checked with the sponsor and/or business leadership.

Revised Policy Completion Process

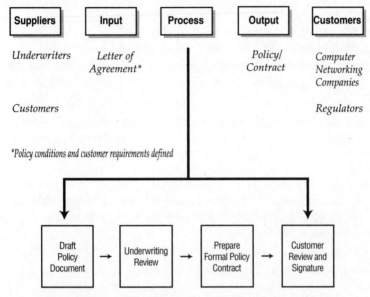

Suppliers	Input	Process	Output	Customers
Underwriters	*Letter of Agreement**		*Policy/ Contract*	*Computer Networking Companies*
Customers				*Regulators*

*Policy conditions and customer requirements defined

Draft Policy Document → Underwriting Review → Prepare Formal Policy Contract → Customer Review and Signature

FIGURE 15.5   COLA POLICY COMPLETION SIPOC DIAGRAM AFTER REDESIGN

▶ **Willingness to change the rules.** Unfortunately, the obstacles to new process ideas often are *unconscious* assumptions or beliefs about how things are or should be done. It can take a concerted effort by a team and by their colleagues who will live in the new process to overcome their old assumptions.

▶ **Creative thinking.** The ability to imagine and find ways to achieve a new level of performance can play a big role. So can creative borrowing of best practices from organizations.

▶ **Technical/implementation knowledge.** As ideas come into focus, the ability to assess their practicality and to make them a reality requires greater performance.

▶ **Assessment/operational criteria.** If the redesign goal is like an airport beacon, then evaluation and operating criteria for the new process are the airport's runway lights: They guide you to the right path for a smooth landing. Defining these criteria in advance can actually help people be more creative, by them giving guidelines and also the security of a good way to evaluate ideas.

▶ **Time.** To quote Thomas Paine: "Time makes more converts than reason." Having the time to think and to get comfortable with new approaches is essential to creativity and buy-in.

▶ **Trust.** Trust is a key principle and ingredient for process design success. For example, many non-value-adding process activities are based on the *possibility* that someone will make a mistake simply because we cannot trust them not to. But a basic premise of smooth process flow is that if people understand what is required of them, and have the proper support and skills, they *will* get the job done.

Case Study #12 Continued: By Adding Meat to the Bones, the New Process Emerges

The COLA group elected to work in two subteams to start building the new process flows. While one of the subteams went right to work mapping a "should-be" process on the wall, the other brainstormed ways to shorten the process time and still get contracts written with adequate input from customers to meet their coverage needs. ("Fast, but wrong, is not an option," commented Bob Tull.) As they developed their new process maps, both teams discussed whether each step was value-adding or value-enabling. Any non-value-adding steps were starred for later review.

Overall, several innovations were envisioned in the new process flow:

▶ Letters of agreement would include a coverage code corresponding to policy templates. The policy contract would be put together more quickly based on the codes and templates.
▶ Policy conditions (i.e., requirements of the client that ensure they will not be an undue risk) would also be defined in "packages." These packages would be described in the LOA so that policy completion would be able to simply include the correct conditions (if any) in the contract.
▶ A policy completion coordinator would be responsible for each new policy assigned to him or her. Each coordinator would work with no more than two sales/underwriter teams, to ensure consistent knowledge of the customer up and down the process.

► Each letter of agreement/new policy would be given a number at the beginning of the process, instead of in the middle as had been the practice. Policies could be tracked in the policy database, with cycle-time guidelines for each step in the process. Alerts would be issued if a policy missed a deadline.

► Legal staff review of policies would be eliminated, except for coverage over a certain amount (which represent a small percentage of policies).

► Meanwhile, a dedicated underwriter group—initially, two people— would be set up in the policy completion group to review questions that did not need to be presented to the customer.

► As already decided, policy contracts would be simplified, with a goal of an average length of eight pages. Review copies would be e-mailed to customers for review, with explicit guidelines and highlighted text to help them review the key points requiring their scrutiny. When the two subteams shared their ideas and merged their should-be process maps, they had reduced the number of steps in the process to 16 from 45.

Process Flow and Management Options

Depending on the product/service and work being done, many options can improve the performance of a process. Some principles that apply in process design situations are described in the following paragraphs.

Simplification. The fewer the steps and the more consistent the path, the better your ability to eliminate defects and control variation. You can have fewer "handoffs," fewer people ("too many cooks . . ." and all), and fewer non-value-adding activities. Simplification can be a reason to *avoid* automation when it is less complex to do work manually.

Straight-Line Processing. Arranging tasks in sequence will help you to avoid communication and coordination issues. The straight-line path is the easiest to track and manage.

A big disadvantage of the straight-line path, however, is that it can add time to the overall process by delaying the start of each task until the previous one is done.

Parallel Processing. Doing tasks in parallel, or concurrently, reduces overall process cycle time. For example, in a new product development effort, several components can be designed independently, then integrated into the completed product. The challenge of parallel flows is what you might call the "right-hand/left-hand" syndrome: Changes or decisions are made in one path of the process that the other paths do not know about. The result is a problem downstream in the process when the paths converge.

Alternate Paths. Preplanned flexibility in how work is done, based on customer needs, product type, technology, and so on, is increasingly important in an environment where every product or order is unique. Alternate paths allow you to handle work according to any number of factors. For example when you go to the hospital, you might take different "paths" to being admitted, depending on the urgency of your condition. The risk of having alternate paths, however, is in keeping track of and managing various ways to handle an item in the process.

Bottleneck Management. In almost any process are points where capacity or cycle time causes a slowdown or backup. In bottleneck management, the process flow is "widened" so as to streamline the entire process. But *beware!* Adding people or equipment may *not* be the best way to widen the bottleneck. Consider also how the product, service, or task/procedure could be changed to eliminate the slowdown. Also, be advised that eliminating one bottleneck may just create another one farther downstream in the process; bottleneck management needs to be undertaken with a "whole process" perspective.

Front-Loaded Decision Making. Because decisions can be challenging, the natural tendency is to defer them until later in the process. But that delay may force a lot of work to be based on assumptions that later are proven to be wrong. Pushing decisions upstream in the process can reduce the probability of rushed efforts or rework later. In our COLA project example, one of their design decisions is to require earlier clarification of policy terms and conditions—a front-loaded decision—so that the actual policy completion process can move forward unimpeded.

Standardized Options. This approach simplifies decisions yet still offers flexibility by defining a fixed number of options and preparing the process to handle them. The output of this design would be a semicustomized product or service. The number of elements to be selected will determine the number of possible end products.

One of the most familiar examples of this approach is found in the car business. Manufacturers offer a set of color packages and other options a buyer can choose from, but getting the beige carpet with the blue exterior may not be possible unless it is one of the packages. In a service example, the COLA team took this approach when they elected to establish set policy components to speed up completion of contracts.

Single Point of Contact or Multiple Contacts. These two ends of the customer-interface spectrum encompass infinite options. In the *single contact* option, a customer and/or order is assigned to a person or group that maintains responsibility for the item as it is processed. Another term for the responsible party is *case worker.* If you call a customer service number and are told to "always ask for Amy," you are dealing with a single-point-of-contact process. (Unless they have a lot of Amys . . .)

Multiple contact processes are usually backed up by strong customer and/or order tracking systems. They allow any person on the system to follow and respond to customer requests and questions. This, of course, is what happens when you key in your account number on the phone before talking to a service representative: if the system isn't down, they have your information ready to review before even saying "hello."

Summary of Process Flow Options. Some of the more common options you should consider when exploring process designs for your organization include variations that have been around for a long time. One of the most important advances in management thinking in recent years has been to define these options more clearly, and to allow for more conscious decisions about which approach works best for a particular organization or process. The most important question, of course, is "Which design will work best for the customer?

Methods of Reviewing and Refining the Design

A variety of useful techniques is available to help you evaluate and improve the initial process design. During this effort, more details and subcomponents of the new process can be developed as well. The following paragraphs describe some of the more helpful methods for the refinement phase. Most critical in all of these testing and refinement activities—and you should choose the ones that will be of most help to your project—is to learn from them and to adapt/improve the process so that it incorporates those lessons.

Process Walk-Throughs and Simulations. Even process "talk-throughs" are a good way to validate how things will work, surface possible problems, determine where greater detail is needed, and so on. Some process-flow software will let you run sample scenarios of different options to see the impact on costs, cycle time, and other relevant factors. More elaborate simulations can be done using sophisticated modeling software, as well, though the work and costs involved can be high.

Moments of Truth Assessment. Identifying and assessing the key points of customer interface in the process should be a priority. You may have a terrific new approach that will provide faster, better products to customers; but if customers are treated badly or ignored during the process, they may end up less happy than they were before.

Focus Groups and Feedback Sessions. Broader feedback, especially from customers and/or people familiar with the process, can surface concerns and issues you never even dreamed of. Much as you may not *like* people to shoot holes in your brilliantly designed new process, it is better to have it happen early, and in a meeting room, than on the day the new process is launched. Seeking input from people also helps gain their support, or at least lets them know their opinions are valued. Be careful, though, not just to listen politely and then totally ignore feedback offered.

Potential Problem Analysis. Every process has plenty of potential problems. A process design team cannot deal with every possible problem, but it can try to identify the big ones and prepare proactive steps to eliminate or mitigate them. In potential problem analysis, the basic strategy is to focus on critical steps or milestones in the process and ask: "What could go wrong?" Then, concentrating on the higher-probability, higher-impact problems, you can develop *preventive* actions (i.e., ones that reduce or block the effect of causes of the problem) or *contingent* actions (i.e., measures designed to contain or overcome the consequences of the problem). In Chapter 17, we review a more detailed variation of potential problem analysis: failure modes and effects analysis (FMEA).

Unintended Consequences Analysis. This approach takes the big-picture view in considering the impacts of a new process and of the various procedures, forms, and systems it will entail. Implementing a new process is like tossing a rock in a pond: The effects spread out to the surrounding water (i.e., people and processes) in all directions. Those waves of change may create other problems you never anticipated, potentially big ones. Understanding the interconnectedness of processes is key to doing a good analysis of potential consequences. You can trace the effects of, say, new requirements upstream to see who they will affect and how. Conversely, new procedures or service changes need to be followed downstream to note where they may cause unforeseen difficulties.

Winning Support for the Plan

An important part of the refinement process, with an eye on effective implementation, is to gain acceptance of a process design or a process improvement. A couple of approaches can help any leader or group to deal with the challenge of gaining support: strategic selling and force-field analysis. These are defined next, followed by a look at how our fictitious insurance company won support for its plan to redesign its policy completion process.

Strategic Selling. By *strategic selling*, we mean focusing your efforts on key influencers and decision makers who can help build support for the plan and offer useful suggestions on how to improve it. It is best to start with people who are likely to look with favor on your ideas. Usually that will mean focusing on the management and executive levels, but you should not necessarily stop there. Important influencers can exist in many parts of an organization.

Force-Field Analysis. This tool is used to identify and analyze the factors, pro and con, to any change or idea. Force-field analysis begins with structured brainstorming and then leads to a discussion and to planning on how to deal with those elements or issues that oppose your new idea. A key premise is to concentrate on changing or weakening the opposing or restraining forces. When you push harder on the driving force side, the other side usually just pushes back harder.

Case Study #12 Continued: COLA Fine-Tunes Its Insurance Policy Completion Process

Though the COLA team was pleased with the new process design, they realized it was not a cinch to get everyone's approval. They also knew that a lot of details would need to be worked out before they could launch anything.

Their first step was to present the plan to the executive group. Actually, they met prior to the presentation with their sponsor, Di Edsota, as well as with the head of sales, Phil Cooler, to review the plan. They felt Phil's support would be especially important because they were asking salespeople to put more detail into LOAs, which might add some time to the selling process. They also knew, though, that Phil was a strong proponent of continuous improvement and would see the strength of their reasoning.

The top managers had some concerns, especially about the notion of eliminating the legal review. It would also mean the likely layoff of about 20 attorneys, which was not the initial objective of the project. In the end the leaders agreed to let the team move forward with the work to refine the process plan and make sure it would operate as envisioned.

Before unveiling the process to any other groups in the organization, the team decided to do some of its own tough evaluation of the process, and gave Bob Tull the go-ahead to start working on the policy contract templates. The first analysis they did was a walk-through of each step in the new process design. By taking an entire day, they were able to flesh out some of the more important procedures for the process and identify where others would need to be developed.

The walk-through also caused one aspect of the new design to be placed on the questionable list: the database tracking of policies. "As busy as things are in the IS (information systems) group," said Toni, the team leader, "this may hold up the entire project—and I'm not sure if manual tracking won't work just as well for now."

Their next step was to divide the work into two main areas:

1. Analyze the process for potential problems.
2. Prepare an initial piloting plan.

Their potential problem analysis turned up a number of possible trouble spots that they were able to address. For example, one was described as follows:

Process Step: Customer Contract Review
Potential Problem: E-mailed review file is edited by the customer online, making it difficult to track revisions and ensure legal validity of the document.

Preventive Action: Send customers a markup file on which they can add comments and changes but not actually edit the document itself.
Contingent Action: None

Getting Focus Group Feedback on the Redesigned Process

The next refinement action was to review the still-evolving process design in a series of focus group–type meetings with COLA associates. A back-and-forth debate arose on whether to have cross-functional meetings or to focus on one department at a time. In the end they split the difference: Three sessions would be held, each with one or two representatives from policy administration, underwriting, sales, accounting, and claims. They decided to do a special session with a couple of folks from legal; in light of the potential layoffs, it was thought not to be a good idea to involve them in the cross-functional sessions.

A lot of preparation went into the sessions. First of all, the team wanted to present the process in a positive light and accurately. Second, they wanted to ensure that people would not clam up and not offer helpful criticism. Most of the reaction was positive, though, and it was clear that the communicating Rute Biere had done since the "mass layoff" rumors hit had helped to prepare people well for the coming changes. At the same time, some stern critiques were issued along with the helpful suggestions. A lot of unforeseen issues were raised, which gave the team more food for thought and led to more ideas on how to make things run smoother.

At the end of a series of revisions to the process, Toni, Bev Ehridge, and an accounting manager prepared a budget for the implementation. It included severance packages and outplacement services for attorneys, and costs for moving some staff locations, as well as salaries for an additional two underwriters. Toni met alone with Rute Biere and Di Edsota and presented the updated plan and budget. She sent an e-mail to the team as soon as the meeting was over: "It's a go!"

Implementing the New Process: Start with a Pilot

To repeat the point about implementing Six Sigma solutions from the last chapter: You should *always* start with a pilot rather than with a full-scale launch. Piloting gives you an opportunity to test the assumptions, procedures, and people-challenges of the new process, try out your measurement systems, and limit any damage that might occur if things go less than perfectly, which they *will*.

Various options are open to you when preparing a pilot. The most sophisticated pilots can be used as experiments to compare different approaches and identify the best combination of factors for effective, efficient performance. Some broad choices for pilot strategies that will also influence how you eventually implement the process permanently are described in the following paragraphs.

Off-Line Pilot. Like a laboratory test, in this approach the pilot is really a "dummy" operation that resembles/replicates the real world. The output of this approach may end up not being sold or delivered to customers, but its quality can still be evaluated to check the effectiveness of the process. In some companies a pilot plant is used to test new processes and equipment or to develop products for test (i.e., pilot) marketing.

Selected Times. A defined-length pilot offers a couple of advantages:

1. Participants know the test has a defined end point, so they may approach it with more of an open mind.
2. The postpilot period offers downtime for corrections or refinements that may be harder to accomplish if the pilot continues to operate.
3. Comparative measures can be even more revealing. For example, if improvements are seen during the pilot period, but then disappear afterwards, it adds validity to the conclusion that the solution (not some other unknown factor) created the gain.

Selected Items or Customers. In essence, this approach creates an alternate path in which a certain type or number of real items is sent through the new process. This piloting strategy can lend itself well to a parallel implementation in which more and more work is moved over to the new process.

Selected Locations. If you have different regions or locations, you can switch one site to the process as the pilot, gather data and refine the operation, and convert other sites as appropriate.

Selected Solution Components. Rather than testing the entire new process, different parts of the change can be tried independently. For more on this approach, which works best as an experimental method, see the information in "Design of Experiments" in Chapter 17.

Choosing a Pilot Strategy. These pilot strategies can all be mixed and matched. For example, you might conduct an off-line pilot of one component of the new process, or you could do a time-limited test at one location. Depending on the scope, complexity, and potential risk of your new process or solution, piloting in several dimensions and/ or phases can be key to ensuring that the full implementation goes as smoothly as possible. Let's see what COLA decided to do with its pilot plan.

Case Study #12 Continued: COLA Develops Pilot Plan of the Old and New Processes Working in Parallel

The Limit Busters' piloting plan called for a selected group to try the new process in parallel with the existing one for a four-week period, taking all the new letters of agreement from two sales associates. The sales and underwriting members of the team had actually already begun preparing their prospective customers for the more detailed decisions that would need to be made before signing the LOAs. So far, clients were showing no resistance to defining their coverage requirements more explicitly in advance of the LOAs, and the extra detail was not adding much time to the sales cycle. "If you can get my policy ready faster," said one Internet services provider CEO, "a little upfront work is not a problem."

The team had agreed that each policy coordinator would keep track and measure the progress of his or her contracts manually (i.e., not on a central database). "This has been a lot of work," Tye Neebublscz of policy administration told the pilot group, "but it's really been fun, too. I'm getting more and more excited as we go."

After the first four-week pilot would be a two-week evaluation period. At that point the decision would be made as to whether a second pilot was needed. Assuming that it was not, the plan was to have the pilot group convert to the new process full time, then shift the rest of the group and make the conversion in two phases.

At the end of the meeting, consultant Art Glass made a brief (for Art . . .) speech about the excellent work the group had done. The design team later explained to the pilot participants that Art actually had been a huge help in their effort. "You just have to get used to him."

Look at This COLA Fizz!

Like almost any pilot, the four-week test of the new policy completion process experienced a few bumps. The predefined coverage categories and the new policy templates were not well matched, so it took the policy coordinators some extra work to clarify just what clauses and endorsements would be needed. Having a team approach made that adjustment go smoother, though, because the coordinators were in close touch with their sales/underwriting partners most of the time. They also found that it had not been routine in the past to get customers' e-mail addresses, so when the time came to send out policy documents for review, they had to call the customer's office first to get the address.

With the COLA people really on their toes and concentrating on getting the policy papers finished in less than eight days, the cycle times were close to the target, especially as the pilot progressed. It was somewhat difficult to manage the client review time; sometimes it would take four or five days to get the papers back. But when the customers did turn their review around in a day, the total cycle times were less than one week.

At the end of the pilot, the full group held an assessment debriefing session. They identified the following refinements:

1. Include customer e-mail addresses on LOA data sheets.
2. Clarify a primary and an alternate person to review the documents on behalf of the client (for a backup if the primary person happened to be out of the office).
3. Adjust the coverage codes and policy templates so that the right items could be included in the policy documents.
4. Inform clients one day in advance of e-mailing policy documents for review, and send a client-reminder e-mail two days after transmission of the review documents.

The team realized that their measures were not as clear as they should be, and that the role of the customer needed to be taken into account. Therefore they resolved to change the cycle time goal to make it more specific, namely:

Maintain a 7-working-day average cycle time per month, with a maximum cycle time (in the event of client delays) of two weeks.

The operational definition for a cycle-time measure was updated to clarify that the clock would start on the day LOAs were signed by the customer, except for those signed after 3 p.m., which would be measured starting the following working day. Any policy contract would be considered a cycle-time defect:

1. Completed in more than 8 days if signed off on by the customer in three days or less; or
2. Completed in more than 10 days if signed-off on by the customer in more than three days.

The other primary output measure of the policy completion process, "contract accuracy," would continue on unchanged.

Over the four-week period the average cycle time was 8.5 days, with only 5 of the 150 policies processed taking more than 10 days. The team—both the design group and those in the pilot process—were confident that these refinements, with some learning curve time, would allow them to meet their goal.

The Final Process Rollout

It is a big mistake to get overconfident after a successful pilot. The pilot is usually a much more controlled situation than real life, with fewer variables to manage and fewer people involved. Other problems are almost sure to arise in the conversion from test to final rollout of a new process. Some of the critical ingredients of a successful launch of a redesigned process include the following:

▶ **Training.** New approaches need to be learned, old habits broken.
▶ **Documentation.** References on how to do things, answers to frequently asked question, process maps, and so on are all important.
▶ **Troubleshooting.** Responsibility needs to be clear with regard to who will deal with the issues that arise.
▶ **Performance management.** Keep your eyes open for needs/opportunities to revise job descriptions, incentives, and performance review criteria.
▶ **Measurement.** Results need to be documented.

Finally, let's look at the results of the COLA team's effort, and then at Exhibit 15.6, which lists the "dos and don'ts" to help you through your own improve phase of DMAIC.

Case Study #12 Conclusion: The COLA Team Declares Victory in the Redesign of Its Insurance Policy Completion Process— from 12 Weeks to 8 Days

Six months after the first pilot of the new policy completion process, the people at COLA were beginning to wonder how they ever could have lived with the old 12-week limit. The rollout of the new process throughout the rest of the company encountered a few glitches. Not all the salespeople were ready to do the extra work on the LOAs the new process required. A couple of them actually had to be let go.

Nor were customers always as quick to turn papers around as had been hoped. Over time, the organization learned ways to better prepare its customers to be ready for the reviews. And even though the shorter policy documents were a huge hit, eventually COLA added to the process a documents review appointment, during which policy coordinators would walk through policy with customers (usually by phone). That new "moment of truth" actually turned out to be a big customer satisfaction-booster.

The before and after report tells the story (see Figure 15.6). Even with a much tighter customer requirement, process performance and capability improved. Staff in policy administration, underwriting, sales, and claims discovered that their work is much more rewarding without the constant confusion over coverage terms that would come up during the 10 weeks it used to take.

In the annual report of International Insurance and Indemnity (COLA's parent), the subsidiary was singled out for its Six Sigma Design effort:

> In one of the fastest-growing markets in the insurance industry, Computer Outage Liability Assurance (COLA) has established itself as the leader in responsiveness, customer focus, and understanding of the needs of its high-tech customers. "Without COLA's work," said the top executive of NetSetGo, the fifth largest ISP in the finance sector, "many

Policy Completion Process:
Comparative Performance Data

Measure:	Before Redesign:	After Redesign:
Total Cycle Time	10.4 weeks	8.2 days
Average Pages/ Contract	26.3 pages	9.2 pages
In-Process Revisions/ Contract	7.1 revisions	.4 revisions
DPMO (rounded)	321,000	75,000*

* Based on new 8–10 day completion requirement

FIGURE 15.6   COLA BEFORE AND AFTER RESULTS REPORT

companies might have had to close because of undue liability risk. Their work is literally keeping us in business." COLA CEO R. O. "Rute" Biere is projecting 35 percent annual growth over the next five years. This year, Biere was named to the III Board of Directors.

Exhibit 15.6

"DOS AND DON'TS" FOR THE PROCESS DESIGN/REDESIGN IMPROVE PHASE OF SIX SIGMA

- Do—*Concentrate on seeing the process in a new way.*
  - Try to identify what rules or assumptions govern today's process and ask: "Are these valid? Why? How can we make them invalid?"
- Do—*Set performance criteria to analyze the design.*
  - Give the team a framework to assess their creative ideas against the practical reality of the process.

- ■ Do—*Refine and enhance the process iteratively.*
  - Get feedback, use simulations, walk through the process, and add detail as you go.
- ■ Do—*Pilot the process, in multiple phases when warranted.*
  - It may take longer, but the chief benefit will be a smoother final implementation.

- ■ Don't—*Run a downtime pilot.*
  - Test the process in a variety of conditions, including when things are really busy.
- ■ Don't—*Assume everyone will love the new process.*
  - Even if it is only unconscious, resistance will come up. Respond to it, and learn from it, but also be ready to enforce new procedures when people are downright belligerent.
- ■ Don't—*Take your eye off the process.*
  - Expect problems, and you will be ready for them. Stay alert throughout the duration of at least one process cycle. Prepare to transition to control.

CHAPTER 16

Expanding and Integrating the Six Sigma System
(Roadmap Step 5)

Imagine you decide to lose some weight by using the new Six Sigma diet plan. With the help of a well-defined problem ("I'm 25 pounds over my optimal weight"), some carefully recorded valid measurements, a review of your eating and exercise processes, and the advice of a doctor and some fitness instructors, you implement a solution of changed diet and increased exercise. You are so successful that you go beyond the goal you set for yourself and lose 27 pounds. And just in time for summer holidays!

How might this success story end? As with Six Sigma, so with diets: It depends.

Old habits are hard to break. Maybe you pile on an extra helping of your favorite food, skip jogging on rainy days, order *whole*-milk lattes instead of nonfat. And before you know it the scale is back up where it started. The alternative takes more discipline: You decide to control your weight by keeping an eye on your eating and exercising processes and by keeping some charts on your weight and eating patterns. You even manage to get your cholesterol down, and people say you are looking great.

Six Sigma companies face much the same challenge as the dieter. When improvement or design projects achieve their goal of reducing defects or waste, discipline is essential to sustain the results. It is more complicated than losing weight, of course, because a process involves many people, not just the dieter. Do Six Sigma gains ever fade when solutions are turned over to full-time operations? Do dieters ever gain back lost pounds?

Even when improvement sticks, a Six Sigma company faces another challenge similar to the dieter's: Those first few pounds tend to come off easily, but they get harder to shed as you go. Without a sustained, focused effort, the beginning drive for improvement will lose energy and your company will become a *former* Six Sigma organization.

In this chapter, we explore both the short- and long-term challenges of sustaining Six Sigma improvement and building all the concepts and methods of Steps 1–4 into an ongoing, cross-functional management approach. The key actions to be taken in managing processes for Six Sigma performance are these three:

1. Implement ongoing measures and actions to sustain improvement (the control phase of DMAIC).
2. Define responsibility for process ownership and management.
3. Execute closed-loop monitoring and drive on toward Six Sigma performance.

Step 5A: Implement Ongoing Measures and Actions to Sustain Improvement (Control)

Our first consideration is how to solidify the immediate gains made through Six Sigma efforts. It is at the end of a process improvement or design/redesign effort that the results achieved are most vulnerable. A team alone cannot keep its efforts from fading away. The ensuing subsections give you the essentials of sustained improvement.

Build Solid Support for the Solution

Being smart about getting others to understand and buy in to your solutions is a recurring theme in Six Sigma, and the need to "sell" the solution doesn't stop. Some of the most important considerations here are described in the following paragraphs.

▶ **Work with those who manage the process.** It helps if those who must manage new and improved processes also participated in their creation. When this is not the case, teams and project sponsors have to carefully explain the benefits of the improvement. Having a process or solution owner to take over responsibility for your change can make the task simpler.

▶ **Use a storyboard with facts and data.** The project storyboard tells the background, plot, and outcome of your Improvement in words and pictures. Being able to show why and how the change you developed makes sense for your organization's customers will go a long way to convince people that the new approach is the right one.

▶ **Treat the people using the new process as your customers.** Tailor your pitch and product to the internal groups who need to embrace the change. Results need to be expressed in terms each group understands. For example, people in customer support will be happy to hear "reduced customer complaints," but may not care much about "additional referral business." When people are being asked to do new or extra work as part of the solutions, explain clearly how other aspects of their job will get easier.

▶ **Create a sense of purpose and enthusiasm.** Sharing credit for the solution and building a sense of participation is not just a good selling tool, it is also realistic. As we noted previously, no Black Belt or team can even hope to make a meaningful improvement happen alone.

Document the Changes and New Methods

In the minds of many people, the thought of documenting a procedure or process—even one they created themselves—falls somewhere between the thrill of dental work and the ecstasy of filing income taxes. But documentation is a necessary evil and can even be a creative undertaking in itself. A successful Six Sigma organization needs to look for new and better ways to make documentation usable and accessible, to get away from the horrors of all those huge procedures manuals and process descriptions guaranteed to cure insomnia.

The following paragraphs provide some general guidelines that will help people to actually follow your directions and/or documentation; then we look at a case study of a home furnishings company that used Six Sigma to transform the way it did business to keep up with changing consumer tastes.

▶ **Keep the documentation simple.** Write in direct, jargon-free sentences. If you must use specific terms that someone new may not understand, include a definition or glossary. Explaining the meaning of TLAs and FLAs (three-letter and four-letter acronyms) is important, too. If a lot of detail is needed, consider including it in the support or reference materials, so that people can get the *basics* easily and more background as needed.

▶ **Keep the documentation clear and inviting.** Using pictures and flowcharts whenever possible can make your message clearer and more accessible. Use of white space, bullets, various fonts, and highlights will make the documents both easier to navigate and more appealing to the eye, which is an important criterion in today's visually oriented world.

▶ **Include options and instructions for emergencies.** One of the ways to ensure that your new processes and procedures are not abandoned is to plan and document ways to adjust them under various conditions. Include information on how to identify problems or issues, too.

▶ **Keep the documentation brief.** Yep! (Actually, there's more. . . .) If you want a good guide to brief instructions, read cake recipes. Usually they are models of clarity and brevity. By contrast, check the operating instructions for a TV. The longer instructions are, the less likely it is that people will have time to read or understand them.

▶ **Keep the documentation handy.** One sign that an organization really is not taking the Control phase seriously is when documents are hard to find, either physically or on-line. Hard-to-locate documentation sends the implicit message that—despite all of someone's hard work and analysis—you can feel free to do any old thing you care to while working on this process. But guess what? That old devil, variation, will be sneaking in whenever this happens, and it won't be for your company's good.

Have a process for updates and revisions. It is not enough to say "have to keep this up-to-date." Documentation, like measurement, is a process that needs to be *designed* and managed, with document tracking and revision as key parts of it. The need for revision should be one of the most important considerations in designing the documents to start with: The more complicated they are, the harder it will be to update. But the less often they are revised, the more likely it is that people will ignore the documentation.

Of course, you face the risk of creating a documentation bureaucracy. Having a "document control" department has worked fine for some companies. Our recommendation, though, is to try to keep ownership of documents close to the work and in the hands of those people who are best able to judge *what* needs to be documented, to what level, and when it should be revised. Guidelines to maintain consistency across the organization are important as well.

Case Study #13: A Home Furnishings Company Uses Six Sigma to Transform Its Business

UpHome is a small but successful chain of retail stores that sells "contemporary country" home furnishings in 17 locations in the Mid-Atlantic states. UpHome carved its niche by being the first store of its kind to sell products that had a country look but had been updated to contemporary tastes. People wanting their décor to be cozy but not old-fashioned have been terrific customers for UpHome.

As the market for home furnishings diversified, however, UpHome began to see some decline in its sales. Looking at their prospects, company leaders and store managers concluded that their *products* could still outshine their competition, but that the real edge would come from the service provided to their customers. UpHome subsequently launched a transformation effort based on the Six Sigma system with the theme "Making People Feel UpHome."

One of the first projects completed was the development of a new furnishings loan-out process. UpHome salespeople (called "neighbors") and folks in advertising began to actively promote the option of trying out items in people's homes to make sure they actually worked well. The "Take It Home" process was piloted at two stores before being implemented chainwide; the tests showed it to be a huge success.

Take It Home was not a simple process, however, because it involved issues such as inventory, delivery, potential damage, and the risk of theft. The team that developed the process worked out as many issues as possible in the design phase, and then fine-tuned the various procedures during the pilot with the active participation of the management and staff of the two pilot locations.

The result was a kickoff campaign for the full rollout of Take It Home that created a lot of excitement throughout UpHome. Salespeople from the pilot stores gave testimonials about the stronger relationships they were able to develop with customers. Sales figures showed an almost immediate 25 percent jump after the launch of the program.

In addition to a series of training programs held at each location to explain the new process and tasks, each store associate was given a personalized "How to Help 'Take It Home'" guidebook. The most useful was an extensive intranet site that provided complete instructions on how to handle questions and issues as they arise, which was linked to an online sharing site where issues and questions were posted. A section with maps of the key process elements was one of the most popular features. A committee made up of representatives from each store was responsible for reviewing and updating the site as adjustments were made to the process.

To make sure no store associate created a problem for customers due to uncertainty about the Take It Home policy and procedures, each staff member was given three "your call" opportunities per month, in which whatever they decided to do was okay. The only requirement was that they be posted on the sharing platform.

Establish Meaningful Measures and Charts

Imagine you are the coach in a football game in which you are not quite sure of the score or how much time is left in the game. How do you know what plays to call? How do you handle that fourth-and-one situation, whether to let the clock run or call time-out? Well, your experience may lead you to some pretty good guesses, which is what many managers rely on much of the time.

Now that you are successfully invested in Six Sigma projects, however, you put your victory in jeopardy if you revert to the management guessing game. You avoid guessing, on the other hand, by employing well-chosen and well-implemented measures to track your process and solution. By now, we expect that you understand some of the basics and tools of measurement covered in previous chapters. Thus the two questions in Step 5 become: "What measures do we continue to use?" and "How do we make them useful?"

Selecting Ongoing Measures. We already looked at several ways in which you can categorize measures: input, process, and output; efficiency and effectiveness; predictors (Xs) and results (Ys). One of the first rules with ongoing measures is to include a balance among these categories so as to give a full picture of the organizational system. For example, measures of defect levels will tell you how well you are meeting customer requirements, but in-process measures are better at giving you early warning of pending problems. Financial measures are useful, but other data can be more indicative of what is happening to drive costs.

Another consideration is rate of change. Things that change more frequently—especially factors that can impact customers, product, or service quality, and costs/profits—should go higher on the measurement priority list. You cannot ignore the more slowly changing factors, but it may be possible to keep an eye on them through different mechanisms than an ongoing measure.

What you measure should also be influenced by what is important at a particular point in time. Some will be long-term maintenance measures of things such as defects, cycle time, and cost per unit. Other measures will be situational. For example, in the first few months after a new process has been introduced you may measure several aspects to make sure it is working well, then phase them out once the success of the improvement seems certain. Still other measures may be improvement-focused. Obvious examples would be those initiated during a DMAIC project to gather data on a problem or causes, or those tied to a business imperative such as a new-product launch.

Finally, you can test each possible measure with our favorite two criteria: *meaningful* and *manageable*. Will the data from the measure really help track the business and lead you to make better decisions, and will the resources and logistical issues behind getting the data be affordable?

Using Your Ongoing Measures. As with any product, the more you can tailor how measures are designed and reported, the better. Some people love the details and are not happy without a full spreadsheet of numbers. Others want the barest synopsis.

As a general rule, however, simpler, graphical measurement reports work best. They are quicker to read, make for easier comparisons, and can be colorful. The kinds of charts we already mentioned, such as run or trend charts, Pareto charts, and histograms, along with many other familiar "data pictures," can be the workhorses of measurement reporting. Another technique, profiled in Chapter 17, is the control chart. This chart helps you to see at a glance how much variation is occurring in a process and whether the process is "in control."

As data are collected at various points throughout the organization, the need to summarize *many* measures becomes critical so that top leaders can effectively get an idea of what is happening in the trenches. One of the most popular and useful tools you can use to reach that high-level view is the *balanced scorecard*, popularized by Robert Kaplan and David Norton.[1] A balanced scorecard (BSC) is a flexible tool for selecting and displaying key indicator measures about the business in an easy-to-read format. Many organizations *not* involved in Six Sigma, including many government agencies, use the BSC to establish common performance measures and keep a closer eye on the business.

One of the strengths of the balanced scorecard concept is the emphasis it places on four categories of measures: innovation, process, customer, and financial. So it can offer some help in choosing what to measure. But whether you use a by-the-book balanced scorecard or develop your own approach, just taking the action of creating an easily digestible array of measurement data can help to ensure that *using* measures becomes a part of the new habits of your Six Sigma organization.

Building Process Response Plans

Given the power of Finnegan's law ("Murphy was an optimist"), we can rest assured that sooner or later something will go wrong in any process, even one that has been improved by a crack Six Sigma team. Having advance guidelines on when to take action and what to do is part of the proactive management practice of any Six Sigma company.

A process response plan includes three major elements:

1. **Action alarms.** With clear standards in place at key points in the input, process, and output phases of a process, and measures tracking performance, *trigger points* can be set at which some action needs to be taken to correct a problem or concern. For example, if test data show circuit boards approaching the edge of their rated

energy consumption, an engineer may want to begin investigating to see what is wrong. Or if no-shows at a hotel get 5 percent above the seasonal normal, some special contingency plans could be implemented.

2. **Short-term or emergency fixes.** By no means can every problem wait for a chartered team or Black Belt assignment. Having some guidelines on quick fixes mean they can be more effective and less likely to cause the collateral damage that often results from haphazard short-term solutions.

3. **Continuous improvement plans.** A process for identifying and prioritizing ongoing or serious problems so they can be acted on feeds into the DMAIC process and other higher-level activities such as strategic planning and budgeting. Guidelines can also be established on how significant a problem or opportunity must be before it qualifies for a continuous improvement action. Continuous improvement plans are a key link in the closed-loop business management system of Six Sigma.

Anticipating possible problems is clearly an important part of an effective response plan. Techniques like potential problem analysis and FMEA (covered in Chapter 17) can support that effort. Let's take a look at how our home furnishing company monitored its new process.

Case Study #13 Continued: UpHome Keeps Its Eyes Open to See How Its New Process Works

Despite the early success of furniture and decorating retailer UpHome's new Take It Home service and process, the company was not ready to declare victory. Each store was asked to keep track of such key variables in the new process as

- ▶ Percent of Take It Home customers who make purchases
- ▶ Dollar volume of Take It Home–related sales, overall and by neighbor (sales associate)
- ▶ Defect data (e.g., missed or wrong deliveries; erroneous billing; etc.), including a Sigma score

> ▶ Damaged/lost merchandise
> ▶ Customer satisfaction index data
>
> The data were reported by each location and then summarized for the UpHome chain as a whole.

To help you with your control phase of DMAIC, Exhibit 16.1 provides a list of "dos and don'ts" for ongoing measures and control, and Exhibit 16.2 provides a checklist of the steps you should follow.

Exhibit 16.1

"DOS AND DON'TS" FOR ONGOING MEASURES AND CONTROLS

■ Do—*Develop good documentation to support the new process.*
  • Keep it simple, clear, and easy to use, and have a plan for updating the document.
■ Do—*Select a balanced mix of measures to monitor process performance.*
  • Look at results, process variables, customer requirements, and costs. Avoid strictly financial measures.
■ Do—*Create measurement reports that convey information quickly and simply.*
  • Charts and graphs usually are preferable to raw texts and tables of figures.
■ Do—*Develop a plan to take action in case problems arise in the process.*
  • Responding in a preplanned, effective manner is much better than reacting in an ignorant panic.

■ Don't—*Leave documents to gather dust.*
  • Designing and finding ways to use documentation helps ensure they are kept up-to-date, and will help keep the process from reverting to bad habits.
■ Don't—*Forget the process maps.*
  • They are the best tools for quick reference and review of workflows, customer/supplier relationships, and key points for measurement. Process maps make changing the process much easier, too.

Control Checklist

5. Control

Instructions:

If you can respond "yes" to each statement, you have completed all key steps in your DMAIC project and are ready to *celebrate* and maintain your improvement.

For our project we have ...

1. Compiled results data confirming that our improvement has achieved the goal defined in our DMAIC team charter. [YES] [NO]

2. Selected ongoing measures to monitor performance of the process and continued effectiveness of our solution. [YES] [NO]

3. Determined key charts/graphs for a process scorecard on this process. [YES] [NO]

4. Prepared all essential documentation of the revised process, including key procedures and process maps. [YES] [NO]

5. Identified an owner of the process who will take over responsibility for our solution and for managing continuing operations. [YES] [NO]

6. Developed (with the process owner) process management charts detailing requirements, measures, and responses to problems in the process. [YES] [NO]

7. Prepared a storyboard documenting the team's work and data collected during our project. [YES] [NO]

8. Forwarded other issues/opportunities we were *not* able to address to senior management. [YES] [NO]

9. Celebrated the hard work and successful efforts of our team. [YES] [NO]

Exhibit 16.2 **CONTROL CHECKLIST**

Step 5B: Define Responsibility for Process Ownership and Management

As your company adopts and implements the steps on the Six Sigma roadmap, you will be positioning your organization to adopt the most promising solution to cross-functional barriers and organizational silos: a *process* management approach. What might this adoption and implementation mean in terms of how your company operates? Well, here are some elements of the process management vision:

▶ Business leaders will concentrate on getting work to move effectively and efficiently *across* functions to the benefit of customers and, ultimately, of shareholders.

▶ Employees will identify as much with the process as with their individual functions/departments.

▶ People at all levels will understand how their work fits into the process and adds value to the customer.

▶ Customer requirements will be known throughout the process.

▶ Processes will undergo continuous measurement, improvement, and redesign.

▶ More energy and resources will be focused on delivering value to customers and shareholders, rather than be wasted on bureaucracy or infighting.

The Process Owner

Perhaps the most essential step in the transformation to process management is designation of process owners.

The Process Owner's Responsibilities

Although there is no official job description for a process owner, the responsibilities described in the following paragraphs are key to the role in a continuous improvement-focused organization.

Maintaining Process Documentation. The process owner is the person who creates and becomes keeper of process design data (i.e., maps, flows, and procedures), background data on customer requirements, and other defining documents of the process. Part of that responsibility includes keeping data and documents up-to-date.

Measuring/Monitoring Process Performance. You may already have wondered: "Who is going to *do* all this measurement and tracking of the process?" Process owners see that the right measures are executed in the right way.

Identifying Problems and Opportunities. As the primary observer of performance data, a process owner is the person who should first see problems as they arise, or to whom other people report the problems or issues they observe. Process ownership ideally involves the authority to take action to address quick fixes and longer-term solutions.

Launching and Sponsoring Improvement Efforts. When projects to improve, design, or redesign a process are identified, the process owner will take up the key role of supporting, if not *leading*, the effort. Just as importantly, the process owner takes the handoff from an improvement team, assuming the responsibility for maintaining the gain.

Coordinating and Communicating with Other Processes and with Functional Managers. One of the most important principles behind the process owner role is that the work coming *into* and especially *out of* the process is just as important as the work *within* the process. Some of the biggest obstacles to serving *external* customers come from poor coordination between *internal* suppliers and customers. It is only through upstream and downstream coordination that the process owner can remove the barriers or us-against-them attitudes that arise in the functional world. A process owner has to work with suppliers and customers to meet the goal of top-level performance. In addition, a process owner needs to align the various groups in the process to make sure the work flows smoothly and is done well.

Maximizing Process Performance. All the responsibilities noted thus far lead to this most-important objective. The process owner becomes the key driver to achieve Six Sigma levels of quality, efficiency, and flexibility.

Process Owners in the Organization

Decades of functional management is not likely to give way to a process management orientation overnight, nor is it clear that it *should*. To maintain the command-and-control advantages of the functional system, a hybrid of process and hierarchical structures may be more effective.

For example, some businesses use levels of process ownership, with a core process owner having two or more subprocess owners engaged in a process management team. Each of these individuals wears a functional hat as well, but the process owner role concentrates on the overall cross-functional operation and on improvement of the process. If these process management layers were to turn into a new reporting structure, it is not clear how much better it might be than

existing organizational hierarchies. This issue poses one of those evolutionary questions about process management that will have to be
answered over time and by each organization based on its own needs
and experiences.

What *is* clear about process ownership is that the emphasis on
measuring, improving, and coordinating flows of work calls for a
somewhat different, if not broader, set of skills than does functional
management. A profile seeking to identify potential process owners
might include these traits:

- ▶ Results-oriented, with an emphasis on "win-win" gains and a focus
  on the customer
- ▶ Respected by senior leaders, middle management, and staff
- ▶ Strong business knowledge, with ability to think and work as a
  generalist
- ▶ Excellent people skills, especially in the areas of team development,
  consensus building, and negotiation
- ▶ Skilled in Six Sigma concepts, measurement, and process improvement and design methods
- ▶ Ability to share credit for success and to take the responsibility for
  setbacks

Strong technical knowledge or statistical expertise also can be helpful, but not if it takes away from that more important generalist
perspective.

Exactly where process owner candidates will be found in an
organization is anyone's guess. It will likely take some creative
talent-scouting to find the right mix of skills and potential to fill the
ownership role in your organization. It is safe to say, though, that
old-style authoritative managers are not right for the role unless they
can change their approach. In fact, one of the reasons that process
management will require a long-term evolution is the fact that many
of today's managers will have trouble adapting to the new "horizontal"
approach. It may take a whole new generation to really develop the
talent needed for the new role.

Where to Put Process Owners?

We laid the groundwork for an answer to this question back in
Chapter 11, where we explored core and support processes. As your

organization prepares its inventory of critical or strategic processes, you are also setting the stage for designating *owners* of those processes. In larger organizations, as in the organization noted previously, having layers of ownership is the best option. No one person can oversee a single large, diverse process. Where responsibility for a larger process is divided, those owners would form what some companies call a process management team (PMT).

It is also important that process owners be deployed at an operating level of a business. We have seen situations in which a company with several divisions created a macro process management system at the corporate level. Unfortunately, even though the different divisions included common processes, each was unique and required focused ownership at the division level. The firm struggled for a while before realizing and correcting its mistake.

Can process ownership reach all the way down to the departmental or functional level? The answer is a qualified "Yes." Clearly, some processes *within* a function can be managed with many of the same methods and measures as cross-functional processes. Nonetheless, we say the shift to process management at the department level is best driven by a change in focus, rather than by creating a new process owner assignment within functions. Individuals are already in place to manage functions: vice presidents, directors, managers, and so on.

Let's take a look at how the company in our case study selected its new process owners.

Case Study #14: UpHome Selects Process Owners to Manage Its New Process

Top management at UpHome was pleased with the results of the design and management of the Take It Home process. They were early in their Six Sigma effort, though, and still unsure whether or how the concept of process management would fit in with a dispersed retail operation.

The launch of the new process seemed to provide a good opportunity to test how the process owner role would work, and to see whether it would add value to the organization and its customers. After a discussion of the idea of creating a Take It Home process owner, top management agreed that it did meet several important criteria:

▶ It was a cross-functional process, involving many of UpHome's departments.

▶ It was a continuing effort, not just a marketing campaign, and hence an appropriate choice for establishment as a key business process.

▶ The ability to measure, assess, and improve the Take It Home process would be key to its continued success. As customer needs, product mixes, competition, and so on changed, it was likely the process would need to adapt.

One question provoked some debate: Could a process owner really oversee an activity being carried out at 17 different locations? The decision was to designate a companywide owner of the process, and to assign a process coordinator at the store level. (Some of the coordinators would cover two or three locations.)

Selecting the process owner was, fortunately, easy. One of the members of the team that had designed the new process, Margy McMahon, had already exhibited the kind of leadership and process perspective that seemed ideal for such an important cross-functional activity.

Margy's first task was to pull together many of the documents and notes prepared by the design team, which no one had touched since the pilot, and create an overall process guidebook. When that was ready, she set out on a tour of UpHome stores to begin selecting process coordinators.

Step 5C: Execute Closed-Loop Management and Drive to Six Sigma

Establishing process management is both the end of our Six Sigma roadmap and the *beginning* of becoming a real Six Sigma organization. Any business or process that has followed the roadmap through at least Steps 1, 2, and 3, will be forming the key elements of the process management approach. Let's briefly review these steps and their contributions:

1. **Identify core processes and key customers.** Defining the process, its key steps, customers, and outputs creates the blueprint for process management.

2. **Define customer requirements.** Process goals and performance standards, determined by market and customer needs, are the *raison d'être* of any process. Understanding those requirements in concrete terms helps you to answer that basic question: "Manage the process to do *what*?"

3. **Measure current performance.** Measurement in the process management system will provide ongoing, essential feedback on results (Ys) and key process factors (Xs).

As your efforts at Six Sigma mature, process improvement and design/redesign (DMAIC) become the strategies that drive work processes to ever-higher Sigma levels and respond to customer demands for new products, services, or capabilities.

Tools for Process Management

Every tool we described or mentioned, as well as those we will review in the next chapter, may play a role in helping to manage processes. A couple of other methods, however, can be of particular value to the process owner who strives to keep a process running smoothly and improving continuously. Let's take a look at two of these process-management methods, and then we check in with our case study company to see how it is managing its new process.

▶ **Process scorecards or dashboards.** The Process scorecard, like the balanced scorecard mentioned earlier, provides a summary update on key indicators of process performance. While the balanced scorecard typically provides organization-wide data, the process scorecard would be designed for a specific process. It can include alarms to show if and when a key indicator is nearing a problem level. For example, by noting the specified delivery time on a cycle-time chart, a process owner could see whether times are close to exceeding the requirements. Some companies, including a number of GE businesses, actually provide tailored process scorecard data to customers, telling them "here's how our process is performing for you."

▶ **Customer report cards.** Timely customer feedback is a key ingredient in optimized process performance. One of the focused tools that can support that need (i.e., an element of the overall voice of the customer system) is a customer report card. Ideally, it provides representative data (i.e., an accurate, unbiased sample) of how well the process is meeting customer needs. The best customer report cards are more than surveys or complaint data; they provide input that is meaningful both to the customer and to the company on performance and concerns. In business-to-business relationships these report cards can be tailored specifically to the client, so that the "grades" or other feedback provided has been selected on the basis of each customer's unique needs and priorities.

Case Study #14 Continued: Process Management Finds UpHome

Six months after Margy McMahon was named the first process owner at UpHome and began overseeing the new Take It Home product trial process, company leaders were becoming convinced that the process management approach could be a big benefit to the organization as a whole.

For one thing, Margy and the network of process coordinators in the stores had made some significant contributions to the Take It Home process's continued success. For example:

▶ Three months after the process was launched, lost items began to climb. Margy and the process coordinators were able to determine that some of the UpHome sales associates were failing to record complete address data and were unable to recontact customers to get the items back. A simple fix solved the problem.
▶ By tracking the types of products where Take It Home led to the highest sales increases, they were able to anticipate additional inventory needs and gear up for higher demand. This change not only allowed for additional sales, but also gave UpHome an opportunity to get discounts from vendors.
▶ In a number of instances where squabbles arose between the sales and product delivery departments, Margy and the process coordinators were able to keep things from getting out of hand. By maintaining the focus on the customer, the issues were resolved to everyone's satisfaction.

> The process scorecard Margy created for Take It Home helped every-one keep up-to-date on the performance of the process (see a sample of it in Figure 16.1).
>
> As a first step in expanding the process management approach, UpHome's leaders scheduled a half-day meeting, to begin mapping out all their core business processes.

Conclusion: Moving Toward Six Sigma

We began this chapter with an analogy of regaining lost weight after a bout of successful dieting. We suggested that some companies, like complacent and undisciplined dieters, are doomed to backslide when they shift their attention to seemingly more urgent issues. We also noted that the gains of Six Sigma will come somewhat easily at first, like those first few pounds in a diet, but that the last few Sigma points will be harder to rack up in the drive for *Six* Sigma.

The process management discipline is where the momentum to "keep losing weight (or defects)" will come from. It is the mechanism

Take-it-Home PROCESS SCORECARD (Quarterly Summary)

	Target	Performance JLY AUG SEP	Notes
New Products Added	6 per Month	● ● ○	Quarterly target exceeded
Defects per TIH Item Loaned (DPU)	.01 (99% Yield)	○ ○ ◒	Total DPU of .031
TIH Volume Growth	6% Month-to-Month	◒ ○ ◒	Quarterly target met
% TIHs Purchased	75%	◒ ○ ○	Average 68% for quarter
% Customers Rating TIH "Excellent"	95%	◒ ● ●	Strong positive comments
Sales Increase Due to TIH (estimate)	20%	● ● ●	25% increase approx. $8 mil.

● - Above Target   ◒ - At Target   ○ - Below Target   **UpHOME**

FIGURE 16.1   UPHOME TAKE IT HOME PROCESS SCORECARD

that ensures your firm will make measures and improvement a daily responsibility, not just an occasional task. Moreover, as your business progresses down the Six Sigma Way, you will find more opportunities to use sophisticated tools to move past Four and Five Sigma. We look at the advanced Six Sigma tools in Chapter 17, but first, let's wrap up with Exhibit 16.3, which lists the "dos and don'ts" to help you manage Six Sigma performance in *your* organization.

Exhibit 16.3

"DOS AND DON'TS" FOR MANAGING FOR SIX SIGMA PERFORMANCE

- Do—*Document the steps and lessons in process improvement and design/redesign projects.*
  - A project storyboard will be helpful to "sell" the solutions and as an aid to future improvement teams.
- Do—*Develop a complete plan to control the process and maintain the gains.*
  - Selling, documenting, measuring, and responding are essential to solidify success, and they become key inputs to the process management system.
- Do—*Carefully define the role and responsibilities of a process owner for your organization.*
  - As a new player on the business landscape, a process owner and those who work with that person need a clear idea of the owner's function and objectives.

- Don't—*Take on process management without careful upfront consideration.*
  - As useful as this discipline and resource can be, an all-out process management implementation may not make sense. If necessary, try it out and learn (i.e., pilot the concept) before you create unnecessary business upheaval.
- Don't—*Create process reports and documentation that end up being just as underused as your current ones.*
  - Focus first on information you know you or others will need, and add to it as need be.

CHAPTER 17

Advanced Six Sigma Tools: An Overview

In our journey along the Six Sigma Way so far, we have concentrated on the fairly simple methods and tools that drive much of the improvement in most organizations and processes. As we've noted, the publicity connecting Six Sigma exclusively with heavy-duty analytical methods has been very much exaggerated. Those who stick with the continuous improvement journey learn that the majority of problems and opportunities can be addressed with techniques nearly anyone can use. At the same time, one of the clear advantages of the Six Sigma system has been the application of more sophisticated tools that bring more power to the learning and improvement efforts.

Our objective in this chapter is not to make you an expert in any of these advanced methods. We will try, though, to make you familiar with *what* some of the most common Six Sigma techniques are, *why* they can be helpful, and *how* they can be applied to process design, management, and improvement. Each of the power tools we cover has one or more specific applications, and like any tool, it can be misused or unproductive if not chosen and applied with care.

These are the methods we'll review, with their most common purpose noted in italics:

▶ Statistical process control and control charts—*problem identification*

▶ Tests of statistical significance (chi-square, *t*-tests, and ANOVA)—*problem definition and root cause analysis*

▶ Correlation and regression—*root cause analysis and prediction of results*

▶ Design of experiments—*optimal solution analysis and results validation*

▶ Failure modes and effects analysis—*problem prioritization and prevention*

▶ Mistake-proofing—*defect prevention and process improvement*

▶ Quality function deployment—*product, service, and process design*

Statistical Process Control, and Control Charts

Statistical process control (SPC) involves the measurement and evaluation of variation in a process and the efforts made to limit or control such variation. In its most common application, SPC helps an organization or process owner to identify possible problems or unusual incidents so that action can be taken promptly to resolve them—in other words, to *control* the performance of a process.

When and Why to Use SPC/Control Charts

Use of SPC and control charts constitutes the ideal way of monitoring current process performance, predicting future performance, and suggesting the need for corrective action. Control charts, which are easily understood after just a bit of instruction, can be an effective communication tool. Numerous companies post control charts for key processes in readily accessible areas, giving visibility to daily activities, trends, and patterns, and warnings of possible problems. This practice can get everyone involved in the company's management and problem solving.

Control charts have three significant uses in the Six Sigma system:

1. In the early measure activities of a DMAIC project, they help teams identify the type and frequency of problems or out-of-control conditions. They can even suggest what type of investigation or corrective action might prove most effective.

2. In piloting or implementing a process solution or change (in the improve or control phases), they help track results, showing how variation and performance have been affected and perhaps even suggesting further areas of work or investigation.
3. Third, control charts act as an ongoing alarm system, alerting the observer to unusual activities in the process and triggering the process response plan discussed in Chapter 16.

You can think of SPC/control charts in that third application as being a smoke detector in your house: When it has batteries, is properly placed, and someone is around to hear it, it can sound the alarm in ample time to keep the place from going up in flames.

What Does the *Control* in SPC/Control Charts Mean?

"Control" means keeping a process operating within a predictable range of variation. The objective is to maintain the stable, consistently good performance of a process. In SPC, we add the notion of *statistical* control to the discussion. Thus to figure out whether a process is statistically in control or out of control, you begin by actually measuring a process over time and then examine the variation in the data you gather. With enough data you can calculate what are called "control limits," thereby taking a first step in checking to see how well the process is working.

Let's take an example. Imagine you are managing your company's e-mail system, and you want to know how much variation exists in the number of e-mail messages sent per hour. To get an answer, of course, you have to gather some data. So, after compiling hourly volume levels over a month (using excellent data-collection methods, no doubt), you plot e-mail traffic volumes on a run or trend chart (i.e., in time order—and described in Chapter 14). Next, you use those data to calculate the control limits (UCL for upper control limit, and LCL for lower control limit), and you add those to your chart along with a line indicating the average or mean. You now have a control chart (see Figure 17.1).

If you continue to gather data on e-mail traffic, the control chart will give you the ability not only to track changes in e-mail volume, but also to be able to see if and when the process is out of control or operating in a way that is no longer predictable.

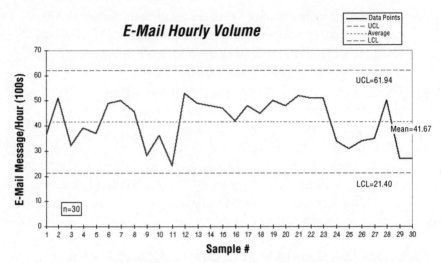

FIGURE 17.1   EXAMPLE: CONTROL CHART OF E-MAIL VOLUME

Control Chart Alarms

Because we expect that variation in a process under normal conditions will be random, several indicators can be used to signal an out-of-control situation:

- ▶ **Outliers**—any point outside the control limits
- ▶ **Trends**—a series of points continually rising or falling
- ▶ **Shifts**, or **runs**—a continuous sequence of points above or below the average
- ▶ **Cycles**, or **periodicity**—a series of points alternating up and down or trending up and down in waves
- ▶ **Tendencies**—situations in which the points continually fall close to the center line or to either of the control limits

Control Charts and Customer Requirements

One of the misunderstandings about control charts is that being "in control" means the same thing as being "good." If a computer repair shop decides to measure its turnaround time on routine repairs, it might create a chart showing a process under perfect control. The problem however is that while their average turnaround is five days, customers want these jobs done in *two*!

Remember that these two types of limits introduced in this book (control and specification, not outer and city) are developed differently:

Control limits are calculated from actual process data; they can change as the process performance changes over time. Specification limits come from the *customer*; they change only as the customer's requirements change.

Using Control Charts

The basic steps for implementing SPC should be familiar by now: Decide on the critical measures, implement a data-collection plan, plot the data, view the results, and take appropriate action. It is much in line with the closed-loop system that is the foundation of the Six Sigma organization. Plotting and testing the data can be easily accomplished using statistics software. Simply enter the data or copy it from a spreadsheet, select the chart type and the tests from menus, and there you have it—a control chart.

Choosing the right type of control chart to use is important. Several factors determine which chart format fits your situation. For example if you have a continuous data measure (weight, time, temperature, etc.) you use one of two types. SPC books usually feature handy guides to selecting the appropriate chart.

No business should be creating new control charts all the time, because they are of real value only in monitoring changes in process performance. Therefore you should only occasionally have to confront the question: "What type of control chart should we use?"

Finally, remember that SPC and control charts are methods for *monitoring* and *understanding* your process. They do nothing to *solve* problems or improve your performance, unless you take corrective actions or apply Six Sigma improvement methods.

Exhibit 17.1 lists some "dos and don'ts" to keep in mind when using SPC and control charts.

Exhibit 17.1

"DOS AND DON'TS" FOR USING SPC AND CONTROL CHARTS

- Do—*Gather, plot, and review data promptly.*
  - A key to the value of SPC is to get early warnings of problems or opportunities. If your data-collection systems and reporting take days or weeks, or if no one looks at them, why waste the resources?

■ Do—*Choose and prioritize measures carefully.*
  • One or two really meaningful control charts can be a big help. Having 10 or 15 mildly interesting ones only mean you will quit looking at them soon.
■ Do—*Set and fine-tune your alarms.*
  • Use what you learn about the process to improve your response plans. The more promptly and effectively you can take action on key events, the more likely you are to keep customers and shareholders smiling!

■ Don't—*Recalculate control limits too often.*
  • Because the control limits are a function of the data, they *could* be adjusted almost continuously, but that would make it much harder to detect alarm conditions. It is best to recalculate the limits only following a known process change. (When using software to present and test the control charts, set your preferences so as to prevent the recalculation of the control limits!)
■ Don't—*Assume perfect data.*
  • Regular checks on the quality of your data collection, using methods such as Gage R&R, are important to ensure that alarms are not based on problems with the data itself.

Tests of Statistical Significance (Chi-Square, *t*-test, ANOVA)

When you measure and analyze a process or product, it is often possible to draw valid conclusions simply by *looking* at the data.

Sometimes, however, the lessons of the data are not obvious or certain. You may look at your data and say, "I don't see anything to help me here!" Or you may have a good hunch about what is going on, but want to be *extra* sure your conclusions are supported by the data. In these instances we can apply more rigorous *statistical* analysis methods to find or confirm trends or patterns in your data.

Tests of statistical significance are some of the most important techniques used by statisticians to look for patterns or to test their suspicions about data. In Six Sigma these tools have various possible applications, including:

▶ Confirming a problem or meaningful change in performance
▶ Checking the validity of data

- ► Determining the type of pattern or distribution in a group of continuous data
- ► Developing a root-cause hypothesis based on patterns and differences
- ► Validating or disproving root-cause hypotheses

Basics of Statistical Analysis: The Null Hypothesis

A 10-day heat wave hits your town and people say: "It's global warming!" You hit two holes-in-one in golf in two weeks, and exult "My game's really coming around!" The phone in the office seems to be ringing constantly and everyone says "It's going to be a busy quarter." You see a group of school kids making a lot of noise in the grocery store and say to yourself: "Kids these days just aren't brought up right!"

How valid are these conclusions? It is easy for us to extrapolate broad explanations from simple observations, and in some cases it is not a problem. The fact is, however, that in many instances, the so-called patterns we think we see are simply random variations. Wait long enough, and we will see just as much evidence for a completely *opposite* conclusion. When the cold spell hits its fourth week, someone is sure to speculate on the coming Ice Age. As you hit your fourth bad round of golf in a month, you figure you are "past your peak." And so on.

In statistics, we guard against the possibility of false patterns tricking us into faulty conclusions by adopting what is called "the null hypothesis." The null hypothesis states that any variation, change, or difference observed in a population or a process is due purely to *chance*. It is much like the attitude of that ultimate skeptic who won't believe anything unless you "prove it." And often the way we convince a skeptic is not to prove *our* theory but rather to *disprove* any other explanation. That is the approach we take in tests of statistical significance.

Testing for Statistical Significance: Methods and Examples

As with control charts, you can choose from several methods as you proceed to statistically test a hypothesis, described in the following paragraphs.

Chi-Square (χ^2) Test. This technique is used with discrete data, and in some cases with continuous data ("chi" is pronounced *kye*). As examples, you could apply a chi-square test so as to

▶ Compare defect rates in two locations to see whether they are significantly different

▶ Check to see if week-to-week changes in customer product choices indicate a meaningful level of variation

▶ Test the impact of various staffing levels on customer satisfaction

The *t*-Test. You use this method to test for significance when you have two groups or samples of *continuous* data. (As we noted in Chapter 13, continuous data measures have more power than discrete ones, but you need to be careful because these tests work only if certain conditions are met in the data.) Assuming that your data qualify, you might apply a *t*-test to:

▶ Compare the cycle time for a key step in your process at two weeks during the quarter, to check for any meaningful change

▶ Examine customer income levels in two regions, to see whether one serves significantly higher- or lower-income customers

▶ Test to see if the seek-time speed in two lots of disk drives is different

Analysis of Variance (ANOVA). ANOVA is another test of significance for continuous data; unlike the *t*-test, however, it can be used to compare *more* than two groups or samples. (If you find a significant difference among three or more groups of data, you have to do more analysis to find out *which* groups are different.) The following examples are the same as those for the *t*-test, but with the number differences shown in italic type:

▶ Compare the cycle time for a key step in your process for *each week* during the quarter to check for any meaningful change.

▶ Examine customer income levels in *four* regions to see whether one *or more* serves significantly higher- or lower-income customers

▶ Test to see if the seek-time speed in *five* lots of disk drives is different

Multivariate Analysis. In the first three methods described, the comparisons are based on a single factor or variable (time, income, speed, etc.). Of course *other* factors may be changing between one group or sample. Multivariate analysis (sometimes called MANOVA)

is used to determine the significance of several factors. (It is usually best to do an ANOVA test before doing a multivariate.)

Basic Steps Taken in Statistical Tests

The good news about applying statistics to business problems these days is that a lot of the grunt-work has been eliminated, thanks to statistical software. The major steps in applying them remain relevant, however, regardless of how quickly the calculations are done. These steps are described here, followed by Exhibit 17.2, which lists the "dos and don'ts" for performing tests of statistical significance.

1. **Identify the issue being analyzed.** What is the key question or concern to which you want to apply a statistical test? Check to make sure statistical validation is really needed; is the answer already fairly obvious?
2. **Formulate your hypothesis and the null hypothesis.** Describe in your hypothesis (known technically as the "alternative hypothesis") what you think is happening, and then negate it by concluding: "It is actually just random probability that this is what we see" (the null hypothesis).
3. **Select the proper statistical test.** Before you make a final choice of a continuous-data technique, you will need to review the data to see whether it will work.
4. **Conduct the calculation and review the results.** Basically, the three possible answers here are: (a) the null hypothesis is proven, meaning these data provide no evidence supportive of your hypothesis; (b) the null hypothesis is *not* true, based on these data, indicating that some significant factor is affecting the data and hence your hypothesis may be correct; or (c) an *error* indicates that something in your data or in the tool you selected is not right.

Exhibit 17.2

"DOS AND DON'TS" FOR PERFORMING TESTS OF STATISTICAL SIGNIFICANCE

■ Do—*Make sure the data being used is valid.*
  • A test done using faulty data is meaningless or even dangerous. If for example your sample size is too small, you find "significant" differences when they don't really exist.

■ Do—*Select the right kind of test.*
  • For example, if it is discrete data, chi-square is the test to use.

■ Don't—*Use your own expertise as a gut check of the statistical analysis.*
  • Statistics and experience are meant to work together.

■ Don't—*Consider yourself an expert too soon.*
  • Plenty of complexities and nuances come with using these tools. Unusual situations actually are typical in the real world, and thus it can take more than a bit of experience to learn the ins and outs of statistical analyses.

Correlation and Regression Analysis

Correlation and regression analysis encompass a family of tools that analyze the relationships among two or more factors. The basics of correlation were introduced with scatter plots in Chapter 14 (see the Overview on p. 273 and the example on p. 315). When two factors are correlated, a change in one will be accompanied by a change in the other. By applying statistical calculations to those data, we can measure the *strength* of a possible relationship among the factors and draw a number of other helpful conclusions besides.

Across the various types of correlation and regression, you will find tools that can help you to:

► Test root-cause hypotheses by finding links between the suspected cause (the X) and the response or output (the Y).
► Measure and compare the influence of *various* factors (Xs) on the results (Y).
► Predict the performance of a process, product, or service under certain conditions.

Correlation and regression can be used *only* when you have data for two or more factors that are matched on individual items. (This contrasts with the statistical tests, which compare *groups* of data.) Table 17.1 shows a situation in which you might test a correlation.

To do a correlation analysis, you would need to have data *both* for time between maintenance *and* for copy defects from copier A, B, C, and so on.

TABLE 17.1   CORRELATION TEST EXAMPLE

Copier	Time elapsing between maintenance	Copy defects

Particularly in analyzing causes, and depending on the nature of your data, correlation and regression tools can bring some important advantages over such tools as chi-square and ANOVA. They allow you to see finer patterns in smaller samples of data, and to see how the changes in different variables directly affect a unit

Types of Correlation and Regression Analysis

Again, computers, spreadsheets, and statistical software have made these tools accessible to many people. The following paragraphs describe some of the common uses and a few key concepts, followed by Exhibit 17.3, which lists the "dos and don'ts" of using correlation and regression analysis.

Correlation Coefficient. The same data used to draw a scatter plot can be crunched into a number—noted r—that tells you whether and how strongly the factors are correlated. The r correlation coefficient ranges from -1 to 1; generally an r score of below $-.7$ or above $.7$ would be worthy of serious further investigation. (Negative r results indicate a negative correlation.)

Correlation Percentage. Another number, r^2, is preferred by many because it reflects the amount or percent of variation in the Y or dependent factor that seems to be caused by the X factor. (You get r^2 just by "squaring" r.) For example, let's say you found an apparent positive correlation for the time between copier maintenance and copy defects, with an r value of .72. Therefore, $r^2 = .52$, which means that roughly 50 percent of the increase in defects correlates with the time between maintenance. Note that how you will interpret and respond to either r or r^2 will depend on the purpose of your analysis and on your type of data.

Regression. The various forms of regression analysis concentrate on using existing data to predict future results. The most common is linear regression (or simple regression), which is used for two variables. We can illustrate with a case study.

Case Study #15: Percy's Copy Repair Analyzes Defect Rates for Its Clients

Percy's wants to show clients the value of its maintenance service contract. Having gathered data on the relationship between time maintenance and copy defects, they found that defect rates tend to increase by 15 percent for every two-week period without maintenance.

Using the tool of linear regression, they were able to predict for a prospective customer that by the third month after their last emergency service call, they would reach about 25 percent "defective" copies. The prediction turned out to be accurate, and now the customer has a biweekly service agreement with Percy's.

Multiple Regression. Multiple regression, like multivariate analysis, examines the relationship among *several* factors and the results. In a process environment, examples could include all those shown in Table 17.2.

Using multiple regression, you would be able to quantify the impact of each of these Xs on the Ys—and to see how they interact. In more advanced applications, multiple regression is applied to create *models* to predict the results when combinations of factors interact under various conditions.

TABLE 17.2   MULTIPLE REGRESSION ANALYSIS EXAMPLES

Software installation	Software package	Size of software (MB)	Number of users on network	Server processor speed (MHz)	System downtime during install (minutes)
Hotel reservation and check-in	Reservation	Hold time to talk to reservation agent (seconds)	Number of days reserved	Number of agents on duty in call center	Time to check in a guest (minutes)

Exhibit 17.3

"DOS AND DON'TS" FOR USING CORRELATION AND REGRESSION ANALYSIS

■ Do—*Make sure you have paired data.*
  • The ability to do correlation and regression is predicated on how you collect and compile data. If the values of the factors being analyzed do not match for a single item, you cannot do correlation analysis.
■ Do—*Use the correlation coefficient and percentage (r and r^2) to better understand scatter plot data.*
  • As one of the easiest statistical indicators, it can be a huge help to you as you try to interpret the mass of dots on a scatter diagram.
■ Do—*Apply more advanced methods—when you're ready—to learn more about your processes and products.*
  • Used properly, correlation and regression can add significantly to your understanding of how and why variation occurs in your business, and how to control it.

■ Don't—*Take predictions drawn from data as fact.*
  • The predictions made from regression analysis are in most cases based on *tendencies*, which means you may still encounter a lot of variation you do not understand, and can lead to results you did not expect.
■ Don't—*Look at the data in only one way.*
  • If a strongly suspected correlation does not show up, it may be hidden. You might want to consider stratifying your data or gathering them over a longer period before you conclude absolutely that no relationship is present.
■ Don't—*Assume that correlation means causation.*
  • As we discussed in Chapter 14, two items that correlate may not cause one another at all—something else may be affecting them both.

Design of Experiments (DOE)

DOE is a method used for testing and optimizing the performance of a process, product, service, or solution. It draws heavily on the techniques just reviewed (i.e., tests of statistical significance, correlation, and regression) to help you learn about the behavior of a product or process under varying conditions. The unique aspect of DOE is the opportunity it gives you to plan and control the variables using an *experiment*, as opposed to just gathering and observing real-world events in the manner known as empirical observation.

DOE has plenty of potential application in a Six Sigma organization. It can allow you to:

▶ Assess voice of the customer systems to find the best combination of methods producing valid feedback without annoying customers.
▶ Assess factors to isolate the vital root cause of a problem or defect.
▶ Pilot or test combinations of possible solutions to find the optimal improvement strategy.
▶ Evaluate product or service designs to identify potential problems and reduce defects right from day 1.

Even though DOE tends to be easier to apply to *things* than to people, it is possible to conduct experiments in service environments. They tend to be real-world tests in which the variables are controlled in the actual process and the results then compared. For example, a large sales organization tested 14 variables over a four-month period in an effort to find the best sales-boosting combination. Based on solutions identified in the field experiment, sales volume jumped by more than 50 percent even in the firm's top-producing region.[1]

Basic Steps in Design of Experiments

The basic steps for you to take in a designed experiment are described here, followed by Exhibit 17.4, which lists the "dos and don'ts" for using design of experiments.

Step 1. Identify the factors to be evaluated. What do you want to learn from the experiment? What are the likely influences on the process or product? As you select factors, keep in mind the importance of balancing the benefit of getting additional data by testing more factors with the increased cost and complexity.

Step 2. Define the levels of the factors to be tested. In the case of such variable factors as speed, time, and weight, you could test them at an infinite number of levels. Thus in this step you choose not only which values, but also how many different levels you want to test. In the case of discrete data, levels may be either/or; for example, in testing a form we could (a) include our e-mail address, or (b) not include our e-mail address.[2]

Step 3. Create an array of experimental combinations. In DOE, you usually want to avoid the one-factor-at-a-time (OFAT) approach, where each variable is tested in isolation. Rather, arrays of conditions are examined to obtain representative data for all the factors. Possible combinations or arrays can be generated by statistics software tools or found in tables, and their use helps you to avoid having to test every possible permutation.

Step 4. Conduct the experiment under the prescribed conditions. A key here is to avoid letting other, untested factors influence your results.

Step 5. Evaluate the results and conclusions. If you are going to see patterns and draw conclusions from DOE data, tools like ANOVA and multiple regression are a must. From the experimental data you may get clear answers, or additional questions may arise that you will then test in additional experiments.

Exhibit 17.4

"DOS AND DON'TS" FOR USING DESIGN OF EXPERIMENTS

- Do—*Be prepared to apply DOE concepts to real-world processes.*
  - Outside of product design, engineering, and manufacturing, most other business activities won't fit in a laboratory. You may need to conduct your experiments on real people (e.g., in piloting a new solution).
- Do—*Take advantage of experimental arrays.*
  - One way that the discipline of DOE can bring you big time and resource savings is by producing more data from fewer tests. Done right, you *can* take the time to conduct experiments you might otherwise not have considered.
- Do—*Include problem prevention in your DOE plans.*
  - If something goes wrong in your experiment, would the consequences be serious? If so, you need to plan preventions and contingencies to make sure an experiment does not backfire.

For example, piloting a solution with customers is fine, as long as you do not put your business with them at undue risk.

■ Don't—*Fail to consider a variety of factors or influences.*
 • It is the unanticipated variables that mess up lots of experiments.
■ Don't—*Get stuck on the experimental treadmill.*
 • As in the analyze phase of DMAIC, you can always do more tests and gather more data. Use DOE as a *tool*, not as an *end*.

Failure Modes and Effects Analysis (FMEA)

Failure modes and effects analysis is a set of guidelines, a process, and a form to identify and prioritize potential problems (failures). By basing their activities on FMEA, a manager, improvement team, or process owner can focus the energy and resources of prevention, monitoring, and response plans where they are most likely to pay off. Borrowed from high-stakes industries such as aerospace and defense, FMEA is a more rigorous application of the potential problem analysis concept discussed in Chapter 15.

The FMEA method has many applications in a Six Sigma environment in terms of looking for problems not only in work processes and improvements but also in data-collection activities, voice of the customer efforts, procedures, and even the rollout of a Six Sigma initiative. The only prerequisite is to have a complex or high-stakes situation in which you want to place a special emphasis on keeping problems at bay.

The steps and key concepts for using FMEA are as follows:

1. **Identify the process or product/service.**
2. **List potential problems that could arise (failure modes).**[3] The basic question is "What could go wrong?" Ideas as to potential problems may come from various sources including brainstorming, process analysis, and benchmarking. They can be grouped by process step or product/service component. Avoid trivial problems.
3. **Rate the problem for severity, probability of occurrence, and detectability.** Using a 1–10 scale, give a score on each factor to each potential problem. More serious problems get a higher rating; harder-to-detect problems also get a higher score. Again, these scores may be judgments or be based on historical or test data.

4. **Calculate the risk priority number (RPN) and prioritize actions.** Multiplying the three scores together gives this overall risk rating. By adding the RPNs from all problems, you get a total risk figure for the process or product/service. (Maximum RPN = 1,000.)

5. **Develop actions to reduce the risk.** Focusing first on potential problems having the highest priority, you then can devise actions to reduce one or all factors: seriousness, occurrence, and detectability. A key benefit of the tool is to make your problem management resources, which always are finite, go to best benefit.

Let's take a look at how FMEA can be used.

Case Study #16: An E-Commerce Company Uses FMEA to Make Sure It Catalogs Are Updated Accurately

Managers and engineers at e-commerce company Nitwit.com wanted to make sure nothing went wrong with its process for updating the online catalog. Here are two of the problems they identified and the analysis they did:

1. The wrong artwork is used with a new item.
   Severity = 5
   Occurrence = 5
   Detection = 3
   RPN = 5 × 5 × 3 = 75
2. Buyers can't place an order for an item.
   Severity = 8
   Occurrence = 5
   Detection = 6
   RPN = 8 × 5 × 6 = 240

Based on this assessment, they focused on the concern about not being able to place orders and developed preventive measures to ensure that all new product numbers are posted to the ordering system.

Mistake-Proofing (or *Poka-Yoke*)

Mistake-proofing can be thought of as an extension of FMEA, or as an extra-disciplined way of shedding those final pounds (i.e., defects) in our Six Sigma diet. Whereas FMEA helps in the prediction and prevention of problems, mistake-proofing emphasizes the detection and correction of mistakes before they become defects delivered to customers. It puts special attention on the one constant threat to any process: *human* error.

The basic ideas behind mistake-proofing—also known by the Japanese name *poka yoke* (*POH-kuh YOH-kay*)—were developed by a management consultant in Japan, Shigeo Shingo. Shingo's ideas were controversial, partly because he proposed a method whereby "inspection" (the word he chose) becomes an integral part of every step in a process, as opposed to being solely a separate responsibility. When one looks more closely, however, one sees that the heart of mistake-proofing is simply to pay careful attention to every activity in the process and to place checks and problem prevention at each step. It is a matter of constant, instantaneous feedback, rather like the balance and direction data transmitted from a cyclist's ears to brain, keeping his or her bike upright and on the path.

Mistake-proofing can be used to:

▶ **Fine-tune improvements and process designs from DMAIC projects.** How can those rare, most challenging errors be avoided or managed?

▶ **Gather data from processes approaching Six Sigma performance.** The more "perfect" a process is, the harder it can be to measure.

▶ **Eliminate the kinds of process issues and defects needed to take a process from 4.5 to 6 Sigma.**

Basic Steps in Mistake-Proofing

Mistake-proofing is best applied after completion of a thorough FMEA prediction and prevention review. The following paragraphs describe the steps in mistake-proofing; then Exhibit 17.5 lists the "dos and don'ts" you should keep in mind when using this tool.

Step 1. Identify possible errors that might occur despite preventive actions. Review each step in the existing process while asking the question "What possible human error or equipment malfunction could take place in this step?"

Step 2. Determine a way to detect that an error or malfunction is taking place or about to occur. For example, an electric circuit in your car can tell if you fastened your seatbelt. E-commerce software is programmed to tell whether any piece of data is missing from a field. In an assembly plant, trays holding parts help the worker to see whether an item is missing.

Step 3. Identify and select the type of action to be taken when an error is detected. The basic types of mistake-proofing device include:

▶ **Control.** An action that self-corrects the process, like an automatic spell-checker/corrector.
▶ **Shutdown.** A procedure or device that blocks or shuts down the process when an error occurs. The automatic shutoff feature of a home iron is one example. Another is sophisticated investment software that bars the entry of certain investments in accounts decreed to be off-limits to those investments.
▶ **Warning.** As the name implies, this alerts the person involved in the work that something is going wrong. A seatbelt buzzer is an example. So is a control chart that shows that a process may be out of control. Warnings too often are ignored, so controls and shutdowns usually are preferable.

Coming up with methods to detect, self-correct, block/shut down, or warn of a problem can require real imagination and creativity. Some common types of mistake-proofing measures include:

▶ Color- and shape-coding of materials and documents
▶ Distinctive shapes of such key items as legal documents
▶ Symbols and icons to identify easily confused items
▶ Computerized checklists, clear forms, best-in-class, up-to-date procedures and simple workflows to help prevent errors from becoming defects in the hands of customers

Dave Boenitz of semiconductor equipment manufacturer Applied Materials (quoted in Chapter 3) says that mistake-proofing has been the focus of their improvement and lean manufacturing efforts. "We've looked for ways to make the assembly so foolproof that it's impossible to assemble it the wrong way. So we've done things like more visual displays; we've got colored schematics of how the part is supposed to go together." Also, a variety of jigs and fixtures are used to make it difficult to assemble items in the wrong way, much like a key that can fit only a certain lock.

Extra care is taken to check the work at each step as well: "Those people who do the work inspect their product before it moves on; then those people who *receive* it inspect the product. Through this orchestrated movement, they are able to eliminate most of the manufacturing assembly errors that can occur."

Exhibit 17.5

"DOS AND DON'TS" WHEN USING MISTAKE-PROOFING

■ Do—*Try to imagine all conceivable errors that can be made.*
  • Here is where the truly negative and paranoid people in your organization can at last be of real help!
■ Do—*Use all of your creative powers to brainstorm clever ways to detect and correct errors as part of the work process itself.*
  • To leave the detection of defects to downstream inspectors, or to the customers, is to court disaster.

■ Don't—*Fall into the "to err is human" mindset.*
  • "To get things right most of the time" is also a human trait. Find out how your people are self-correcting problems that are not prevented upstream, and share best practices.
■ Don't—*Rely on people to catch their own errors all the time.*
  • If your process is chugging along at just 2 Sigma, you cannot eliminate the safety net of downstream inspection.

Quality Function Deployment (QFD)

Quality function deployment is a method for prioritizing and translating customer inputs into designs and specifications for a product, service, or process. Although the detail of the work involved in QFD can be both complex and exhaustive (not to mention exhaust*ing*), the essentials of the QFD method are based on commonsense ideas and tools we have already seen.

QFD is a robust method having many variations, so its uses can be quite broad. It can be applied to:

▶ Prioritize and select improvement projects based on customer needs and current performance.

▶ Assess a process's or product's performance versus competitors.

▶ Translate customer requirements into performance measures.

▶ Design, test, and refine new processes, products, and services.

QFD is by no means a stand-alone tool. To work well, it relies on a variety of other methods from voice of the customer input to design of experiments.

Basics of Quality Function Deployment

A special multidimensional matrix, dubbed the "House of Quality," is the best-known element of the QFD method. A full QFD product design project will involve a series of these matrices, translating from customer and competitive needs all the way down to detailed process specifications. Among all the detail included in the QFD documentation, however, lie two core concepts:

1. **The QFD Cycle.** An iterative effort to develop operational designs and plans in four broad phases:
   a. Translate customer input and competitor analysis into product or service features (basic design elements).
   b. Translate product/service features into product/service specifications and measures.
   c. Translate product/service specifications and measures into *process* design features. (How will the process deliver the features per specification?)
   d. Translate process design features into process performance specifications and measures.
2. **Prioritization and correlation.** Detailed analysis of the relationships among specific needs, features, requirements, and measures. Matrices like the House of Quality or the simple L-Matrix (see Figure 17.2) keep this analysis organized and document the rationale behind the design effort.

In essence, the QFD cycle develops the links from downstream Ys (customer requirements and product specifications) back to upstream

	Choice of point sizes	Variety of ink colors	Choice of finishes	3 price levels ($12, $40, $75)	Available neck chain	Nontoxic ink	Retailed at jewelers	Sold direct online
Stylish			●	△	△		●	△
Multiple choices	●	●	●	●	○		○	○
Safe to use			△		△	●		
Value for money	△		△	●			△	●
Hard to lose			△		●			

CONTRIBUTION: ● Strong ○ Moderate △ Weak

FIGURE 17.2 EXAMPLE: SIMPLIFIED L-MATRIX FOR DESIGNING A PEN

Xs (process specifications) *right in the design process.* With an existing process or product, it can be used to clarify and document those relationships never investigated before. Another benefit of the House of Quality is a "diagonal" relationship test afforded by the matrix, testing combinations that may not have been considered by our standard human linear thought processes.

Exhibit 17.6 lists the "dos and don'ts" to keep in mind when using quality function deployment.

Exhibit 17.6

"DOS AND DON'TS" FOR USING QUALITY FUNCTION DEPLOYMENT

- Do—*Adapt the complexity of the method to your situation.*
  - Designing a complex product can involve many layers and much detail. Simply creating measures for an existing process should be much simpler. (Software packages are available for simpler or detailed House of Quality matrices.)
- Do—*Concentrate on getting good input and data, not just on "filling boxes."*
  - A QFD matrix can have a lot of white space. Often, you will fill it in best just using your own judgment; if however you are putting something in a box merely to fill the space, don't.

- Do—*Use the competitor analysis feature of QFD to factor other external data into your designs and specifications.*
  - Design for the customer, with an eye on the competitor.

- Don't—*Forget to apply other tools to the method.*
  - For example, design of experiments can be critical to maximizing performance on various design features. You also can use tools such as project charters to help lay the foundation for a design effort.

Twelve Keys to Success

As we approach the end of our journey along the Six Sigma Way, we hope it is a beginning for you. In some ways, this book has just scratched the surface in outlining the ideas, tools, and disciplines that make up this system for management. (Some points we likely repeated often enough that the diligent reader by now is saying "Enough! I get it!") To wrap up, we summarize some of the key points of this book and the experiences of various organizations trying to become master Six Sigma methods and build a culture of continuous improvement with a list of keys to success. Hopefully, this list will make up for the areas we did not cover in greater depth, and help you glean the key points from topics covered in detail.

Keys to Success

1. Tie Six Sigma Improvement Efforts to Business Strategy and Priorities

Even if your first efforts focus on fairly narrow problems, their impact on key business needs should be clear. Show how projects and other activities link to your mission, customers, financial performance, and competitiveness whenever possible.

2. Position Six Sigma as an Improved Way to Manage for Today

The methods and tools of Six Sigma make sense for successful organizations in the twenty-first century. They are a product of lessons learned by enlightened companies and managers, which address the challenges of rapid change, intense competition, and increasingly demanding customers.

3. Keep the Message Simple and Clear

Beware of alienating people with strange terms and jargon that create classes in a Six Sigma environment. Although new vocabulary and skills are obviously part of the Six Sigma discipline, the core of the system and your company's vision for improvement should be accessible and meaningful to everyone.

4. Develop Your Own Path to Six Sigma

Your themes, priorities, projects, training, and structure all should be decided based on what works best for you. Think about it: Why would a rigid formula for an approach create a more flexible, responsive organization?

5. Focus on Short-Term Results

The proof is in the power of what Six Sigma can do to make your organization more competitive and profitable and your customers more loyal and delighted. Develop and push forward a plan that will make initial achievements concrete in the first four to six months.

6. Focus on Long-Term Growth and Development

Balance the push for early results with the recognition that those gains must lay the foundation for the real power of Six Sigma: creation of a more responsive, customer-focused, resilient, and successful company for the *long term*.

7. Publicize Results, Admit Setbacks, and Learn from Both

Don't expect—or claim—that Six Sigma works perfectly in your company. Recognize and celebrate successes, but pay equal attention to challenges and disappointments. Be ready to continuously improve and even redesign your Six Sigma processes as you progress.

8. Make an Investment to Make It Happen

Without time, support, and money, the habits and existing processes in your business will not change much. The results are likely to bring a quick return on investment, but first you have to *make* the investment.

9. Use Six Sigma Tools Wisely

No single tool or discipline in the Six Sigma system can create happier customers or improve profits. Statistics can answer questions, but cannot deliver outstanding service. Creative ideas may hold potential, but without processes to develop and deliver them, they are just dreams. Your success in Six Sigma will depend on applying all the methods, in the right balance, to maximize your results. And using the *simplest* tool that works rather than the most complex should be highly valued.

10. Link Customers, Process, Data, and Innovation to Build the Six Sigma System

These core elements are brought together in the Six Sigma approach. Understanding your markets and your operations and being able to use measures and creativity to maximize value and performance create a *potent combination that can make life miserable for your competitors.*

11. Make Top Leaders Responsible and Accountable

Until senior managers of the organization, unit, or even department accept driving improvement as an integral part of their jobs, the true importance of the initiative will be in doubt, and the energy behind it will be weakened. To get there, they will need to examine and improve *their own* management processes and leadership habits.

12. Make Learning an Ongoing Activity

A few months of training, however intensive, cannot cement all the new knowledge and skills needed to sustain Six Sigma. Over time, you should look outside the continuous improvement discipline for other methods and ideas that complement the tools reviewed in this book.

BONUS—Make Six Sigma FUN!

Yes, this stuff about business survival, competition, and measurement is serious, sometimes confusing, and even a bit scary. But the Six Sigma Way opens the door to new ideas, new ways of thinking, and a new breath of success. Putting humor into it and having a good time with Six Sigma will only *raise* your chances for success: Any time people enjoy something, they almost automatically put more energy and enthusiasm into it.

A Final Word

In business-speak we are compelled to use short phrases to describe complicated ideas. "Six Sigma" is no more a *thing* than is "economic policy" or "organizational excellence" or any dozens of other short-hand terms we use every day. As we noted from the start of this book, what we label Six Sigma is really a *system* that encompasses many concepts, tools, and principles. It's not the label that's important, but how you use and adapt it to meet the needs and goals of your organization.

We believe, and we hope you agree, that the elements of the Six Sigma system are essential, powerful, and valuable in some way as part of *every successful business*. At the same time, we strongly encourage you to adapt the discipline and methods of Six Sigma to best influence your unique culture, industry, market position, people, and strategy. Our biggest fear is that people will accept or reject Six Sigma as if it were a *thing* (falling victim to the Tyranny of the Or) and not use it as a flexible system.

Finally, having worked with this big topic and the companies applying it for quite a few years now, we are continually startled at how much we still have to learn and how many new perspectives emerge. We would be thrilled to hear your comments, new ideas, and your thoughts on whether and how *The Six Sigma Way* has helped you. You can reach us via e-mail at *ssw@pivotalresources.com*.

We hope to hear about your successful journeys on the way to Six Sigma.

Sigma Calculation Worksheet

Sigma levels of a process can be determined several ways. The steps below use the simplest method, based on number of defects at the *end* of a process (usually called, appropriately, "process sigma").

STEP 1: Selecting the Process, Unit & Requirements

➤ Identify the process you want to evaluate: _____ (process)

➤ What is the primary "thing" produced by the process? _____ (unit)

➤ What are key customer requirements for the unit? _____

_____

_____(requirements)

STEP 2: Defining the "Defect" and "Number of Opportunities"

➤ Based on the requirements noted above, list all the possible *defects* in a single unit (e.g. late, missing data, wrong size, delivered to wrong address, etc.). Be sure the defects described can be identified *objectively*._____

_____

_____ (defects)

➤ How many defects could be found on a *single* unit? _____ (opportunities)

STEP 3: Gather Data & Calculate DPMO

➤ Collect end-of-process data: _____ (units counted) _____(*total* defects counted)

➤ Determine Total Opportunities in data gathered:

Units Counted x Opportunities = _____ (total opportunities)

➤ Calculate Defects per Million Opportunities:

(# Defects Counted ÷ Total Opportunities) x 10^6 = _____ (DPMO)

STEP 4: Convert DPMO to Sigma

➤ Use Sigma Converstion table on reverse and note estimated sigma here: _____

NOTES: 1) The table will give you a very rough range of your sigma level 2) Your sigma figure can vary significantly based on the accuracy of your data and the number of opportunities you identify on a unit.

NOTES

Introduction

1. James Collins and Jerry Porras, *Built to Last* (New York: Harper Business, 1994), p. 44.
2. Since the first edition of this book, author Pande expanded on the "Genius of the And" concept as a theme for a book on leading a changing organization, entitled *The Six Sigma Leader*, also published by McGraw-Hill.

Chapter 1

1. Address to General Electric Company Annual Meeting, Cleveland, Ohio, April 21, 1999.
2. Six Sigma was adopted as the theme linking all of AlliedSignal's diverse quality initiatives in about 1995. In a sense Allied's decision, and its influence on GE, is what brought Six Sigma back to its original role at Motorola where, as we've noted, it was a full culture-change process.
3. AlliedSignal, *1998 Annual Report*, p. 8.
4. GE Annual Meeting, April 24, 1996, quoted in Slater, p. 209.
5. *AlliedSignal Annual Report*, 1998, p. 2.
6. Quoted in *Fortune* (September 27, 1999), p. 132.

Chapter 2

1. We owe credit for this phrase to our friend and colleague Chuck Cox, whom we will be quoting later in the book.
2. The curve metaphor is reflected in a core concept presented by Intel chairman Andy Grove in his book *Only the Paranoid Survive:* the "strategic inflection point." Grove points out that a company's failure to adjust its strategy at the right moment can mean disaster. We suggest that many smaller "inflection points" can have a huge impact

on a corporation or its business units, and that Six Sigma is a way to better negotiate both the strategic and the daily curves. See Andrew Grove, *Only the Paranoid Survive* (New York: Currency Books, 1996), p. 32.

3. A couple of points to make our comments more precise: First of all, σ is used to represent the standard deviation of a population or an entire group. Usually, standard deviations are calculated based on a sample from the population, for which the notation is *s* (for sample standard deviation). Thus you'll usually see *s* in statistics formulas, and not σ.

   Second, the letter *z* gets used in this context, too. The distance from the mean in numbers of standard deviations is measured in what statisticians call *z units*, but the scale is the same (e.g., 1.65 *z* units from the mean equals 1.65 standard deviations). Also, the percentage of the sample or population represented by a slice of the bell-shaped curve is often called the *z*-score. So when we noted that 34.1 percent of your trips were between 18 and 20.7 minutes, 34.1 percent is the *z*-score.

4. Deming called this the *Shewhart Cycle*, after his friend and mentor, Walter Shewhart. It is sometimes called PDSA for Plan-Do-Act-*Study*-Act.

5. This particular model got its start at GE Capital and was later adopted by all of GE. The original model—still used in some companies—included only four steps: measure, analyze, improve, control.

6. Interview with Devin Rickard of Adobe Systems, June 2013.

Chapter 3

1. The discipline of activity-based accounting is giving finance people new perspectives and tools to help them link costs and process tasks more closely.

2. ISO9000 is an internationally recognized set of standards used to validate the consistency of processes, usually in product manu-facturing and design but in other areas as well. A company is certified by a recognized independent auditor, primarily indicating that (a) the company has properly documented processes, and (b) the processes are being followed as documented. A number of other industry- and customer-specific certifications can be sought by

manufacturing organizations as well—usually as a basic requirement for consideration as a potential vendor.

Chapter 4

1. We know of a car dealer who visited Detroit in the 1970s to plead for more fuel-efficient, well-made economy vehicles. After listening (or seeming to), the Big Three executives patted the dealer on the shoulder and sagely counseled: "Just sell what we build."

Chapter 5

1. These figures are drawn from the presentation "Training Six Sigma Quality in a Service Organization," given at a meeting of the American Society for Training and Development National Conference in Atlanta, Georgia, on May 26, 1999.

Chapter 7

1. We've seen some *good* change marketing efforts, too. For example, when a major bank was moving a regional headquarters to a new building and shifting people from offices to cubicles (a jarring change), the switch was accompanied several months in advance by a slogan ("It's Your Move"), sweatshirts, parties, brochures, etc.—all just to help people feel better about the new environment.

Chapter 8

1. The roles and structure noted here are common to Six Sigma and quality efforts in a number of organizations, including GE.
2. Note that we are focusing here only on Black Belts as the workhorse role in most Six Sigma initiatives. Some of the same considerations apply to preparing and deploying Master Black Belts.

Chapter 10

1. This great analogy is borrowed from a book by consultant Jill Janov, who actually came across the "dried peas" effect while learning to write billboard ad copy. See Jill Janov, *The Inventive Organization* (San Francisco: Jossey-Bass, 1994), pp. 11–12.

Chapter 11

1. See a classic study: Alfred Chandler, *The Visible Hand: The Managerial Revolution in American Business* (Cambridge, MA: Harvard University Press, 1977), p. 462.
2. Michael Porter, *Competitive Advantage* (New York: The Free Press, 1985), p. 36.
3. Porter, p. 38.

Chapter 12

1. We use the single term *voice of the customer* throughout the book to signify *both* efforts to understand current and future needs of existing and prospective customers, *and* activities to gather information on competitors, new technologies, etc.—also called *voice of the market* systems.
2. *Note:* Although most of this chapter uses a focus on external customers and markets, we encourage those in *internal* organizations or support processes to adopt a similar perspective, which will help them to better understand customers and markets.
3. Jan Carlzon, *Moments of Truth* (Cambridge, MA: Ballinger, 1987).
4. We learned of this performance standard from Barbara Friesner, director of training for Loews Hotels, which uses "10, 5, First and Last" extensively in their evaluations of service performance. In the next chapter, discuss how Loews measures against this standard.

Chapter 13

1. Bob Lawson and Ron Stewart, *Measuring Six Sigma and Beyond: Continuous vs. Attribute Data* (Schaumberg, IL: Motorola University Press, 1997), p. 16.
2. A warning for the technical types: PPM and DPMO are not really synonymous, so be careful. Many people assume or intend PPM to signify defectives units—so 6σ would mean 3.4 "bad" units for every million produced. In our electronic components example, however, we noted that each item has roughly 4,000 opportunities. Using the DPMO calculation, you would therefore reach 6σ performance with 3.4 defects for every 250 units (250 units × 4,000 = 1,000,000 opportunities). If defects were one to a unit, your yield would be 98.64 percent and your total *defectives* for every million electronic

components would be 13,600. Pretty good for a complex product, but a lot more than 3.4!

3. For our discussion and examples here, we assume only *one* defect opportunity in our   Sigma calculations. Determining opportunities gets trickier for internal process measures.

4. Another method to calculate the internal yield is called "rolled throughput yield." YRTP is generated by multiplying the yields from each of the substeps. In our example, this would be: $.98 \times .99 \times .97 = .94$.

5. Cost of poor quality (which we introduced in Chapter 5) also is known as price of nonconformance (PONC). The related measure, cost of quality, includes the costs of *both* rework and defects (i.e., poor quality), as well as the costs of solutions, prevention, and appraisal/prevention (i.e., achieving good quality).

Chapter 15

1. See "GE's Quality Gamble," *ComputerWorld*, June 8, 1998.

2. Like the one in Chapter 14, this scenario is based on several real organizations. It has been fictionalized for the reader's enjoyment and to avoid inflicting any embarrassment on real people.

3. Other "value" dimensions influence organizational decisions as well, including, for example, integrity, respect for diversity, environmental consciousness, support for employees' personal lives, and so on. These other factors may serve to justify activities not technically value-adding to the customer.

Chapter 16

1. Robert S. Kaplan and David P. Norton, *The Balanced Scorecard* (Boston: Harvard Business School Press, 1996).

Chapter 17

1. See "Numbers Tell the Story," *Selling Power* (July–August 1999), pp. 58–64.

2. If we wanted to test *where* on the form to put the e-mail address, several more possible levels could be included. Few factors are *really* binary, but it is often simpler to handle them that way.

3. Some practitioners differentiate between "failure modes," which refer to system and equipment problems, and "*error* modes" (or EMEA) that refer to human error. We prefer to combine the two into a single analysis.

GLOSSARY

Affinity chart (diagram) Brainstorming tool used to gather large quantities of information from many people; ideas usually are put on sticky notes, then categorized into similar columns; columns are named giving an overall grouping of ideas.

Analyze DMAIC phase where process detail is scrutinized for improvement opportunities. Note that (1) data are investigated and verified to prove suspected root causes and substantiate the problem statement (*see also* Cause and effect); and (2) process analysis includes reviewing process maps for value-adding/non-value-adding activities. *See also* Process map; Value-adding activities; Non-value-adding activities.

Balanced scorecard Categorizes ongoing measures into four significant areas: finance, process, people, and innovation. Used as a presentation tool to update sponsors, senior management, and others on the progress of a business or process; also useful for process owners.

Baseline measures Data signifying the level of process performance as it is/was operating at the initiation of an improvement project (prior to solutions).

Black Belt A team leader, trained in the DMAIC process and facilitation skills, responsible for guiding an improvement project to completion.

Cause-and-effect diagram Also known as a "fishbone" or "Ishikawa diagram"; categorical brainstorming tool used for determining root-cause hypothesis and potential causes (the bones of the fish) for a specific effect (the head of the fish).

Charter Team document defining the context, specifics, and plans of an improvement project; includes business case; problem and goal statements; constraints and assumptions; roles; preliminary plan; and scope. Periodic reviews with the sponsor ensure alignment with business strategies; review, revise, refine periodically throughout the DMAIC process based on data.

Checksheet Forms, tables, or worksheets facilitating data collection and compilation; allows for collection of stratified data. *See also* Stratification.

Common cause Normal, everyday influences on a process; usually harder to eliminate and require changes to the process. Problems from common causes are referred to as "chronic pain." *See also* Control charts; Run chart, or time plot; Special cause; Variation.

Continuous data Any variable measured on a continuum or scale that can be infinitely divided; primary types include time, dollars, size, weight, temperature, and speed; also referred to as "variable data."

Control DMAIC phase C; once solutions have been implemented, ongoing measures track and verify the stability of the improvement and the predictability of the process. Often includes process-management techniques and systems including process ownership, cockpit charts and/or process management charts, etc. *See also* Process management. Also, a statistical concept indicating that a process operating within an expected range of variation is being influenced mainly by common-cause factors; processes operating in this state are referred to as "in control." *See also* Control charts; Process capability; Variation.

Control charts Specialized time plot or run chart showing process performance, mean (average), and control limits; helps determine process influences of common (normal) or special (unusual, unique) causes.

Cost of poor quality (COPQ) Dollar measures depicting the impact of problems (internal and external failures) in the process as it exists; include labor and material costs for handoffs, rework, inspection, and other non-value-adding activities.

Criteria matrix Decision-making tool used when potential choices must be weighed against several key factors (e.g., cost, ease to implement, impact on customer.). Encourages use of facts, data, and clear business objectives in decision making.

Customer Any internal or external person/organization who receives the output (product or service) of the process; understanding the impact of the process on both internal and external customers is key to process management and improvement.

Customer requirements Defines the needs and expectations of the customer; translated into measurable terms and used in the process to ensure compliance with the customers' needs.

Cycle time All time used in a process; includes actual work time and wait time.

Defect Any instance or occurrence where the product or service fails to meet customer requirements.

Defect opportunity A type of potential defect on a unit of throughput (output) that is important to the customer; e.g., specific fields on a form that create an opportunity for error that would be important to the customer.

Defective Any unit with one or more defects. *See also* Defect.

Define First DMAIC phase defines the problem/opportunity, process, and customer requirements; because the DMAIC cycle is iterative, the process problem, flow, and requirements should be verified and updated for clarity throughout the other phases. *See also* Charter; Customer requirements; Process map; Voice of the customer (VOC).

Discrete data Any data *not* quantified on an infinitely divisible scale. Includes a count, proportion, or percentage of a characteristic or category (e.g., gender, loan type, department, location, etc.); also referred to as "attribute data."

Downstream Processes (activities) occurring after the task or activity in question.

DFSS Acronym for "Design for Six Sigma." Describes the application of Six Sigma tools to product development and process design efforts with the goal of "designing in" Six Sigma performance capability.

DMAIC Acronym for a process improvement/management system, which stands for define, measure, analyze, improve, and control; lends structure to process improvement, design, or redesign applications.

DPMO, or defects per million opportunities Calculation used in Six Sigma Process improvement initiatives indicating the amount of defects in a process per 1 million opportunities; number of defects ÷ by (the number of units × the number of opportunities) = DPO × 1 million = DPMO. *See also* DPO; Six Sigma; Defect opportunity.

DPO, or defects per opportunity Calculation used in process improvements to determine the amount of defects per opportunity; number of defects ÷ (the number of units × the number of opportunities) = DPO. *See also* Defect; Defect opportunity.

Effectiveness Measures related to how well the process output(s) meets the needs of the customer (e.g., on-time delivery, adherence to specifications, service experience, accuracy, value-added features, customer satisfaction level); links primarily to customer satisfaction.

Efficiency Measures related to the quantity of resources used in producing the output of a process (e.g., costs of the process, total cycle time, resources consumed, cost of defects, scrap, and/or waste); links primarily to company profitability.

External failure When defective units pass all the way through a process and are received by the customer.

Force-field analysis Identifies forces/factors supporting or working against an idea; restraining factors listed on one side of the page, driving forces listed on the other; used to reinforce the strengths (positive ideas) and overcome the weaknesses or obstacles.

Goal statement Description of the intended target or desired results of process improvement or design/redesign activities; usually included in a team charter and supported with actual numbers and details once data has been obtained.

Handoff Any time in a process when one person (or job title) passes on the item moving through the process to another person; potential to add defects, time, and cost to a process.

Histogram, or **frequency plot** Chart used to graphically represent the frequency, distribution, and centeredness of a population.

Hypothesis statement A complete description of the suspected cause(s) of a process problem.

Improve DMAIC phase in which solutions and ideas are creatively generated and decided upon; once a problem has been fully identified, measured, and analyzed, potential solutions can be determined to solve the problem in the problem statement and support the goal statement. *See also* Charter.

Input Any product, service, or piece of information that comes into the process from a supplier.

Input measures Measures related to and describing the input into a process; predictors of output measures.

Institutionalization Fundamental changes in daily behaviors, attitudes, and practices that make changes "permanent"; cultural adaptation of changes implemented by process improvement, design, or redesign, including complex business systems such as HR, MIS, training, etc.

ISO-9000 Standard and guideline used to certify organizations as competent in defining and adhering to documented processes; mostly associated with quality assurance systems, not quality improvement.

Judgment sampling Approach that involves making educated guesses about which items or people are representative of a whole, generally to be avoided.

Management-by-fact Decision making using criteria and facts; supporting intuition with data; tools used include process measurement, process management techniques, and rational decision-making tools (e.g., criteria matrix).

Measure DMAIC phase M, where key measures are identified, and data are collected, compiled, and displayed; a quantified evaluation of specific characteristics and/or level of performance based on observable data.

Moment of truth Any event or point in a process when the external customer has an opportunity to form an opinion (positive, neutral, or negative) about the process or organization.

Multivoting Narrowing and prioritization tool; when faced with a list of ideas, problems, causes, etc., each member of a group is given a set number of votes, and those receiving the most votes get further attention/consideration.

Non-value-adding activities Steps/tasks in a process that do not add value to the external customer and do not meet all three criteria for value-adding; includes rework, handoffs, inspection/control, wait/delays, etc. *See also* Value-adding activities.

Operational definition A clear, precise description of the factor being measured or the term being used; ensures a clear understanding of terminology and the ability to operate a process or collect data consistently.

Output Any product, service, or piece of information coming out of, or resulting from, the activities in a process.

Output measures Measures related to and describing the output of the process; total figures/overall measures.

Pareto chart Quality tool based on Pareto principle; uses attribute data with columns arranged in descending order, with highest occurrences (highest bar) shown first; uses a cumulative line to track percentages of each category/bar, which distinguishes the 20 percent of items causing 80 percent of the problem.

Pareto principle The 80/20 rule; based on Vilfredo Pareto's research stating that the vital few (20 percent) causes have a greater impact than the trivial many (80 percent) causes with a lesser impact.

Pilot Trial implementation of a solution, on a limited scale, to ensure its effectiveness and test its impact; an experiment verifying a root-cause hypothesis.

Plan-Do-Check-Act (PDCA) Basic model or set of steps in continuous improvement; also referred to as "Shewhart Cycle" or "Deming Cycle."

Precision The accuracy of the measure you plan to do, which links to the type of scale or detail of your operational definition, but can have an impact on your sample size, too.

Preliminary plan Used when developing milestones for team activities related to process improvement; includes key tasks, target completion dates, responsibilities, potential problems, obstacles and contingencies, and communication strategies.

Problem/Opportunity statement Description of the symptoms or the "pain" in the process; usually written in noun-verb structure; usually included in a team charter and supported with numbers and more detail once data have been obtained. *See also* Charter.

Process capability Determination of whether a process, with normal variation, is capable of meeting customer requirements; measure of the degree a process is/*is* not meeting customer requirements, compared to the distribution of the process. *See also* Control; Control charts.

Process design Creation of an innovative process needed for newly introduced activities, systems, products, or services.

Process improvement Improvement approach focused on incremental changes/solutions to eliminate or reduce defects, costs or cycle time; leaves basic design and assumptions of a process intact. *See also* Process redesign.

Process management Defined and documented processes, monitored on an ongoing basis, which ensure that measures are providing feedback on the flow/function of a process; key measures include financial, process, people, innovation. *See also* Control.

Process map, or **flowchart** Graphic display of the process flow that shows all activities, decision points, rework loops, and handoffs.

Process measures Measures related to individual steps as well as to the total process; predictors of output measures.

Process redesign Method of restructuring process flow elements eliminating handoffs, rework loops, inspection points, and other non-value-adding activities; typically means clean-slate design of a business segment and accommodates major changes or yields exponential improvements (similar to reengineering). *See also* Process improvement; Reengineering.

Project rationale (aka "Business Case") Broad statement defining area of concern or opportunity, including impact/benefit of potential improvements, or risk of not improving a process; links to business strategies, the customer, and/or company values; provided by business leaders to an improvement team and used to develop problem statement and project charter.

Proportion defective Fraction of units with defects; number of defective units divided by the total number of units; translate the decimal figure to a percentage. *See also* Defect; Defective.

Quality A broad concept and/or discipline involving degree of excellence; a distinguished attribute or nature; conformance to specifications; measurable standards of comparison so that applications can be consistently directed toward business goals.

Quality assurance (QA) Discipline (or department) of maintaining product or service conformance to customer specifications; primary tools are inspection and statistical process control (SPC).

Quality council Leadership group guiding the implementation of quality or Six Sigma within an organization; establishes, reviews, and supports the progress of quality improvement teams.

Random sampling Method that allows each item or person chosen to be measured is selected completely by chance.

Reengineering Design or redesign of business; similar to process redesign, though in practice usually at a much larger scale or scope.

Repeatability Measurement stability concept in which a single person gets the same results each time he/she measures and collects data; necessary to ensure data consistency and stability. *See also* Reproducibility.

Reproducibility Measurement stability concept in which different people get the same results when they measure and collect data using the same methods; necessary to ensure data consistency and stability. *See also* Repeatability.

Revision plans A mechanism (process) for updating processes, procedures, and documentation.

Rework loop Any instance in a process when the thing moving through the process has to be corrected by returning it to a previous step or person/organization in the process; adds time, costs, and potential for confusion and more defects. *See also* Non-value-adding activities.

Rolled-throughput yield The cumulative calculation of defects through multiple steps in a process; total input units, less the number of errors in the first process step number of items "rolled through" that step; to get a percentage, take the number of items coming through the process correctly divided by the number of total units going into the process; repeat this for each step of the process to get an overall rolled-throughput percentage. *See also* Yield.

Run chart, or **time plot** Measurement display tool showing variation in a factor over time; indicates trends, patterns, and instances of special causes of variation. *See also* Control chart; Special cause; Variation.

Sampling Using a smaller group to represent the whole; foundation of statistics that can save time, money, and effort; allows for more meaningful data; can improve accuracy of measurement system.

Sampling bias When data can be prejudiced in one way or another and do not represent the whole.

Scatter plot or diagram Graph used to show relationship or correlation between two factors or variables.

Scope Defines the boundaries of the process or the process improvement project; clarifies specifically where opportunities for improvement reside (start- and end-points); defines where and what to measure and analyze; needs to be within the sphere of influence and control of the team working on the project; the broader the scope, the more complex and time-consuming the process improvement efforts will be.

Should-be process mapping Process-mapping approach showing the design of a process the way it *should* be (e.g., without non-value-adding activities; with streamlined workflow and new solutions incorporated); contrasts with the "As-Is" form of process mapping. *See also* Process redesign, Value-adding activities; Non-value-adding activities.

SIPOC Acronym for suppliers, inputs, process, outputs, and customer; enables an at-a-glance, high-level view of a process.

Six Sigma Level of process performance equivalent to producing only 3.4 defects for every 1 million opportunities or operations; term used to describe process improvement initiatives using sigma-based process measures and/or striving for Six Sigma–level performance.

Solution statement A clear description of the proposed solution(s); used to evaluate and select the best solution to implement.

Special cause Instance or event that impacts processes only under special circumstances (i.e., not part of the normal, daily operation of the process). *See also* Common cause; Variation.

Sponsor, or **champion** Person who represents team issues to senior management; gives final approval on team recommendations and supports those efforts with the quality council; facilitates obtaining of team resources as needed; helps Black Belt and team overcome obstacles; acts as a mentor for the Black Belt.

Statistical process control (SPC) Use of data gathering and analysis to monitor processes, identify performance issues, and determine variability/capability. *See also* Run charts; Control charts.

Storyboard A pictorial display of all the components in the DMAIC process, used by the team to arrive at a solution; used in presentations to sponsor, senior management, and others.

Stratification Looking at data in multiple layers of information such as what (types, complaints, etc.), when (month, day, year, etc.), where (region, city, state, etc.), and who (department, individual).

Stratified sampling Dividing the larger population into subgroups, then taking your sample from each subgroup.

Supplier Any person or organization that feeds inputs (products, services, or information) into the process; in a service organization, many times the customer is also the supplier.

Systematic sampling Sampling method in which elements are selected from the population at a uniform interval (e.g., every half-hour, every twentieth item); recommended for many Six Sigma measurement activities.

Upstream Processes (tasks, activities) occurring prior to the task or activity in question.

Value-adding activities Steps/tasks in a process that meet all three criteria defining value as perceived by the external customer: (1) the customer cares; (2) the thing moving through the process changes; and (3) the step is done right the first time.

Value-enabling activities Steps/tasks in a process enabling work to move forward and add value to the customer but not meeting all three of the value-adding criteria; should still be scrutinized for time and best practices—can it be done better?

Variation Change or fluctuation of a specific characteristic that determines how stable or predictable the process may be; affected by environment, people, machinery/equipment, methods/procedures, measurements, and materials; any process improvement should reduce or eliminate variation. *See also* Common cause; Special cause.

Voice of the customer (VOC) Data (complaints, surveys, comments, market research, etc.) representing the views/needs of a company's customers; should be translated into measurable requirements for the process.

X Variable used to signify factors or measures in the input or process segments of a business process or system.

Y Variable used to signify factors or measures at the output of a business process or system; equivalent to "results"; a key principle of Six Sigma is that Y is a function of upstream factors; or $y = f(x)$.

Yield Total number of units handled correctly through the process step(s).

REFERENCES

Process Improvement and Design/Redesign

Ashkenas, Ron, Dave Ulrich, Todd Jick, and Steve Kerr. *The Boundaryless Organization: Breaking the Chains of Organizational Structure.* San Francisco: Jossey-Bass, 1995.

Cross, Kelvin E., John J. Feather, and Richard L. Lynch. *Corporate Renaissance: The Art of Reengineering.* Cambridge, MA: Blackwell Publishers, 1994.

Davenport, Thomas H. *Process Innovation: Reengineering Work Through Information Technology.* Boston, MA: Harvard Business School Press, 1993.

Hammer, Michael. *Beyond Reengineering: How the Process-Centered Organization Is Changing Our Work and Our Lives.* New York: HarperBusiness, 1996.

Hammer, Michael and James Champy. *Reengineering the Corporation: A Manifesto for Business Revolution.* New York: HarperBusiness, 1993.

Harrington, H. James. *Business Process Improvement: The Breakthrough Strategy for Total Quality, Productivity, and Competitiveness.* New York: McGraw-Hill, 1991.

Holpp, Lawrence. *Managing Teams.* New York: McGraw-Hill, 1999.

Ramaswamy, Rohit. *Design and Management of Service Processes: Keeping Customers for Life.* Reading, MA: Addison-Wesley, 1996.

Stalk, George Jr. and Thomas M. Hout. *Competing Against Time: How Time-Based Competition Is Reshaping Global Markets.* New York: The Free Press, 1990.

Voice of the Customer

Carlzon, Jan. *Moments of Truth*. New York: HarperCollins, 1989.

Gale, Bradley T. *Managing Customer Value: Creating Quality and Service That Customers Can See*. New York: The Free Press, 1994.

Heil, Gary, Tom Parker, and Deborah C. Stephens. *One Size Fits One: Building Relationships One Customer and One Employee at a Time*. New York: John Wiley & Sons, 1999.

Kaplan, Robert S. and David P. Norton. *The Balanced Scorecard*. Boston, MA: Harvard Business School Press, 1996.

Treacy, Michael and Fred Wiersema. *The Discipline of Market Leaders: Choose Your Customers, Narrow Your Focus, Dominate Your Market*. Reading, MA: Addison-Wesley, 1995.

Learning and Innovation

Imparato, Nicholas and Oren Harari. *Jumping the Curve: Innovation and Strategic Choice in an Age of Transition*. San Francisco: Jossey-Bass, 1994.

Janov, Jill. *The Inventive Organization: Hope and Daring at Work*. San Francisco: Jossey-Bass, 1994.

Senge, Peter M. *The Fifth Discipline: The Art and Practice of The Learning Organization*. New York: Doubleday, 1990.

Organizations and Six Sigma

Breyfogle, Forrest W. *Implementing Six Sigma: Smarter Solutions Using Statistical Methods*. New York: Wiley-Interscience, 1999.

Porter, Michael E. *Competitive Advantage: Creating and Sustaining Superior Performance*. New York: The Free Press, 1985.

Rummler, Geary A. and Alan P. Brache. *Improving Performance: How to Manage the White Space on the Organization Chart*. San Francisco: Jossey-Bass, 1990.

Slater, Robert. *Jack Welch and the GE Way: Management Insights and Leadership Secrets of the Legendary CEO*. New York: McGraw-Hill, 1999.

Tichy, Noel M. and Stratford Sherman. *Control Your Destiny or Someone Else Will: Lessons in Mastering Change—from the Principles Jack Welch Is Using to Revolutionize GE*. New York: HarperBusiness, 1993.

Voice of the Process

Brassard, Michael and Diane Ritter. *The Memory Jogger II*. Methuen, MA: GOAL/QPC, 1994.

Fraenkel, Jack, Norman Wallen, and Enoch I. Sawin. *Visual Statistics: A Conceptual Primer*. Needham Heights, MA: Allyn & Bacon, 1999.

Kume, Hitoshi. *Statistical Methods for Quality Improvement*. Tokyo, Japan: The Association for Overseas Technical Scholarship, 1985.

ACKNOWLEDGMENTS

For the Second Edition

Updating and revising a book turns out to be a tricky proposition: You don't want to lose the essence of the original, but it has to bring new insights and information. Completing this second edition would not have been possible without the expert guidance and significant contribution of Ruth Mills, a veteran editor who (we think) helped find the right balance and who shouldered a lot of the work to make it happen.

The other major acknowledgement for this Edition goes to the many readers, clients, and colleagues who have helped us continue to learn and see the challenges of Six Sigma in new ways. There have been times when we thought the over-hyping of Six Sigma and the criticism leveled at it (often justified, even if too harsh) would combine to send Six Sigma the way of the dinosaurs. But many others have looked past these extremes to find that the good parts of Six Sigma are not ephemeral and offer significant value, when done right. Without these people, a second edition would not have been worth doing at all.

For the First Edition

We now understand why the awards shows on TV always run long. Partly, of course, it is due to slow delivery of canned jokes by the presenters. Usually, though, it is that the winners need to thank so many people. We have not won an award, but we could go on for a while thanking people. Our friends at McGraw-Hill have threatened to cut to a commercial if we run long, however, so we will try to keep this brief.

The most important acknowledgment is to the person who put in hours of tireless, good-natured, and indispensable work to make this book a reality: Percy Madamba. She kept everything organized, proofread, offered countless suggestions, laughed at jokes (we are hoping her sense of humor is representative of the general reading public), did graphics and countless other small acts, including shipping out the manuscript. (Our worry now is that Percy will quit and go write her own d—n book.)

Carolyn Talasek, Kelly Fisher, Carla Queen, Chet Harmer, Mona Draper, and Amanda Dutra—along with other members of the great team at Pivotal Resources—contributed graphics, editing help, suggestions, and research, as well as many ideas and insights. That group (the "Pivotal Pack") has been instrumental in bringing together a vast amount of experience and success that we channeled into these pages. Other key contributors to that well of knowledge include Pamela Schmidt-Cavaliero, Fred Kleiman, Mercie Lopez, Greg Gibbs, Jane Keller, and Rosalie Pryor. Also thanks to our colleague Larry Holpp, for advice and publishing contacts that helped us to bring this book to life.

We owe special thanks to dozens of people in our client organizations, practicing Six Sigma here and in other parts of the world. These people are making Six Sigma pay off and are learning how to make it work in many different environments. Some of the individuals we thank in particular for their support include all our friends at GE Capital's Center for Learning and Organizational Excellence—Mike Markovits, Mo Cayer, Hilly Dunn, Jenene Nicholson, Kelly Babij, Mike Mosher, and many others. This book would not exist without the terrific work the folks at GE have done, and without their commitment to Six Sigma. Thanks also to the great people at Employers Reinsurance, including Kaj Ahlmann, Alan Mauch, Tom Felgate, Lee Tenold, Julie Hertel, Mike Nichols, and many others; John Eck and the QNBC people at NBC, where we got to watch the *Tonight Show* live and help introduce Six Sigma to a prime-time organization; at Cendant Mortgage, a whole group of great people including our pal Pat Connolly, Tanya DeLia, Suzanne Wetherington, and many others; at Auspex Systems, where process redesign has been part of quality for years, Tamas Farkas and Charlie Golden (who is actually now at Genentech).

People who offered special insights into this book and who we want to thank for their time include Dave Boenitz, Chuck Cox, Bob Golitz, Barbara Friesner, Aldie Keene, Alan Larson, Rich Lynch, Celeste Miller, and Jessica Shklar.

At McGraw-Hill, much appreciation to our editor, Richard Narramore, for coaching us through, getting this project off the ground, and put to bed. We are aiming for Six Sigma performance!

Our families deserve loving mention, and sincere thanks, for putting up with the hours of time spent watching daddies and husbands hunched over a computer. (To Olga, Stephanie, and Brian Pande: *Now the book is finished. Let's go play!*)

Finally, we make a special dedication of this book to the memory of our great friend and colleague, Bill Lindenfelder. Bill was not only our partner in helping teach people about Six Sigma, but taught everyone who knew him about enthusiasm, encouragement, and boundless energy. We are among the many people who miss Bill enormously, and we hope he would be proud to see some of his ideas and so much of his influence in these pages.

INDEX

ABOUT THE AUTHORS

Peter S. Pande

Pete Pande is founder and president of Pivotal Resources, Inc., an international consulting firm focused on supporting transformational change, performance improvement including Lean Six Sigma, and leadership development. Pete has worked in the organization improvement field for more than 25 years, supporting change initiatives for large and small organizations including high tech, financial services, manufacturing, health care and government. He is author of the *Six Sigma Leader*, and co-author of *What Is Six Sigma?* and *The Six Sigma Way Team Fieldbook*.

Robert P. Neuman, Ph.D.

Bob Neuman is a senior consultant and noted speaker in the area of business improvement methods and Six Sigma. His background in Six Sigma and quality systems includes two years with a major California health care system, and consulting work with such Pivotal Resources clients as Macy's NBC, GE Capital, Cendant, and many others.

Roland R. Cavanagh, P.E.

Roland Cavanagh is a professional engineer who has an extensive background in improving manufacturing and service business processes. His areas of expertise include process measurement and applied statistics, business reorganization, and Six Sigma methods. He has worked with such organizations as America West Airlines, Commonwealth Edison, GE, and Tencor Instruments.

www.pivotalresources.com